SEXUAL CITIZENSHIP

In *Sexual Citizenship*, David T. Evans argues that analyses of the social construction of sexualities have tended to ignore the material contexts in which gender construction occurs. The main negative effect of this is that the sexual has been detached from mainstream power relations and interests. Building upon Foucauldian and Interactionist perspectives, Evans maintains that the progressive sexualisation of modern capitalist societies is primarily shaped by the complex interrelated material interests of market and state. The inherent individualism and amoralism of the consumerist market inevitably leads to the commodification of that which is most 'personal', 'private', 'individual' and 'natural'. Capitalism encourages us to purchase our sexual identities and lifestyles and impels us to conclude that we are right to do so. In response the state is not a passive actor. It neither simply resists nor retreats. Rather it concedes relative and partial rights to 'deviant' sexual minorities, investing them with particular, limited forms of gender/consumer power, i.e. sexual citizenship. After a detailed discussion of the theoretical issues, the argument is developed through the specific instances of male homosexuality, bisexuality, transvestism, transsexualism, paedophilia and children's sexuality.

Sexual Citizenship is the first book to approach sexuality from the perspective of citizenship. It raises fruitful and disturbing questions that will be of interest to all academics, students, counsellors and practitioners (sexologists, social workers) with an interest in and concern for sexuality in all its forms.

David T. Evans lectures in Sociology at the University of Glasgow.

SEXUAL CITIZENSHIP

The material construction of sexualities

David T. Evans

London and New York

First published 1993
by Routledge
11 New Fetter Lane, London EC4P 4EE

Simultaneously published in the USA and Canada
by Routledge
29 West 35th Street, New York, NY 10001

© 1993   David T. Evans

Typeset in 10/12 pt Baskerville by
NWL Editorial Services, Langport, Somerset

Printed and bound in Great Britain by
T.J. Press (Padstow) Ltd, Padstow, Cornwall

British Library Cataloguing in Publication Data
A catalogue record for this book is available from the British Library.

Library of Congress Cataloging in Publication Data
Evans, David T. (David Trevor), 1945–
Sexual citizenship: the material construction of sexualities /
by David T. Evans
p.   cm.
Includes bibliographical references and index.
1. Sexual ethics.   2. Capitalism.   3. Sex.   4. Sexual deviation.
I. Title
HQ32.E95   1993   92–28812
306.7 – dc20   CIP

ISBN 0–415–05799–X
0–415–05800–7 (pbk)

FOR CHRIS, IN LOVING MEMORY

Christopher David Parker 2.12.46–29.3.91

CONTENTS

INTRODUCTION

... with the collapse of other social values (religion, patriotism, family and so on) sex has been forced to take up the slack, to become our sole mode of transcendence, and our only touchstone of authenticity. The cry for scorching multiple orgasms ... impeccable and virtuoso perform- ance, the belief that only in complete sexual compatibility lies true intimacy, the insistence that sex is the only mode for experiencing thrills, for achieving love, for assessing and demonstrating personal worth ...

(White 1980: 282)

The second half of this century has seen a pronounced escalation in the already well established sexualisation of developed capitalist societies at all structural levels, from day-to-day interactions and relationships to long-term market planning and state policy formation (Armytage *et al.* 1984; Gebhard 1984). Of course 'sexuality has always been of central concern to human beings' (Brake 1982: 13) because of its associations with procreativity, its credited though usually unspecified 'mysteries' and apparently unsocialised animality, but never before has this concern been in explicit and coded terms, so widely and incessantly discussed, so prominently marketed and consumed, so repeatedly the site of contests over 'permissiveness', 'liberation', the pursuit or infringement of rights and freedoms. If, as Sontag (1969: 46) has claimed, 'since Christianity focused on sexual behaviour as the root of virtue everything pertaining to sex has been a "special case" in our culture', then never before have there been so many 'special cases'. We have become hooked on the Sexual Fix (Heath 1982), worshippers at the altar of Sex

1

Religion (Greer 1984) as sexuality has become 'the medium through which people seek to define their personalities and . . . to be conscious of themselves' (Foucault and Sennett 1981: 183).

If this 'sanctification of the sexual as "sexuality" indeed is one of the major characteristics of our culture' (Heath 1982: 147), it surely is not one that is so in isolation, discretely segregated from other social, political and economic structures and associated cultures. Many of the critiques which stress that sexuality has 'become our sole mode of transcendence . . . our only touchstone of authenticity' (White 1980) perpetuate traditional dominant ideologies of the sexual as individual, personal, private, definitively divorced from material structures and power relations. Yet, as merely passing references to the civil, political and social rights of various sexual minorities, and the marketing of sexual imagery and commodities make clear, this is manifestly not the case. There has been a sexualisation of late twentieth-century first world capitalist cultures but, behind the distracting verdicts of experts who claim via labels such as the Sexual Fix (Heath 1982) and Sex Religion (Greer 1984) that sexuality is a private escape from the alienation of the public material world, it is clear that in many and various guises, it is formally and customarily institutionalised and incorporated within the latter. Sexual minorities have progressively become distinct, formal, though not necessarily formally clear, participants within the citizenship of developed capitalism, whilst simultaneously becoming, not surprisingly for of course the two are closely connected, legitimate consumers of sexual and sexualised commodities marketed specifically for their use and enjoyment. It is with the general and particular characteristics of the major specific forms of sexual citizenship that this text is concerned.

The initial and requisite emergence of civil citizenship within capitalism encompassed a relatively limited set of rights enabling citizens to engage in the productive activities of the economy and avail themselves of the protection of the legal system (Marshall 1950; Berger 1977; Tushnet 1991), and whilst the subsequent development of further civil, plus political and social rights has been marked by weak, imprecise and overlapping legal categorisation and practice (Tushnet 1991; Weinreb 1991), it is nevertheless clear that in the first world economies of the global chain citizenship has increasingly focused on the rights of citizens as consumers.

In Britain since the late 1980s citizenship has become a major preoccupation of the main political parties and prominent public figures. As elsewhere during this period the moral and ideological running has been made by the Conservative Party, despite or perhaps because of a steady decline in social or welfare rights since the late 1970s, the increased social and economic strains of the Thatcher era, growing levels of unemployment, inner city riots, increases in recorded crimes, lengthening hospital queues, etc., and doubts about the legal safeguards of existing rights such as freedom of information and of speech and from stop and search policies, etc.

Oliver (1991) notes how during the 1970s and 1980s the balance of citizenship rights shifted away from social rights of welfare towards civil rights of an economic kind (i.e. market access related) such as the right to buy council houses and to purchase shares in privatised industries. She claims that to include these rights which are 'essentially directed to promoting the individual persona and private autonomy of the individual rather than citizenship in the sense of the relationship between the individual and the state or the community' is to stretch citizenship to breaking point (p. 160). However, citizenship has been effectively so stretched, through a considerable political exercise in redefinition throughout the Thatcher era whereby it has become, by the beginning of the 1990s, primarily a matter of civic responsibility and cost-effective duty, with British citizenry becoming 'a kind of secular Salvation Army' (Heater 1991: 147).

The formal legal content of citizenship in Britain amounts to very little for basically the term 'citizen' is used to differentiate the entitlements of citizens (to reside, work, claim social rights, etc.) from 'aliens' of various types (Dummett and Nicol 1990), thus whilst citizenship in generalised terms has occupied a central symbolic and structural place in British political culture it has also been wide open to interpretive colonisation and refinement. As Oliver (1991: 162) argues, this became ever more likely with post-1945 changes to local economies, the disintegration of stable manufacturing communities, increased social and geographical mobility, redevelopment of housing estates, the increase of women in waged labour, greater fragility of marriage, etc., all of which caused 'networks of local co-operation and support [to] weaken', as did the promulgation of ideologies of competition and individual self-reliance within a consumerist economy, which further eroded community attachments and sensibilities.

Thus, by its 1988 Annual Conference, the Conservative Party was prepared to launch its commitment to what it chose to call 'the "active" citizen' forged out of traditional Tory values: 'underpinning our social policy are those traditions – the diffusion of power, civil obligation, and voluntary service – which are central to Conservative philosophy. . . . The diffusion of power . . . the key to active and responsible citizenship' (*New Statesman* 1 April 1988). In this sense 'active' citizenship is presented as a way of encouraging responsibility to the community and becomes a close complement to the enterprise culture; 'Public service may once have been the duty of an elite, but today it is the responsibility of all who have time or money to spare. Modern capitalism has democratised the ownership of property, and we are now witnessing the democratisation of responsible citizenship' (Hurd in Heater 1990), meaning with due regard to what the country can afford. Margaret Thatcher (*Guardian* 26 Sept 1989) proclaimed: 'When you have finished as a taxpayer, you have not finished as a citizen', whilst Chris Patten opined 'the active citizen is someone making more than a solely economic contribution to his or her community; nothing more nor less'. In February 1990 John McGregor, the then Secretary of State for Education, identified three fundamental aspects of citizenship which should be the responsibility of the national curriculum: '. . . the individual's rights and responsibilities within a democratic society . . . the organisations and structures of society, including the rules and laws within which it functions . . . [and] the role of the individual . . .' (Heater 1991) though he warned that the school should not encroach on the responsibilities of other key institutions: voluntary associations and, most crucially, the family.

This Tory use of 'active' citizenship reiterates earlier Thatcherite visions of individual and family civic responsibilities and duties to nation and community subverted by a 'nanny state' which had promoted 'passive' citizenship and civic irresponsibility as demonstrated most disastrously by the 'permissive 1960s'. 'Active' citizens are givers, not takers, committed to the national and communal good; normal, moral and nationalist. The good citizens of this absolutist vision of consensus and uniformity have been progressively released via monetarism into

4

a free and fair competitive participation as consumers in the private market but deserved further protections in the public sector which remained an iniquitous mire of inefficient state monopolies against which consumers were powerless. Thus by July 1991 in the glossy format of the government White Paper *Citizen's Charter: Raising the Standard*, citizenship had become overtly and succinctly crystallised around the twin statuses of consumer and taxpayer. Obligations to absolute moral and political values deserved the legal rewards of protections against the remnants of the dread state which had done so much to undermine them.

> The Citizen's Charter is about giving more power to the citizen. But citizenship is about our responsibilities – as parents for example, or as neighbours, as well as our entitlements. The Citizen's Charter is not a recipe for more state action: it is a testament for our belief in people's rights to be informed and choose for themselves.
>
> (*Citizen's Charter* 1991: 2)

Not only did the citizen become a consumer but the commodities on sale became the entire machinery of citizenship: 'Where the state is engaged in regulating, taxing or administering justice, these functions too must be carried out fairly, effectively and courteously' (p. 4). The modern citizen's prime rights are to have the freedom to make a well-informed choice of high quality commodities and services in public and private sectors, and to be treated with due regard for their 'privacy, dignity, religious and cultural beliefs' (p. 10).

This pure and idealised representation of the citizen as free consumer/taxpayer with 'privacy, dignity, religious and cultural beliefs' clearly fails to accurately address, as have other key weapons in the Conservative Party's 'hegemonic thrust' (Hall 1985), the structural diversity of the world it purports to describe and the fundamental moral contradictions within it, and that of course is in part its purpose. In particular, behind the rhetoric of universal rights of 'privacy, dignity, religious and cultural beliefs', there stands a citizenship machinery which effectively invades and corrals those who by various relative status shortcomings are deemed to be less than fully qualified citizens. The state's management of these 'moral aliens' is exercised in social, political and economic arenas. Under certain legal and moral constraints the market may be said to be amoral in the sense that as long as one has the purchasing power, one can demand and consume the specific commodities that one wants but, in practice, legal and moral constraints adjudicate and differentiate between the legitimacy of varieties of marginal or minority groups who are clearly not allowed the privacy and dignity to pursue their religious and cultural beliefs or economic needs in equal measure. The full weight of civil, political and social rights machineries is employed to define degrees of citizenship or, to be more precise, the non-citizenship of those manifestly outwith the absolute reified standards of the moral community. Furthermore, these degrees of non-citizenship incite the further fragmentation of communities with sectionalised access and activity to and in specialised markets, they define degrees and forms of consumer status and lifestyle.

Clearly religious and ethnic minorities are located within this marginal matrix of citizenship, but so too are sexual minorities. By the 1990s the burgeoning fragmentation of identities into forms of 'multiple citizenship' (Heater 1990) through ethnic, religious, regional and sexual allegiances in complex inter-relationship with each other and the familiar processes of social class has become very marked. These are sub-collectivities which experience informal and formal discrimination consonant with their credited lower social worth and, in the case of sexual minorities in particular, their relative immorality within the British moral community. Campbell (1987a) has explained how in the 1980s the Conservative Party articulated a somewhat ambiguous family-centred sexual/moral ideology at the centre of its broad monetarist and anti-statist policies

Rather than waging an ideological offensive to consign women to their separate sphere within the home, thus reuniting women and the family, Thatcherism was concerned with something bigger than both of them: the family as the anchor of the new right's anti-statism and economic liberalism. Citizens were to realise themselves not in their social being, not through politics, but through consumerism.

(Campbell 1987a: 159)

As Campbell continues, this ideological strategy has not involved any explicit designation of the role of women as only

6

homemakers, nor prescribed women's expulsion from the labour market. Similarly, Thatcherism has not formally reversed or repudiated the existing rights and freedoms of sexual citizens outwith the conventional family but rather has engineered elaborate panics around their moral difference and threat, to confine them socially, economically and morally. Throughout, Thatcherism's family strategy has 'clearly been about the family as its moral bulwark against degeneracy and dependence, and as its economic barricade against the state' (p. 159). It was a strategy which effectively redefined citizenship through consumerism tied to moral conformity and in so doing formalised degrees of citizenship according to categories of sexual difference.

Sexual minority groups have as a result, with growing momentum, developed socioeconomic 'community' infrastructures of varying degrees of complexity around their particular identities, 'types', 'kinds', 'status groups', 'minorities', etc. Each produces its political parties concerned with challenging the moral boundaries behind which it is confined but most members exercise their partial rights within the socioeconomic and moral spaces permitted. Representative groups of homosexuals and lesbians, for example, may publicly organise to attain further housing, insurance, medical, parenting, marital rights, etc., but they do so whilst the gay community's majority spends significant proportions of their income on gay commodities in pursuit of distinguishable gay and lesbian lifestyles in segregated specifically gay social and sexual territories. Comparable patterns of secondary material citizenship are manifest amongst other sexual minorities, albeit at lower levels of organisational and associational development.

Perhaps this account of citizenship underemphasises continuing general debates about broad principles as well as campaigns and battles over specific sexual rights. Other political parties have attempted to respond to the Conservative Party's colonisation of citizenship as consumer choice twinned with civic obligation: the SLD, SDP and Labour parties have all at times stressed the need to extend and formalise citizenship in a bill of rights, advocating for example 'democratic citizenship' (Plant 1988) in a Citizens' Britain with a welfare secure, politically active yet culturally diverse population, to replace what some have called the Citadel Britain of oppressed, stressed people in a closed political system (Ashdown 1989). Considerable efforts have been made by specifically sexual political parties to influence such programmes, but when moral push has come to manifesto and electoral shove, mainstream parties have backed away from overt commitments to the sexually immoral.

Also, numerous specific sexual campaigns, from the respectably reformist to the radically unpredictable, have achieved high-profile media interest and so it would be wrong to portray citizenship as solely a key element in right-wing hegemony, or as merely a distracting device whereby minority access to minority markets may be monitored. It is an arena of potential conflict within which over time there have been notable victories for rights reform, resistance and dissent. However, it is also noteworthy that for most sexual minorities, citizenship advance beyond the limited constraints of permitted legal participation in segregated, privatised social and economic territories, is either of no great concern or entails moral costs which are simply too high to pay. Through formal enforcement and informal incorporation specific forms of sexual citizenship are largely confined to the moral and economic and largely part-time leisure and lifestyle spaces which encircle the moral community between the boundaries of illegality and immorality. Particular political campaigns may question and seek to breach these moral boundaries but, for the majority, incorporation into discrete social territories and markets would appear to be sufficient to guarantee political and economic acquiescence. Sexual citizenship, to the extent that it guarantees differential market access, commodification of sexual immorality within 'private' environments, has served to largely maintain the purity of the moral community, conceal impurities and fragment and distract potential dissent, and to quite clear material and ideological ends. Central to such a process has been the further social construction of sexualities within these by now well established material parameters.

In this text these themes will be explored by way of various specific examples of sexual citizenship: the homosexual, the bisexual, the transvestite, the transsexual, the child and the female. Given that at the heart of the discussion will be the central importance of consumer power and commodification, and of established formal civil, political and social rights, there will inevitably be a tendency to debate these issues from the male, masculine, i.e. more economically and politically powerful point

8

of view. The history of citizenship is a history of fundamental formal heterosexist patriarchal principles and practices ostensibly progressively 'liberalised' towards and through the rhetoric of 'equality' but in practice to effect unequal differentiation.

Before particular forms of sexual citizenship can be discussed, however, it is necessary to address the context in which their material construction has taken place. In particular attention has to be given to the 'permissive' 1960s which, in all senses, loom large as the watershed which enabled the subsequent emergence and development of material forms of secondary sexual citizenship (Hall 1979). However, this watershed stands not as a single radical turning point but as a a key moment in an ongoing sexualisation process which has characterised the capitalist epoch, within which the heightened preoccupation with sexuality in all manner of explicit, implicit and diverse forms has effectively saturated populations, structures and cultures with constellations of immanent sexual power/knowledge (Foucault 1981) ripe for commodification. Accordingly the discussion will commence with a review of the major existing analyses of the sexualisation of modern societies.

1

SEXUALITY AS DISCOURSE AND SCRIPT

It is quite true. Most people are other people.
Their thoughts are someone else's opinions,
their lives a mimicry, their passions a quotation.
(Bartlett 1988: 190)

At the time of his death in 1984 Michel Foucault had completed four of his planned six volumes on the history of sexuality in Western civilisation (Foucault 1981, 1987, 1986, 4th vol. unpub. but see 'The battle for chastity' in Kritzman 1988), an exploration of the history of subjection in terms both of the creation of the subject and the internalisation of normative control into the deepest recesses of subjectivity: the sexual. As such it was an exercise which required 'a reconceptualisation of the logic of history' (Poster 1984: 127) in the particular instance of the sexual, as well as 'a re-elaboration of a theory of power' (Foucault 1981: 187).

Once past the first volume: *La Volonté de savoir* or *The Will to Know* which addressed the modern world, 'a sort of prelude to explore the keyboard, sketch out the themes ... to see how people react' (Foucault 1985: 8),[1] Foucault's focus on the sexual part of the equation weakened temporally and thematically, being used in the subsequent volumes' dense examinations of antiquity as the means of exposition rather than the object. It is this first volume therefore which has most influenced analyses of sexuality in the modern world.

Throughout *The Will to Know* Foucault is at great pains to undermine all notions of power in the formal juridical sense of negative constraints located in laws and legal institutions; as something which excludes, prohibits and punishes. Rather, power is an all pervasive, normative and positive presence, internalised by and thus creating, the subject. Indeed, the subject seems not to exist outside of immanent patterns of normative knowledge derived from language, objects and practices, i.e. discourses. 'Subjectivity' in the Foucauldian sense is always discursive, it refers to general subject positions, conceived as empty spaces or functions occupied by particular individuals in the pronouncement of specific statements.[2] We are what we learn, internalise and reproduce as knowledge and the language through which it is understood. We are subjects of the power immanently installed in that knowledge.

In his earlier *The Archaeology of Knowledge* (1972), Foucault argued that discourses operate through rules of exclusion and classification, which determine discourse content; what is to be excluded, included, privileged, disqualified and why, as well as by rules governing the who, when and where of their use. In *The History of Sexuality* these rules have become less formally identifiable, discourses and discursive power seemingly altogether less substantial but more insidiously pervasive. However, the same patterns of power/knowledge exclusion, classification and aptness, constructing rather than sanctioning or banning the sexual, may be discerned.

In *Madness and Civilisation* (1965) Foucault traced the systematic exclusion of the 'insane' since the eighteenth century through ever more elaborate classifications of madness, 'into the realm of the Other, into a space previously occupied by death' (Lash 1985: 5). In *Discipline and Punish* (1977a) he demonstrated how within the prison system, power is exercised not solely in a prohibitive way, but more importantly imprints identities on categories of non-citizens set apart as 'criminals' or 'delinquents', and to categorically differentiate between them as 'sex', 'high security' or 'political' prisoners, etc. So too in *The Will to Know* this growing imperialism of a society seeking to attribute a social status and definition to everything, even the unclassifiable, eventually reaches precisely that, the epitome of the 'personal', 'private', 'mysterious' and natural, that which most naturally resists the cultural: sexuality, *the* most important source of identity for modern subjects, and therefore the ultimate means of their complete subjection.[3]

Thus this re-elaboration of a theory of power was simultaneously a demonstration of 'how the subject is "created"

11

by [the] power–knowledge complexes of history' (Shiner 1982: 387), and in particular how sexual subjects in modern societies are constructed out of their obsessive pursuit of ever greater knowledge about their innermost individual 'essential' sexual selves, ironically so, being that aspect of self considered to be the most resistant to explanation through discourse. Thus for Foucault

> Sexuality . . . is not a domain of nature which power tries to subjugate, and which academic disciplines set out to explore. It is merely a name which one may give to a historical artefact – rather a . . . hybrid mechanism which links together the stimulation of the body, the intensification of pleasures, incitement to discourse, the formation of knowledges and reinforcements of controls and resistances to it.
>
> (Hussain 1981: 178)

It is precisely because sexuality is an historical artefact defined as a private 'essence' which transcends history and culture, and therefore unregulated by juridical power, which enables it to serve unrecognised as 'an especially dense transfer point for relations of [immanent] power' (Bailey 1988: 118) in the modern world.

La Volonté de savoir raised its concerns in questioning terms. How have modern men and women come to regard their sexualities as the hidden secret of their beings? Why is sexuality at the centre of their struggle for the control of themselves and others? Why has sexuality become the central bearer of power relations in the second half of the twentieth century? Why do people believe that knowledge of their sexualities will provide them with *true* knowledge about themselves? What is the relationship between increasing knowledge of the sexual to sexual liberation? Is the history of sexuality a history of progress and if so of what kind? And so on.

That modern societies are increasingly sexualised is accepted, but dominant explanations in terms of the gradual 'liberation' of repressed innate instincts and desires, or of the granting by enlightened states of extended rights and freedoms to sexual minorities, are completely rejected; indeed for Foucault they are central to the deception. Possibly in disillusioned reaction to his first-hand experience of the so-called 'revolution of desire'

12

(Weeks 1978: 9) of Paris in 1968, Foucault argues that, as a social construct of transparent substance and clandestine detail, sexuality has become so ubiquitously part of our mundane everyday lives that to seek or to gain 'liberation' is merely to embroil us further in the discursive web rather than to free us from it.

> All objects and human beings exist within relations of power even those who resist, who set their faces against what appears to be the norm (homosexuals to take one example) participate in the production of the norm in the very act of opposing it, by allowing the norm to be articulated against its abnormal opposite.
>
> (Haug 1987: 196)

Foucault's frequent references to 'counter-discourses', 'counter affirmations', 'reverse discourses', may suggest forms of resistance but his analysis allows little if any room for them in any literal sense, as he himself acknowledged with some regret in his last writings (1978; O'Higgins 1982–3). 'Counter-discourses' exist but apparently as little more than demonstrations by subjects of their successful internalisation of knowledge/power and their ability to police themselves.

This post-eighteenth-century discursive explosion on and around the sexual was not confined to sexuality in the contemporary narrow sense but rather functioned as an instrument of domination in the modern regime of 'bio-power' which 'group[ed] together, in an artificial unity, anatomical elements, biological functions, conducts, sensations, and pleasures and . . . [made] use of this fictitious unity as a causal principle, an omnipresent meaning, a secret to be discovered everywhere' (Foucault 1981: 154).

Pre-capitalist societies were characterised by the 'deployment of alliance', their populations integrated through kinship, possessions and wealth in essentially static structures. Modern societies by contrast are characterised by the dynamic 'deployment of sexuality' with populations controlled by ever more specific definitions of sensations, needs of the body and qualities of pleasure. Whilst 'bio-power' has the narrowly sexual at its core, it opens out to a wider focus on the body as a machine, its 'disciplining, the optimisation of its capabilities, its integration into systems of efficient and economic controls' (Foucault 1981: 139).

Foucault's unwillingness to do more than credit the emerging bourgeoisie with almost inadvertently 'discovering' this bio-political focus due to its interest in wealth, self-preservation and inheritance, is tantalising, but his purpose is clear; all of us, no matter how much we may apparently differ in our tangible and formal powers, are but bit players in the grand march of discursive history.

'Bio-power', he argues, emerged simply as health improved and more people lived longer.

> Death was gradually ceasing to torment life so directly. . . . Western man was gradually learning what it meant to be a living species in a living world, to have a body, conditions of existence, probabilities of life. . . . For the first time in history no doubt, biological existence was reflected in political existence; the fact of living was no longer an inaccessible substrate that only emerged from time to time, amid the randomness of death and its fatality; part of it passed into knowledge's field of control and power's sphere of intervention.
>
> (Foucault 1981: 142–3)

While death still tormented the lives of the poor, there emerged amongst the rich the later pervasive belief that it was in the public interest to manage the body, and through the body, the population; its birth rates, marriage rates; its health or proneness to illness and disease, sexual disease in particular; the protection of its children's innocence; the need to identify manifestations of threat, abnormalities, deviations, etc., not managed in a juridical sense, or solely through 'expert' discursive practice, but through normative infusion into everyday knowledge and experience.

Precisely who manages and intervenes and who is thereby managed is not of importance, for Foucault effectively dispenses with the human subject as 'sovereign' creator or bearer of historical continuity. Whilst conventional liberal conceptions stress independent individual sovereignty bound by rights in public, and respectfully unregulated by juridical laws in private,[4] Foucault's 'sovereign' subject is no more than the complex product of colonising discursive knowledge. As sexuality has pervaded modern societies, human subjects' increased obsession with the sexual has been not as self-determining beings but as beings in sexual subjugation, if not cultural dopes, cultural dupes, culpably passive in the face of this discursive onslaught, unable to escape its consequences.[5]

> ... the subject is merely a derivative product of a certain contingent, historically specific set of linguistically infused social practices which inscribe power relations on human bodies. Thus there is no foundation for critique oriented around the notions of autonomy, reciprocity, recognition, dignity and human rights.
>
> (Fraser 1983: 56)

Foucault reached the construction of sexual subjects as ensnared receptacles by way of his critique of the dominant 'repressive thesis' as most prominently promulgated by Freud and post-Freudian psychoanalysis (Freud 1905), the Freudo-Marxist syntheses of Reich (1961, 1969), Marcuse (1964, 1969) and by such conventional histories as Marcus' *The Other Victorians* (1966). This thesis, which assumes the existence of 'human nature', the natural subject and sexuality beyond the constraints of language and culture, proposes that prior to capitalism there had been relative freedom and openness about all manner of sexual forms including the illicit. However, from the transition onwards and with gathering momentum through the nineteenth century especially, sexuality had become increasingly repressed by prohibition, denial and censorship, subordinated to the procreative function within conjugal monogamy where it was addressed in terms of secrecy, silence and euphemism. Sexuality was obliterated from cultural recognition, forced into the collective unconscious.

Proponents' explanations of this developing 'repression' tend to be developed out of the recognition of a simple conjunction:

> By placing the advent of the age of repression in the seventeenth century, after hundreds of years of open spaces and free expression, one adjusts it to coincide with the development of capitalism; it becomes an integral part of the bourgeois order.
>
> (Foucault 1981: 5)

Thus it is argued that capitalism required an efficiently exploitable, reproductive, malleable, undistracted labour-force with non-procreative 'wasteful' sexuality repressed, the mode of

15

production dictating a particular mode of reproduction in turn dependent upon a culture of silence about the sexual.

For radical commentators such as Reich and Marcuse, sexual liberation therefore becomes a necessary concomitant to any general revolutionary programme, whilst for liberal critics the twentieth century has witnessed, especially within neatly packaged notorious decades such as the Roaring Twenties and the Permissive Sixties, the progressive relaxation of earlier repressive sexual and moral constraints. Thus, as Poster relates, a conventional view is that during the Roaring Twenties:

> popular culture in Europe and the United States shifted away from the pre-war Victorian ethos of respectability and rushed towards a more uninhibited way of life, one that acknowledged openly the pleasures of the flesh. In the context of the Roaring Twenties, psychoanalysis was taken as a support for overturning constraints on sexuality. Freud appeared to demonstrate the validity of the new middle-class ethos; restrictions on sexual activity were harmful mentally and physically.
>
> (Poster 1984: 121)

Foucault's counter-hypothesis not only rejects the history of 'repression', but also dismisses 'liberation' for, 'the irony of this deployment of sexuality is in having us believe that our "liberation" is in the balance' (Foucault 1981: 159). Rights language and sentiments merely mystify the processes of social domination, falsely constructing autonomous self-determining subjects.

In particular, Foucault attacks Freudo-Marxist syntheses. As Morris has noted (1982), Reich and the early Marcuse believed not only that a sexual input into radical politics was essential but that it would secure a popularising impact, as indeed was fleetingly suggested during the late 1960s when both attained transitory 'guru' status amongst the radical young. The view was that the 'affirmation of our sexual repression is perhaps the one way left, given the experience of history, to discreetly associate the revolution and happiness, or the revolution and pleasure' (Morris 1982: 267). On the contrary Foucault, 'nihilistic and despairing' (Gandel 1986: 121), asserts that our visions of freedom, liberation and our pursuit of perpetual spirals of pleasure are inevitably 'complicit with the powers we would oppose' (Gandel 1986: 121); they manifest 'a liberationist conceit,

16

a millenarian blindness entangling us all the deeper in the networks to be escaped ... [and] ... a yearning for transcendence' (Comay 1986: 111).

Foucault's bleak view, in its implications though not in its rejection of material forms, is akin to the pessimism to be found in Marcuse's (1964) later presentiments of 'one-dimensional' liberation as no more than the manipulated frantic sensualism of 'repressive desublimation'; having freedom to be immediately gratified (i.e. re-repressed) through the pursuit and consumption of commodified 'false' sexual needs and desires. Foucault's rejection of liberation is more comprehensive and less concrete; 'to dream of escaping from the system ... is to long for a point of transcendental privilege (therefore in complicity with what we oppose); to participate in the system is to reconfirm our complicity once again and so on' (Comay 1986: 112), but it is his rejection of repression which marks his 'complete re-conceptualisation of the logic of history' (Poster 1984: 127) for 'what is peculiar to modern societies ... is not that they consigned sex to a shadow existence, but that they dedicated themselves to speaking of it *ad infinitum* while exploiting it as a secret' (Foucault 1981: 35).

Given the all-pervasive nebulousness of these sexual power/knowledge constellations can it be possible to identify any pattern to this exploitation? Foucault assures us that it is, claiming that four 'great strategic ensembles or channels' may be clearly discerned (1981: 104–5).

1 The hysterisation of women's bodies, whereby female bodies become saturated by sexuality, medically defined as reproductive so that they become 'domestic clearing houses'. 'Mother' becomes along with 'housewife' the controlled and acceptable opposite to the nervous, hysterical woman.

2 The pedagogisation of children's sexuality. Children become defined as pre- or a-sexual, innocent beings with, however, a sexual potential that must be protected by a wide range of guardians, doctors, teachers, nurses and, of course, parents.

3 The socialisation of procreative behaviour. Economic and social pressures elaborate the need to procreate and to be 'responsible' parents *vis à vis* children's safety, security, well-being, etc. These particular discursive forms relate to such issues as fertility, sterility, contraception, inheritance, etc.

4 The psychiatrisation of perverse pleasure. The sex instinct becomes isolated as a distinct and seperate biological, psychological instinct or perverse type.

These strategic channels merely give us the most summary guidance, they do not necessarily work in tandem, indeed within all four, at all levels from the Mandarin to the mundane there are likely to be disjunctions, ambiguities, contradictions, even conflicts. In general, however, they all mark the progressive deployment of 'bio-power' and the dismantling of 'alliance' machineries so that the most fiercely disputed contemporary 'transfer points for relations of power' (Foucault 1981: 4) attend such issues as family privacy, autonomous parental control over children, female sexuality and the sexuality of children; sex education in schools; child sex abuse within the family; age of consent; the economic responsibilities of separated or divorced fathers; the rights of non-family formations (e g. gay and lesbian couples) to family and adoptive 'parental' status; the rights of transsexuals to marry; access to and control of reproductive technologies, etc. One way or another all of these conflicts denote the persistent encroachment of the state on a diminished 'family', ostensibly to safeguard it.[6] The irony is striking for whilst 'family behaviour has become the most private and personal of all areas of behaviour . . . almost totally free from external supervision and control' (Anderson 1979: 67) its protection, especially from sexual threats, has demanded enhanced state intervention.

Foucault's rejection of the repressive model is clearly an acknowledgment of its discursive dominance in distracting us from sexuality as a target of power; '. . . the image of the imperial prude is emblazoned on our restrained, mute and hypocritical sexuality' (Foucault 1981: 3). Behind the prude, however, have developed elaborate practices of *scientia sexualis*, the mechanism by which the proliferation of discourses has effected asymmetrical procedures of coercion, intimidation and surveillance by and of oneself and others.

Whereas the *ars erotica* of traditional civilisations drew the 'truth' of sexual pleasure from accumulated personal experience, *scientia sexualis* delivers the truth from 'experts' and 'saviours' in instructional discourse. Bodies in all their dimensions are measured; symptoms and treatments isolated; 'types' catalogued; acts 'accounted'; orgasmic dysfunctions and potentials treated; all

18

as forms of secularised confessional sites in the exercise of 'bio-power'.[7] Through them we find our innermost sexual souls cleansed through the verbalisation of desires and practices in medical, psychoanalytic, criminal, educational, sociological, philosophical and historical examinations. Indeed Foucault's own analysis, intended though it clearly was (as evidenced by its self-consciously unconventional form and language) to 'by-pass' existing discourse, inevitably also becomes an exemplar of the entire process, a secular confessional demonstrating the ultimate futility of resistance.

As a result sex becomes associated with everything requiring explanation no matter how minor or apparently non-sexual. We demand redemption through knowledge and understanding of our sexual souls in terms of elusive, mysterious, unfathomable feelings of guilt, shame, embarrassment, innocence, content-ment, happiness, fulfilment as mediated by the diagnostic and curative powers of 'experts' to whom all is at great cost revealed. These systems of (sexual) ideas become systems of power and by internalising them we truly become sexual subjects.

If *La Volonté de savoir* 'dramatically changed the field of sexual history' (Gilbert 1979: 1020) its influence on the sociology of sexuality has been no less great, despite being anti-sociological in many of its precepts and implications. Ensconced within the highest levels of social constructionist meta-theory, sexuality is transformed from the singular, coherent, constant essential given of dominant discourse into sexualities, historical artefacts multifarious and dynamic in form and context. More specifically, the obsessive pursuit of sexual knowledge as the all pervasive prime source of subjugation in modern societies becomes irrevocably a legitimate object of sociological enquiry, galvanising existing fragments of interactionist and factual accounts of 'sexuality as an objective reality' (Plummer 1975: 46) of formal laws and institutions, into potential complex unity.

The bravura force and commitment of Foucault's counter-thesis are also, however, the source of its sociological weaknesses, for *La Volonté de savoir* is largely a work driven by negation, an exer-cise in deconstruction rather than construction. Ironically, all social constructionist accounts are more concerned to deconstruct taken-for-granted essentialist notions than with developing alternative constructionist frameworks, but this is especially so with the discourse obsessed polemics of *The Will to Know*, specifically designed not to carry 'the function of proof' (Foucault 1972: 193). The result is a world of as much apparent 'fixity and truth' (Weeks 1989: 200) as any arrived at from essentialist reasoning, a superstructural immaterial world without active human agents, formal hierarchies of control or material substance.

Inevitably, given its fundamental prominence, the radical reformulation of power is at the heart of these problems. Within sociological analysis it is of course by no means radical to argue that power is immanently present in, and exercised through, norms,[8] folkways,[9] mores, institutions[10] or 'ideological state apparatuses'.[11] In all these ways the terrain is clearly marked out with the potential for power/knowledge constellations in the Foucauldian sense. However, what must most concern the sociologist in this latter scheme is the radical denial of 'active' self-determining human agents in a material world. Specifically, Foucault's emphasis on complete subjectivity brings his analysis into direct confrontation with the most basic sociological equation; social structure plus social consciousness equals social action. Sociologically social beings cannot be simply regarded as 'passive agents' in the determinate flow of events.

Sociology is 'a science which attempts the interpretive understanding of social action in order thereby to arrive at a causal explanation of its cause and effects' (Weber 1947: 110). By action, Weber meant all human behaviour to which the acting individual attaches subjective meanings, action being social when 'by virtue of the subjective meanings attached to it by the acting individual (or individuals) it takes account of the behaviour of others and is thereby oriented in its course' (p. 110). Accordingly the basic unit of sociological analysis is actor orientation, the anticipation of the reciprocal significance of action, which bestows upon them a social quality. Weber employed the term 'social relationship' to denote

> the behaviour of a plurality of actors in so far as, in its meaningful content, the action of each takes account of that of others and is oriented in these terms. . . . Thus, as a defining criterion, it is essential that there should be at least a minimum of mutual orientation of the action of each to that of the others. Its content may be of the most varied nature: conflict, hostility, sexual attraction, friendship, loyalty or economic exchange.

> (Weber 1947: 118)

For Marx, too, human activities might be constrained, limited, determined by aggregate forces and material conditions which lie beyond their individual wills, but still they are conscious activities; 'Man makes his life activity itself an object of his will and consciousness. He has a conscious life activity. Conscious life activity distinguishes man from the life activity of animals. Only for this reason is his activity free activity' (Marx quoted in Frankl 1974: 22).

Foucault's discourse-colonised agents are not, of course, animals but nor are they conscious human actors, being robotically unconscious and unfree. Admittedly academic sociology has on occasion driven the free human agent into some tight corners. Parsons (1971: 7), for example, talks of 'acting units' in hyper-elaborate normative systems leaving little apparent scope for subjective agency and *en passant* even employs examples which serve as interesting precursors of the Foucauldian *scientia sexualis*, by arguing that within medical professions, norms and rules not only define conditions of entry, demarcation of professional boundaries, the prescription of rights and obligations of practitioners in relation to wider society, etc., but also serve as rules of 'etiquette', which dictate the inter-personal relations between practitioners and clients leaving those involved with little room for independent self-determined manoeuvre (Parsons 1952). In these terms Parsons too understands power as 'an attribute of the *total system*' (Parsons 1959: 81) comparable, he argues, making a potent comparison in contrast to Foucault's immaterialism, to the circulating medium of the economy: money. Even Parsons, however, cannot obliterate 'free activity' and the 'active subject' albeit because inherent systemic deficiencies require dynamic reformulations of restrictive norms. The social system's ubiquitous drive for enhanced economic adaptive capacity inevitably strains the system into new dynamic equilibria with dysfunctional consequences, especially in the key discourse-inducing process of socialisation, itself always wanting for greater efficiency. In these circumstances Parsons' immanent power is of necessity reinforced, symbolically and practically, by elaborate hierarchies of formal power in which, on occasion, human agents must take decisions over other agents who, on occasion, may 'resist', perhaps due to incomplete socialisation and centrally expressed through relative access to his key circulating medium of power: money.[12] On the former point Parsons notes that in addition to

> the relatively unconditional loyalties of the population to society, support . . . can be mobilised by those exercising power, [through] the facilities they have access to [notably the control of the productivity of the economy] and the legitimation that can be accorded to the positions of the holders of power.
>
> (Parsons 1959: 81)

Foucault's attempt to achieve an 'intricate local understanding of the workings of power' (B. Marshall 1989: 268) certainly provides a welcome corrective to analyses based solely on objective juridical forms (Dreyfus and Rabinow 1983), but his preoccupation with the *completeness* of power in these 'micrological aspects' eradicates human agency and 'blinds him to the perseverance of traditional forms of domination . . . economic, political and cultural' (Wolin 1986: 80). To similar effect his eagerness to attack the naive determinism of the repressive relationship between capital accumulation, the capitalist state and sexuality, questions the survival and discursive impact of the first, denies the role of the second and leaves sexuality detached from both, which is unwarranted and illogical given the multifarious ways in which sexual discourses formally and informally inhabit both state and market relations.

Some might argue that this verdict is harsh and certainly his work is not unambiguous. In *The Archaeology of Knowledge* (1972) he argued that 'a specific discursive practice provides a number of available subject positions from which it is possible for a specific individual to formulate or enunciate linguistic statements' (O'Higgins 1982–3: 12) but such formulation remains the product of discursive rather than subject input, for the enunciating subject he tells us 'should not be regarded as the author of the formulation' (p. 15). Also, in some of his later observations he acknowledged, mostly indirectly, that whilst sexual power/knowledge is predominantly immanent, there is a monitoring and controlling requirement. In the following extract from a 1982 interview we find not only a re-statement of his anti-essentialism and his anti-juridical position but also hints that the latter is not entirely exclusive.

22

Sexual behaviour is not, as is too often assumed, a superimposition of, on the one hand, desires which derive from natural instincts, and, on the other hand, of permissive or restrictive laws which tell us what we should or shouldn't do. Sexual behaviour is more than that. It is also the consciousness one has of what one is doing, what one makes of the experience, and the value one attaches to it.

(Foucault in O'Higgins 1982–3: 10–11)

In the same interview Foucault states that 'sexual acts like rape should not be permitted' (p. 12) and that 'In a society like ours ... homosexuality is repressed, and severely so' (p. 15). Clearly we have to ask by what means other than juridical are the required control and regretted repression to be effected? As Weeks suggests, Foucault's dematerialisation of sexuality is primarily due to his polemical purpose.

It seems clear [that] at certain times some political and social regimes are more 'repressive' both ideologically and physically (as in the case of Nazi Germany) than others. The polemical rejection of the repression hypothesis obscures the very real formal controls that can be exercised and ... implemented ...

(Weeks 1981b: 9)

Implicitly Foucault recognises the influence of Mandarin discourses as means of formal control but again these 'experts' and the knowledge they peddle are seemingly detached from any hierarchy of power despite the fact that they are inextricably linked to the exercise of juridical power over the sexual. What is more, compared to other forms of juridical power, 'Sex law is the most adamantine instrument of sexual stratification and erotic persecution. The state routinely intervenes in sexual behaviour at a level that would not be tolerated in other areas of social life' (Rubin 1984: 285).

In his last observations, gleaned mostly from interviews, Foucault agreed that he had concentrated too much on the problems of truth and power at the expense of individual action (1985: 8) within sites of formal as well as immanent power, asserting that 'sex is not a fatality, it is a possibility for creative life' (1984a: 400). Even in Volumes II and III of *The History of*

23

Sexuality concerned with antiquity, following his 'journey to Greece' (Daraki 1986: 87), 'there is a recognition . . . that forms of subjectivity are the socio-historical creations of human actors and not merely the effects of some structural configuration' (Harrison 1987: 136). Indeed the central task of any history of thought has by this stage become the definition of 'the conditions in which humanity [*l'être humaine*] problematises what is, what human beings do and the world in which they lived' (Foucault 1987: 16).[13] Perhaps the most revealing insights into his understandings of discursive power attend his self-deprecation over the discursive status of his own writings on gay politics, which leaves the homosexual subject some distance short of complete subjection.

> I am wary of imposing my own views, or of setting down a plan or program. I don't want to discourage invention, don't want gay people to stop feeling that it is up to them to adjust their own relationships by discovering what is appropriate in their situations.
>
> (Foucault in O'Higgins 1982–3: 23)

Overall, however, Foucault's commitment to a postmodernist vision incorporating a decentred subject as a mere switching centre for immaterial networks of discursive influence, fails because he does not recognise the latter as the 'superstructure' generated by the base of late capitalism. Postmodernism's 'cheerful mishmash of quotations' (Reynolds 1991: 59) may be dominated by the mass media and information technology but it remains driven by and experienced within structures determined by late forms of capital accumulation, multinational circuits which leave the first world to pursue leisure and lifestyle commodity forms in insular xenophobic ignorance. Thus modern societies are characterised by *apparent* fundamental shifts in social structure with new forms of sectionalism adding to, if not replacing, traditional ties to class so that 'labour or work itself, and the sphere of production seems to be becoming less central to the identity and consciousness of workers' (Lukes 1984: 270). Dominant discourses and consumerism undermine class consciousness in what is depicted as an increasingly middle-class society. Accordingly, sexually differentiated populations take up their place amongst numerous other alternative sources of individual and group reference.

24

Within such a fragmented world Foucault's 'bio-power' is inevitably all-conquering but it is bereft of source, purpose, focus and momentum; here his determined negation is at its most perplexing. As Hussain (1981: 172) notes, we are told that 'there are a set of disparate discourses which are normally not put together', but by refusing to present a mechanism that drives them Foucault preserves their disparateness and leaves us without any ideas as to how they form or where they come from. The wilful disregard for contemporary material developments bemuses but does not convince for if modern societies are characterised by deployment of sexuality surely their deployment of consumerism and citizenship are implicated? If we are in pursuit of spirals of pleasure are we not most likely to realise them through purchase? If modern societies have dedicated themselves to speaking of sex *ad infinitum* while exploiting it as a secret, surely this exploitation has been in commodified and commercial forms? And if sexual obsessiveness is manifest in these material forms surely their realisation and the market's exploitation of them are monitored by the juridical and citizenship interventions of the moral state? Consumerism directs our energies to the purchase of private pleasures and happiness; modern capitalism incorporates expanding 'middle classes' into privacy: 'The desire for privacy has grown in recent years as a reaction to market society' (Younger 1972: para 78). Only sexuality can serve as the link between private desire and its public expression in and through the market. Modern capitalism's ability to pander to happiness and pleasure through consumption clearly underpins the pervasiveness of what in effect is material 'bio-power': 'nearly all enjoyments . . . are in private lives; the immense majority forever excluded from power, necessarily take only a passing interest in their public lives' (Constant cited in Lukes 1973: 65).

Sexuality serves as an especially dense transfer point for relations of immanent power precisely because it crystallises around the distraction of a natural individual personal mystery all the material economic and political strands which tie the individual to both state and market, and it is through such material distractions that capitalism clearly demonstrates yet again its ability to confuse us (Williams 1975: 327).

Perhaps as Poster (1984) argues, if Foucault had devoted detailed attention to the family as a major channel for

25

burgeoning sexual discourses, the latter would have been firmly anchored in 'traditional forms of domination [and] very real formal controls' (p. 138), rather than the free-floating finely spun gossamer things that they are. He continues, 'if the emotional structure of the family is taken into account, differences between the classes regarding sexuality become intelligible' (p. 138). In particular close observation of the family reveals increasing state deployment in and around it to maintain it as the private sphere set apart from public and material life.

> ... the family has acquired a particular strong set of social connotations (haven, retreat from bustle and pressures of the competitive public world, the 'little kingdom' of private virtues, feminine qualities and concerns and the realm of domesticity). It has in many ways become the *essentially* private institution, the heart and centre of everything we associate with what is *not* the state.
>
> (McIntosh 1984: 205)

This *essentially* private institution also marks out the conventional sphere of female/feminine existence and the discursive deployment around patriarchy. Just as Foucault ignores other traditional forms of domination so too he ignores patriarchy, concentrating on the 'obsessive male sexual discourse that runs through the centuries from St Augustine to Philip Roth' (Snitow 1983: 2), failing to acknowledge that 'Women's relationship to the sexual ... has been very different [from men's]' (p. 2).

> While it is no doubt true that all subjects, male and female are structured through discourse, and are in that respect passive, men enjoy another kind of discursive association as well, which is not available to women – an 'acting' or 'speaking' association.
>
> (Silverman 1984: 324)

Again this omission is so obvious it must be intentional but one is at a loss to know why, for it allows feminist critics to claim in some sense that patriarchal power over female/feminine sexuality is outside discourse, and if male–female differences are not the product of power/knowledge formations, and it is interesting that Foucault doesn't even refer to them when dealing with their seemingly relevant strategic deployment around the hysterisation of women's bodies, then they can only exist through the 'sovereign' exercise of power by male subjects (Seidler 1987: 103). If, on the other hand, all manifestations of the sexual are the product of discourse then, logically, sexist[14] knowledge can only be discursive too. If so, where does it come from and what are its relations with other discursive forms? Why does Foucault not deal with it, especially as contemporary feminist analysis which so forcefully presents sexuality as an aspect of patriarchy, parallelled, indeed underpinned other radical critiques of sexuality from the late 1960s onwards, from which Foucault himself emerged and against which his thesis is so clearly a reaction? Once more one can only conclude that his silence on this matter is due to his exaggerated avoidance of implicated material and juridical forms of domination to safeguard his polemical thrust.

In the circumstances it is unsurprising that, once freed from the hypnotic completeness of Foucault's scheme, the arbitrariness of many elements becomes all too apparent. For example, given the criticisms made by feminist commentators in particular, why are the strategic channels of discourse the four selected (Wolin 1986)? Is there really no element of sovereignty within subjects, no opportunity for opposition that doesn't simply reaffirm the oppressive inevitability of power/knowledge, leaving us with political engagement without liberal hope or comfort (Hiley 1984: 192)?

Earlier it was noted that Foucault's analysis has been credited as a radical departure. If that is so, it is in three ways: his humans are devoid of agency; his social systems are immaterial, being lodged in discourse; nor do the latter have or require formal juridical monitoring and enforcement, populations being so effectively subjected to discourses that they have no active decisions to take. In itself, therefore, this particular radical departure goes nowhere, but injects remarkable energy into critiques of it.

It has been suggested that many of the inherent shortcomings of Foucauldian analysis are partially eased by the addition of symbolic interactionist and psychodynamic analyses (Weeks 1981b: 4–6). The former's passionate commitment to an almost hyperactive subject, and the latter's concentration on the emergent modern 'sexual' and sex-obsessed individual certainly provide some of the required analytical support. However, symbolic interactionism[15] is clearly antagonistic to Foucauldian analysis in one key sense; its practitioners reject any analysis which assumes that

> human society or social action can be successfully analyzed by schemes which refuse to recognise human beings as they are, namely, as persons constructing individual and collective action through an interpretation of the situations which confront them.
>
> (Blumer 1969: 192)

However, interactionist approaches to the sexual (Gagnon and Simon 1967, 1969, 1970, 1973a, b, 1986, etc.; Simon and Gagnon 1969; Plummer 1975) share with Foucault an uncompromising anti-essentialism, claiming that 'the sexual area may be precisely that realm wherein the superordinate position of the socio-cultural order over the biological level is most complete' (Gagnon and Simon 1973a quoted in Altman 1981: 100); that sexuality is subject to 'socio-cultural moulding to a degree surpassed by few other forms of human behaviour' (Gagnon and Simon 1973a: 26) so that 'nothing is sexual but naming makes it so. Sexuality is a social construction learnt with others' (Plummer 1975: 30). But whereas for Foucault (1981: 85) sexuality does not result from the choice or decision of an individual subject, for interactionists individual choice and determination have considerable, indeed in earlier versions, seemingly unlimited scope. People, it is argued, behave towards each other and things according to the imputed meanings that both have for them, e.g. through labelling;[16] these meanings are derived from 'scripts' learnt in primary and secondary socialisation[17] but performed through negotiation by actors in interaction with significant others in a range of situational contexts. The subject is active in script interpretation and in the social construction process itself. 'Sexual behaviour is socially scripted behaviour and not the masked or rationalised expression of some primordial drive. The individual learns to be sexual as he or she learns sexual scripts, scripts that invest actors and situations with erotic content' (Gagnon and Simon 1969).

However, clearly much depends here on the extent to which the subject interprets meanings and behaves accordingly. In their more recent work Gagnon and Simon (1986) are emphatic that the sexual becomes significant through its definition as such

28

within *either* 'collective life (which gives sociogenic significance) *or* when individual experiences or development assign it to a special (ontogenic) significance' (p. 104). Presumably the one co-ordinates with the other and so perhaps it should be not *either/or* but *both*. Whatever, Simon and Gagnon here are seeking to solve what has been a perennial problem for interactionists, namely that their focus on the social world as 'intersubjective, emergent and negotiated . . . renders [the source of] sexual meanings as fundamentally problematic' (Plummer 1975: 47–8). Plummer's own solution is a re-statement of Berger and Luckmann's (1967) suggested 'dialectical' relationship between the 'externally coercive, reified and objectified society and the ever-changing, emergent historical forces of men in action' (p. 47). 'Objective' reality as a social construct is enacted upon, internalised and reinterpreted or resisted by subjects. However, whilst Simon and Gagnon and Plummer clearly demonstrate their awareness of the problem, neither can, through symbolic interactionism's implicit ahistoricism, provide a satisfactory solution.

Superficially interactionist 'scripting theory' appears potentially compatible with Foucault's thesis, for even ontogenic significance, it could be claimed, is found within the adoption of microscopic fragments of sexual power/knowledge, and at face value both Foucauldian and interactionist analyses are primarily concerned with micrological aspects of power. But Simon and Gagnon are adamantly pledged to their 'active' subject although in their later work, through direct reference to Foucault, they have been obliged to place rather more constraints on him/her, by recognising the dominant norms, mores and institutions, i.e. 'cultural scenarios', which:

> instruct in the narrative requirements of specific roles [and] provide for the understandings that make role entry, performance, and/or exit plausible for both self and others: providing the who and what of both past and future without which the present remains uncertain and fragile.
>
> (Gagnon and Simon 1986: 98)

However, Gagnon and Simon argue that such collective scripts, even in the most traditional social contexts, are rarely entirely predictive of actual behaviour because their inherent generalisations deny specific relevance. Thus additional

29

'inter-personal scripts' transform the subject from the passive re-enactment of 'cultural scenarios' to partial scriptwriter or adaptor 'as he/she becomes involved in shaping the materials of relevant cultural scenarios into scripts for context-specific behaviour' (p. 99).

If restricted to 'cultural scenarios' and 'interpersonal scripts' the subject's self-scripting could still be limited to the pre-determined expression of colonising discourses but Gagnon and Simon go further and insist that, when actors are faced with alternative outcomes and the need to rehearse the possibilities which thereby become available to them, a third layer of 'intrapsychic scripts' comes into play, enabling decisions to be made through the 'symbolic reorganisation of reality in ways that make it complicit in realising more fully the actor's many-layered and sometimes multivoiced wishes' (p. 99).

Thus Gagnon and Simon's 'subject' has recently become, in response to earlier criticisms of over-individualisation and self-determination, constrained by layers of scripts, which at their most general, seemingly meet up with the sexual power/ knowledge complexes of Foucault. But the latter's fundamental premise of subject creation 'fixed' by discourses which leave people 'powerless to make discriminations in their sexual experiences and with a false sense of freedom that anything goes' (Seidler 1987: 103) stands as a firm barrier between the full integration of the two. Whilst Foucault 'does not help illuminate the difficulties in personal and sexual relations or the problems people face in changing themselves' (p. 103), symbolic inter-actionists have no such difficulties, indeed theirs are of a different order, for so concentrated is their focus on interactional process that the larger socio-cultural context is largely taken as given and ignored, and to strange effect in that, e.g. 'deviant sexual socialisation is so well acounted for that one can barely see the overall pressures towards conformity' (Barrett 1989: 61).

This is the major deficiency of symbolic interactionism. The world is seemingly one of flux, fluidity and unstable unpre-dictable negotiation. Certainly attempts have been made to calm down the hyperactivity of the world and its citizens through the disposition of such artificial sounding stabilisers as 'self-lodging' (Denzin 1971), 'commitment' (Becker 1971), 'perspective' (Becker 1971) and 'emergence' (Plummer 1975), whereby through actors' familiarisation with recurrent meanings and adopted solutions, their recurrent investment of energy in actions which make the adoption of alternatives costly, the actors' world is stabilised into one 'taken for granted' (Schutz 1962 referred to in Plummer 1975: 16), experienced in routinised and unquestioned ways. Symbolic interactionist logic appears to undercut such stases as no more than temporary, especially in modern societies where routinisation appears less realisable, but such arguments have even so been particularly well demonstrated in accounts of 'status passage' (Glaser and Strauss 1971) from 'primary' to 'secondary' stages in such deviant moral careers as the prostitute (Rock 1973), the male homosexual (Dank 1971; Plummer 1981, etc.) and the lesbian (Ettore 1980). Unfortunately what these accounts omit are structural mechanisms, other than the actor's own ability to 'self-lodge', etc., mechanisms specific to particular historical and cultural contexts.

Of course there are 'cultural scenarios' but where do they come from? Are they uniform and consistent or do they demonstrate conflicts in the script writing? Why are certain scripts available and not others? Why are some scripts available only to some and not to others? In whose interests are particular scripts? How do they represent and reproduce existing power relations? Are their effects universal throughout stratified and differentiated populations and if not why not? Are scripts available and negotiated solutions dependent upon the relativities of material power and citizenship status? These are some of the questions left unanswered by symbolic interactionism.

Symbolic interactionism gives us back the 'active' though not necessarily 'sovereign' subject, occupied by discourses to a degree but still able to improvise his or her scripts, and to this extent the perspective's value in the sphere of the sexual has been demonstrated amply by its major proponents, especially in examination of the complexities of adult sexual socialisation and career deviance and status passage.

Even so, concern with the intricacies of deviant interactional processes has led symbolic interactionism to also ignore their structural setting. Clearly given the role of 'cultural scenarios' and lesser scripts in framing actors' behaviours we have emergent on-going negotiations with cultural standards, norms, values, etc., but, as with Foucault, the latter are resiliently detached from hierarchical material relations and associated

31

forms of political and juridical dominance. It is not necessarily assumed of course that such contextualisation is unimportant, it is simply not the object of interactionist interest. Simon and Gagnon's three script levels may be intended to bridge the gap between individual and society, but the traffic seemingly moves in one direction only: towards society from the individual, rather than the other way about, and the destination is never reached.

Thus, whilst there is the potential for a relationship between discursive and interactionist analyses, albeit a problematic one given the head-on conflict over the status of the subject, it remains ephemeral due to the common failure to establish the material contexts within which sexual discourses and scripts occur; those of capital, class and the state. 'Strategic channels' and 'cultural scenarios' depict a world of innumerable free floating, possibly chaotic and incoherent colonising 'ideas' and expressions which construct sexual subjects who have no material existence. It is not surprising, therefore, that those who press the case for a strong complementary relationship between discursive and symbolic interactionist approaches, overstate the randomness of sexual discourses and the individualism of their effects.

> ... the meanings we give to sexuality in general ... are socially organised, but contradictory, sustained by a variety of languages which seek to tell us what sex is, what it ought to be, and what it could be. Existing languages of sex embedded in moral treatises, laws, educational practices, psychological theories, medical definitions, social rituals, pornographic or romantic fictions, popular assumptions and sexual communities, set the limits of the possible. We in our various ways try to make sense of what we are offered.
>
> (Weeks 1989: 208)

On the contrary, whilst fully accepting that we are likely to encounter different sets of sexual instructions and that a common ideological theme built into them all is that no pattern to them exists, not only may such patterns be discerned, so may their structural origins, their means of promulgation and their effects, not least because increasingly the most important discursive input to sexual power/knowledge is that which formalises sexual minority status into particular forms of citizenship, which in turn govern access to specifically sexual and sexualised markets. It is especially interesting that whilst neither discursive nor symbolic interactionist accounts have any doubt that sexuality is socially constructed, neither credits this construction to economic or state interests. Nor, less surprisingly, does a third social constructionist school, psychodynamic analysis, which provides much of the discursive or scripting groundwork for the high market exchange value which has increasingly accrued to the sexual in the latter decades of this century. If sexuality is 'exploited as a secret', psychodynamic analysis has constructed the secret as one worth pursuing to the commodity limit.

The significant intellectual break with biological determinist reasoning occurred within the works of Freud (1905). Consistently they mark a rejection of numerous essentialist assumptions about gender and sexuality: e.g. the assumed equivalence between maleness and sexual activity and femaleness and sexual passivity, though admittedly Freud was only able to do this by describing 'active' females in terms of male/masculine characteristics; the view that sexuality consists of a biologically instinctive drive towards heterosexual genital forms; that sexuality manifests itself only after puberty; that sexuality and genitality are necessarily the same thing and therefore that sexuality is normally and naturally restricted to procreativity.

Sexuality thereby became rooted in polymorphous sensations and diffuse pleasures which emerge at birth, subsequently becoming subject to learned rules of cultural expression within the family unit, both positively, albeit unnaturally, channelled and negatively repressed into the unconscious. Thus psycho-analysis identifies a psychic domain with its own sexual rules and autonomy through the conjunction of awareness of the body and the constraints and demands of culture, which is also sensitive to mental activities within constructive and repressive experiences and developments. The behavioural results are thus but part of the sexualisation process, for much else is consigned to the unconscious 'the way in which we acquire the rules of culture through the acquisition of language' (Weeks 1985: 132). For Lacan (1968), possibly the most influential of recent psychodynamic theorists, the unconscious is primarily marked out by the internalisation and repression of symbols and ideas immersed in language which carry with them deep and dark sexual memories and desires. Given that the unconscious is a product of repression it follows that the varieties of the sexual thereby constructed are manifestations of power.

33

Mitchell's (1975) attempt to develop a materialist feminist theory of gender and sexuality observes that in Freud's work 'psychoanalysis is not a recommendation for a patriarchal society but an analysis of one' (p. 15). Thus within the patriarchal family triad (father, mother, child) such Freudian cornerstones of the female child's psychodynamic development as penis-envy should be interpreted, claims Mitchell, as an emerging awareness not of physical, anatomical difference and inferiority but of how the penis is culturally defined as superior in a world governed by the law of the Father. Similarly the Oedipal conflict is not a real conflict, but the crisis point at which sexual mores and institutions require the forced 'forgetting' of culturally unacceptable desires and their consequent consignment to the unconscious whence they may later erupt to displace identities. Thus desire 'is not reducible to an appetite, a drive, an instinct: It does not create the self, rather it is part of the process of the creation of the self' (Gagnon and Simon 1986: 100–1) through the internalisation (sublimation) of the sexual immersed in symbols and language.

Psychoanalytic theory has proved a major source of inspiration for some sociological accounts of primary socialisation (Parsons and Bales 1964); 'the internalisation of the culture of the society into which the child is born' (p. 17). Parsons and Bales incorporated into the Parsonian systemic paradigm a refined form of Freud's account of psycho-sexual development but, as with Foucauldian, symbolic interactionist and Lacanian psychodynamic analyses, they perceive this process as largely one of reifying the ideological over and above the material, claiming, for example, that the 'most important part of this [socialisation into] culture ... consists in the patterns of value which ... constitute the institutionalised patterns of society' (p. 17). Such analyses address important links in the social construction chain but, despite exhaustive (and exhausting) attempts to prove otherwise, they can be no more than hypothetical in their detailed exposition of precisely how we learn cultural standards in general, and sexual standards in particular.

As with Foucauldian and symbolic interactionist analyses, no convincing attempt is made by psychodynamic analysts to address relations between spheres of production, distribution and exchange, consumption and the state. The only structure recognised, seemingly for the obvious reason that it is the immediate site of construction and repression, is the nuclear family, which whilst it *could* serve as the bridgehead into more substantial structural forms, is not so used, largely because of psychodynamic analyses' lack of historical or cultural specificity. Mitchell (1975) has argued that Freud's own analysis is specific to patriarchal bourgeois forms within capitalism, but this is an uncommon and generous view for clearly Freud in such works as *Totem and Taboo* (1950) and *Civilisation and its Discontents* (1963) addresses psychodynamic demands in transhistorical, universal, indeed mythic terms.

Discourses, scripts, language; sexualities appear in all these accounts, Foucauldian, symbolic interactionist, and psychodynamic, to be the product of and to exist within ideologies divorced from material relations. There is commitment to sexualities as social constructs so that even within the unit of class and citizenship, the family, sexuality's psychodynamic construction is detached from material constraints and circumstances. As Foucault insisted, the main significance of psychodynamic analysis is not its discovery of repression but its role as major perpetrator of comprehensive clusters of power/ knowledge, the 'cultural scenarios' of *scientia sexualis*. As such, psychoanalytic scripts are responsible for the subsequent segregation of sexual from material worlds, establish sexuality as an individual mysterious domain and establish the imperative that its pursuit as the essence of our innermost deeply personal and individual selves is the means by which people seek to be conscious of themselves.

Foucauldian, interactionist and psychodynamic approaches to the social construction of sexualities frame the ideological processes involved with commendable vigour: the psychodynamics of learning of sexuality as a unique secret, the saturation of sexual power and knowledge around the pursuit of its discovery or disclosure, and consequent negotiation of actions within particular social contexts. However, the sexualisation of modern societies cannot be fully comprehended without attention being given to the material dynamics of late capitalism and their repercussions upon the state and the material relations through which populations relate to both.

2

SEXUAL RIGHTS AND COMMODITIES

The material construction of sexual citizenship

The fact that American capitalism can co-opt almost anything no matter how ostensibly subversive is a truism so bizarre, so fascinating in its implications, as to give many sensitive souls perpetual culture shock.

(Blachford 1981: 185)

In discussing the relative merits of discursive, symbolic interactionist and psychodynamic approaches to sexuality, Weeks (1981b: 3) observes that they all positively reject 'sex as an autonomous realm', as 'a natural force with specific effects'. In doing so, however, all three construct sexuality as autonomous in a different and negative sense, as discretely separate from material relations and hierarchies of control. Populations appear to be identified by their sexualities alone, as though the sexualisation of modern societies has severed commitments to class, market and state and purged any related consciousness of kind. Despite advocacy of social constructionist principles, all three fail to apply them to the material specificities of time and place. The social, economic and political emergence and organisation of sexual status groups in modern societies *has* been notable, but within not outwith the complex processes, structures and power relations of capitalism. Sexuality is inextricably tied to capitalism's requirements for reproduced labour of different values, the buoyant consumerism of the metropolitan economies and, as with all capitalist social relations, sexuality's material construction is effected not only directly through the market, but also mediated through the state's formal machineries and practices of citizenship, and in all these arenas sexuality is, albeit attenuated, a channel of class relations.

36

Marx's dialectical materialism demonstrates how social beings have no nature prior to material history and struggle and are the product of an ensemble of the social relations determined by the mode of production. Matter is the primary reality:

> The mode of production in material life determines the social, political and intellectual life processes in general. It is not the consciousness of men that determines their being, but on the contrary, their social being that determines their consciousness.

> (Marx 1904, Preface)

For Marx social 'entities' and 'events' are not segregated, disparate things 'existing in a set of eternal, external spatial relations' (Fletcher 1971: 375), but mutually interdependent parts of one vast continuous process, giving rise to qualitatively new forms of social reality determined by the mode of production. The existence of forces of production requires that social beings be related to them and through them to each other. The making and distribution of commodities determines forms of property relations amongst social beings, the existence of *definite* means of production requiring *definite* forms of social relations. Thus material products embody human relationships, alienated and commodified.

The significance of sexuality to such a scenario is apparently oblique but in practice fundamental in that the 'maintenance and reproduction of the working class is, and must ever be, a necessary condition to the reproduction of capital. But the capitalist may safely leave its fulfilment to the labourer's instincts of self-preservation *and of propagation*' (Marx 1938: 571, my emphasis).

Capitalism's requirement for the commodity of maintained and reproduced free wage labour provides this earliest sexual commodity form, whilst capitalism's subsequent need for labour quality rather than quantity in first world economies, has devalued procreative sexuality and progressively released the commodity potential of non-procreative forms. In such circumstances Foucault's avoidance of the material context of the late nineteenth-century 'discursive explosion' through his four strategic channels of sexual discourse seems wilfully perverse, for in part all four are reflections on procreation as the primary commodity form. More significantly perhaps, they are also concerned with women's prior commitment to propagation, privacy and domesticity expressed through the ideology of essential femininity. Women are 'naturally' mothers and unnaturally waged labour, women's sexuality primarily procreative, not recreative. Masculine sexuality by comparison is relatively free from alliance constraints just as male labour is waged, public, alienated and free. Propagation as the first sexual commodity determines that female waged labour will initially be less free and of lower value than that of men. Given that other sexual minorities deviate from this primary sexual commodity form and are accordingly constructed out of their supposed gendered as well as sexual differences their labour too, is potentially less free and of lower value than that of men, as well as qualitatively different to that of both men and women.

The value of free wage labour is normally interpreted as uniformly average, but in *Capital* (1938) Marx cites as determinants of concrete differences in the value of labour powers such criteria as training expenses, natural diversity and the part played by the labour of women and children. Waged work in every advanced capitalist society continues to be sharply differentiated along sex and gender lines (Hakim 1979),[1] reflecting the persistence of material definitions of propagation as the first sexual commodity and women's prior responsibility to the family.[2]

Within the material constraints of: the 'use-values' of female domestic labour;[3] the sexual division of labour and skills;[4] the state's role in reproducing the position of women within the family and in circumscribing forms of employment available to women;[5] the elaboration of exploitative ideologies of housewife and mother;[6] the extension of modest forms of property to working-class families which reinforce the material dependency of women upon men;[7] the extension of the law as a mechanism for regulating the working-class family[8] and the forms and extents of welfare state involvement in the reproduction of labour power;[9] etc.; within all these constraints free female wage labour is distinguished by being less free than male labour and of lower value. Contemporary trends may be towards greater female participation in wage labour and prominent are the flagship campaigns to counter discrimination and equalise opportunities, but apart from selected professional and managerial employment fields, these deep-rooted distinctions between gender differentiated labour forms persist (Hakim 1979; Beechey 1986a, b).

'Natural' female domesticity underpins the 'natural' differentiation between female and male skills. Women attract restricted training and employment opportunities;[10] are more prone to deskilling;[11] are more flexible (i.e. more disposable) in terms of time, availability and tolerance of conditions;[12] are politically less well organised;[13] have some reserve army capacities[14] though largely deployed in secondary labour markets.[15] All this results in considerable vertical and horizontal employment segregation (Hakim 1979, 1981) in part justified by the inevitable, because natural, intervention of motherhood.

Whatever the enormously complex debates about the origins and extents of these characteristics of female free wage labour they demonstrate, as do those of other labour forms, e.g. 'racialised class fractions' (Miles 1982) that labour types differ in value, and that their values, qualitative and quantitative, are institutionalised within citizenship machineries, so that the political and social unity of labour is fragmented. The development of women's civil, political and social rights testifies to their progressive emergence as free labour, different and of less value to that of men. Of course they testify too to the struggles and conflicts fought at the work-place and through the state to alleviate exploitation, win freedoms, enhance protective legislation and maximise welfare support, for state citizenship principles and practices have become a major site of displaced struggles over the qualitative and quantitative requirements of capitalism (Gordon 1976). Anti-discrimination legislation (1975) is a testament to female citizenship's origins in lower labour value arising out of capitalism's exploitation of women's 'natural' work in reproducing labour including its propagation.

For some committed monetarists, free markets break down such discrimination because 'bigots are weak competitors' (Bolick 1988: 49). Marx proposed that where possible 'individual capitals will purchase labour powers . . . below the average social value' (1938: 599). Similarly it is argued that markets have an amoral tendency to commodify and commercialise all and everything, but such possibilities are severely circumscribed by discriminatory practices based on the qualitative criteria and goals of both commercial enterprises and the monitoring state. Markets by definition incorporate the norms and practices of advantaged groups (Sunstein 1991), devalue the products and enterprises of identifiable minorities (Dipboye *et al.* 1974, 1977), whom they are less inclined to employ and to whom they are less inclined to sell. Far from such discriminatory behaviour irrationally placing a self-imposed tax on operations (Sunstein 1991), it rationally respects the material power of, and prevents market withdrawal by, offended third party participants. There is a mutually reinforcing effect among the various sources of market discrimination *vis à vis* all minority labour types: 'The effect of discrimination on preferences and beliefs fortifies existing prejudice, produces a decrease in human capital, leads to more in the way of statistical discrimination and increases the unwillingness of third parties to deal with blacks and women' (Dipboye *et al.* 1977: 288).

Sexual difference clearly is of a different order to those of gender and ethnicity in that it is not overt but has to be declared or exposed, but mainstream market pressures supported by legal judgements discourage revelation and exposure in both production and consumption relations. Sexual minorities' abilities to minimise discrimination through concealment, aping dominant values and/or seeking work in more appropriate and tolerant gendered employment sectors testifies to these market effects and confirms employers' views of the discriminated through their lower and specific forms of visibility. Formally and informally sexual minority presence in 'sensitive' medical, educational and military employment is rigorously policed, revelations of deviance mobilising discriminatory market effects. Alternatively certain areas of work, e.g. gender typed 'feminine' and/or servicing work, less free and lower paid, are more accessible to and tolerant of sexual minorities. Whether revealed or not, employment practices constrain and attribute lower value to the labour of sexual minorities, reinforcing dominant legal and moral sexual standards. To argue that propagation is the first sexual commodity within capitalism is not to argue that propagation's sexual primacy is solely determined by material interests, as Foucault's examination of alliance discourses makes clear, but to argue that from this original colonisation of reproductive sexuality, all subsequent diverse sexual social forms have material influences and implications, mediated and contested through citizen–state struggles. Since the 1970s the material construction of sexualities has been most spectacularly manifest not only through consumerism's colonisation of specialised sexual leisure and lifestyles, but also through its deployment of covert coded sexual messages to further the comercialisation of all commodity forms.

D'Emilio (1983a, b) has pursued such arguments, but in a slightly different sense. He claims that capitalism's requirement for differentiated free wage labour is directly linked to the sexualisation of modern societies in that free labour is potentially and symbolically as free morally and sexually as it is economically, politically and legally. For him the fundamental contradiction between capitalism and the family, partially manifest in the specific instance of lower female wage labour value, has become a general channel of material sexual discourse. As the material basis of the family has been undermined through its loss of economic functions, so too have relations between its members.

> As more adults have been drawn into the free wage labour system, and as capital has expanded its sphere until it produces as commodities most goods and services we need for our survival, the forces that propelled men and women into families and kept them there have weakened.
>
> (D'Emilio 1983a: 148)

Capitalism's requirement for free wage labour initially freed male labour from pre-capitalist alliance constraints of economy and kin, so too in the late twentieth century its requirements for cheaper and different female wage labour forms has contributed to the weakening of females' alliance attachments. Female sexuality has, as a result, been the focus of diverse, often contradictory, discourses which contest the residue of pro-creation and domesticity within a consumer capitalism no longer content with such restricted definitions. Thus the whole range of female self-determination, liberation and independence issues carries weighty sexual power/knowledge tensions concerning self-determination and self-control away from procreative sexual meanings. Women, in the broadest and simplest of senses, as they have become free wage labour have become socially and morally freer to be sexual, or, more accurately, to negotiate with competing sexualising discourses. Still severely proscribed by femininity, female sexuality has nevertheless become active, recreational, material, independent, consumerist and consumed, a key site of conflict, resistance and division. The sexualisation of

41

women in the post-war period may have been largely in the interests of men (Jeffreys 1990; Faraday 1981) but men's interests have been mediated through the market, and there have been sufficient reverse discourses to suggest that this sexualisation has not been one-dimensional or irresistible.

It is in logical extension of this argument that D'Emilio (1983a) makes the intriguing claim that late twentieth-century changes to capitalism's 'free labour system . . . [have] allowed significant sections of the population to call themselves gay' (p. 148), and, by implication, transvestite, transsexual, bisexual, etc. Conversely the loss of many of its economic functions, not least its reduced significance as the site of propagation in the face of the commoditising market, has meant that the family has become first and foremost a 'social, political and natural unit of great effective and *symbolic* power' (p. 148). As the pursuit of profit maximisation drives the amoral market to eat away at moral and legal constraints, so the family has increasingly been mobilised to serve the integrative hegemonic interests of the state. Crudely the market has no morality other than its pursuit of profit, but still requires a state to maintain the fetishised conditions within which that profit may be accumulated: consensus, law, order, justice, freedom, morality. It is in this sense that sexuality's peculiar quality in the modern world would appear to consist of complex uneven dialogues between economy and state over the quantitative benefits of commodification and the qualitative costs of immorality and decadence, dialogues conducted through a population of apparently great structural complexity.

For some the diverse and contradictory metropolitan social relations of late twentieth-century capitalism signifies the demise of class relations, even of capitalism itself, and within such arguments the emergence of sexual minorities, associations, parties, affiliations, communities and lifestyles is, with comparable ethnic, religious, regional and other examples, much quoted in evidence. Post-industrial utopianism has been notoriously tempted to view the differentiation of modern populations as indicative of deep structural fragmentation and disintegration:

> There seems to be a tendency to believe that, just because social movements articulate legitimate values and concerns which are not identical with those of traditional labour movements, then somehow all these women, gays, Greens,

etc., are not living in the same society, not encountering similar problems to do with war, economic power, public administration, religion, education, poverty, legal rights and other overlapping and interconnecting public issues.

(Frankel 1987: 184)

Since Westergaard's 'pioneering critique' (Blackburn 1972: 119) over twenty-five years ago, the 'myth of classlessness' (Westergaard 1973) of late capitalist Britain has been repeatedly asserted via all manner of clichés from 'the affluent society', 'home centred society', 'mass society', 'post-capitalism', to the ultimate 'postmodernism'.[16] Then as now evidence belies the easy assumptions behind these claims. Changes there have been in first world social relations of production but globally the capitalist dynamic persists. Capital has not been significantly dispersed or democratised,[17] rather it has been transferred from less profitable (i.e. industrial manufacture increasingly consigned to 'developing countries') to more profitable (i.e. tertiary sector, service, banking, finance, pension funds, etc.) sectors of first world economies,[18] where the relatively affluent 'enjoy' the consumerism by which their own economies are sustained.

There have inevitably been diversifying effects on social relations of production in these first world populations. Industrial development based on technological advance has required a first world labour force increasingly differentiated by education, skill and training, with commensurate forms and levels of rewards.[19] Large portions of the economically active enjoy relatively high levels of occupational status, and leisure time.[20] Expansion of higher-grade employment and educational provision has increased opportunities for achieved and perceived social mobility in private and, despite the 'rolling back of the state',[21] public employment. Conversely this overall 'upgrading' has been accompanied by increased unemployment and deployment of sections of the work-force into 'secondary' labour markets based on non-standard types of work (Goldthorpe and Payne 1986). Under such conditions, first world populations are more differentiated, less likely to experience capitalism collectively through production relations, more likely to experience it through consumption relations and via citizen–state relations. Within this scenario egoism, privatisation, individualism, competitive, pecuniary, 'in short capitalist values'

(Lukes 1984), effect populations' lifestyle integration into society as consuming citizens, as members of status-group communities rather than solidaristically as collective sellers of labour (Moorhouse 1983).

> ... in present day society, consumer conduct (consumer freedom geared to the consumer market) moves steadily into the position of simultaneously the cognitive and moral focus of life, integrative bond of society, and the focus of systematic management. In other words it moves into the self-same position which in the past ... was occupied by work in the form of wage labour. This means that in our time individuals are engaged (morally by society, functionally by the social system) first and foremost as consumers rather than producers.
>
> (Bauman 1988: 807)

In Britain this moral engagement through consumer citizenship has by the 1990s been formally acknowledged by the *Citizen's Charter*'s (1991) explicit specification that modern citizenship is a matter of twin responsibilities: those of consumer and taxpayer, protected in the private sector by free market competition and in the public by the neutral state. Whatever else this ideological push signifies, it is indicative of political struggle being further fragmented and displaced from class towards status criteria within which sexual status has become one crucial focus.

Whilst there has been this diversification of social forms: 'many sub-collectivities within the societal community ... the typical individual [participating] through membership in a wide variety' (Parsons 1965: 1015), recent evidence comprehensively 'challenges the view that novel and fundamental changes in the structure of social hierarchy have altered the basis of distributional conflict in modern Britain' (Marshall *et al.* 1988: 9). How could this be otherwise for 'Capitalism's version of society can only be the market ... its purpose is profit in particular activities rather than any general conception of social use' (Williams 1975: 327). Class remains the prime determinant of opportunities for the acquisition of 'goods and opportunities for income ... under the conditions of the commodity and labour markets' (Crompton and Gubbay 1977; Weber 1967: 181), though qualified by status identities and affiliations which, despite being located in hierarchies of moral worth, prestige and honour, are not divorced from capitalism, but in diverse complex forms clearly tied to it. Status 'communities' are constructed and expressed through the market, for 'status groups are stratified according to the principles of their consumption of goods as represented by special styles of life' (p. 182). This stratification of status groups in general, and sexual status groups in particular, is accordingly an inevitable concomitant of capitalism's first world consumerism. The proliferation of status groups generally and sexual status groups in particular is only possible with their entry into formally adjudicated moral status and material needs of legal, free, though unequal, citizenship.[22]

As consumers we are unique individuals with needs, identities and lifestyles which we express through our purchase of appropriate commodities. If therefore our sexual identities are our imperative, inescapable and the deepest reality with which it is our duty to come to terms, then we must come to terms not only with sexuality as bio-political acts, drives, dysfunctions, 'the Big O' (Heath 1982), health, pleasure and happiness, but also with sexuality as commodities. If 'Reality as the consumer experiences it is the pursuit of pleasure' (Featherstone 1983: 19), as 'on display . . . [we] move through the field of commodities' (p. 29) in 'search [of] personal and private satisfactions above all else' (Hobsbawm 1981: 2), the latter are increasingly sexual, their construction and realisation are forged out of material circumstance. The pursuit of the commodified self is the pursuit of the sexual self; individual, private, innermost, accomplished through the acquisition and conspicuous manifestations of style.

The material construction of sexualities within consumerism lies at the very heart of the modern era's instrumental self-interest for whilst consumption and sexual identity and expression are pursued in public, both their objectives remain resolutely fetishised as 'personal' and 'private'.

> Finding their jobs boring, most people do not seek fulfilment through paid labour, but elsewhere. . . . In so far as people have any sense of control over their own destinies, this is more likely to be experienced in the private than the public domain. The private domain may therefore be as crucial for the formation of social identities as the more public milieux of work and production.
>
> (Marshall et al. 1985: 272–3)

Material pressures represent these identities as 'narcissistic', protean, and marketable (Sennett 1980; Lasch 1979), and burden sexuality 'with the tasks of self-definition and self-summary' (Sennett 1980: 95) because:

> sex remains one of the few areas of life where we feel able to be more than passive spectators. . . . It is a feature of modern life that we increasingly define achievement in terms of immediate gratification and the move to burden sexuality with greater expectations is closely related to the stress on ideas of 'self-fulfilment' and 'personal actualisation' . . . ours is a time of increasing demands for private and immediate gratification often without realising how these values are in large part the product of modern consumer capitalism.
>
> (Altman 1982: 82)

'Individual', 'private', 'immediate gratification', are all fetishised consequences of consumerist alienation. As capitalist social relations deprive labour of property and meaningful work, labour is degraded, dehumanised and alienated. Alienated from commodities produced, labour is also alienated from 'false needs . . . superimposed . . . by particular societal interests in his repression; . . . needs which perpetuate toil, aggressiveness, misery and injustice' (Marcuse 1964: 5).[23] Alienation is a source of conflict and struggle amongst a population battling to be conscious of its social interests, unities and political purposes, but too often accounts of consumerism convey a Foucauldian immanence and pessimism akin to Marcuse's vision of our passive colonisation by 'material and intellectual needs that perpetuate obsolete forms of the struggles for existence' (1964: 4). His 'one-dimensional man' (p. 10) needs to buy, possess and consume, in the process perpetuating conformity and alienation, whilst sharing his consuming passion with everyone else: 'mass consumption claim[s] the entire individual' (Fromm 1955: 131), the 'process of consumption . . . as alienated as the process of production' (p. 120). Through it we become more alone and isolated, tools in the hands of overwhelmingly strong forces outside of ourselves; 'individuals' but bewildered insecure individuals, our insecurities soothed by the transient pleasures of self purchase, 'idiots' of McLuhan's Brave New Global Village (Sturnock in *Independent on Sunday* 8 July 1990). Such accounts

leave us powerless, 'lost in objects ... man ... lost to himself'
(Frankl 1974: 24).

> The processes of capitalist relationships reproduce
> themselves in the consciousness of man and, in turn
> reproduce a society that reflects an image of man as the
> seller and buyer of work, talent, aspiration or fantasies.
> Everything has its price. A man's ability is merely a
> commodity. It has to be sold in accordance with the
> demands of the market.
>
> (Frankl 1974: 26)

But the market is itself an arena of choice, and the
contradictions experienced within it (in the selling of labour of
qualitatively different values and the consumption of
commodities as expressions of identities and status affiliations),
and between it and the state, are the source of complex and
diffuse tensions, struggle and conflict. Certainly within such a
terrain economic, political and moral choices may be
circumscribed by the alienating and distracting effects described
but, as evidence demonstrates all too clearly, these power
relations and the effects which serve to conceal them may
nevertheless be resisted, even subverted. Everything may have its
price but that price need not be paid.

Alienated propagation may be sexuality in its first
commodified form but all sexualities have commodity potential.
If Foucault's discursive explosion on and around sexuality charts
subjects' unquenchable pursuit of knowledge about their true
beings, then in consumerism's high-intensity market setting
knowledge is purchasable and material. What distinguishes
sexuality's presence in the market is its dual specific and general
commodification roles. Specific forms of sexuality are commodified, but all commodities are subject to the coded presence
of sexual messages and imagery. Why should this be so? In brief
the market's pecuniary egoism appears inherently sexual. It is in
this context that Foucault's contribution to any analysis is at its
most persuasive, for surely both market and sexual values are
united in the ultimate fetishisation of the individual as a unique
being. Simultaneously sexuality is both the least apparently
commodifiable aspect of social life, being 'natural', 'personal' and
'private', and for these very reasons it is that part of ourselves
with the greatest commodity potential. We must consume to find

47

and express our natural unique selves, it is beholden upon us to do so. This 'bias to material commodities' (Kline and Leiss 1978: 9) pervades all forms of 'bio-power', sustained by mass culture, advertising, leisure, entertainment, sport, saturated with signs, messages and spectacles, recycling consumer demand and consuming society itself. Fashions, tastes, toys, sports, games, tourism, restaurants, bars, discos, architecture, interior design, shops, cars, all that 'constitutes the very facade of advanced capitalism' (Kellner 1983: 66).

> Not only do the media shape our vision of the contemporary world, determining what most people can or cannot see and hear, but our very images of our own body, our own selves, our own personal self-worth (or lack of it) is mediated by the ominpresent images of mass culture . . .
>   (Kellner 1983: 66)

images which define the legitimacy and privacy of our sexual search for self, and provide us with purchasable alternatives. 'In contemporary consumer societies sex is . . . equated with "private" as distinct from "public" life and seen as the solvent of all problems' (Altman 1982: 82), eminently suited to consumerist ethics because sexuality (especially male/masculine sexuality) is itself objectified and objectifying.

In terms of 'dress, gesture . . . occupation' (Oakley 1972: 16) and sexuality, ideal masculine qualities are of dominance, activity, autonomy, impersonality and rationality. Sexually there is a focus on release, needs, experience, fantasy and achievement (McIntosh 1978a), that is central to self-identity and esteem, yet detached from other aspects of self (Gross 1978; Pleck 1981; Reik 1960). Males are scripted to believe they need sexual release for natural 'hygienic' reasons, 'just as they need three meals a day' (Gross 1978: 94). This detached, discreetly managed, male sexuality is learnt through masturbation-centred childhood and adolescent games which 'focus the male sense of sexual feeling or desire in the penis, giving the genitals centrality' (Simon and Gagnon 1969: 13), and entail heavy peer pressure to demonstrate, especially in the telling (Lees 1986: Wood 1984), potency through numbers of orgasms and conquests (Kanin 1967). In contrast 'innately it seems women have sexual attractiveness . . . men have sexual urges. . . . Men consciously experience and express sexual "needs" that go beyond

48

monogamy' (McIntosh 1978a: 54). Men accentuate the physical aspects of the sexual, 'erotica, pornography, sexual fantasy and objects associated with coitus' (p. 63), whilst in women it is 'more often the relational aspect that has become elaborated. Women have "sexual relationships" whereas men engage in "sex acts" ' (p. 63), and both ideologies reflect the material inequalities which exist between men and women. Women need to attract men because legally, economically and socially their status and security remain primarily found through men. As institution-alised, prostitution highlights men's comparative material superiority, objectifies their sexuality in already alienated forms through the purchase of wife or prostitute, or indeed child, magazine, video or inflatable doll.

This alienated 'dismemberment' of masculine sexualities is abundantly exploited in consumer scripts (Goffman 1976; Coward 1984; Soble 1983; Root 1984):

> I am alone in the underground waiting for a train. All around me are huge images of female parts: giant rubbery peach tone breasts, wet lips, denim bums, damp looking stomachs, long legs in high heels. . . . I don't know where to look that doesn't make me feel vulnerable or angry. A man comes into the tunnel and looks me up and down. All these ads are . . . telling him I am a cunt-thing, a leg thing, a breast thing and that I am waiting for him.
>
> (*Spare Rib* letter quoted in Root 1984: 56)

All masculine sexualities are inherently objectifying, com-modifying and commodified sexualities, even though differentiated by the relative moral worth and market access of their particular forms.

Feminine sexuality in its traditional alliance, procreative form is less obviously commodifiable in comparable objectifying terms, but it was as domestic consumers-in-chief that women played such a crucial role in the first world economies' transformation into consumerism, and the transition in their exposure to objectifying commercial discourses. Simultaneously the post-Kinsey (1948, 1953) and Masters and Johnson (1966, 1970) era has seen a dramatic escalation of fiercely contested 'liberating' recreative and commodifying feminine sexual discourses. Women have greater potential for physical sexual fulfilment than men, they have a right to sexual pleasure, self-determination and independence and, increasingly, the material means to exercise these rights. Definite means of production require definite means of social relations and the material construction of feminine sexualities has placed women in the frontline tensions between amoral market and moral state. The latter's ideological mobilisation of the ideal family has required the reification of traditional alliance feminine virtues and their expression through consonant commodity forms, whilst enabling the market's requirement for free female wage labour and the exploitation and construction of non-domestic female commodity forms. This underlying contradiction between moral state and amoral market contextualises all types of sexual citizenship but it has been nowhere more pronounced or significant than in female/feminine forms, as the many dramatic contests over citizenship rights and duties (abortion, rape in marriage, equal pay, taxation, etc.) testify.

If status groups are 'communities' with common rights and privileges determined by relative moral worth, 'stratified according to the principles of their consumption of goods as represented by special styles of life' (Weber 1967: 181), one must expect the consumerist 'search for private and personal satisfactions above all else' (Hobsbawm 1981: 169) to be reflected in forms of differential sexual citizenship.

Many accounts of the state's relationship to capital reduce its structural and theoretical core and its dynamic excrescences to over-simplifications such as the 'laws of motion' and/or the interests of the bourgeoisie (Hall 1984). Whatever general criticisms may be made of such mechanical models it is clear that given capitalism's oblique commodification of sexualities, state policies towards sexual status groups and sexual issues have been marked by obfuscation. Indeed a state relatively autonomous of capital or bourgeois influence has responded to the complex integrative demands placed on it by effecting a confusing variety of discursive developments. On the broadest level these consist of a liberalising incorporation of sexual minorities into specified legal rights and freedoms, offset by the mobilisation of core moral values to achieve ideological integration, outside of which these newly legalised sexual citizens emphatically remain. Thus, it is intended, is modern society 'brought into line with fundamental trends or tendencies in the social formation' (Hall 1984: 34).

The conditions in which this 'reconstruction' can come about are however, conditional on the effective mastery of the political and ideological, as well as the economic terrain; also on the formation of a social bloc, comprising sections of different classes, which forms the necessary underpinnings of the state; and on the winning over to the bloc of a significant section of the popular classes.

(Hall 1984: 11)

Jessop *et al.*'s (1988) examination of four specific state foci enables a clearer appreciation of these contradictions. The 'social base' includes the 'set of social forces which support – within an accepted institutional framework and policy paradigm – the basic structure, mode of operation and objectives of the state system in its role as the official representative of civil society' (p. 156). It includes normative consensus on values and beliefs as well as institutionalised means and forms of social and political integration. Given that objective material experiences are mediated by populations through interpretations influenced by state ideological interventions and the experience of state structures, sexual issues will, unless negotiated beyond absolute cultural standards, readily mobilise conservative popular sentiments across class and status lines. Also given that, within any one population, experience of sexual issues will be fragmentary and specialised, resistance to the social base will be comparably sectionalised and perhaps 'single-issue'. Battles over sexual rights are invariably limited accordingly, given that sexual minority groups have reduced access to state and political institutions. Only rarely have coalitions of minorities been successfully mobilised to attain sexual reforms in the face of state sexual hegemony.

'Accumulation strategies', from elaborate corporatist economic plans to *ad hoc* inertia, are managed as part of the 'state strategy' which, in addition, determines 'the access of key sectors and social groups to sites of political and economic power' (p. 159). Modern states manifest two key sexual accumulation strategies: first the legalisation of previously illegal and thus non-consuming sexual status groups, for example, most spectacularly, male homosexuals, thus 'releasing' considerable consumer power and enabling the development of considerable specific minority commodity markets. Such 'accumulation strategies' are facilitated by minority status group claims for consumer status and are not simply the consequence of amoral market pressure. Second, the state has to enable 'accumulation strategies' in ways which safeguard qualitative concerns, i.e. do not subvert absolute moral sexual standards. A major strain between sexualised consumerism and state managed 'accumulation strategies' requires the state to somewhow respond to the inherent amorality of the market whilst maintaining the state's fetishised moral authority. This has largely been accomplished in the post-Wolfenden era (the *Wolfenden Report* being the period's most influential statement) by the distinction elaborated between illegality and immorality, whereby in the latter instance the state condemns but permits on grounds that the populations concerned are willing and the behaviours 'private' and victimless. Minority sexual status groups have thus emerged in this legal–moral limbo characterised by specialist 'hidden' community territories and markets within which commodification is strictly policed into a 'privacy' to minimise encroachment on the moral community, but once permitted such a moral and economic space, contests over the relativities of both boundaries have inevitably ensued.

This 'privately legal yet immoral' state policy response has been effective if studies of public attitudes are to be believed, no doubt because overall state strategies reify the state's neutral, unifying, liberal-democratic, detachment from capitalism (Offe 1984).

'Hegemonic projects' concern facilitation of the accumulation process through making economic concessions to the masses of the social base. Jessop *et al.* (1988) distinguish between 'one-nation' and 'two-nation' projects, the former concerning an inclusive conception of the societal community, the latter exploiting a clear division between the majority who deserve to share in the economic benefits, and those who do not. We are all consumers but power differentials are considerable. There is a moral dimension to such strategies too for the New Right has prominently mobilised sexual as well as economic ideologies in 'one-' and 'two-nation' terms. In particular divisive economic strategies have been overlaid by the repeated reification of a one-nation morality to reinforce the social segregation of legal sexual minorities from the moral community and its champion the state. The *Citizen's Charter* (1991) pursues this strategy

52

explicitly with, at its centre, the 'active' but responsible citizen. State strategies do not pass unopposed of course, and inevitably the state has become the site of multiple schisms and tensions around sexual issues, but the combination of legal access for sexual minorities to specialised predominantly leisure and lifestyle markets with, simultaneously, their reiterated 'second nation' moral status has, for the majority, led to political incorporation and maintained their socioeconomic invisibility.

The basis upon which these legal–moral distinctions have been made should be briefly elaborated. The watershed discourse, the *Wolfenden Report* (1957), distinguished between crime and sin as follows: 'it is not the function of the law to interfere in the private lives of citizens, or to seek to enhance any particular pattern of behaviour' (p. 10). Even so it was still the law's duty to:

> preserve public order and decency, to protect the citizen from what is offensive and injurious, and to provide safeguards against the exploitation and corruption of others. . . . Unless a deliberate attempt is made by society, acting through the agency of the law, to equate the sphere of crime with that of sin, there must remain a realm of private morality and immorality which is not the law's business.
>
> (*Wolfenden Report* 1957: 9–10, 24)

It was argued that there was a need for 'more effective regulation of sexual deviance' (Weeks 1981b: 242) for existing legislation encouraged 'disrespect and cynicism' (D'Emilio 1983a: 145).[24] The recommended shift of legal emphasis was from moral to causal judgements (Davies 1975). Rather than appraising behaviours by their moral worth: 'immoral, wrong, wicked' (Davies 1975: 3), legal judgements were to be concerned with proven effects: 'if it turns out that more harm is done by forbidding an activity than by allowing it, then Parliament will permit it, even if most of the members consider the activity to be wrong or immoral' (p. 3). Thus the conjunction of illegality with immorality was severed, and between their boundaries a social, economic and political space created for those newly legalised but still morally reprehensible.

This distinction between illegality and immorality certainly was not intended to weaken moral values, for whilst recommending legalisation of male homosexual behaviours between consenting adults in 'private' Wolfenden deplored the decline in moral standards, defining homosexuality as 'reprehensible from the point of view of harm to the family' (*Wolfenden Report* 1957: para 124) and contemplated the retention of buggery, 'particularly objectionable because it involves coitus and thus simulates more nearly than any other homosexual act the normal act of sexual intercourse' as a separate offence (para 124). Above all else, therefore, public manifestations should be severely restricted:

> We do not think that it would be expedient at the present time to reduce in any way the penalties attaching to homosexual importuning. It is important that the limited modifications of the law which we propose should not be interpreted as an indication that the law can be indifferent to other forms of homosexual behaviour or as a general licence to adult homosexuals to behave as they please.
>
> (*Wolfenden Report* 1957: para 124)

Accordingly the policing of this moral boundary through recourse to a variety of often grossly antique 'receptacle' laws has, in the post-reform period, been notably increased.

The emergent causalist emphasis was in accord with high classic liberal utilitarian principles, proponents claiming Mill as their own, but the removal of criminality from certain victimless sexual behaviours introduced a causal relativism into the equation of sexual citizenship with regard to both citizen–state and consumer–market relations. 'Discourses hierarchise and distribute the various categories of sexual deviance around the norm of marriage, the family and procreation, which provide the particular "regime of truth" ' (Mort 1980: 44). Rather than all non-monogamous heterosexual behaviours being equally illegal, within this new social space which is 'not the law's business', 'no hard and fast line' can be drawn, some becoming more immoral than others, there developed 'incommensurate and irreconcilable conceptions of the [*sexual*] good' (*Wolfenden Report* 1957: para 124) and accordingly incommensurate and irreconcilable concept-ions of consumable identities, lifestyles and communities. The result has been a considerable fragmentation of the boundaries of immorality and legitimacy (Weeks 1985: 55) with commensur-ate inconsistency in enforcement practices, and immense possibilities for battles over further citizenship gains and losses.

In a minimal classical sense 'citizens . . . are all who share in the civic life of ruling and being ruled' (Aristotle 1972: 45), having the right to be consulted on the conduct of the political society 'and the duty of having something to contribute to the general consultation' (Brogan 1960: 4), being 'bound by the results [for] . . . duties flow from . . . rights' (p. 5). Thus idealised citizenship is a matter of simple inclusionary principles of a respectful contractual relationship between autonomous moral subjects and their state. In practice citizenship has developed as elaborate tariffs of partial or complete exclusion according to adjudicated standards of status conformity (Parsons 1965: 1011).[25]

The British approach to citizenship has traditionally been a negative one. With no Bill of Rights 'freedoms' are what is permitted because no common law specifically prohibits them (Dicey 1965). In British constitutionalism it is assumed that Parliament and the legislature are inherently defenders of liberty and that therefore formal legal declarations are unnecessary.[26] By contrast, written constitutions record bills of individual and collective rights and liberties plus basic preconditions for their enjoyment and these 'constitutional guarantees of individual freedom, civil liberties, and political, social, legal, and participatory rights represent the quintessence of constitutionalism in the sense of limited, responsive and accountable government' (Duchacek 1973: 36). Both customary and recorded forms serve as 'symbolic expressions of the unifying forces in a community' (Burdeau 1949: 145),[27] and 'the form by which the group finds its unity in submission to law' (Duchacek 1973: 37). Alternatively, they create an image of ideal citizenship against which the partial qualifications and achievements of peripheral minorities can be measured and towards which aspirations may be directed (p. 3).[28]

Of all the shopping lists of rights and liberties perhaps the most important from the British point of view, given some form of European Union in 1992, is that of the European Convention on Human Rights (1948), ratified by Britain in 1951, and yet to be incorporated into British law,[29] but under which several successful claims against British injustice have been made.[30] Apart from their political and moral contextualisation of citizenship battles, such shopping lists are of limited value, and certainly do not equate with the experiences of citizens. In order to understand how citizenship operates as machinery for formalising exclusion as opposed to idealising inclusion we need to look elsewhere: e.g. to Rawls' contractarianism (Rawls 1972, 1987) and T.H. Marshall's 'justly famous essay' (Ginsburg 1981: 38) *Citizenship and Social Class* (1950).

Rawls (1987) identifies four socially valued stages in the emergent properties of citizenship rights in their constitutional and institutional forms (p. 21). The first consists of those primary goods (*social* and *natural*) which any rational person would want 'whatever his plan of life or social orientation would be' (p. 31). Social primary goods form the basis of all citizenship and include 'the basic liberties' (p. 22) freedom of thought and liberty of the conscience, indispensable to the protection of determinate conceptions of the good within the limits of justice; freedom of movement and free choice of occupation against a background of diverse opportunities; powers and prerogatives of offices and positions of responsibility which 'give scope to various self-governing and social capacities of the self' (p. 23); and income and wealth defined broadly as 'all purposive means' (pp. 22–3) having an exchange value and, finally, the social bases of self-respect – in general those aspects of basic institutions normally essential 'if citizens are to have a lively sense of their own worth as persons and to be able to develop and exercise their moral power and to advance their aims and ends with self-confidence' (p. 22).

Natural primary goods include health and vigour, intelligence and imagination, qualities which are clearly dependent upon primary social goods (Rawls 1972: 62, 303). Rawls locates these primary goods in their specific social contexts as he moves through his other three stages, the second consisting of two 'principles of justice', the first of which is phrased as a right:

(1) Liberties are to be arranged so as to achieve the most extensive justifiable set of equal basic liberties for each and everyone.

(2) Social and economic inequalities are to be arranged so that (a) they are structured by social roles and offices, which are open to all under conditions of 'fair equality of opportunity' and such inequalities in wealth, income and position serve (b) to improve, ideally to maximise, the life situation of the least adavantaged group.[31]

(Rawls 1972: 60, 83, 250, 302–3)

Rawls' third stage is the identification of how (and the extent to which) these two principles of justice are brought to bear on the distribution of primary goods, through any particular society's economic, political and other institutions so that rights and duties are assigned and monitored.

Rawls' fourth stage is in many ways the most interesting for it concerns the 'legitimate expectations' of populations; the extent to which a particular citizenship culture is accepted as given and in which injustices are challenged. Such injustices may be perceived in terms of constitutional rights or state institutional practices (e.g. the jury system, employment practices, welfare accessibility, etc.).

To these four stages Rawls adds the general 'method of effective equilibrium', meaning that in any particular society rights machinery will be mediated by accumulated historical and cultural assessments of what is being done, how and why, in terms of which rationales, etc.

This exposition of universal primary goods institutionalised as extensively as justifiably possible immediately isolates the existing machineries and experiences of citizenship as restrictive on particular subjects' 'self-confidence' and 'sense of self-worth', 'plan of life', 'scope for self-government', realisation and expression of 'social capacities of the self' on the basis of their particular disqualifying, in this instance sexual, 'orientation'. Similarly, linking these 'egalitarian' principles of justice to market constraints of wealth and income, as together part of overall 'legitimate expectations', underlines the close relationship between the two spheres. Also a causal relativism is implicitly incorporated, for once such citizenship principles are established, the history of citizenship rights, whatever the peculiarities of any one society's 'method of reflective equilibrium, consists of battles over the legitimacy of relative claims. The post-Wolfenden reforms therefore legalised citizens who were inevitably released into the causalist fray. Of course Rawls addresses principles of a 'just' citizenship outside and beyond the 'just' effects of the market alone and thus exposes the monetarist crudity of the New Right's 'active' citizen, but already informally most members of sexual minorities, through their willing embrace of the consumer role in secondary markets, have suggested that in practical terms the New Right is not wrong.

T.H. Marshall's (1950) analysis also ties citizenship to the demands and constraints of capitalism. Specifically it was inspired by Alfred Marshall's (1873) observation that the more skilled and affluent artisan members of the working class were learning to value education and leisure more than 'mere increase of wages and material comforts' (p. 5). They were

> developing independence and a manly respect for themselves and therefore a courteous respect for others; they are steadily acquiring the private and public duties of a citizen; steadily increasing their grasp of the truth that they are men, and not producing machines. They are steadily becoming gentlemen.
>
> (A. Marshall 1873: 16)

A. Marshall therefore advocated increased state provision of education for 'only the educated can freely choose and appreciate the good things' (T.H. Marshall 1950: 6), whilst insisting that money provided 'the best measure of motives that no other competes with it' (Pigou quoted in T.H. Marshall 1950: 7). State intervention should not go beyond educational provision however, for 'free choice takes over as soon as the capacity to choose has been created' (p. 6). For A. Marshall, therefore, citizenship rights are primarily rights of market access and choice.

In pursuit of such arguments T.H. Marshall claimed 'there is a kind of basic human equality associated with ... full membership of a community; citizenship, which is not inconsistent with inequalities which distinguish the various economic levels in the society' (1950: 8). Inequalities of class may be made acceptable and not necessarily threatened by citizenship rights in which all may share. Through formal recognition of common citizenship, all, whatever their class differences, could enjoy the one culture as consumers in the one market. Citizenship commences in capitalist societies with the state's duty 'to appoint in what manner ... contracts between Subjects (as buying, exchanging, borrowing, letting and taking to hire)' should be carried on (Hobbes 1963: 96). Formal legal equality is the basis of the labour contract and a necessary pre-condition for the inequalities of the class system.

Following a logic of evolutionary democratisation, T.H. Marshall traced the successive emergence of civil, political and social rights; 'the modern drive towards *social* equality is ... the latest phase of an evolution of citizenship which has been in continuous progress for some 250 years' (1950: 10).[32]

Civil rights emerging in the eighteenth century prior to the Reform Act of 1832 include individual rights to liberty, freedom of speech, thought, faith and association, rights of property ownership, to 'follow the occupation of one's choice in the place of one's choice' (1950: 15–16) and to justice, which in turn provides the right 'to defend and assert *all* one's rights in terms of equality with others and by due process of law' (p. 10). These most basic of civil rights establish the precedence of citizenship status over any other particular status differences or interests.

Political rights emerged from the early nineteenth century and include rights of participation in the exercise of political power as party member and elector. Whilst successive Reform Acts extended the franchise and dropped economic disqualifications for universal adult suffrage, in the nineteenth century political rights were subject to qualification through ownership of sufficient wealth. It was the 1918 Reform and Women's Suffrage Acts that transferred the basis of political rights from economic substance to personal status.[33] In contemporary practice political rights extend beyond such formal elements of enfranchisement and include the right to influence through free speech and assembly, the lobbying of political leaderships via pressure groups and media. With contemporary fragmentation and sectionalism political rights extend well beyond the institutional parameters of government.

Making their first appearance in Britain with such legislation as the Factory Acts of the 1840s,[34] *social rights* were extensively institutionalised in the Beveridge Plan.[35] These rights of welfare, education and social security, minimum wage protection for the low paid, disabled, old and unemployed, and health care established 'the right to share to the full in the social heritage and to live the life of a civilised being *according to the standards prevailing in the society*' (T.H. Marshall 1950: 28, my emphasis), thus recognising the possibility of legitimate exclusionary principles and practices arising out of adjudicated non-conformity to prevailing standards.

It is a crucial component of liberal accounts of 'the nature and the limits of the power which can be legitimately exercised by society over the individual' (Mill 1910: 1) that equal citizens have different indeed incommensurate and irreconcilable conceptions of the public good (Dworkin 1978) and so 'standards prevailing in the society' rubrics set utilitarian limits; the duties required to satisfy aggregate benefit, general or national economic, political and moral welfare.

> ... the sole end for which mankind is warranted, individually or collectively, in interfering with the liberty of action of any of their number is self-protection ... the only purpose for which power can be rightfully exercised over any member of a civilised community, against his will, is to prevent harm to others
>
> (Mill 1910: 13)

So whilst all citizens of democratic states are 'free and equal persons' (Rawls 1987: 18) with 'the right to act in the public realm this leaves us with the burning question: what precisely is the public realm?' (Kelly 1979: 27). The state is necessarily 'both immanent and instrumental' (p. 27) and citizenship enables the expansion of its immanence on grounds of preventing harm to the moral community. The European Commission on Human Rights (1950) is no different: it guarantees such rights as 'freedom of thought, conscience and religion' (Art. 9), 'freedom of expression' (Art. 10) and 'of peaceful assembly and to freedom of association with others (Art. 11) but all are subject to

> such formalities, conditions, restrictions or penalties as are prescribed by law and are necessary in a democratic society, in the interests of national security, territorial integrity, or public safety, for the prevention of disorder or crime, for the protection of health or morals, for the protection of the reputation or rights of others, for the disclosure of information received in confidence, or for maintaining the authority and impartiality of the judiciary.
>
> (Ewing and Gearty 1990: 14)

Such qualifications of citizenship are clearly demonstrated throughout. Social rights are routinely means-tested according to calculations of scale and form of need, economic and social costs and the moral status of claimants, deriving exclusionary practices from inclusionary principles, accompanied by conditions for re-inclusion after appropriate acts of atonement. For example:

Social rights of citizenship can be forfeited if labour power is not offered as an exchange value in some circumstances. In many areas the definition of the rights of welfare consumers is left to the discretion of the administrators or professionals and the actual encashment of social rights is sometimes made very difficult or conditional on submissive forms of behaviour.

(Ginsburg 1981: 38–9)

Similar means of disqualification occur formally and informally in the other political and civic citizenship spheres. For example, with 'equal' access to the law:

Today, everyone is equal before the law, whatever his race, colour or creed . . . there are *no* outlaws. . . . Everyone is entitled to equal protection, and the judiciary, appointed independently of government, has a duty to apply the law fairly to all, rich and poor, public institutions and private citizens [but] equality before the law is an illusory equality [because] the very neutrality of the law becomes an instrument of inequality, it defers to the power of the stronger party and enforces his legal rights against the weak.

(Lester 1970: 15, 18)

Furthermore, interpretations of the national good lead to one person's qualification being another's exclusion. For example, children's rights can only develop at the expense of those of parents and teachers, whilst conversely:

the right of women to control their own bodies has been expressed through a variety of legal developments such as abortion reform. However, women's rights over their own bodies may conflict with the rights of children, especially unborn children. The right of abortion has raised the problematic issue of when a fertilised embryo is a legal person and involves a political decision about the citizenship rights of unborn children.

(Turner 1986: 105)

So status criteria are employed by state agencies to set relative rather than absolute standards of citizenship. The responsible, tax-paying, morally conforming consumer can expect full membership, but status or 'orientation' difference justifies partial restricted membership as both citizen and consumer. Post-Wolfenden (1957) legal sexual minorities, on the grounds of their continuing immorality have, to quote Rawls, been given only limited scope to develop 'social capacities of the self' and their ability to self-govern limited to self-confinement within the 'private' immoral territories granted, in the name of 'public safety', 'public order', health, morals, 'the rights of others' even 'national security',[36] and especially the family, *the* symbol of national purity and survival and the site of propagation.

Most constitutions specify the family's survival and defence as being at the heart of rights legislation: for example in (West) Germany where

> (i) Marriage and the family are under the special protection of the state (ii) care and the upbringing of children are the natural rights of parents and their duty incumbent upon them primarily. The state watches over their performance of this duty.
>
> (Art. 6 quoted in Duchacek 1973: 116)

Within the liberal tradition the gradual extension of rights to women, ethnic, religious and sexual minorities is interpreted as indicative of real gains made by those who have pursued them via democratic reformism (T.H. Marshall 1950; Parsons 1965). Alternatively, such rights are the 'bourgeois freedoms' by which 'formal democracy inserts the dominated classes into the power equation in a permanently secondary or subordinate position' (Hall 1978), as in their relationships to the 'ostentatiously egalitarian' (Rae 1979) welfare state.

> Social rights are a powerful legitimation of the state creating a form of unwritten contract between the individual and the state, exemplified in social insurance and reinforcing the apparent neutrality of the state as the repository and guardian of the equal rights of all citizens.
>
> (Ginsburg 1981: 38)

Sexual struggles clearly reflect this reformist and radical conflict over citizenship as exemplified by the current battles in Britain between Stonewall and OutRage and FROCS[37] over gay rights, and the best means to achieve them. These are but a few of the many active specifically gay parties whilst gay and other sexual issues have increasingly become agenda items for general political parties contributing to the increasingly complex diversity of political alignments and attachments:[38]

> In recent decades public and private disputes over education, law, gender relations, family forms, gay rights, religion, the role of the media have resulted in new splits within traditional Left and Right parties: the 'cultural contradictions of capitalism' (Bell) have also polarised new social movements such as the Moral Majority and feminists, as each side puts forward irreconcilable views on public and private life.
>
> (Frankel 1987: 147)

However, whilst there is no doubt that through 'community' and general media coverage minority sexual rights are no longer ignored, most within sexual minority groups do not actively participate in 'out' campaigns or explicitly gay political parties. Rather, for them commitment to their sexual citizenship rights is chiefly expressed through their 'out' participation in commercial 'private' territories.

This political fragmentation of sexual issues has enabled the state to legitimately police civil society to ensure that freedoms granted do not contaminate the moral community but, in so doing it has also been required to constrain the market's eagerness to exploit these segregated commercial and commodity settings. As with other minority citizenship forms, sexual citizenship 'sits awkwardly across all three elements' (Roche 1987: 370) of the T.H. Marshall scheme, in the moral–legal limbo referred to earlier.

The much vaunted assertion that there are immoral victimless consensual sexual behaviours which are not the law's business does not of course mean that they are simply consigned to absolute personal privacy. Within the Trojan horse of 'privacy' state and commercial penetration of private lives has continued apace. Conventional liberal wisdom is that the modern state *frees* civil society (personal, family and business life, 'everything that affects daily life' (Hobbes 1963)) from political influence. However, the extension of rights to sexual minorities demonstrates how citizenship machineries enhance state management of this 'life-world'. The logic of the distinction between private and public behaviour was that the legal penalties for *public* displays of sexuality could be strengthened as private behaviour was decriminalised, but given the strict definition of 'private' elaborate policing of civil society became *de rigueur*. By concentrating on public manifestations of sexual deviance in the buffer zone between moral and immoral communities, this policing has effectively penetrated all 'private' territories with immanent self-regulating material forms of power/knowledge, the legitimate expression of which is mediated via the 'privacy' of commercial establishments which have done so much 'to structure the person-focused, pleasure-seeking and often apolitical nature of . . . [their] . . . commercial culture' (Mort 1980: 43).

If 'Citizenship involves essentially the question of access to scarce resources in society and participation in the distribution and enjoyment of such resources [so that there is] social membership and participation in society as a whole' (Turner 1986: 85), sexual citizenship involves partial, private, and primarily leisure and lifestyle membership. Bauman (1988) contends that state penetration of civil society in consumer capitalism means that instead of capital domination being grounded in a civil society colonised to the ends of reproducing labour, now civil society is colonised by the state to the ends of reproducing consumers, 'men and women whose needs are permanently redirected to fit the needs of the market', in their obsessive pursuit of sexuality 'the medium through which . . . [they] . . . seek to define their personalities and . . . to be conscious of themselves' (Foucault and Sennett 1981: 183).

3

THE 'PERMISSIVE' WATERSHED

It's when authority won't allow something that I dig in. I'm against anything that interferes with individual freedom. As a non-conformist I won't accept what other people say is right. And there are hundreds like me, thousands.
(Mick Jagger quoted in *Guardian* 1969)

Commentators of all political persuasions are inclined to agree that it was the 'sexual revolution' of the 'fab' and 'groovy' 1960s (Hewison 1990), myth or reality, which served as the sea-change in the sexualisation of modern capitalist societies. On the Left many question whether 'real' sexual freedoms were gained whilst on the Right there is no doubting them as indicative of grievous moral decline, whilst across the spectrum of opinion there has emerged a considerable volume of literature, stimulated, even when unconvinced, by this 'permissive' decade.

As noted earlier, Foucault's discursive analysis was, in part, a personal intellectual response to the failed events of Paris 1968 in which 'sexual liberation' and 'sexual freedom' were central issues and slogans. In America, too, eminent 'post-industrial' theorists raised criticisms against the backdrop of Cold War polemics, civil rights upheavals, anti-war and generally 'counter-cultural' claims (Frankl 1974: 3). In Europe and North America there also emerged the 'strange stirring of feminist sentiment' (Coote and Campbell 1982) with the publication of many high-profile texts (Friedan 1965; de Beauvoir 1972; Millett 1972; Greer 1970, etc.). For example, on its twentieth anniversary *The Female Eunuch* received rapturous accolades: '. . . it changed women's lives all over the world . . . [Greer] made it clear that women could be strong and argue back. They didn't have to put up with things'

(Callil 1990). Sociological interest in gender and sexuality blossomed in Britain with the appearance of such key works as Oakley's *Sex, Gender and Society* (1972) and the 'landmark article' (Vance 1989: 20) by Mary McIntosh (1968) on the homosexual role, whilst academically the freeing of symbolic interactionism from the strictures of rigid role analysis and psychologism, especially in the study of deviance, had considerable impact on sociological interest in especially unconventional sexualities (Gagnon and Simon 1967, 1970, 1973a; Plummer 1975). Clearly, whatever else might be claimed for the changes effected in the everyday experience of sexuality during this period, a mighty array of challenging Mandarin discourses were spawned.

Whether this 'permissive moment' (Weeks 1981b: 249) affected the lives of ordinary people has proved a major preoccupation of these discourses. Altman for one, in the pre-AIDS late 1970s at least, believed that in the long run 'the whole set of challenges to the dominant value system of liberal capitalism that emerged in the late sixties may prove to offer the most important contemporary prospects for change in Western societies' (Altman 1981: 115).

Others, such as the populist Talese (1980), concurred, claiming a revolution which, from his observations of the seemingly *Playboy* dominated war-zone, he asserted enabled the 'freed' to abandon 'possessive monogamy', to 'swing' and to experiment with 'recreational' and 'varietal' forms of sexual expression. 'Where there had been only marriage, there were now "life-styles" featuring a bewildering multiplicity of relationships, all shored up by the seemingly inexhaustible affluence of the sixties' (Biskind and Ehrenreich 1980: 113).

Some lifestyles bred momentuous demonstrations of political dissent, not least the Stonewall Bar riots in Greenwich Village New York City of 28–29 June 1969, which for some commentators marked the 'symbolic beginning of the modern struggle for gay liberation . . . when gay male bar-users in Christopher Street, New York, rioted against police raids. These events were a symbol of gay people resisting the attacks of straight society' (Gough and McNair 1985: 90).[1] Others have been more sceptical, for example Plummer (1975) whilst accepting that 'Homosexual experiences in the Western world would appear to have undergone somewhat dramatic transformations since the early 1960s' cautions that even so 'the evolution of the modern homosexual is a process that began a good while back' (pp. 11–12).

Other lifestyle eruptions are also given low-key treatments by some: for example O'Sullivan describes the feminism of 1969–72 as 'a relatively cohesive time' (1987: 43) and others have argued that the upheavals merely signified new forms of dominance and submission, the feminist outburst merely a stage in the emergence of 'post-feminists [with] "interesting" jobs, but [who] still wear make-up. They are the women in advertisements who don't really exist . . . our new role models – another impossible ideal . . . men can fancy them without having to alter their own ideas' (Waugh 1990), or that the 'sexual revolution's' primary accomplishment was the compulsory conscription of women into active heterosexual sex, introducing 'a new language of liberation and pleasure which can befog the observer and make the political function of sexual intercourse (i.e. patriarchy) less easy to spot' (Jeffreys 1990: 5).

New Right moralists have had no doubts about the dramatic extent of changes diagnosed as symptomatic of moral subversion. There was a narcissistic flight from commitment (Lasch 1979), a gay anarchy and hedonism which threatened the family and social order (Elshtain 1982/3). In Britain numerous scandals during these 'exciting, turbulent years' (Elliott and McCrone 1987: 491) underlined the general sense of moral panic: the Profumo affair, the arrest of Mick Jagger of the Rolling Stones on drugs charges, the *Lady Chatterley's Lover* trial, and the growing reputation of Britain as an abortion Mecca. Whilst proponents trumpeted 'liberation', opponents derided a 'permissiveness' which has become a major element in the New Right's ideological programme as illustrated by the then Chairman of the Conservative Party, Norman Tebbitt, who in 1985 called for an official end to the 'permissive society' to which he ascribed 'today's outburst of crime and violence . . . the era of post-war funk which gave birth to the "permissive society" ' (1985 quoted in Marshall 1986: 30). He continued:

> The permissives scorned traditional standards. Bad art was as good as good art. Grammar and spelling were no longer important. To be clean was no better than to be filthy. Good manners were no better than bad. Family life was derided as an outdated bourgeois concept. Criminals deserved as

much sympathy as their victims. Many homes and class rooms became disorderly – if there was neither right nor wrong there could be no basis for punishment or reward. Violence and soft pornography became accepted in the media.

(Tebbitt quoted in Marshall 1986: 30)

Perhaps it has something to do with our 'sliced bread view of the past' (Green 1989) but as we forget the 'sour' (Hewison 1990) and 'boom-boom' (Wolfe 1979) 1970s and leave behind the Thatcherite 1980s, it is to 'the golden past of the swinging' (Greenwood and Young 1979) or iniquitous 'permissive' 1960s that analysts of the sexual look for guidance in understanding all that has followed. The 1960s are back in fashion (Gottfried 1988), partly it seems as an exercise in disavowal by former radicals, many turned academics, called to account for their past sins (Bunzel 1988; Hollander 1988),[2] but mainly through continued attempts to disentangle reality from myth, for example, by drawing keen distinctions between the 'good early period and the ... insanity of the late sixties' (Breines 1988: 529) when the advance of American society 'towards higher levels of democratic self-actualisation' was ruined ... by 'malodorous adolescents [who] began to urinate on their professor's rugs' (Gottfried 1988: 28). In a sense it no longer matters, for in our sexually obsessed world we cannot fail to constantly reflect upon the decade that, by reputation at least, made it so. Whether 'hymned by ageing hippies, still wreathed in rosy fantasies, or vilified by contemporary politicians, desperately hunting an easy scapegoat for over-complex ills, the image remains: something happened' (Green 1989: 115). That 'something' was more than 'counter-cultural' promiscuity, psychedelia and the defiant rejection of middle-class values by the young (Hall et al. 1976), it marked the culmination of a period of unprecedented juridical reform, affluence, and leisure and lifestyle consumerism which challenged fundamental norms of monogamous marital hetero-sexual love and relational fidelity, and asserted sexuality as an 'autonomous sphere of pleasure and self-expression with its own intrinsic value and justification ... in the context of mutual consent and respect' (Seidman 1989: 298). The 1960s were the catalyst in the emergent political, economic and moral battles for discursive dominance over sexual citizens and sexual consumerism.

Of most political and legal significance was the dismantling of many formal controls which had survived since the Victorian era. Home Office reformism as part of the 'consensus politics' of successive Labour and Conservative post-war governments extended beyond the economic, through the social to the moral (Kavanagh 1987). Just as in foreign affairs there was broad agreement on Britain's nuclear role, NATO membership and decolonisation, and domestically accord on full employment budgets, the incorporation of trades unions, public ownership of basic monopoly services and industries, state provision of social welfare, and interventionist market management through commitment to a large public sector, so too, under Conservative Home Secretary R.A. Butler and his Labour counterpart Roy Jenkins, despite opposition at all levels of the legislative process, there was majority support for liberal utilitarian principles of moral reform.

As the date of the era's most outstanding legal document, the *Wolfenden Report* (1957), demonstrates, this 'permissive' period was not neatly confined to the 1960s, the 1950s accounted for much of the spadework by Royal Commissions and numerous lobby organisations collating evidence on issues such as divorce, obscenity, theatre censorship, male homosexuality, etc. As Hall (1980) has noted, the end of this era of the 'legislation of consent' was marked by the Misuse of Drugs Act (1971) which 'legislated in a thoroughly reactionary direction' effectively overturning the causalist utilitarian recommendations of the *Wootton Report* preceding it (1968). Significantly, further reforms affecting married women's legal rights continued into the 1970s, 1980s and 1990s.

Several of the reforms were not specifically concerned with sexual or gender matters but were indicative of general changes in the moral climate: the Homicide Act (1957) and the Murder Abolition Act (1965) removed the death penalty from the statute books; the Suicide Act (1961); the Betting and Gaming Act (1960) legalised casinos and betting shops (following the setting up of a public lottery; the Premium Savings Bonds in 1956), and Sunday entertainments were legalised in 1968. Pleasure and conditional self-determination in the pursuit of it were, broadly, new orders of the day.

As far as the juridical reconstruction of sexual morality was concerned the major statutes were of two kinds: those which specifically addressed the form and standing of the nuclear family, especially the ties of women to and within it, and those which considered wider non-familial and largely male/masculine sexual issues.

The most outstanding of the former were the National Health Service (Family Planning) Act (1967) which permitted family planning advice to be given on the NHS and prescription of contraception to married women (later extended to unmarried);[3] the Abortion Act (1967) legalised abortions under certain circumstances, i.e. if two registered doctors agreed that the continuation of pregnancy would be more injurious to the mental or physical health of the woman or her existing children than termination, or if there was a substantial risk that the baby would be mentally or physically handicapped; the Divorce Law Reform Act (1969) (the 'Casanova's Charter') abolished 'matrimonial offence' and established 'irretrievable breakdown' as grounds for divorce, allowing divorce after a separation of three years where both partners agreed or after five where one partner agrees.[4] The Matrimonial Property Act (1970) recognised women's rights to a share of family property on divorce, and the 1973 Matrimonial Causes Act reformed the marriage ceremony by removing the term 'obey' from the woman's vows.

The most significant reforms of specifically sexual offences were inevitably more notorious. Two were direct consequences of the Wolfenden Committee's recommendations derived from the distinction made therein between 'public good' and 'private morality'. (The Sexual Offences Act (1957) decriminalised prostitution but simultaneously increased maximum penalties for persistent soliciting in public, repeated offences and call-girl agencies, etc.) The Sexual Offences Act (England and Wales) (1967) legalised some male homosexual behaviours i.e. between men over the age of 21 in 'private' excluding those in the armed services or merchant marine, but likewise strengthened policing of public moral space to prevent manifestations of the still gravely immoral homosexuality, via the use of non-specific 'receptacle' or 'residual' laws; i.e. against vagrancy, soliciting, loitering with intent, breach of the peace, etc.[5] Despite these qualifications the 1967 Act's principal recommendation was 'sufficiently "permissive" to make the nation draw a deep breath' (Hall 1980: 11).

The period's other major sex law reform also addressed male sexuality by indirectly recognising the legitimacy of male sex needs for pornographic stimulation. The Obscene Publications Act (1959) relaxed laws of censorship over published material on grounds of obscenity, unless deemed 'likely to deprave and corrupt', another example of the causal relativism of this era's reforms. Another Obscene Publications Act (1964) followed and theatre censorship was removed from the Lord Chamberlain's office by the Theatres Act (1968). Of some notoriety and significance, too, were the trial and acquittal of the publishers of *Lady Chatterley's Lover* (1960) and the quashing of the initial conviction of the publishers of *Last Exit to Brooklyn* in 1967 (although there had been few attempts to enforce the initial conviction preventing the book's distribution), indicative of state moral uncertainty.[6]

These reforms explicitly restructured the moral sphere, particularly with regard to male/masculine sexualities through the underlying assumptions of homosexual, prostitution and obscene publications law reform and women's economic and sexual status, within and outwith the nuclear family. The impact of affluence on the 'consuming housewife' (Marshall 1986), 'shopper in chief' in the new consumer economy' (Coote and Campbell 1982),[7] reconstructed women domestically as more technologically effective managers, with responsibilities for turning past luxuries into contemporary necessities.[8] Simultaneously, abortion and birth control reforms released women symbolically if not in practice, from the confinement of reproductive sexuality, just as new marriage and divorce laws enabled some degree of economic and financial independence from the parental family and men. As such it has been argued that 'women were the key interpellated subject of the new legislation' (Hall 1979: 20).

> Overwhelmingly it was the position of women in the field of sexual practice which provided the legislation with its principal object/subject. What it proposed in sum was a measure of relaxation in the social and legal control of selected aspects of female sexual practice. It meant in effect a new modality of 'control' over these aspects – a more privatised and 'person-focused' regulation, tacit rather than explicit, invisible rather than visible.
>
> (Hall 1979: 21)

However, whilst Hall is correct insofar as these changes altered female sexual practice, they also marked an even more 'tacit' and 'invisible' reconstruction of the legal, if not moral, validity of adult consensual non-procreative and recreational sexualities for men as well as women. In this sense the interpellated subject was not women but all sexual citizens of whatever legal type and, given the commodification implications of sexualities released into the market from their confinement in monogamous marital procreativity and criminality, the sexual citizen as consumer. The legislation of this period initiated women's movement into sexual citizenship, but as one exemplary form in a more general strategy.

If this was the formal juridical reality of 'permissiveness' during the late 1950s, 1960s and early 1970s, 'permissiveness' was to become subsequently both less and more, less in that what was effected was not solely new 'freedoms' but also new forms of legislative penetration of civil society through a juridical 'double taxonomy'; greater 'private' formal sexual freedoms contained by reinforced moral sanctions and rigorous policing of 'public' outcrops. This 'public'/'private' moralities strategy (Hall 1979: 17) released consumerist discourses on the purchase of a wide range of sexual lifestyles and commodities but within the strict moral conditions which crystallised around the ideological myth of 'permissiveness' by the beginning of the 1970s, a myth which has subsequently been a key weapon in the New Right ideological armoury.

In 1971 John Selwyn Gummer, later a prominent front-bencher in the Thatcher and Major governments, noted that:

> Permissiveness is, more often than not, a term of abuse by one generation for all those things it dislikes in another ... as such it can be simply dismissed as the modern term for those changes in society that happen every generation and of which a band of sterner and older moralists always disapprove.

> (Gummer 1971: 1)

Behind the normal permissiveness of the late 1950s and 1960s, however, Gummer warned there lurked new, deep and threatening changes:

There *has* been a real change in society since the Second
World War . . . more fundamental than either the novelties
to which in every generation the young flock and the old
object, or the mere change to a society prepared to admit
publicly the things which privately have always been true.

(Gummer 1971: 2–3)

This 'real change' made Britain by the 1970s the Permissive
Society incarnate. His analysis somewhat belied the blanket
assertion of this sobriquet however, for Britain's deplored moral
decline was tied to a regrettable lack of freedom in the market.
In both the state was culpable. Using proto-Thatcherite rhetoric,
invoking Victorianism as the measure of Britain's decline,
Gummer argued that in contrast to the nineteenth century of
economic permissiveness and moral repression, the 'twentieth
century has increasingly reversed that position . . . restricted and
cosseted us economically while leaving us more and more free to
do as we like in bed' (p. 5).

Today we are much more preoccupied with a man's
economic effect on others. . . . We protect the individual
from every possible material harm which may come to him
. . . and restrict his freedom of material decision . . . [yet] we
increasingly deny, at least in theory, that private sin makes
for public danger. Whereas the Victorians believed that the
State had to be restrictive in the field of private moral
actions or society would suffer, we believe that a man's
private life is his own and the State need take no account of
it.

(Gummer 1971: 5)

Post-war Britain was 'corporatist', 'welfare-statist' and
therefore, inherently morally lax to the extent that, 'the
traditional moral standards of western Christian civilisation are
not merely found difficult or merely ignored – they are actively
challenged' (p. 7).

Gummer's explanation for this new and virulent
'permissiveness' largely coincided with those of left-wing, gay and
feminist critiques (Weeks 1985; Jeffreys 1990; Elliott and
McCrone 1987): the appearance of an employed, free-spending
younger generation with weakened family ties due to greater
social, moral and geographical freedoms. Gummer specifically

73

warned of the deleterious effects of greater privacy amongst the young quoting in evidence one of the most touted 'gurus' of this era's voxpop, Wilhelm Reich, who, in his SexPol Clinics in Vienna and Berlin during the 1920s and 1930s, had advocated that a successful sexual revolution depended on greater privacy, access to contraception and greater flexibility with expenditure (Reich 1969). Reich's revolution was Gummer's nightmare and he singled out modern motherhood for particular blame for preaching the virtues of independence. Also, regardless of the structural changes well under way, he prosaically laid blame at the door of the 'advertising man and the marketeer' (Gummer 1971: 15), of 'market-oriented industries' (p. 5) determined to woo and to mould the needs and caprices of the newly affluent young, and in so doing he revealed the deep tensions between state and capital at this time.

The creation of these mass markets encouraged a 'throw away lifestyle' (Hotchner 1979: 347), the rapid turnover in superficial and soon-outmoded fashions and superficial and soon-outmoded values in pursuit of excitement, change and novelty to the detriment of continuity and order, values which 'requiring not discipline or discrimination merely energy' (Gummer 1971: 8) increasingly permeated sexual relationships.

Continuity and order were not only threatened by the affluent young, educational expansion was also a dangerous influence. The increased university population of welfare-state funded, campus dwelling and thus similarly family-detached idealist students, were also targeted. The first 'sit-in' at a British university was in 1967 at the London School of Economics and several others followed at campuses around the country. Nowhere did they as seriously provoke and represent the overt mood of rebelliousness as in May 1968 in Paris, which provided:

> the most potent symbols of the efforts to contest established relationships and practices. For many young people they continued to shine as beacons of hope, of possibility: for many of their elders, for those in authority, they were no less powerful as symbols of threat.
>
> (Elliott and McCrone 1987: 492)

Gummer's peroration was of course neither the first nor only critique of 'permissiveness' in Britain, nor was 'permissiveness' of solely British concern. In America too, affluence and the growing independence of the young, particularly campus populations, were blamed for specific outbreaks of dissent over black civil rights and America's involvement in the Vietnam war with seemingly little opposition from federal state authorities and the 'colossal permissiveness [exhibited] by faculty and administration' (Nesbit 1970).[9] In 1967 one visiting academic noted that

> In this university building where I am now writing, the students gather names and money for a campaign against the war. Peacefully, every day and throughout the day this goes on, with no one doing or saying anything to the contrary.
>
> (Marias 1968: 301–2)

This author noted the impatient mood for change reduced to three letters: *now*; 'right *now*', 'civil rights *now*', 'freedom *now*', 'get out of Vietnam *now*', 'war on poverty *now*', 'all power to the people *now*' (pp. 301–2).

Commentators in Britain and America noted 'anti-ascetic' and 'anti-social' values amongst the young (Marias 1968: 418) plus a growing individualism referred to in America by some as a New Sentimentality set against the 'Old' (Wright 1971: 67). The latter had values which 'all could see, bywords that meant the same to all: Patriotism, Love, Religion, Mom, The Girl' (Benton and Newman 1969: 399), whilst 'New' values were:

> out there emblazoned on banners. They differ slightly from man to man, because one of the definitions of New Sentimentality is that it has to do with you, really just you, not what you were told or taught, but what goes on in your head, *really* and in your heart *really*.
>
> (Benton and Newman 1969: 400)

But as the 'change now' slogans demonstrated, the 1960s mobilised, with some acceleration, popular discourses over the changed economic, political and legal, social, sexual and moral structures of advanced capitalist societies. In particular they reflected a momentary fracture in the apparent coherence of economic and political strategies. Again right- and left-wing critics broadly agree that the widespread rejection of conventional forms was facilitated because the latter no longer appeared to be acknowledged or imposed with any degree of conviction by state bodies and representatives, seemingly out of touch and uncertain about their value, and the significance of the changes underway. In all senses, from the affluent and hedonist to the questioning and idealistic, there was an individualisation of reasoning: a 'raising of the demands a man may make on life and a lowering of the demands life can make on him' (Whiteley and Whiteley 1964: 21).

Some of these 'men' making demands were gay, others women, reacting to the 'fetishised femininity of the previous decade' (Coote and Campbell 1982: 12) by making claims against the constraints of gender relations reified in the 'bourgeois' family,[10] demanding the right to define and control their own bodies and sexualities, again in spectacular discursive subversions of public events, such as the dumping of bras and other undergarments into a 'freedom trash bucket' at the Miss America pageant in Atlantic City in 1968.

For Gummer, however, all these demands were mainly due to welfare state irresponsibility, releasing women from family commitments, conspiring in their pursuit of liberation: 'the whole concept of courtship and capture has been broken down' (1971: 24). Here, as throughout, Gummer's text is a curiously honest combustion of concern for events seen as rapid, incoherent, threatening, virtually unstoppable.

Perhaps the panicked tone was because by the end of the decade 'permissiveness' was most spectacularly manifest in the 'expressive revolution' (Martin 1981) of diverse youth subcultures signalling their new consumer status and social independence through dress, music and lifestyles. As a 'revolution' of style and culture, unsurprisingly media influence was specifically blamed for subverting that of the traditional family into whose home it could transmit subversive messages, and by the mid-1960s vociferous opponents of media influence appeared on both sides of the Atlantic, none more so in Britain than Mary Whitehouse, who for three decades has remained a permanent and formidable fixture in extra-parliamentary British politics. She began her Clean-Up TV campaign in 1964, generally derided by the popular press and the main object of her wrath, the BBC. By 1974 Conservative Party minister Sir Keith Joseph still described her as 'that admirable . . . unknown woman' (1974 quoted in Campbell 1987a). Whitehouse deployed a prototypical 'enemy within' thesis (McWhirter quoted in Elliott and McCrone 1987) by claiming that, as with other institutions of the 'nanny state', the media was dominated by 'small groups of people ... committed to the new permissive morality in a position to sway a large body of opinion because they [are] vociferous and regarded as "experts" by those who [are] not always in full possession of the facts' (Whitehouse 1967: 52).

For Whitehouse and others of the NVLA (National Viewers and Listeners Association) and Moral Re-armament, the newly popular medium of television was literally the 'enemy within' the family home. 'Men and women and children listen and view at the risk of serious damage to their morals, their patriotism, their discipline and their family life' (Whitehouse 1964 quoted in Tracey and Morrison 1979). Specifically 'from the BBC a spiritual sewer flows ... into the homes of Britain ... [and] ... infects the community' (Gordon 1969: 304) with sex and to a lesser extent violence; pre- and extra-marital sex, homosexual sex, promiscuous and pornographic sex, adolescent sex and violent sex. Thus to the National Secretary of Moral Re-armament in a 1962 speech it seemed 'that the aim is to foster and increase a taste for sex so that the more leisure people will have that is all they will want' (Wilson 1963 quoted in Tracey and Morrison 1979: 62):

If you soften the people of a nation limitlessly by feeding them with sex, you may so reduce the power to say 'No' that there are certain other things to which they will be unable to say 'No', such as dictatorship and tyranny.

(Wilson quoted in Tracey and Morrison 1979: 62)

In the United States opposition to 'permissiveness' was largely organised around the reality and symbolism of pornography which, through the rapid expansion of multi-million dollar men's magazines such as *Penthouse* and *Mayfair*, providing 'pin-ups without hang ups' (Talese 1980: 147), became perhaps the most prominent public sexual issue. It demanded and produced the *Report of the Presidential Commission on Obscenity and Pornography* (1970), a massively funded, elephantine, multi-disciplinary attempt to assess the impact on American life and the public of exposure to all manner of materials possibly pornographic or obscene. Congress decided that the matter was 'of national concern', but on the whole the Commission did not agree although minority Commissioners such as Charles H. Keating

Jnr, the founder of the Citizens for Decent Literature, Cincinnati, and the Reverend Morton A. Hill, President of Morality in the Media, New York, warned that 'The Commission's majority report is a Magna Carta for the pornographer' (Barnes 1970: ix). Keating rose to the crude euphemism challenge which permeates all such disputes, by claiming, 'Credit the American public with enough common sense to know that one who wallows in filth is going to get dirty' (p. ix), reminding us lest we forget that a consistent feature of opponents of 'permissiveness' is their ready embrace of defecatory metaphors.

Opposition to materials deemed to be corrupting of or offensive to the 'moral community' inevitably gave rise to debates over censorship and free speech. The Majority Report of this Commission was most concerned to safeguard such constitutional 'freedoms' unless there was good cause so not to do, for in such an emotive climate it was believed they could so easily have been swept aside:

> Censorship is a dirty word – perhaps the dirtiest. The easiest thing to censor – or if you prefer it to suppress – is something of a sexual nature. You merely have to say that it offends you morally, and in breathless, bible-tapping guilt, a considerable part of the community is likely to support you.
>
> (Barnes 1970: xiv–xv)

By the end of the decade therefore, in America and Britain debates about the form and scale of threat posed by 'new morality', the 'new permissive age' and 'counter-culture' were widespread. The intoxicating brew of 'freedoms', 'liberties', hedonism, living 'now' rather than later, decadence, patriotism, 'filth', 'spiritual sewers' and 'breathless bible-tapping guilt' signified popular and Mandarin responses to considerable socio-cultural upheaval not least, momentarily, between state and capital. Affluent consumerism demanded state assistance in the construction and exploitation of individual leisure and lifestyle needs, commodities and moralities, and in one sense that is precisely what the 'legislation of consent' delivered, but the state's reintegrative response was inevitably more tardy, ultimately through the construction of a 'one nation' moral state to offset the causalist relativism of citizenship liberalisation, and the development of the means to police it. This 'interventionist permissiveness' (Greenwood and Young 1979) restructured state authority by striking a new balance between liberalisation and control (Hall 1979), which relied upon close monitoring of degrees of citizenship acccording to the moral worth of the minority groups concerned. It has probably been the successful assertion of Victorian values as the arbiter of this new moral certainty, which has been the most signal achievement of Thatcherism. The skill with which the embryonic glorification of Victoriana by Gummer has been wrought into the elaborate falsehood of neo-conservative morality has been skilful and nerveless, trumpeting unity, essential purity and normality, whilst simultaneously facilitating the exploitation of specialised and hidden diverse forms of impure, immoral pleasure.

In this moral transformation of the state, 'permissiveness' has served as a most potent summary symbol. In the late 1960s and 1970s the term was unsettled as to meaning. In a sense it meant everything and anything that this period represented, with seldom any critical introspection on the growth of 'personal liberty' (McCrone *et al.* 1989), but even by the end of the 1960s some recognised that what the term loosely represented was a sham: not the winning of greater liberties or freedoms, nor the erosion of moral standards, but the permitting of whatever by those with the power to permit. The latter may not have intended such lassitude but their security, and the extent of their material and moral dominance was, for these critics, never seriously threatened:

> Permission is *Fanny Hill* available only in an expensive edition. Permission is the BBC showing *The War Game* to an audience of war correspondents (who are used to asking permission to print the stories they hear at briefings) rather than TV critics. Permission is the deportation of Lenny Bruce, the Home Office file on Stokeley Carmichael. Permission . . . is still – Please sir, may I leave the room, sir? . . . Permission implies the wisdom of an officially appointed elder brother. Permission, however, you shake it, satisfies only the powerful (who don't need it) and the timid (who ask little else from life).
>
> (Mitchell 1969: 40–1)

Maybe this was what permission was, but 'permissiveness' was soon hijacked by the New Right and primed for 'moral panic' duty, to emotively summarise nebulous, omnipresent, deep-rooted moral decay, which had to be uncovered, exposed and controlled if the nation was not to be undermined, and to that end stronger policing and state authority was essential. As long as the decriminalised but immoral were contained, socially, politically and economically, public spheres could be emphatically 'moral'. The boundary between the two is in many senses 'permissiveness', firmly inserted in the necessarily fragmentary and contradictory 'nature' of common sense, its material and cultural details distorted or ignored, its coherence requiring complete detachment from its economic base (Rock 1973: 27).

Almost at a stroke considered reflections by figures such as R.A. Butler and Roy Jenkins (Jenkins 1959),[11] on the quest for a more open, tolerant, humane and life-enhancing society were short-circuited by the spectre of drugs, crime, withdrawal from work, rampant sex, promiscuity, perversion, pornography, anarchy, libertinism and violence.

> By the 1960s 'permissiveness' had become a political metaphor, marking a social and political divide. . . . Those who were chief advocates of the 'permissive society' would rarely have used the term; while for the defenders of 'traditional' (and largely authoritarian) values 'permissiveness' became an almost scatalogical term of abuse.
>
> (Weeks 1981b: 249)

A term of abuse which, once the general scatalogical spectre has been raised, enables a multitude of specific, fragmented and seemingly disparate inheritances to be identified and countered, from increased crime and violence, pornography, decline in family standards, lack of discipline in schools, even bad grammar and bad art (Tebbit) to teenage pregnancy, herpes, AIDS, 'declining worker productivity and the loss of US hegemony in world politics' (Wallerstein quoted in Piccone 1988). This ideological strategy, wherein judgements of minority status and secondary citizenship are justified and strengthened through reference to a 'false' national moral consensus, may not have been unopposed but, whilst political resistance has been at times relatively high in media profile, it has largely remained fragmented and with only minority support from the 'communities' concerned, for for most the right to consume in private would appear to be sufficient to effect their incorporation.

If this 'permissiveness' programme has succeeded in persuading general populations, it should be possible to obtain evidence from researched attitudes and values. Such research is bedevilled by dissensus over definitions and methodology (Harding *et al*. 1986), even answers to such basic questions as 'What *are* moral values?' and 'How are they to be identified?' have proved inconclusive (Halsey 1985: 6). Understandably therefore, those working in the field seriously qualify any claims which may be drawn from their findings:

> the moral character of an individual cannot plausibly be represented as a conscious recapitulation of the long history of moral reasoning. Attitudes and opinions typically owe less to individual reflection than to the social processes of upbringing, custom, and habituation.
>
> (Halsey 1985: 7)

If so, then given the limited details accrued in attitudes research about 'upbringing, custom and habituation', much has to be imputed. However, despite these difficulties, data on sexual attitudes does at least provide snapshots of population moods, and the moods of sub-sets within, allowing some modest assessment of the success of the New Right 'permissiveness' ideology.

Generally, evidence suggests that populations treat most sexual issues in a conceptually similar manner so that, for example, tolerance of homosexuality tends to be consistent with tolerance of other deviant behaviours such as abortion, divorce, etc. There are predictable variations too, according to respondents' structural locations and other non-sexual values held, so that the more elderly, religious, less well-educated and politically right-wing are more censorious, whilst those younger, irreligious or less religious, politically left-wing and educationally more highly qualified are more tolerant (Harding 1988; Harding *et al*. 1986; Abrams *et al*. 1985).

This last criterion is of course class implicated. Abrams has noted that there is a greater laxity among middle-class than working-class respondents on issues such as homosexuality, prostitution and abortion but that 'even so solid majorities also condemn these practices' (Abrams *et al*. 1985: 35). He also argues that it is amongst the young that endorsement of traditional values is at its weakest, although not on all aspects of sexual morality, for instance there is much higher inter-generational agreement over the sexual standards expected of married people. As for extra-marital issues, the gap between younger and older adults is much wider, the former less condemnatory of prostitution, homosexuality and abortion.

Such findings are not in themselves surprising but they become more provocative in the context of 'post-materialist', 'post-industrial' and 'postmodernist' theses (Inglehardt 1977, 1978) which suggest that with continuing affluence, secularisation and increased educational opportunities amongst the young, moral attitudes will be less likely to correlate with 'old style' class consciousness, and more likely to demonstrate 'an abundance of lifestyles' (Toffler quoted in Frankel 1987: 161), 'detached' concerns and 'single-issue tolerance' or intolerance. However, despite some evidence of single-issue fragmentation, the broader trends exhibited in research amongst the young suggest that, in terms of class, religious commitment and ethnic background, sexual and moral attitudes still tend to cluster in traditional patterns. More importantly perhaps, whilst attitudes research is not sufficiently sophisticated to allow the pursuit of confident detailed conclusions, a brief perusal raises interesting inconsistencies and ambiguities, as possible legacies of the 1960s watershed.

The annual *Survey of British Social Attitudes* (Jowell and Witherspoon 1986) shows that, with one notable and other very minor exceptions the 'consistency' of attitudes to 'personal–sexual' issues remarked upon has continued, revealing a 'rock steady Britain, changing as imperceptibly as the White Cliffs of Dover' (Barker in *Daily Telegraph* 2 Nov. 1986). Nonetheless there are signs of subcutaneous changes. There has been stability in attitudes towards sex before marriage, but increased censure for sex outside marriage and an even more dramatic increase in the proportion critical of homosexuality (Harding 1988), an increase which cannot be laid unambiguously at the door of 'AIDS as a gay plague'.

American findings dating back to the early 1970s show that following a decade in which there was a liberalisation of attitudes, by approximately 1982 this trend had halted. As Table 3.1 demonstrates, the aforementioned hardening of British attitudes has been towards greater consistency with American, the latter having throughout been more inclined to the censorious.

Table 3.1 Selected 'personal–sexual' attitudes[1]

% saying 'always'/'mostly' wrong	Years of surveys					
	1983	1984	1985	1986	1987	1989
Pre-marital relations						
USA	36		36	36		
GB	28	27	23		25	22
Extra-marital relations						
USA		87	87		89	
GB	83	85	82		88	84
Homosexual relations						
USA		75	77		78	
GB	62	67	69		74	68

Source: Harding 1988: 37. 1989 figures from 'British social attitudes', The Times 14 November 1990.
1 British attitudes were investigated using a similar set of questions to those used in the USA General Social Survey. Respondents were given a range of five options ranging from 'always wrong' to 'not wrong at all'.

What is perhaps most revealing about these findings is their consistency given the margin of error inbuilt in such research, and in particular the consistently high opposition to extra-marital behaviours. The most notable trends are the marginal decline in opposition to pre-marital sex and the hardening of especially British, but also American attitudes to male homosexuality. Attitudes to some other aspects of sexual culture also show increased hostility to pornography (with the proviso that respondents have very varied understandings as to what exactly pornography is), 38 per cent favouring an outright ban in 1987 compared with 33 per cent in 1983, 42 per cent in 1988 and 52 per cent four years earlier favouring its availability in 'adult shops but not displayed to the public'. This increased hostility to pornography occurred amongst males aged 35–54 and younger females, i.e. between the ages of 18–34 (Harding 1988).

As far as artificial fertility measures are concerned there is wide acceptance of artificial insemination by husband and in vitro fertilisation but there has been a decline in percentages of populations prepared to favour artificial insemination by donor and either unpaid or paid surrogate motherhood, although it should be noted that half of those sampled were in favour of donor insemination.

Presumably the strength of feeling against surrogacy in Britain has been to some extent inspired by the recommendations of the Warnock Committee (Warnock 1985) which were partially (i.e. through the banning of commercial surrogacy agencies) made law in the 1985 Surrogacy Arrangements Act. Harding wonders whether the 'precipitous' fall in support amongst women aged 18–34 for all forms of surrogate arrangements has been due to adverse publicity surrounding some cases in Britain and the US, or connected to the increasing fear of AIDS, and it is perhaps unsurprising that the latter is credited by most such surveys with the responsibility for this general movement towards an intolerance for non-monogamous and non-marital forms of sexuality.

However, the backlash against homosexuality in particular appears to have preceded wider public knowledge about, and instruction on AIDS, but such data cannot really bear the weight of anything other than the most basic interpretations of 'moods', anything more is surmise.

It is with attitudes to abortion that we find the most dramatic inconsistency within this overall drift towards greater censoriousness there being a continuing trend towards liberalisation as Table 3.2 demonstrates.

If there is any conclusion to draw from this exceptional trend on abortion attitudes it could be that abortion is now considered less an aspect of sexual morality, more one of women's rights. If

Table 3.2 Selected attitudes to abortion

	Years of surveys		
	1983	*1985*	*1987*
% agreeing that abortion should be allowed when:			
the woman decides she does not want the child	37	49	54
the woman is unmarried and does not wish to marry the man	44	54	56
the couple agree that they do not wish to have the child	46	55	59
the couple cannot afford any more children	47	58	58
there is a strong chance of a defect in the baby	82	87	89
the woman became pregnant as the result of rape	85	89	93
the woman's health is seriously endangered by the pregnancy	87	91	94

Source: Harding 1988: 41

so abortion has been 'desexualised' within a sexualising culture which has simultaneously increased its formal juridical acknowledgement of the citizenship rights of women, and suggests that pro-abortion lobbies have successfully countered opponents' claims that abortion involves both the infringement of foetus rights and female sexual promiscuity.

These findings on single sexual issues reveal little, you get no more than you see, except when set against other data which suggests an ongoing shift away from absolute moral standards, towards ' "moral relativism" marked by a subjective evaluation of prevailing circumstances' (Harding *et al.* 1986: 225). As traditional Christian theological moral schemata lose plausibility, internally consistent alternatives are apparently neither available nor adopted (Brown *et al.* 1985; McIntyre 1981; Gerard 1985). Perhaps here we do have one legacy of the 'legislation of consent' with its emphatic differentiation between morality and legality, crime and sin. Some recent findings suggest that the erosion of absolute moral standards is most pronounced on issues where moral choice is deemed to be essentially a personal concern, as with sexual behaviour and close relationships. Explanations for such 'moral secularisation' link it to individualisation, privatism and consumerist leisure principles. Wilson, for example, argues that the demise of an absolute moral code is inevitably linked to the move towards mass society in which personal relationships are based on the playing of numerous cross-cutting designated roles, so that 'a kind of functional rationality comes increasingly to govern human affairs' (Wilson 1982: 157). Absolute moral principles are poorly adapted to a fragmented society, whereas moral relativism or 'situational ethics' are more appropriate (Harding *et al.* 1986: 227).

The viability of such explanations is limited, however, by the poor quality of the evidence, but the latest British and American data does suggest that there might be a tendency, albeit slight, towards single-issue relativism *vis à vis* the discrepant findings on homosexuality and abortion, pre- and extra-marital sex, etc.

More intriguingly, other analysts have suggested that trends towards moral relativism not only increasingly allow populations to hold single-issue values about specific aspects of sexuality, they may well hold different and seemingly contradictory views about different aspects of any particular one. Normally the simplicities of attititudes research conceal such contradictions by asking

85

blanket questions limited to degrees of approval or disapproval. However, those few which have required respondents to judge sexual behaviours *and*, separately, the moral status of those associated with them, are more revealing. This is at least the claim of Rayside and Bowler (1988) using British, American and Canadian data of the past two decades which, they claim, show a consistent drift towards ambivalence, but which could be something rather different. Their concern is with the particular issue of homosexuality, and they claim that survey findings show an across-the-board increase in support for citizenship rights of male homosexuals and lesbians (i.e. to be homosexual or lesbian), but coinciding with a marginal strengthening of moral disapproval through a tenacious retention of traditional negative stereotypes of both, especially the male, as illegal, sick and deviant (Levitt and Klassen 1974). As has so often been the case in the past two decades, the homosexual test-case is both likely to be in some ways typical of comparable other 'deviant' sexual categories, behaviours and types, whilst at the same time being quite exceptional in that there is, apart perhaps from prostitution, no other comparable, elaborate sexually deviant category. As data on attitudes to abortion show, populations can and do make a number of distinct judgements around particular sexual–moral issues rather than there being one-dimensional intolerance or tolerance. But is this ambivalence, or something rather more conscious and intentional?

Rayside and Bowler set their collation of Canadian, American and British attitude research findings *vis à vis* homosexuality alongside each other as shown in Table 3.3.

This data is unfortunately not as recent as one might wish given the subsequent bombardment of populations with presumably influential anti-gay, anti-AIDS messages, but within this limitation their claim is not without interest; 'evidence in Canada as well as in Britain and the United States indicates that support for gay equality has survived the onset of the AIDS crisis' (Rayside and Bowler 1988: 651). They support this observation by referring to Sniderman's (1986) comparison against 1985 surveyed attitudes in California which showed that, during a period marked by public prominence of AIDS as a 'gay plague', 'on a range of issues dealing with discrimination . . . [there was] a shift to more liberal positions'.[12]

Instead of ambivalence, however, perhaps Rayside and Bowler

Table 3.3 Canadian, American and British poll results

	Canada	US	Britain
Support for gay equality rights	70% ('80/'85)	65%[1] ('83)	73%[2] ('79)
Homosexual relations thought wrong	69% ('80)	76%[3] ('80)	69%[4] ('85)

1 *Newsweek*-Gallup poll in *Newsweek* (8 Aug. 1983) 'In general do you think homosexuals should have equal rights in terms of job opportunities?'
2 Gallup Poll in the *International Gallup Polls* (1979: 266) 'As you know, there has been considerable discussion in the news lately regarding the rights of homosexual men and women. In general do you think homosexuals should or should not have equal rights in terms of job opportunities?'
3 National Opinion Research Centre poll in Index to *International Public Opinion* (1979–80: 228) 'What about sexual relations between adults of the same sex – do you think it is always wrong; almost always wrong; only sometimes wrong or not wrong at all?' (Ans 70%; 6%; 6%; 14%).
4 Jowell *et al.* (1986: 152) 'What about sexual relations between two adults of the same sex? [What would your general opinion be?] Always wrong; sometimes wrong; rarely wrong; not wrong at all; DK?' (Ans 59%; 10%; 7%; 4%; 13%; 7%).

have inadvertently located a two-tiered drift in attitudes. Populations have become more censorious over unconventional sexual behaviour, but also more willing to accept that many types of 'deviant' consenting adults have the right to be what they are, indeed should have the rights to realise specific sexual lifestyles, but only insofar as they do not impinge upon and appear to threaten the reified moral community. To this extent differential sexual citizenship rights appear to have become, in complex interaction with commodity structuration through the market, fundamental to the wider contemporary construction of sexuality.[13]

Thus far the discussion has been contextualising and largely abstract. I have been concerned to set out the broad parameters within which varieties of sexual citizenship have developed, been permitted and exploited, but also organised and fought for by those involved. In the remainder of the text particular categories of sexual citizen will be examined. In the broadest of senses, of course, sexual citizenship is first a matter of conformity to core conventional sexual standards, marital, monogamous, heterosexual and procreative but, for those so defined, transgressions of standards do not implicate the person in a citizenship sense, unless liberties are forfeited due to the interventions of the law, and certainly there will not be allegiance to an alternative status group, 'community', lifestyle or identity. The particular explorations which follow, however, concern sexual allegiances of this latter type, from arguably the most complex and developed, that of the male homosexual, to the least, that of the sexualised child. Given that men have greater economic, social, political and moral power than women it is inevitable that specific forms of sexual citizenship have developed, as did general citizenship before, more dramatically amongst men than women. This dominance is reflected in the chapters which follow, including the final chapter which in general terms seeks to summarise the particular sexual citizenship status of women.

4

HOMOSEXUAL CITIZEN
ECONOMIC RIGHTS

> I'm beginning to lose patience
> With my personal relations:
> They are not deep,
> And they are not cheap.
> (Auden 1977: 51)

As has been noted great claims have been made for the dramatic impact and symbolic breakthrough of the 1969 Stonewall Riots, 'when gay pride took a quantum leap forward' (Jackson and Persky 1982: 1),[1] on subsequent gay male politics. Bronski (1984: 2–4) argues that they 'established a homosexual militancy and identity in the public imagination that was startling and deeply threatening . . . [so that] the American press and public could no longer ignore the movement for liberation among lesbians and gay men'. For Bronski these riots were a 'defiant, innately political act' that changed 'the status quo between "queers" and "straights" ' (p. 87), for others 'oppressive Law and Order were from then on increasingly challenged' (Tucker 1979: 12).

As with so much else of this period, Stonewall has passed beyond history into myth. Understandably, most interpret the riots as the combustion of justified dissent, the culmination of much small-scale but concentrated rights campaigning and consciousness-raising especially in territories with high density gay populations.[2] Accordingly freedoms were gained by the efforts of those in the political front-line of the gay community. Only rarely is there recognition that of comparable and considerable impact were changes in the legal climate and associated pressures of affluence and consumption. The riots were, after all, a response to insensitive policing in and around

89

y commercial settings. In this sense the 'gay community was
iscovered in the early 1970s for similar reasons to the discovery
of teenagers in the 1960s' (Seabrook 1976: 205). The political,
social and sexual advance of male homosexuality has been a legal
advance of sorts, a citizenship space cleared and occupied, but it
has not been a moral advance, and the space itself has
subsequently largely become one through which self-
preoccupied individuals pass, commodified and de-politicised.
The 'largely' here is important, for the exceptions are notable
and suggestive of widespread activism, whereas the reality for
most gay men is somewhat different. Even so the winning of at
least certain rights of sexual citizenship has ensured that gay
status, identities, lifestyles and cultures have become permanent
items on the sexual/political agenda, and hence persistent
battlegrounds between homosexual citizen and state. Within
some but not all, and especially not in 'reverse' discourses, the
homosexual citizen is male.

Before the latter's peculiar qualities may be considered it is
first necessary to briefly consider accounts of the development of
the male homosexual role and subculture within the capitalist
epoch. Key stages in the emergence of both have been
well-documented by McIntosh (1968, 1981), Weeks (1977,
1981a, b, 1985) and Marshall (1981); committedly constructionist, each emphasises different stages of homosexual role
development. McIntosh's (1968) essay insisted that 'the
homosexual should be seen as playing a social role rather than
having a condition' (p. 184) and her historical documentation
demonstrates the rudimentary emergence of such a role and
acompanying subcultural forms in the notorious 'mollies' clubs of
late seventeenth and early eighteenth-century London (see also
Bray 1982; Trumbach 1987). McIntosh's essay was mould-
breaking because it argued that the homosexual condition is not
an essence but an historical construct. Subsequently historians in
particular have disputed the universality or cultural specificity of
homosexuality, inspired most recently by the work of Boswell
(Boswell 1989), but from a sociological perspective, although
note should be taken of warnings against crude constructionism,
McIntosh's stance has become a given: ' "sexuality" is no more a
fact of life than "dieticity" . . . one of those cultural fictions that in
every society give human beings access to themselves as
meaningful actors in their world' (Halperin 1991: 42).

For McIntosh (1968) earliest manifestations of a homosexual role 'do not coincide *exactly* with the modern conception. There is much more stress on effeminacy ... to such an extent that there seems to be no distinction at first between transvestism and homosexuality' (p. 187). The subsequent gradual unravelling of distinct sexual types (homosexual, bisexual, transsexual, transvestite, paedophile, etc.) out of this initially single composite discourse is a major theme in analyses of the homosexual role, but as her reference to 'exactly' makes clear, McIntosh is content to hint at this subsequent discursive differentiation. It is also important to remember that the much debated 'masculinisation' of male homosexuality has largely occurred since the McIntosh essay first appeared.

Drawing on the crucial distinction between sexual behaviour and sexual role, the latter being 'expectations (which may or may not be fulfilled)' (p. 184), McIntosh (1968) shows within the Kinsey *et al.* data (1948, 1953) evidence of male and female homo- and heterosexualities being differentially determined by the relative strengths of cultural definitions. Kinsey's findings were presented through the well-known seven-point continuum, which despite numerous faults (McIntosh 1968; Faraday 1981; etc.), dramatically represented sexual behaviours as dynamically varied at any one time, or over time, for populations and individuals. McIntosh concluded that for males 'the incidence of a despised role operates at all ages to inhibit people from engaging in occasional homosexual behaviour, but does not have the effect of making the behaviour of many "homosexuals" exclusively homosexual' (p. 191). Also, given the less developed cultural definition of a distinct homosexual role for women, due in part to freed wage labour being initially mostly male, enabling the construction of personal lives independent of attachments to women who, however, remained domestically dependent upon men, she noted that 'fewer women than men engage in homosexual behaviour' (p. 191). McIntosh also argues that the more developed role for men actually leads more men than women to become concentrated in the exclusive homosexual category.[3]

Through such behavioural comparisons McIntosh argues that one can clearly detect the constructionist impact of cultural definitions and the different forms of social control with which they are associated. The development of a stigmatised

91

homosexual role not only serves to identify the deviant, it also establishes clear boundaries between what is and what is not permissible (whether in moral and/or legal terms) and socially justifies the segregation of those so labelled. By implication, too, the existence of the role presents an elaborate 'objective presence' which under certain conditions may be 'learned' or adopted either through self-labelling or imposed labelling by others, a complex interactional process subsequently identified as that of 'coming-out', or to be more accurate as that of a 'homosexual' career in which many of those involved 'stay in' (Dank 1971; Plummer 1975: 135–153).

McIntosh has been criticised on several counts (Whitham 1977a, b).[4] Three are of particular importance. First, 'her conception of the homosexual role suffers from all the deficiencies of mainstream structural-functional role theory; reification, over-determination, consensual absolutism' (Plummer 1981: 23). Second, observations on the embryonic effeminate male homosexual subculture of taverns and 'houses' ignores 'public' territories which in current parlance would be identified as 'outside cruising' areas, many of which it would seem from archive material remain informally occupied by like-minded and interested individuals such as the Tuileries Gardens in Paris (Coward 1980; Gilbert 1974, 1981; Saslow 1991; Trumbach 1987; Huussen 1991). Third, McIntosh uncritically subscribes to dominant male/masculine definitions of sexuality as deployed by Kinsey (genitally and 'outlet' focused rather than non-specifically genital in focus or 'nurturing') which have effectively led to the academic marginalisation of lesbianism (Faraday 1981). In mitigation, despite such problems, this one short essay's timely foresight made a dramatic and lasting impact on the sociology of sexuality and 'Like all landmark articles, it raises many more questions than it resolves' (Plummer 1981: 23). As Vance has noted (1989: 23) the essay's

> many suggestive insights about the historical construction of homosexuality in England . . . vanished like pebbles in a pond until they were engaged with by mid-1970s writers clearly motivated by the questions of feminism and gay liberation. An identifiably constructionist approach dates from this period, not before.
>
> (Vance 1989: 23)

Weeks' and Marshall's contributions are firmly of this later era. Weeks (1977, 1981a) pursues a Foucauldian and latterly post-modernist focus on the impact of the sexological/medical discursive explosion of the late nineteenth century as inventing the 'homosexual' as a congenital condition of intersexuality rather than as learned behaviour and identity:

By the late nineteenth century . . . medicine was replacing the Church as the moulder of public opinion. The identity that was emerging . . . was defined in terms of . . . madness, moral insanity, sickness and disease. And increasingly in the twentieth century the 'medical model' of the homo-sexual has cast an enveloping shadow over homosexual consciousness.

(Weeks 1977: 23)

Weeks (1981a) is especially keen to identify the emergence of popular socio-cultural and rudimentary political reactions to this medicalisation and the criminalisation which accompanied it,[5] noting that around such events as the Boulton Park scandal of 1871 (p. 111), the Cleveland Street scandal of 1889–90 (pp. 113–14) and the Oscar Wilde trials of 1895 (pp. 109–17) there surfaced power/knowledge constellations which defined the homosexual 'type' at popular as well as Mandarin levels. In these terms for Weeks '1895 is a particularly symbolic year because the reaction to Wilde's downfall was indicative of the new mode in public discourse' (p. 92).

Marshall (1981) expresses convincing doubts, however, pointing out that whilst there were scandals around the notorious behaviours of a certain type of debauched male involved in the seduction of other younger and usually working-class males, it was more usually associated with the behaviour of 'Bohemian intellectuals' (p. 141), as specifically with Wilde, rather than of homosexuals. Marshall quotes from the London *Evening Times* of 25 May 1895 which described Wilde's 'diseased *intellectual* condition' (p. 141). Whichever inter-pretation is correct, the publicity attending these events certainly raised in the public imagination representations of behaviour which, combined with the aforementioned medical discourses, could only give considerable momentum to the appearance of a more clearly recognised and distinguishable homosexual status.

Marshall's own concern is to identify a later distinctly

twentieth-century moment in homosexual role development, when homosexual status no longer necessarily carried with it implications of gender inversion, intersexuality, congenital perversity, even of diseased intellectual condition. Distinguishing between biological sex, gender identity (the 'self-knowledge and conviction that one is a man or a woman' (p. 134)), gender role ('the behaviour, personality traits and general societal expectations usually associated with the masculine and feminine role' (p. 134)), sexual behaviour and the meanings given to them by the actors involved, Marshall compares the homosexual role's earlier forms, as 'pansies' and 'perverts', with 'new styles in homosexual manliness' (Humphreys 1971).

Marshall (1981) argues that whereas before this 're-write' of the homosexual script, men engaging in homosexual behaviours could only identify themselves as homosexual by making the cross-gender interpretive step demanded by expert discourses and conventional stereotypy, if they didn't or couldn't their homosexual experiences could only be interpreted as the denial of that status: as simply a male need or outlet (McIntosh 1978a; Humphreys 1970). This 'new' homosexual of the late 1960s was a 'quite different conception based not upon gender ideas but upon the notion of "sexual object choice" or "sexual orientation" . . . defined independently of gender identity' (Marshall 1981: 133–4). As others noted with an irony now dulled by familiarity, there emerged the homosexual as 'butcher than thou' (Nichols 1979), a 'macho' male and 'it is probably fair to say that this conception is now firmly established in our own culture' (Marshall 1981: 134).

Marshall overstates his case, however, for the 'macho' male did not fully supplant the 'pansy' or 'pervert' in the popular or much of 'expert' medical and legal imagination, nor indeed within the gay community itself. Even so this 'masculinisation' of the homosexual male was a dramatic accompaniment to the 'freeing' of him into 'private' leisure and lifestyle consumerism and, whatever its earlier 'camp' credentials, as yet another camp comment on the tyranny of conventional role models, soon served to conceal the immoral male homosexual's presence in public commercial settings. It was also a newly virilised homosexuality compatible with the alienating and objectifying values of the market. With AIDS the 'virilised' homosexual male has passed into popular debates, a cruel joke to reaffirm his status as pervert, but the masculinising discourses have become an established signpost in the ever more complex, ambiguous and fragmentary identities, lifestyles and commodities of male homosexuality in modern societies.

The appearance of the virilised homosexual male occurred in the context of and out of the 1960s, when legal changes constructed 'a new type of homosexual subject, understood as operating in the private sphere: a subject who in matters of sexuality and morality is defined as consenting, privatised and person-focussed' (Mort 1980: 42). Legal status enfranchised his consumer status, to purchase, to market and exploit, the homosexual commodity. Necessarily the gay male did so in individualised virilised style.

In 1971 *Esquire* commented that no sooner had the public become familiar with the 'camp' and 'swish' male homosexuality of *The Boys in the Band* (Crowley 1968),[6] than it was confronted by a new homosexual male 'indistinguishable from the heterosexual hippie' (Humphreys 1971: 70–1). Marshall (1981: 149) refers to an exposé of London 'old style' gay pubs in the *Sunday People* of 24 March 1968 wherein 'effeminate-looking men disappear into the "ladies" to titivate their appearance and tidy their waved, dyed hair before going into the back room to dance and cuddle with their boyfriends'. By 1971 American observers were noting 'the increasingly masculine image of the gay scene (Humphreys 1971: 70).

> Few gay bars are now distinguished by the presence of limp wrists and falsetto voices. Increasingly, these centers for the homosexual subculture are indistinguishable from other hangouts for youths of college age.... Beards, leather vests, leather jackets and boots have their place alongside the more traditional blue-jeans and t-shirts. If any style predominates it is that of the turned-on, hip generation.
>
> (Humphreys 1971: 70)

Humphreys describes this new homosexuality as a deconstruction of existing homosexual stereotypy within a general youth subcultural adoption of alternative lifestyles ('we learned how to stop pretending from the hip revolution' (Wittman 1977: 330)) rather than the exaggerated construction of potent masculine sexuality it was later to become.

The new generation in gay society is more apt to sleep with a girl than to mock her speech or mannerisms. Many of these young men . . . frown upon an exclusive orientation to homosexual or heterosexual activity. The ideal is to be a 'swinger' sensitive to ambisexual pleasures, capable of turning on sexually with both men and women.

(Humphreys 1971: 71)

The bisexual implications here will be pursued in a later chapter, but it is clear that out of the 1960s' hiatus of fluid social and sexual definitions, including those of the established 'pansy' and 'pervert', new structures (and strictures) rapidly emerged so that by the early 1970s the 'macho' male homosexual's appearance was worthy of comment. What needs to be asked, therefore, is whether this transformation signalled opposition to changes in the dominant order, the commencement of its incorporation or, and this is much more likely, an ambiguous reaction to the contradictory pressures of legalisation, sexualisation and commodification, accompanied by persistent moral exclusion. If subcultures are 'massive problem solving devices' (Blachford 1981: 184) then what new problems were being 'solved' by this 'virilisation' and 'masculinisation' (p. 187)? In turn, have the AIDS-dominated 1980s resulted in a reaction to both transformations sufficient to question the continuing use of the epithet 'new' to describe them? In order to answer these questions it is necessary to examine the male homosexual role beyond that of Marshall's 'macho-men' and into the formalised structures of the modern male homosexual citizen, but to do this it is also necessary to look behind the facade of the 'camp' 'old-style' and supposedly superseded subculture.

There have been some excellent dissections of the meanings, experiences and practices of 'camp' as 'gay sensibility' (Sontag 1967; Babuscio 1977; Blachford 1981; Britton 1979). Babuscio isolates four characteristics: irony, aestheticism, theatricality and humour. Irony refers to use of dramatically incongruous conjunctions (e.g. masculine/feminine; youth/age; beauty/ugliness; straight/gay, etc.) to mediate the incongruity of gayness itself, the mutual defining quality of status group members. Aestheticism marks the presentation of irony in exaggerated styles which subvert conventional decorous tastes. Sontag, prior to the virilised rejection of 'camp', and with more than a touch of

96

the Upper East Side in her tone, argued that 'homosexuals have pinned their integration into society on promoting the aesthetic sense' and that homosexual irony and aestheticism are key elements generally in the 'modern sensibility' (p. 290). Theatricality is manifest in 'camp's' concentration on the superficial outward appearances of roles to parody conventional role playing, constructing the public presentation of the 'gay' self as a self-consciously symbolic style, without inner substance and performed by experienced actors talented in the careful monitoring of interactional presentations in contexts as and when required, most commonly with the facile 'passing' as 'straight' in certain 'non-gay' contexts. Finally humour, inherent in all ironic incongruities, theatricality and aestheticism, is 'the strategy of camp, a means of dealing with a hostile environment and, in the process, of defining a positive identity' (Babuscio 1977: 47).

As such, 'camp' is an oppositional mediation of 'pansy' and 'pervert' stigma. It may be little more than an anaesthetic, providing the feeling of opposition without directly challenging dominant conventions (Britton 1979: 12), but it would be wrong to confuse its artificial and exaggerated style of inverted gender references with a simple or straightforward reification of gender and sexuality, the ingratiation into conventional sexual culture through the embrace of 'jester' or 'fool' roles (Klapp 1958) or with the actual lives and perceptions of the male gay subculture's members.

'Camp' has never been real femininity, as extreme manifestations of 'exhibitionistically effeminate "screaming queens" ' (Sagarin 1970: 41) surely show. 'Camp' is a defensive manouevre by a group so oppressed that it has no other socio-cultural or political alternative. In coded terms it denies the means of its oppression whilst enabling the necessary underlying masculinity and mutual sexual self-interest of its participants to survive. The majority of homosexual men, despite their willingness, indeed need, to revel in this 'camp' sensibility, were and remain first and foremost male and masculine, not least with regard to the one thing that gives them any sense of 'community', their sexual interest in other men.

Gay male sexuality is masculine sexuality in all but sex object choice. It too is organised by 'male sex needs' ideology; objectifying as to fact and fantasy. It is central to personal identity and yet compartmentalised, not necessarily implicated in other aspects of life apart from the need to conceal it. It is, in short, as easily commodified. 'Permissive' icon Joe Orton provides many succinct graphic accounts of virile male homosexual detachment such as the following diary extract:

> He had a white body. Not in good condition. Going to fat. Very good sex though, surprisingly. The bed had springs which creaked. First time I've experienced that. He sucked my cock. Afterwards I fucked him. It was difficult to get in. He had a very tight arse. A Catholic upbringing I expect. He wanted to fuck me when I'd finished. It seemed unfair to refuse after I'd fucked him so I let him. We lay in bed and talked for a while. He showed me a photograph of his fiancée. Not a particularly attractive piece. As I lay in bed looking upwards, I noticed what an amazing ceiling it was. Heavy moulding, a centrepiece of acorns and birds painted blue. All cracked now. Must have been rather a fine room once.
>
> (Orton 1986: 45)

The process of becoming and being gay involves varieties of negotiations with heterosexual gender-differentiated roles; mimicry, modification and perhaps ultimately rejection (Dank 1971; Plummer 1975), but this 'coming-out'[7] is mainly the management of appropriate forms of eroticism. The male homosexual may not experience his sexuality exactly as heterosexual men do (Bell and Weinberg 1978: 101, 111), being 'boy watchers' rather than 'girl watchers' (Plummer 1975: 158), but the expression of 'masculine' homosexualities in a culture without strict sanctions on male promiscuity and where the boys watched enact the same scripts means that male homosexuals as 'sexual outlaws' (Rechy 1977) are inevitably more virile than their heterosexual counterparts.

Thus as Blachford (1981) has noted, from the general gay male subcultural style manifest in favoured language ('fish', 'fag hag' derogations of women) to 'sexual cruising and pick-ups': objectified, anonymous, silent, fleeting, promiscuous (Bell and Weinberg 1978; Delph 1978; Humphreys 1970; Hooker 1967; Cavaan 1966; Reiss 1961; Pitman 1971) these 'masculine' characteristics pre-date the 'virilisation' and 'masculinisation' of the late 1960s and 1970s. Of course with legality the latter aspect became in a sense more visible, certainly within specific social and commercial homosexual territories, but the earlier secrecy of the illegal homosexual world was as inclined to objectification, indeed in one sense more so, for the imposed silence, secrecy and anonymity became indelibly imprinted on modern gay sexual scripts of simulated danger and studied anonymity as re-enactments of this oppressed heritage. The masculinisation of the homosexual subculture following legalisation was in part constructed out of the need to fabricate the conditions within which gay sexuality had been learned but which no longer prevailed. If gay machismo is not 'real' heterosexuality, as 'camp' is not 'real' effeminacy, is not the self-conscious irony of gay machismo an attempt to retain the familiar sexual distance, anonymity and, in the leather scene especially, the danger that defined the homosexual experience in pre-legal days?

Commentators seldom refer to the sexual implications of 'camp', presumably because as a style it demasculinises, apparently taking gay men onto an asexual or solely sexually passive plane. Some have suggested that men who participated in the pre-legal 'camp' subculture were by necessity 'camp' themselves, i.e. sexually 'passive' as the rigid re-interpretation of conventional gender and sex roles of the time dictated, and that they necessarily found their sexual partners amongst 'active' men not part of the subculture, nor defined themselves as homosexual for the reasons given by Marshall (1981). However, there are in 'camp', its form rather than content, basic characteristics – the cool detachment with which it distances and dissects both the condemning straight and resisting homosexual worlds – which match male sexual objectification with a savage objectification of the spirit, baroque in expression because the object of interest is forbidden by and hidden from the dominant order.[8]

Therefore 'new' styles of homosexual manliness differ from the 'old' most significantly at the level of 'expressive artefacts and concrete objects' (Blachford 1981: 190), which have in the past twenty years been transformed into a 'bricolage' (Hebdige 1979: 103–4) of clothes (leather, denim, plaid shirts, overalls, hard-boots, but also a pronounced male 'fashion' consciousness), mannerisms (in extreme instances self-conscious masculinsation, as in the 'no smiling' and strict clothing codes of some 'leather' and 'denim' bars) and the values both represent: 'toughness', 'aggression', 'strength', 'control' and all the other idealised qualities of masculinity referred to earlier. These masculine traits are not 'real', they are consciously enacted by men who have failed to fully complete the conventional course in masculinisation, and who construct this fabricated form quite specifically around performances in part-time, highly controlled sexual scenarios, the purpose being exaggerated sexual potency (Fernbach 1981).

There is understandable doubt, therefore, as to whether this masculinised assemblage of symbols represents a 'new' role or an extension of the 'old' 'camp' subversiveness. Is the heightened conjunction of masculine artefacts to the point of 'camp' incongruity or is it the means by which the majority of gay men who do not take it to dramatic extremes 'pass', become 'invisible' in still hostile public territories, and thereby a sign of at least partial incorporation? [9]

Certainly 'new' styles, by comparison with the 'old', are explicitly sexual in ways that seemingly replicate, indeed heighten rather than challenge, existing oppressively homophobic dominant gender roles and institutions, but gay men are still not to be confused with the real thing. 'New' styles of homosexual manliness are not conventionally masculine but 'masculine' to a quite studied and specifically homosexual effect and purpose. The term 'masculinisation' is thus misleading in a way that 'eroticisation' and 'virilisation' are not.

So what were the changed conditions upon which this subcultural 'virilisation' emerged? As noted, those of most note include the 1960s 'alternative' or 'counter' cultural environment; partial and spasmodic, but nevertheless juridically real, legalisation in all modern societies and entry into formal citizenship. There was no winning of equal rights; on the contrary, this particular citizenship form was conditional upon strictures of enforced privacy. Male homosexual citizenship is predicated on the conjunction of individual consenting adult freedoms including, indeed particularly, those of a consuming market, and the reinforced stigma of immorality which bans this citizen from the 'moral community' and polices him into privacy. As gay men claimed their leisure and lifestyle market, the market claimed them, colonised and exploited gay sexuality. The potency of the modern homosexual male's 'virilisation' is as much economic as it is sexual, allowed to exercise his rights as consumer but denied 'equal' rights elsewhere, and on the whole he doesn't seem to mind.

Old style effeminacy confined the emasculated 'pansy' to a criminal twilight world in which the denial of the homosexual man's sexual potency was matched by the restraints placed on his open expenditure of income. In this sense 'pansy' and 'pervert' labels decommodified male gay sexuality, or at least stood in the way of its commodification. Legalisation and market exploitation thus required the modified incorporation of the male homosexual into the 'active' sexual and economic 'free' masculine world of sex needs, commodifiable through the legacy of earlier scripts of criminality, secrecy, anonymity and enforced fleeting promiscuity.

When illegal, gay male sexuality was objectified but not commercialised. With legalisation gay male sexuality was inevitably affected by material discourses commensurate with men as potent earners, independent workers, with possibly more disposable leisure and lifestyle income than their married counterparts. Commodification of the sexual socially constructs because it requires active, objectifying commodifiable eroticism. The sanctity of the moral order, however, requires that this homosexual consumer, as citizen, knows his moral and social place.

In a very basic sense the partial legalisation of male homosexuality in the late 1960s simply served to transfer hitherto banned and illegal behaviours into the bar and the bath-house. While for some critics Stonewall realised and symbolised a political breakthrough, subsequent gay history, with but a few exceptional outbursts of dissent, has seen deferential incorporation. In 1969 the homophile movement in the United States was of only peripheral concern to most homosexuals (Sagarin 1969). Although social and counselling aspects of the movement were to grow considerably in the 1970s, the bulk of gay interest was in the dissemination of information about subcultural venues of various kinds, and the prerequisites of the specific homosexual lifestyles for which they catered. To the extent that a journal such as *Gay News* could appear in 1972 in Britain, there was the ability to recognise and identify with a gay subculture of sorts, but for all the dissemination of rights news and political information, such journals have predominantly been devoted to charting the growth of homosexuality as a commodity and how to obtain it. As Shiers (1988) has observed, the gay political movement's influence on the lives of most gay

101

men has been indirect; it may have politically broadened out options but of greater importance to the majority of gay men has been

> the very factor which early 1970s Gay Lib thought impossible. Business interests started tapping into a seemingly ever growing 'gay market' and provided far better social facilities for gay men to meet in. The signs were all there from the mid-60s onwards . . . sex was becoming a marketable commodity – the gay market was particularly lucrative because gay men had nowhere else to go and were prepared to pay more for often a lot less in the way of provision than a heterosexual market would accept.
>
> (Shiers 1988: 230)

In America the consumption of homosexual sex within the legitimate bath-house proved politically central as 'the almost perfect symbol' of changed expressions of homosexuality, being 'clean, luxurious and sensual, replete with the latest technology' (Biskind and Ehrenreich 1980: 113). Legitimacy integrated the pursuit of gay sex into the market-place and nowhere more so than in this packaged environment, where prior to AIDS it was the consumer base for 'a whole way of life' (Altman 1982: 79). In 1982 Altman described the Midwest's largest and most luxurious sauna as 'not just a bathhouse, for you can eat snacks here, buy leather gear and inscribed t-shirts, even watch live cabaret performances on certain nights' (p. 79), in a building that additionally contained saunas, dance-floors and numerous darkened small cubicles which facilitated 'sexual democracy' and 'camaraderie', a 'sort of Whitmanesque democracy' of promiscuous, anonymous sex (p. 79). Even so this 'camaraderie' was fractured by commodified homosexual imagery, desire and self-presentation which differentiated in terms of 'age' and 'beauty' and set up 'their own hierarchies and barriers' (p. 80).

This description portrays a 'microcosm' of the post-legalisation pre-AIDS 1970s and early 1980s gay life of increased sexual expectations and their efficient realisation through the commercialisation of desire (Gassman 1986). For Shiers (1988) the bath-house provided 'a fantasy world where . . . [gay men] . . . could be whoever or whatever they wanted to be, without fear of anybody outside finding out' (p. 234); for Altman (1982) it enabled gratification of sexual desire without either emotional or financial consequences, all involved having paid the same entrance charge and having the same sexual values and interests which are essentially those of the anonymous, brief, unhindered multiple 'zipless fuck' (Jong 1973). 'Going to the baths to have sex integrates sex into the market-place in ways that park and street encounters do not' and whilst the former continue 'reliance on the market-place for sex and sexual encounters increases' (Altman 1982: 81).

In these terms the gay virilised community was politically incorporated into the unfetterd pursuit of commodified sex, and by the 1980s the formula for gay bars had been worked out: 'they were dark, they played very loud fast music, they had good light shows and above all they felt like sexually charged environments' (Shiers 1988: 240). Some critics claim that this was not solely a passive exploitation, arguing that the provision of safe private territories enabled a positive appreciation of these defensible homosexual forms as well as providing the environment within which a 'new gay solidarity' could be forged (Shiers 1988), and Altman (1982: 94–5) disagrees with Seabrook's pessimistic view that 'we *are* simply because we are a market' (1976: 80), claiming that such arguments fail to recognise that opportunities for sexual consumption provide a release from constraints previously the cause of so much unhappiness. All three are right of course but the need to avoid the latter was surely not the main *raison d'être* for the success of the gay bath-house or back room. Both facilitated the pursuit of homosexual encounters with consummate efficiency, and the incorporating effects do not need to be stressed. Some critics sought to defend these specific stylistic features of gay sexual promiscuity as somehow manifestations of a sexual democratisation along Whitmanesque lines. For example Edmund White's (1980) *States of Desire* concludes:

> Homosexuals, now identified as the element in our society most obsessed with sex, will in fact be the agents to cure the mania. Sex will be restored to its appropriate place as a pleasure, a communication, an art; it will no longer pose as a religion, a reason for being. In our present isolation we have few ways besides sex to feel connected with one another; in the future there might be surer modes for achieving a sense of community.
>
> (White 1980: 282)

White's idealism should not force us into the opposite and equally untenable position of arguing that the persuasive and efficient pressures towards commodification, whilst tending towards depoliticisation, automatically have that effect. As has been stressed several times, all forms of minority sexual citizenship occupy social and moral spaces which are constantly under review through the competing and ambiguous pressures of both amoral market and fetishised state. As a result each becomes potentially a moral, political and economic battleground within which the populations concerned, even if by default given the contradictory pressures they experience, have active roles to play. The very existence of homosexual citizenship delimits permitted space, establishes the need for greater space, economic, moral social and sexual, the potential for opposition to dominant forms of power.

Due to the intervention of AIDS one will never know the extent to which White's optimism was misplaced but certainly it would seem that because of AIDS other, whether 'surer' only time will tell, modes have emerged. AIDS itself has of course mobilised gay community power as at no other time, especially within the United States, but again this has been a necessary subcultural response with strong, indeed for some commentators heightened, commodification implications away from the specifically sexual towards more developed lifestyles. Under the headline 'GAY INC: The Surprising Health of Gay Businesses' Vandervelden *et al.* (1987), writing in *The Advocate*, targeted 'the swinging self-confident affluent homosexual male who lives in the pages of *The Advocate*', (Weeks 1980: 11) with an article on the health of the post-AIDS 'gay dollar'.

> The devastating force of the AIDS epidemic has brought warp-speed change to every aspect of gay life. These wrenching adjustments are being felt most acutely in America's gay urban enclaves, where everything but the neighbourhood geography itself has been transformed. Many of the once thriving microcosms of gay life and commerce have bowed out; shuttered bars, baths, and boutiques have become the social and economic relics of a vanished era.
>
> (Vandervelden *et al.* 1987: 43)

The AIDS era demands 'new choices. And in this economy,

when new choices are made it isn't long before someone moves quickly to capitalise on them' (Vandervelden *et al.* 1987: 45), thus there have been basic shifts in the gay economy, especially in such gay enclaves as San Francisco's Castro Street and New York's Greenwich Village, with high proportions of 'guppies': gay men at the peak of their earning power and with 'more disposable income than ever' (p. 45). This income is directed at the essentials of the relatively affluent gay lifestyle: gym memberships, vitamins and health-care, home entertainment (CD players, videos, home computers, etc.), food, fashion and travel. The article claims that gay leisure territories have been 'de-sexualised' or 'de-virilised' in that 'socialising bars' and restaurants have been commercially far more successful than those fewer bars which have sought to maintain the 'virilised' style. Howard Bennett of San Francisco's *Gay Book* commercial directory identifies these changes as being 'slightly ahead', but even so part of the general 'yuppie' trend so that, as in other gentrified urban areas, those with large gay populations have elicited a willingness on the part of large national chainstores to develop premises 'eager to tap gay dollars' (p. 44). R. Sager of the San Diego Business Association is quoted as saying that 'We are seeing . . . the broadening of how the gay leisure dollar is being spent' (p. 45) with slicker advertising being directed at a more sophisticated gay consumer who is not only interested in the accoutrements of a lifestyle, but also in the manner of its achievement. Jeanne Cordora of the *Community Yellow Pages* in Los Angeles claims that

> The sector that has experienced the most growth in the past year or two has been the blue-collar and professional services sector. Gay people have become aware that they can purchase from other gays all the services that they need in the home.
>
> (Vandervelden *et al.* 1987: 46)

In language typical of American Mammon's pseudo-religiosity, Cordora continues 'What gay consumers want from gay *providers* are personal services . . . whenever you may have to reveal to your *providers* your lifestyle, that is when the gay consumer wants to deal with a gay *provider*' (p. 46).

It is also reported that in areas with relatively large numbers of homosexuals *de facto* gay chambers of commerce have been established 'encouraging gays to spend gay dollars in our community. . . . Most gay people if they are aware that it is a gay business, and assuming the business is competitive, would rather deal with another gay person' (p. 47). Also the generally higher commercial profile of the 'guppie' has led, it is claimed, to greater tolerance of the gay community, not surprisingly for its economic diversification post-AIDS, away from bars and bath-houses towards more conformist material forms must have injected a considerable boost to several local economies as well as the national economy, whilst providing a more reassuring image than that given by the bath-house *habitué*.

Homosexually oriented businesses such as bath-houses, escort agencies and backroom bars have done less well, for 'safe sex' culture has undercut demand for such explicit sexual products, but claims of their demise have been somewhat exaggerated, perhaps for political as well as commercial reasons. Certainly 'safe sex' does not necessarily mean less sex or less promiscuous sex as 'jerk-off' clubs and parties held in the larger American cities and European 'gay capitals' such as Amsterdam testify, and there would still appear to be a considerable market for the most extreme of the fetishised homosexualised commodities of the 'virilised' era: leather, rubber, denim clothing and 'toys' as sold in Britain through the Expectations catalogue (1990).

The few sweat/check 'Polo' shirt items advertised are described as 'leisure wear' suggesting that leather, denim and rubber items are designed for 'work'. There are twelve types of leather jacket (with macho names such as the Bronx Belted £165; American Patrolman £185); thirteen types each of leather and rubber waistcoats (from £35.50 to £75), and jeans: 'Cod Piece Jeans' and 'Rubber Track Suit Bottoms' (from £48–£160); leather and rubber chaps (£95–£105); shirts (from £110 'long sleeved leather with epaulettes' down to singlet styles for £39.50); Levi-style leather shorts (£75); caps (with or without chrome peaks up to £44.50), belts, arm and wristbands, collars, bootstraps, braces and restraint harnesses, studded or plain. There are thirty forms of full or partial body harness: 'Upper link to ring' (£39.50), 'Lower body C ring' (£24.95), 'Upper body with snaps' (£35) and 'Suspension' (£95); various head harnesses (with 'detachable solid gag' for £54 or 'inflatable gag' for £62.50 and the 'Dildo harness' £45). Restraints number twenty-six from 'collar to wrist' at £29.50 to 'executioner's mask' for £27.95 and 'toys' range from the 'Elasticated ball bag and sheath' for £18.95; the 'Absolutely anti-erect' at £29.95, the 'Meat tenderiser' at £26.95 and the 'Erection trainer' for £56. Advertised under S/M are canes, handcuffs, 'short studded wangers', 'tit weights large' and 'rubber straightjackets', the latter at £149. There are also heavy metal items such as wrist and ankle manacles and the 'Headcage with mouth hole' for £129.50 plus seventeen types of stainless steel 'tit rings' and two of gold, the more expensive, the Barbell, costing £81.95.

Accessories offered include mirrored sunglasses, rubber sheeting, leather gloves, 'poppers', key chains, tattoos, leather duffle bags, condoms (Black Knight, Red Stripe and Mates), lubricants (Elbow Grease) and saddlesoap for boots which come in five types from Timberland at £39.95 to 'Short engineers' at £65. Finally there is a relatively small ladies' rubberwear section. Phone lines are listed which give details of (i) Great Britain's leather and rubber scene (ii) Amsterdam's leather and rubber scene (iii) the Expectations product and information guide and (iv) Manfest '90 Information line. Needless to say all the major credit cards are taken.

Under the weight of such leather and rubber wear from but one of many similar sources it is hard to believe that diversification of gay consumption has meant the demise of 'virilised' commodification. Of course such materials do not necessarily indicate pre-AIDS sexual lifestyles but they certainly depend upon the costly adoption of what one leather exponent calls 'one more sensuous skin' (Tucker 1987: 40). Even so it is claimed that bath-houses and backroom bars have gone into social and economic decline. For example, estimated numbers of the former nationwide in the States are down from 400 in 1981 to 150 in 1986 (p. 42). However, there has been a slight but continuing recovery during the latter part of this period. 'We eliminated the orgy room, the glory-hole rooms, slings and things of that nature' replacing them with 'gyms, exercise equipment and even health food bars' (p. 45). Prominent emphasis on 'safe sex' helps of course with 90 per cent of clubs providing free condoms and 'AIDS-related educational material'. Even so it is estimated that business has fallen 25 per cent on the peak year of 1980 (p. 49).

Escort agencies have lost customers and escorts. One unnamed head of a New York agency reports that at $200 an hour most customers are wealthy, prominent and closeted: 'We lost people who threw parties and had 10 or 12 boys, that's gone' (Tucker 1987: 108), especially as 'safe sex' regimes reduce the 'quality' of the commodity purchased. By contrast the sale of 'safe' substitutes such as pornographic materials, magazines, videos and chat lines, condoms and masturbation devices such as the Orosimulator have risen, as has the trend towards settled relationships.

Finally one of the great commercial gay growth areas has been in tourism. In the United States the International Gay Travel Association (IGTA) has approximately 250 members providing gay holidays of all kinds and types, fewer now to the 'mecca locations' of old such as Fire Island and San Francisco, but more along the patterns of tourism generally, except again in this instance the *providers* are also gay or lesbian. Denise Mitten of Minneapolis Woodswomen provides outdoor holidays, hiking, camping, mountain climbing, etc. She says

> Especially with lesbians in the 1960s and 1970s it was like you had to be downwardly mobile. . . . Now we realise its OK to have money; its OK to travel; its OK to treat ourselves really nicely. That doesn't mean we're necessarily agreeing with or buying into all the trappings of the patriarchy.
>
> (quoted in Vandervelden *et al.* 1987: 48)

For gay males, however, despite such claims to the contrary by those quoted in this particular article, tourism remains mainly organised around the paramount interest in the erotic.

In one sense tourism directly draws together processes of commodification, consumer capitalism and citizenship in that 'Being able to go on holiday, to be obviously not at work, is presumed to be a characteristic of modern citizenship which has become embedded into people's thinking about health and well-being' (Urry 1990b: 24).

The conversion of tourist services into a satisfactory holiday involves a great deal of 'work' by both those determined to have a 'good time' and those selling the services provided who, to varied degrees, try to guarantee a particular holiday experience. Specifically

> . . . part of the social experience involved in many tourist contexts is to be able to consume particular commodities in the company of others. Part of what people buy is in effect

> a particular social composition of other consumers and this
> is difficult for the providers of the services to ensure.
>
> (Urry 1990b: 25)

Thus if in the most general sense holidaymakers having a 'good time' means not individual consumption but consumption with appropriate like-minded and interested others, 'community' familiars with comparable lifestyles, nowhere is this more likely to be effectively accomplished, sought as well as provided, than in tourism based on the pursuit of gay sexual pleasure in resorts with like-minded pleasure-seekers. For gay men such holidays are marketed and consumed on a world-wide scale, and *pace* Urry it would seem that it is not difficult at all for the providers of gay holidays to guarantee the effective social composition of their consumers, not least because of the uniformity of the international gay community and the consistency and commonality of its core values and interests.

As much can be gleaned from twenty years of *Spartacus International Gay Guides* (1970–   ). As in all editions the first, of 109 large print pages, listed bars, clubs, hotels, cinemas, beaches, saunas, restaurants, bookshops, local health services, gay organisations and 'outside cruising' areas, advising on dangers of their use (i.e. 'AYOR', 'at your own risk' (1970)). Almost half of the pages dealt with venues in the USA. By 1988 the Guide had become a testament to the view that 'new consumption practices can take place anywhere . . . eminently transportable as part of the new export economy' (Zukin 1990: 39). Its 1000 pages (85 on the USA) of closely printed details provide for each country thumbnail sketches in English, French, German and Spanish, detailing area, population size, language, currency and the moral as well as physical climate. This 'international gay community' (*Spartacus* 1988: 8) extends from Abu Dhabi to Zimbabwe via Burundi ('We know little about this little central African agricultural country between Lake Tanganyika and Lake Victoria, but what we've heard sounds interesting. . . . The country is governed by the Tutsi tribe, for whom bisexuality is the norm . . .' (pp. 129–30)); Comoros ('The islands of this former French colony are a heavenly refuge, hardly touched by tourism . . . . A gay scene in western terms does not exist here, but gay sex nonetheless does not appear to be unknown' (p. 161)) and North Korea ('. . . governed by a socialist dictatorship . . . with no democratic freedoms. . . . We assume that in accordance with Stalinist custom elsewhere [homosexual behaviour] is illegal and that no gay scene exists' (p. 534)).

Inevitably Western Europe and the USA provide the bulk of the now highly codified entries;[10] 'LJ' = predominant leather or denim dress codes; 'C' = 'clones';[11] 'sb', 'sol' and 'wh' = the availability of steam baths, solaria and jacuzzi respectively. Even air-conditioning is coded. In total, 59 symbols indicate venue characteristics from 'A', i.e. 'regular art exhibitions' through to 'YP' meaning 'young and progressive' (p. 15).

The *Guide*'s introduction underplays its function as an entrée into gay commercial tourism, instead emphasising goals of health and well-being whilst inevitably taking on board the AIDS health and commercial crisis.

SPARTACUS is a Guide compiled by gay men, for gay men. What do we mean by that? SPARTACUS enables gay men to get closer during their vacations as well as to have international contacts. By this we do not merely mean the joys of sex. Although it is true that we list in SPARTACUS addresses of places where sexual encounters are possible, it is not our aim to propagate the sex-oriented tourism. In view of the disease AIDS, threatening mankind, we relinquish to mention the dark-rooms which can be found in some gay bars. But we are thoroughly convinced that the place is not a determining factor leading to a risky behaviour: everybody is responsible for himself, his own behaviour and for his partner. However, by mentioning the dark-rooms, some institutions could arrive at the wrong conclusions.

(*Spartacus* 1988: 14)

As for AIDS, the editor states whilst 'Gay men are especially well educated about AIDS, through the gay press . . .', and that 'everyone assures me that he only does safe sex', even so 'I have lost count of the number of invitations I have had, and refused, to engage in unprotected sex with strangers, during my travels in 1987 alone' (p. 15). So 'the responsibility lies with the individual to take care of himself and those with whom he has sex experiences [for] those who provide gay venues are not likely to close down their popular back-rooms, baths or prostitution services' (p. 16). As for AIDS 'it can be conquered' (pp. 29–31);

'safe' and 'unsafe' sex are defined, instructions are given on condom use, as is advice on whether to take the HIV antibody test: 'Before testing it is worth considering the enormous emotional strain that a positive result can bring with it' (p. 30). Early symptoms of AIDS-related illnesses are also listed. Finally appeals are made to the sense of solidarity gay men should feel with those of their acquaintance who might become ill with AIDS

> ... it is a matter of self-esteem not to treat the victims of this disease like wrongdoers. A friend who is suffering from AIDS has the right to expect that your friendship will remain steadfast throughout this crucial period.
>
> (*Spartacus* 1988: 30–1)

In brief, Spartacus wishes its readers 'a safe and healthy gay lifestyle, filled with safe pleasures, as you enjoy the gay scene with *The Spartacus Guide*' (p. 16), with its summarised local gay rights (e.g. whether legal and at what age), venues and territories for sex of various kinds, in a consumption package including guidance on 'gay' cultural capital such as restaurants, bookshops and clothes stores. Such sexual 'symbolic consumption practices provide a "real" base for the social processes of capital accumulation' (Zukin 1990: 38), in the gay global village of Le Garcon and Seven Up in Fukuoka, Japan; Napoleon and the Pickwick Bar in Beirut; the Queen's Head in Amsterdam; Bacchus in Goteborg; the North Dakota Saloon in Valencia, and New York and Why Not? bars seemingly everywhere.

Several venues provide for composite consumption, 'Socio-spatial prototypes of a new organisation of consumption' (Zukin 1990: 38), comparable to the American bath-houses in their prime. Al Peter's Sun-Deck Sauna and Fitness Club in Bern, for example, offers a Bistro, Bistro-Bar, Sauna, Whirlpool, Television Room, Video Room, Fitness Gymnasium, a Sun Terrace and 'Relax-Room', advertised through universal symbols of the more than perfect male body; handsome moustachioed 'masculine' face, eyes locked onto those of the viewer. Other bars and clubs cater for other tastes, for younger (and in some parts of the world, e.g. Thailand, boyish) perhaps androgynous, the 'rough' and the 'respectable' in terms of social class and adopted styles. As we have seen in our discussion of the commodification of homosexuality generally, gay tourism offers not particular aspects of homosexual interest, but specific arenas and stages

111

within which selected and highly controlled cosmetic performances may be given with the minimum of biographical revelation
or personal cost. Whichever context selected, whatever the
specific performance given, the common commodity is
homosexual sexual pleasure.

> ... the tourist is interested in everything as a sign of itself.
> All over the world the unsung armies of semioticians, the
> tourists, are fanning out in search of the signs of
> Frenchness, typical Italian behaviour, exemplary oriental
> scenes, typical American thruways, traditional English
> pubs.
>
> (Culler 1981: 127)

The gay tourist is rather more single-mindedly in pursuit of
pleasurable sex, encoded in terms of generalised physical and
performance principles; build, hair, colour of skin and eyes,
dress, etc. which set up their own hierarchies of esteem and
social, economic and sexual barriers. As *Spartacus* guides
demonstrate, the gay tourist pursues gay commodities to the
most esoteric of places, where the commodity sought is
significantly different from that to be found in developed gay
tourist resorts. To know that Sitges in Spain guarantees summer
sun, good food, hotels and unlimited opportunities for gay sex
('Few places have such a concentration of excellent gay hotels and
apartment buildings, so many busy gay bars, and a choice of gay
beaches' (*Spartacus* 1988: 743)) is not enough for the better-off for
whom Indonesia, Costa Rica, or such Muslim strongholds as
Bahrein and Bangladesh offer locations which, as with general
mass tourism in the Mediterranean, have not been physically and
socially devalued (Bataille 1988; Millot 1988). Gay or straight, for
those who can move elsewhere, mass tourism sets up its own
hierarchies of consumer wealth and esteem (Mishan 1969). In
the global gay context, however, such tourism involves the
pursuit of what in a sense is a 'pure' gay commodity: sexual
pleasure with those for whom gay roles, community and lifestyles
are meaningless, and where the commodification of gay sexuality
is initially experienced through tourist influence. The guarantee
of gay sexual pleasure in Sitges is confidently expected because
of the common scripts of its tourists, but the gay visitor to Bahrein
('... a Moslem country [where] homosexuality is illegal, but
nevertheless traditionally practiced. Its better not to carry this

guide or other gay material in your luggage' (*Spartacus* 1988: 87)) is seeking sex in a context within which mutually understood scripts do not exist. There might be homosexual behaviour, but not homosexuality, and in tourist terms it appears that the former is of greater value than the latter and obtainable through the complicit, amoral market to the extent of considerable local social and moral tensions.

If as Warde (1990: 4) suggests there are four key stages in the cycle from tourist commodity production to use – production/provision, conditions of access, manner of delivery and the environment of enjoyment – gay tourism may be described as being universally characterised by the pursuit of commodified homosexual pleasures, but that in the more expensive venues, precisely those without developed homosexual subcultural forms, the specifically economic 'conditions of access' to these particular sexual markets are unconstrained by the citizenship developments which serve as damage-limitation mechanisms in modern societies. This enables the exploitation of a form of homosexual commodity, provided rather than produced through discourse or script in a manner and a locale that heightens the consumer's enjoyment. Sahlins (1976: 169) has noted that an object produced doesn't take on its full meaning until consumed. In the case of third world gay tourism the commodity's meaning is often solely provided by the consumer and the manner of consumption. The consumer's commoditised understanding of the sexual transaction effectively commences the commodification of homosexuality or, where it applies, any other form of material sexual power/knowledge introduced to the native population.

In this sense there clearly *is* specifically homosexual consumption in a global gay market and it is largely in this sense that the 'international gay community' with common norms and values exists. One doesn't know of course just how part-time the gay tourists' participation in solely gay territories is, but there is no doubt that the material discourses on homosexuality have, with modest provisos over local constraints on the expression of these subcultural values, effectively reduced the world to the dimensions of Earls Court or Christopher Street, which is no mean feat.

5

... AND POLITICAL OBLIGATIONS

'We hear such strange things about England, that so many things are forbidden there that are permitted here. And then that books are banned. Is it true . . . ? Doesn't anyone protest?' . . . Paul tried to explain the attitude of the British authorities. But all the explanations sounded ridiculous even as he said them.

(Spender 1988: 66)

If Stonewall provoked a significant practical as well as symbolic impetus it was theoretically built upon by the various Gay Liberation Groups and manifestos which appeared between 1969 and 1972 in the USA, Britain and elsewhere.[1] Their principles and aims were on the grand scale, concerned with the 'political significance of sexuality as a system of social control, on the levels . . . of social structures and belief' (Watney 1980: 64), and the oppressive role of 'bourgeois models of mental health' (p. 65). As is inevitable in such short-circuiting rallies to arms, these manifestos were more expressions of faith than analytical starting points. Sexism, heterosexuality, patriarchy, imperialism, oppression,[2] capitalism, raised passions but closed off rather than opened up debates as indeed did the term 'liberation' itself, stretched to the tensile limit of meaning, and signifying the complete transformation of societies' economic, political institutions and cultures, as well as the gay self from 'self-oppression'. One result was that 'political identity (gay liberation) and personal identification (gay liberationist) became hopelessly confused' (p. 71). Even so such liberation and liberationist concerns did extend within this radical rhetoric to statements of basic citizenship intent, the extension of concrete rights and

114

freedoms feasible without radical upheaval. As much is clear from the following example of a broadsheet produced by the London GLF in 1970.

THE PRINCIPLES OF THE GAY LIBERATION FRONT

1 GLF's first priority is to defend the immediate interests of gay people against discrimination and social oppression.

2 However, the roots of oppression that gay people suffer run deep in our society, in particular the structure of the family patterns of socialisation and the Judeo-Christian culture. Legal reform and education against prejudice though possible and necessary, cannot be a permanent solution. While existing social structures remain, social prejudice and overt oppression can always re-emerge.

3 GLF, therefore, sees itself as part of the wider movement aiming to abolish all forms of social oppression. It will work to ally itself with other oppressed groups while preserving its organisational independence.

4 In particular we see these groups as including:
   (a) The women's liberation movement. The roots of women's oppression are in many ways close to our own (see 2).
   (b) Black people and other national minorities. The racism that these people are affected by has a similar structure of prejudice to our own, but on the basis of racial instead of sexual difference. They are socially and economically the most oppressed group in our society.
   (c) The working class, i.e. all productive, manual and mental workers. Their labour is what the whole of society lives off, but their skills are misused by the profit-oriented economy, and their right to organise and defend their interests is under increasing attack.
   (d) Young people who are rejecting the bourgeois family and the roles and lifestyles offered them by this society, and attempting to create a non-exploitative counter-culture.
   (e) Peoples oppressed by imperialism, who lack the

115

national, political and economic independence which is a pre-condition for all other social change.

5 We don't believe that any existing revolutionary theory has all the answers to the problems facing us. GLF will, therefore, study and discuss all the relevant critical theories of society and the individual being, to measure them against the test of our own and historical experience.

The Gay Liberation Front demands . . .

- that all discrimination against gay people, male and female, by the law, by employers, and by society at large should end,

- that all people who feel attracted to a member of their own sex should know that such feelings are good and natural,

- that sex education in schools stop being exclusively heterosexual,

- that psychiatrists stop treating homosexuality as though it were a problem or a sickness, and thereby giving gay people senseless guilt complexes,

- that gay people should be legally free to contact other homosexuals, through newspaper ads, on the streets, and by any other means they wish, as are heterosexuals, and that police harrassment should cease right now,

- that employers should no longer be allowed to discriminate against anyone on account of their sexual preferences,

- that the age of consent for homosexuals should be reduced to the same age as that for heterosexuals

- that gay people be free to hold hands and kiss in public, as are heterosexuals.

Present organisation:
co-ordinating committee, office collective, media workshop, street theatre group, action group (actions and social events), youth group, counter-psychiatry group, communes group, education and research group, women's group, awareness groups.

Our meetings are held every week on Wednesdays at 7.30 p.m. at All Saint's Church Hall, Powis Gardens, Notting Hill, London W11. Further information can be obtained from the GLF office at 5 Caledonian Road, Kings Cross, N1. Phone 837-7174.

The conjunction of apocalyptic visions and modest reformist claims for citizenship advance within the oppressive status quo is normal during periods of social and political upheaval, but it is salutary to note that whilst in the subsequent twenty years gay and lesbian formal rights have increased, none of this broadsheet's seemingly modest demands have been met.

GLF, experimenting on a broad front, organisationally, culturally, sexually, economically and politically, was short-lived, but less extreme British gay organisations: CHE (Campaign for Homosexual Equality) and SHRG (Scottish Homosexual Rights Group, formerly Scottish Minorities Group), though still in existence, have gone into progressive decline in the past two decades, suggesting a lack of gay 'community' political interest and activism. In a sense the reformist wing of gay politics has been 'glitzed' in the wake of Section 28 (Local Government Act 1988) which mobilised considerable opposition from media, theatre and entertainment 'stars' and by show business dominated organisations such as Stonewall,[3] with the respectful media coverage of its leaders such as Sir Ian McKellan and his tea-time *tête-à-tête*s with the Prime Minister at No. 10. The Stonewall spirit is one of responsible elitist representation and not of mass mobilisation. By contrast spontaneous, combustive and combative minority radical gay politics in the GLF mould have recently surfaced around such specific issues as Section 28, police harassment, the failure of the police to protect gay citizens from assault in public spaces, sex education in schools, the willingness of celebrity McKellan to accept the proffered knighthood, and the threatened 'outing' of celebrities in Britain as earlier accomplished in America.[4] Such groups as FROCS,[5] OutRage,[6] Act Up[7] and Charter 88[8] periodically surge on broad zapping tactics to highlight specific lacks of freedoms and rights so that overall, in media terms, gay claims, if not all of a conventional citizenship kind, are of considerable contemporary significance, not least because of elaborate ongoing debates over gay rights in response to medical, political and moral consequences of AIDS. Even so the proportion of gay men and lesbians actively involved is a small minority, the majority apparently conforming to the moral, political and economic constraints placed upon them.

However, issues of citizenship are repeatedly aired in the gay media and whilst the majority may not be openly political they will be well informed especially through the freely available magazines and newspapers in bars, clubs, etc. Gay citizenship issues are disparate and vary in specificity and levels of support but they cluster around the core disputes listed in the next paragraph. Space forbids detailed or numerous examples but one case in each rights instance is given, with the broader discussion following through a more detailed account of what, in Britain, has proved the catalyst in recent rights battles since its inception as Clause, and subsequent institutionalisation as Section 28.

The recurring issues of citizenship conflict are: *legal status* in terms of specifically anti-gay statutes concerning age of consent, marriage, adoption, discrimination in employment, etc., as well as the police use of receptacle laws particularly against gay people concerning, for example, offences such as soliciting, vagrancy and indecency; *law enforcement and police practices* over 'cottaging' and 'outside cruising', failure to provide protection against 'queer-bashing', over-zealous policing of gay demonstrations and generally hostile police attitudes to gay men and lesbians; *censorship of gay oriented materials* by Customs and Excise and the police and by media watchdogs; inadequate controls on *anti-gay media coverage*; *anti-discrimination employment rights*; the infringement of rights related to AIDS such as HIV testing, drug experimentation, insurance rights, financial and social rights generally of HIV+ individuals, travel and migration restrictions; *sex education* in schools and, finally, the *'promotion of homosexuality'*.

Legal status is inevitably a major focus of citizenship dissent. Tatchell's guide to lesbian and gay rights in thirty European countries shows that nine countries which have repealed the complete ban on homosexual contacts still enforce a discriminatory age of consent which is higher for homosexuals than for heterosexuals; 'on average it is 18 years for same sex relationships compared with 15 years for sex between men and women'[9] (Tatchell 1990). The United Kingdom and Bulgaria, at 21, have the highest ages of consent for homosexuals in Europe; Spain, with 12, has the lowest age of common consent. In total, sixteen countries have common ages of consent, the average age being 15. In Britain, therefore, it is not surprising that age of consent is a major focus for formal citizenship claims such as the Private Member's Bill sponsored by Peter Ashman on behalf of Stonewall (*The Times* 13 Feb. 1990).[10] In Britain in 1988 twenty-three men were sent to prison for up to four years for sexual contact with a consenting male partner aged between 16 and 21 (*Gay Times* March 1990).[11]

The National Executive of the Labour Party, somewhat reluctantly it seems, 'has given up opposition to the idea of legislation to reduce the age of gay male consent to 16',[12] but still refuses to incorporate this reform into its general manifesto. In answer to a question from Conservative back-bencher David Martin at Prime Minister's Question Time as to whether the then Prime Minister agreed 'that for various reasons, including the spreading and contracting of AIDS, any proposal to reduce the age of consent to homosexual activities is wholly unacceptable and crackers', Margaret Thatcher replied 'any such proposal would give totally the wrong signal at this time. It would give offence to many people and worry many more and would give us great problems in the future. I would be very much against reducing the age of consent' (reported in *Gay Times* March 1990). However, her successor's willingness to invite Sir Ian McKellan to put a case for reform has suggested that perhaps signals are crossed in the Conservative Party.

Attempts to change other legislation, given the deep hostility to this most basic of legal changes, invariably looks unlikely to succeed although the Stonewall Group's commitment includes eradication of the laws that have seen escalating police harassment of gay men.

A San Francisco law which would have given gay couples (in the first instance city employees) the opportunity to register their relationships to give them the same rights as married couples was rejected in a city referendum in 1989 (*Gay Times* Dec. 1989: 7). In Denmark homosexual couples have the right to civil marriage at a registry office and enjoy all the rights of married heterosexuals except that of adopting children. 'Until the law is changed in that respect lots of lesbian couples will not bother [to register]' (p. 7). In Britain, despite much opposition, there have been cases of 'successful' fostering by gay and lesbian couples though predictably accompanied by tabloid expressions of deep concern (*Gay Times* 8 Dec. 1990). In Sweden lesbian and gay couples who live together enjoy 'the same substantial legal rights as cohabiting heterosexual couples' (Tatchell 1990: 4), whilst Italy, France and the Netherlands also give partial legal recognition of gay couple status.

Police activities inevitably arouse considerable dissent in that large numbers of homosexual men run the risk of encountering the policing of their everyday sexual, social and political lives. In a sense the lengthy and complex negotiations of the 'coming-out' process take gay men through numerous public contexts in which their sexual identities are being tested and formed. The law operates as though the men concerned are either straight or gay and that, if the latter, are unproblematically so. The boundaries of gay private territories thus provide rich pickings for zealous police officers. Battles over police activities tend to concentrate on the seemingly random use of existing legislation, the means employed to enforce such legislation and the failure of the police to provide protection to gay citizens subjected to physical and verbal abuse. For example, the numbers of 'indecency' cases between males reported in England and Wales have risen steadily over the past three years from 857 in 1985 to 1306 in 1988 and to 2022 in 1989 according to Home Office statistics (*Gay Times* June 1990: 6), the 1989 figure being the third highest in fifty or more years after 1954 and 1955 when all gay sex was still illegal. The year 1989 also saw 'the biggest increase in the numbers of offence in this category in any one year' (*Gay Times* Aug. 1989: 9).[13] At the time of writing, the British government is facing stiff opposition to Clauses 1, 2 and 25 of the Criminal Justice Bill, currently before Parliament, which seek to formalise police powers over various 'gay relations', some public some private; sex between merchant seamen; 'living off the earnings of a male prostitute', etc., all defended by the intention to 'protect the public from serious harm', and to that end proposing stiffer sentences for these victimless crimes (*Gay Times* March 1991).

Police action against a gay presence in public territories is not limited to sexual behaviours of course. On 6 October 1989, 200 San Francisco Police Department tactical squad officers attacked AIDS demonstrators in the Castro and Market Street district.

Similar action was also taken in nineteen cities against a nationwide protest over police policies, underfunding of AIDS research and exorbitant cost of drugs such as AZT and DDI.

Reports of police use of *agents provocateurs*: 'good looking police officers dressed in casual clothes ... to harass men in public toilets and to incite acts of indecency' (*Gay Times* 6 Dec. 1989), regularly appear in gay and general media. In December 1989 MP Keith Vaz accused the Leicestershire police of employing such tactics whilst in June of the same year there was a London protest by OutRage against similar practices and the following summer *Gay Scotland* carried reports of similar activities in Glasgow, and at Prestwick beach (June 1990: 3).[14]

Police action around gay clubs and pubs at closing times, with an obvious overspill from 'private' gay territories onto public pavements has been a regular focus of rights conflicts and one in which those with an interest in the selling of the gay commodity clearly have an interest. Accordingly police liaison with the gay 'community' seems most developed when such interests are taken into account. *Gay Times* (Sept. 1990: 20–1) reported that London police want more meetings with representatives of the Gay Business Association established in 1986 after a police raid on a South London gay pub. The GBA and the organisation Friend have been conducting lesbian and gay awareness sessions for police trainees in response to criticism of the police for not doing enough to protect London's gay population from increased queer-bashing and murder (*Gay Times* Dec. 1986).[15] Similar increases in these so-called 'bias crimes' have been reported in other cities world wide (*Gay Times* July 1990: 16; *Independent on Sunday* 29 July 1990).[16] There are also regular complaints about police harassment of gay men in their enquiries into such crimes as murder (*Gay Times* Aug. 1990: 14).[17]

The imprisonment of sex offenders has become a rights issue of some importance in Britain with campaigners focusing on Rule 43 which segregates sex from non-sex offenders whilst offering them no real protection. Violence against sex offenders is common and the prisoners concerned (2500 in British prisons by 1989) understandably seek protection via this rule, which merely serves to label sex offenders as legitimate targets of abuse for other inmates (Prison Reform Trust 1990; *Gay Times* Aug. 1990: 15).

As for *censorship*, individuals and retail outlets repeatedly find that materials with discernible gay themes (as discerned by the authorities), may be confiscated or destroyed whatever their literary, photographic, 'obscene' or 'artistic' merits. Artist Philip Core had slides to be used in his paintings, sent by himself from America to his home in London, and a copy of the Tom of Finland Retrospective catalogue (personally dedicated to him by the author) requisitioned by Customs and Excise for being 'repulsive, filthy, loathsome, and lewd' (*Gay Times* Dec. 1988: 12).[18] In late 1989 the London bookshop Gay's The Word lost its long-running battle to change the censorship rules applying to lesbian and gay books imported from overseas. 'Magistrates at London's Bow Street Court decided . . . that six books deliberately imported by Gay's The Word as a "test case" ', after a raid on the shop in April 1984 by Customs and Excise officials, were 'blatantly erotic and obscene', the court declaring that it must direct its mind to what 'ordinary decent people' think about obscenity (*Gay Times* Dec. 1989: 7).[19] In Britain and the USA gay culture is regularly banned or at least bans are sought: for example, in 1990 the Director of the Center for Contemporary Art in Cincinnati, Ohio, faced charges of obscenity in connection with an exhibition of the late Robert Mapplethorpe's photographic work.

Television representations of what some consider to be positive gay themes have inevitably been subjected to strong informal controls especially after the generalised inhibiting pressure of Section 28, but the Conservative government's proposals for a new Broadcasting Bill included guidelines which would bring both television and radio into line with the provisions of the Obscene Publications Act (1959), 'and will give new powers to a Broadcasting Standards Council to determine general standards of good taste and decorum' (*Gay Times* Jan. 1990: 5). Such restrictions would apparently receive the support of the majority of viewers for a survey of those of Channel 4, not perhaps the most numerous or typical although reputedly inclined to be more liberal, found that as many as 61 per cent of its viewers are opposed to even occasional programmes about homosexuality; 'the survey found that "a strong anti-homosexual current runs through the public's attitudes, even among those who seek to articulate, in the abstract, the rights of such groups" ' (*Gay Times* Nov. 1987: 10).

Press coverage of gay issues in Britain, from the tabloids especially, has been uniformly hostile, to the extent that most gay press present permanent reports on such coverage. As Quentin Crisp has observed (*Observer Scotland* 28 Jan. 1990), 'There is no more vulgar sight in the civilised world than a shabby journalist chasing a poof' and the Press Council at times agrees. In 1990 it censured *Sun* TV critic Gary Bushell for arguing 'It must be true what they say about nobody being all bad . . . even Stalin banned poofs' (*Sun* 21 March 1990).[20] Bushell's defence was: 'I make no apology for the language I use. It is the language of *Sun* readers, and indeed the majority of British people' (*Gay Times* May 1990: 14–15). Four European countries, Denmark, Eire, Norway and Sweden, have laws against incitement to hatred on the grounds of sexual orientation, and the introduction of such legislation in Britain is part of the Stonewall Group's proposals for private member sponsorship in the Commons.

As for *anti-discriminatory legislation covering employment and employment practices*, Europe's tolerant countries are the same, as are the not so tolerant, including Britain, where repeatedly homosexual status is deemed an acceptable cause for dismissal, and not just from sensitive areas of employment. Employment protection laws do not apply to people in the armed forces following the Sexual Offences Act (1967), hence one gay airman who admitted his homosexual feelings but who was guilty of no offence, was dismissed from the RAF in 1987 (*Gay Times* Nov. 1987). American laws on gayness in the armed services are infamous given the notable challenges that have been made to them (e.g. Matlovich),[21] but even so crackdowns are frequent, for example, again in 1987 there was a witch-hunt at US airbases in the UK, justified officially on the grounds that the lifestyle of gay people is 'incompatible with military work and conditions', and between ten and twenty personnel were sent home (*Gay Times* Nov. 1987: 29). In Britain recent moves by both the armed forces and the police to liberalise employment and recruitment practices in this regard have been made but the effects have yet to be seen, and the furore over public exposure of gay judges (*Sun* 19 Jan. 1990)[22] does not exactly inspire confidence.

Industrial tribunals forced to consider gay status set against the attitudes of discriminatory employers and other employees have tended to work on the understandable prejudices of common sense. One such tribunal of 3 April 1990 in Bedford, ruled that it is acceptable to sack gay men from their jobs because their workmates are afraid of catching AIDS (*Gay Times* Nov. 1987: 3). The case concerned a 43-year-old projectionist who had worked at the same cinema for seventeen years, but the other employees claimed they did not want to work with him because he was gay and he was, therefore, sacked. Despite government guidelines contained in Ministry of Employment pamphlets distributed to all employers in April 1989 stating that HIV+ status should not 'normally' be valid grounds for job discrimination (*Gay Times* Nov. 1987: 3) and that employees sacked would have a case for unfair dismissal, employment practice has been somewhat different. In this case the tribunal decided that given the sacked man's conviction for 'gross indecency' his 'lifestyle exposed him to above average risk of HIV infection and he knows that other people would avoid associating with him as a result' (*Gay Times* Nov. 1987: 3).

Gay Times (Aug. 1990: 5) reported: 'Employment Appeals Tribunal reverses a previous judgement that a teacher who was sacked after raising homosexuality in a sex education class was unfairly dismissed'. The Appeals Tribunal accepted Birmingham City Council arguments that the original tribunal had adopted the wrong test of reasonableness (i.e. had his introduction of the topic into the class been reasonable, rather than was the City of Birmingham reasonable to sack him?). The teacher concerned was reportedly not gay.

AIDS has provided a wide range of specific rights debates concerning rights infringements of all gays vulnerable to AIDS moral panics, and of course those specifically designated as HIV+, or ARC or AIDS patients.[23] Testing patients without their consent has been justified on grounds of medical knowledge and protection of medical personnel. More dramatic rumours such as those which suggested that certain West German cities planned 'pavilions' with electric fences (i.e. 'electronic access control') and that Norway intended off-shore island 'retreats' for HIV+ patients and AIDS sufferers (*Gay Times* Nov. 1987: 14), have done nothing to calm fears about patients' rights of consent over testing, especially when further rights, e.g. to life insurance, mortgage access, etc., are automatically eroded once tests have been made. Even the 1991 statistics on the greater spread of HIV infection amongst heterosexual populations than homosexual, has not disposed insurance companies to modify their anti-gay questionnaires (*Gay Times* Aug. 1989: 5).[24]

Travel freedoms have also been affected; the Australian government has introduced HIV tests for all potential immigrants ('Testing for HIV is an extension of the medical examination and should not be viewed as a breach of basic human rights and civil liberties' (spokesperson for the Australian High Commission reported in *Gay Times* Dec. 1989)). Immigration Control in Britain, the United States and elsewhere regularly stop and send back those suspected of being 'medically undesirable' although the USA has recently introduced a special limited visa restriction on HIV+ tourists where before there was a simple ban for those admitting this status. The US Immigration and Naturalisation Service (INS) uses when it wishes Section 212 (b) of the Immigration and Naturalisation Act which bars those afflicted with psychopathic personality, sexual deviancy or mental defect from entry, if they are certified as such by an officer of the Public Health Service.

Given the fluidity, detail and cross-cultural variations in the statutory status of homosexuals and lesbians, the above discussion is bound already to be inadequate and out of date in specific aspects. In order to understand British legal developments in more detail it is perhaps better to examine the most important recent legal initiative, Section 28, in greater depth.

Clause 28 was successfully introduced into the Local Government Bill (1987) by Tory MP David Wilshire, despite heated parliamentary debates and intense mass demonstration and lobbying opposition.[25] By the time the Clause became law as Section 28 of the Local Government Act on 24 May 1988, it was already being authoritatively dismissed as a particularly weak piece of legislation, the wording ambiguous, contradictory and sometimes quite meaningless, and although fear of prosecution has claimed some notable victims, there have as yet been no prosecutions. This is largely because Section 28 is a demonstrably poor law but nevertheless remarkably effective as a concentrated affirmation of neo-Conservative morality set against that most powerful real and symbolic 'subversive' threat to it: homosexuality. Simultaneously a number of other profoundly significant ideological motifs familiar to the student of New Right philosophy are mobilised; local authority power; the teaching profession; sex education;[26] childhood innocence and suggestibility; the sanctity of the family and illness of plague dimensions, all galvanised under the banner threat of 'permissiveness'.

According to some (e.g. de Jongh in *Guardian* 8 April 1988) Thatcher was herself the driving force behind Clause 28, and certainly her public pronouncements suggest that if this was not the case, she was at least highly sympathetic. At the 1987 Tory Party Conference she noted that 'Children who need to be taught to respect traditional moral values are being taught that they have an inalienable right to be gay' (reported in *Capital Gay* 16 Oct. 1987), and elsewhere she argued that there was 'a real concern that local authorities were targeting some activities on young people in schools, and outside, in an apparent endeavour to glamorise homosexuality' (quoted in Davies 1988). This 'real concern' arose specifically from exaggerated and inaccurate press reports about the activities of some Labour councils, notably Haringey in North London, where the policy of 'positive images' of homosexuality, intended to respect diversity ('We are trying to help people form a humane approach to what is essentially a human rights issue' (*Gay Times* May 1988: 8)), had led to violent clashes between parents and gay rights supporters. 'It all sounds like an Ealing comedy' intoned Norman Tebbit (quoted in Babuscio 1988: 28), but it was rapidly becoming clear that eddying with increasing impetus around this relatively specific and modest affair were persistent generalised neo-Conservative diagnoses of the moral decline of modern Britain with homosexuality once more specified as the synonymous agent.

A *Spectator* editorial sought to represent the moral–political agenda with disarming candour:

> The belief that some sexual acts are perverted accords with the emphasis – essential in a civilised society – on the dignity of man. Acts which stray from those for which the human body is designed and which defy the chief purpose of sexual intercourse impair that dignity. Homosexuality is morally ... a dead end.... Homosexual acts ... are beneath human dignity.... What is needed is a repudiation of homosexuality.
>
> (*Spectator* 14 March 1987)

Such a repudiation is both more necessary and effective, if that which is repudiated can be directly associated with a 'mysterious' life-and-society-threatening disease: AIDS. Geoffrey Dickens MP of the Conservative Family Campaign (committed amongst other

126

objectives to the repeal of the 1967 Sexual Offences Act's partial legalisation of adult male homosexuality), was reported in May 1987 as saying that:

> Public opinion demands that we do control this killer disease ... people are quite appalled at the way homosexuality is spreading throughout Britain. ... Once we introduced legislation in Parliament to make ... [homosexuality] respectable for over 21-year-olds between consenting adults in private, we gave it a sort of currency, a sort of respectability that it was OK. But it's had a roll on effect on the young ... not only with teaching and indoctrination in schools, but we've seen set up, gay and lesbian clubs all over the place. ... They entice and corrupt and bring others into their unnatural net.
>
> (reported in Davies 1987: 12)

Dickens' elision of gays with AIDS with death because unnatural, is by now commonplace rhetoric; e.g. 'AIDS is a self-inflicted scourge' to be 'blamed on degenerate conduct' resulting in 'people ... swirling around in a cesspit of their own making' (Anderton reported in Smith 1987: 114). Dickens' concern was particularly exercised by what he considered to be the too high public profile of homosexual lifestyles and culture which indeed the 1967 Act had not been intended to encourage. The 'sort of currency' referred to by Dickens was of a debased kind, for the 1967 reform did not legalise homosexuality but narrowly decriminalised certain aspects as not the law's business, whilst reaffirming its immorality,[27] as was demonstrated by a Lords ruling of June 1972 on the lawfulness of contact advertising by homosexuals in newspapers and journals, which stated that 'The 1967 Act merely exempted from criminal penalties but did not make it [homosexuality] legal in the full sense' (Weeks 1981b: 274–5).

Numerous examples demonstrate that homosexuality is not 'legal in the full sense', amongst them being the following observation from David Waddington, then Home Office Minister, reacting to the Labour Campaign for Lesbian and Gay Rights' demand that discrimination on the grounds of sexual orientation should be prevented by law:

> I cannot imagine anything which is more likely to damage

the Equal Opportunities Commission than for it to become identified in the public mind with such crankish notions as that it should be wrong to discriminate against people on the grounds of homosexuality.

(Waddington quoted in Davies 1987: 12)

Thus the 1967 Sexual Offences Act conferred upon homosexuality a 'less than' rather than 'equal to' status as long as privacy and thus the sanctity of the moral community were observed and preserved. Deference was what was expected, as was made clear by this appeal by Lord Arran who had helped guide the legislation through the House of Lords: 'I ask those who have as it were been in bondage and for whom the prison doors are now open, to show their thanks by comporting themselves quietly and with dignity' (quoted in Hyde 1970: 303).

Public manifestations were not merely offensive but a threat to the purity of the moral community, especially those most pure, the young. Paul Johnson, speaking on BBC's *Weekend World* in January 1988 stated:

I have known a great many homosexuals . . . many of them would not stop short at seducing someone under age and that is how many of them acquire their perversion. . . . Male homosexuals feel themselves outside the law . . . they know what they are doing is unnatural. If you break the moral and natural law, you are tempted to break it in other ways. . . . My advice to homosexual leaders is not to ask for equality . . . [but] to keep their heads down. . . .

(BBC Radio 4 Jan. 18 1988)

'Tolerance can only exist when disgust is kept at bay. Flaunting breeds disgust. Flaunting a habit which spreads a fatal disease breeds rage' (*Spectator* 1987), a rage presumably made all the greater if the flaunting is perpetrated on behalf of the *habitués* by local council official and teacher representatives of that 'new class', 'enemy within': the bureaucratised intelligentsia (Elliott and McCrone 1987), those most responsible for the 'permissiveness' of the 1960s. Section 28 was aimed at 'public' homosexuality, its promotion and positive 'open' representation, but its target was broader than that, for it reified conventional morality, and identified the source of moral threat as being larger than the specifically gay constituency but the same 'nanny state' which had shackled the market, stifled individual enterprise, and weakened moral fabric as effectively as Gummer (1971) had warned it would.

When Clause 28 was first introduced into the Local Governmnent Bill (1987) Eric Presland of the Organisation for Lesbian and Gay Action warned 'in one year's time there could be no gay pubs, no gay clubs and no gay press left in this country' (quoted in Smith 1989). There were also loudly voiced fears of increased censorship of representations of homosexuality in the arts and media generally. These fears were raised by the initial draft wording of the Clause which, in addition to the provisions finally ratified, also proposed that local authorities be banned from giving 'financial or other assistance to any person promoting homosexuality'. This last component was removed by the Lords, according to SLD peer Lord Falkland, the government being fearful that 'a lot of loony groups mainly financed from the United States and mostly born again Christian paramilitary groups would jump in' (reported in *Gay Times* 8 Aug. 1988).[28] Thus the key provisions of Section 28 that became law on 24 May 1988 were as follows:

28–(1) A local authority shall not
(a) intentionally promote homosexuality or publish material with the intention of promoting homosexuality;
(b) promote the teaching in any maintained school of the acceptability of homosexuality as a pretended family relationship.
(2) Nothing in subsection (1) above shall be taken to prohibit the doing of anything for the purpose of treating or preventing the spread of disease.

(Scottish Current Law Statutes 1989:
Local Government Act 1988)

The weaknesses of the statute were recognised even before the Section became law by legal representatives of opponents and supporters alike. Manchester City Council received a legal opinion, commensurate with another obtained from Michael Barnes QC by the Association of London Authorities, which concluded that the Council's funding of a £150,000 gay centre was legal because it was considered to be a welfare provision and did not constitute, therefore, the promotion of homosexuality.

Even the Department of the Environment's advisers expressed their doubts too in guidance to relevant officers and departments:

> Local authorities will not be prevented from offering the full range of their services on the same basis as to all their inhabitants. . . . The responsibility for sex education continues to rest with school governing bodies by virtue of Section 18 of the Education (No.2) Act (1986). . . . Section 28 does not affect the accountability of school governors nor of teachers. It will not prevent the *objective* discussion of homosexuality in the classroom nor the counselling of pupils concerned about their sexuality.
>
> (*Pink Paper* 2 June 1988: 2)

Of course 'objective' here is a can of worms but even so the doubts expressed by this document were considerable and justified as a detailed analysis of the Section by Norrie and others makes amply clear (Norrie 1989).

First, the Section is aimed solely at local authorities. Thus any individual, organisation or institution that is not a local authority can promote homosexuality as much as he, she or it likes and there will be no breach of this Section, which applies solely to regional, islands or district councils and their committees, including local education committees.

Second, the three opening words of paragraph (a) are all potential pitfalls for the over eager prosecutor. For example, 'promote', even though it has been widely used in statute formulations, has never been subject to formal judicial interpretation, rather it has been customarily interpreted by the courts, as Norrie makes clear, in a manner commensurate with everyday usage: i.e. 'to encourage, to develop, or to bring about an increase in'. Doubts over 'promote' lay behind many of the initial concerns about the scope of Section 28 as has already been noted and were recognised by one Environment Minister who, however, did not enlighten with his subsequent attempt at clarification:

> We *think* 'promote' has a *clear* meaning. If one promotes something one is deliberately doing something to give what is promoted more favourable treatment, more favourable status or wider acceptance than other things or than that thing hitherto.
>
> (Lord Caithness quoted in Wolmar *Observer* 21 May 1988)

Legal judgements, however, are spun from finer silk, as Norrie (1989) elucidates with telling examples:

> Certain local authority activities clearly are beneficial to lesbians and gays such as giving grants to gay groups, licensing gay venues and stocking libraries with books with gay themes. However, none of these things is the intentional promotion of homosexuality. There is a surprising legal authority for this. In the famous Gillick case, the House of Lords held that to provide contraceptives to girls under the age of 16 did not break the law by 'promoting, encouraging, or facilitating unlawful sexual intercourse'. For a local authority to fund gay groups or to license gay venues will undoubtedly make it easier for people to come to terms with themselves, and more likely that they will meet gay people and have gay sex (which *is not* illegal) just as the provision of contraceptives to people under 16 may make it more likely that they will have non-gay sex (which *is* illegal). For a local authority to be caught by paragraph (a) it must provide the grants or issue the licences with the express intention of promoting or facilitating or bringing about an increase in homosexuality, rather than the intention of making life easier for lesbians and gays. It will probably be impossible for a prosecutor to show that the local authority acted with this intention.
>
> (Norrie 1989: 9)

In any case a local authority promoting homosexuality in this sense would in all probability be risking prosecution for what amounts to conspiracy at common law (Howard League 1985).

More problematically Norrie argues that because homosexuality is a state of being 'like femaleness and blackness' it is logically impossible to encourage or further the growth of homosexuality. He explains:

> One can only encourage the acceptability of or the teaching about homosexuality, but paragraph (a) does not prohibit any of that. Because it prohibits the promotion of that which cannot be promoted, paragraph (a) prohibits a local authority from doing the impossible.
>
> (Norrie 1989: 9)

This essentialist contention that homosexuality is a condition 'like femaleness and blackness' is clearly misconceived, though it is also clearly an interpretation that accords with most conventional medical and legal judgements and he is thus accordingly correct to conclude that the Section's paragraph (a) is on this count unenforceable.

However, an even more tantalising interpretation of this paragraph (a) could be that, albeit in a legal context that is muddied by all kinds of wording problems, for the first time in a British legal statute, it has been recognised that homosexuality can be 'promoted', precisely because it is not a condition but a learned status adopted to extents dependent upon a range of social, situational and interactional circumstances. It is highly unlikely, however, that this was recognised by, let alone the intention of, the Section's formulators.

Third, there are obvious problems with the wording of paragraph (b). To begin with, whatever the interpretation given to 'homosexuality' in paragraph (a) it is clear that it can be manifest in a range of ways, whereas paragraph (b) only prohibits homosexuality 'as a pretended family relationship', thus the promotion of promiscuous or presumably, for example, exaggeratedly effeminate male homosexual behaviour is not prohibited by this Section. This is to say the least curious because it undercuts the sub-section (2) which states that 'Nothing in the subsection (1) above shall be taken to prohibit the doing of anything for the purpose of treating or preventing the spread of disease.' It would seem that paragraph (b) is specifically formulated to prohibit one-to-one, long-term i.e. 'pretended family', and thus from the point of view of AIDS transmission, relatively safer social forms of homosexuality only.

A fourth shortcoming relates to the fact that in England and Wales, as the result of the Education Act (1986) it is Boards of Governors rather than local education authorities which have the control and responsibility for a school's curriculum. As Geoffrey Robertson QC explains:

> ... teachers cannot be disciplined or dismissed for discussing homosexuality sensibly and truthfully. Even where local authorities have an advisory role Section 28 must be read subject to the Education Act (1986) whereby the need 'to encourage pupils to have due regard to moral

considerations' may justify references to the morality of tolerance towards those with the same gender preference.

(quoted in *Pink Paper* 9 June 1988: 4)

However, despite this reassurance it should be noted that the 1986 Act intended these 'moral considerations' (p. 4) to be of a conventional kind (hence its sobriquet The Love and Marriage Amendment), for it added 'and the value of family life' (Section 46). Also in 1986 a Circular from the Department of Education and Science, whilst not legally binding, stated 'there is no place in any school in any circumstances for teaching which advocates homosexual behaviour, which presents it as the norm or which encourages homosexual experimentation' (see Davies 1988). In Scotland the right to direct teaching lies, at present, with local education committees. Even so, for a local authority to be in breach of the Section, it would have to be proved that the authority had, for example, instructed teachers to teach pupils that homosexuality is as acceptable as heterosexuality, i.e. encouraged to teach, and thus promoted the teaching of the acceptability of homosexuality.

A strictly legal review of this legislation thus tends towards the conclusion that it adds nothing to existing law and that 'In reality there is little to fear from Section 28 except fear itself. . . . Section 28 is largely redundant. Its most potent effect is as a symbol of the prejudice of the present Parliament' (Robertson 1988), a view not altogether shared by either Lord Gifford the noted civil rights lawyer or by Norrie. The former believed that 'while Clause 28 does not actually ban a local authority from funding welfare schemes for lesbians and gays, the clause is so badly worded that it is virtually impossible for a local authority to know whether it is in fact breaking the law' (quoted in Johnson 1989) and the latter warns

unfortunately courts have a quaintly naive reluctance to accept that the words of Parliament can be inept or meaningless, and they will without hesitation distort words used in statutes to find some meaning but . . . real and substantial distortion will be necessary.

(Norrie 1989: 9)

Finally the likelihood of any action against councils is also reduced by the complex and expensive procedures any objector would have to go through. Anyone feeling that a council is contravening the law would have to go to the High Court to seek an injunction or judicial review of the council's actions, and an unsuccessful applicant might well be liable for large costs. Even so, as we have seen, it has been recognised that right-wing pressure group sponsorship of a test case could be forthcoming.

Despite the fact that Section 28 is, on the grounds rehearsed, almost unworkable at the level of formal law enforcement, it has certainly encouraged a number of significant acts of self-censorship either through fear or enthusiasm.[29] Conversely some initial bans and delays posed on lesbian and gay initiatives have been overturned.[30] So whilst Section 28's very ambiguities and contradictions in formulation suggest that it is an ineffectual basis for practical law enforcement these very same ambiguities and contradictions have ensured that apprehension has been sown in the minds of some funding bodies, local education authorities, school boards, teachers and others whose work involves the treatment, intellectual, financial or otherwise, of homosexuality. As such it undoubtedly continues to stifle new initiatives, restrict opportunities, inhibit aid and welfare and ultimately constrains how we critically look at the society of which homosexuality and that which it is taken to so forcefully threaten are a part, suggesting that the greatest significance of Section 28 is as a codification of prejudice of almost mythic proportions in that 'it cannot be refuted since it is at bottom identical with the convictions of a group, being the expression of these convictions in the language of the movement' (Sorel 1961 quoted in Kumar 1971: 190).

The ideological core of Section 28 is encapsulated in the phrase 'homosexuality as a pretended family relationship'. One of the Conservative Party's great sources of strength in the Thatcher and Major years has been its ability to represent itself as the party to save and to protect, indeed *of* the family, an ability as manifest in the major philosophical tracts of Gummer (1971), Mount (1983), Scruton (1984) and Anderson (1982), as it has been in the populist rhetoric of her ministers and the leaderene herself. The promotion of the family as that which demands allegiance above all else has underpinned most of the major moral panics of the past decade from scares about surrogate motherhood, extra-marital sex, child sex abuse, and teenage promiscuity to attacks on the 'scrounger state', the fight against crime, and the need to resist attacks on the family itself from feminism and homosexuality.

In New Right morality it is the individual and the family of which, usually he, is inevitably a member, and not society nor especially the state, that must take responsibility for their own economic and moral well-being. This view of the family is of a universal, traditional, self-reliant, autonomous, homogeneous social form because biologically natural and God-given. But it is also a view of the family as seriously weakened in the post-war period prinicipally by the actions of a state which has encouraged moral and economic over-dependency; 'I think we've been through a period where too many people have been given to understand that if they have a problem, its the government's job to cope with it' (Thatcher quoted in Keay 1987: 10).

This weakening through over-dependency has resulted, it is argued, in a degenerate family with what might be described as compromised immunity, vulnerable to a whole range of potentially debilitating infections. Thus social demoralisation threatens the natural order '[We] the defenders of the family . . . assert always the privacy and independence of the family, its biological individuality and its right to live according to its natural instincts' (Mount 1983: 12). 'What is the driving force in our society? It is the desire for the individual to do the best for himself and his family. There is no substitute for this elemental human instinct' (Thatcher quoted in Campbell 1987a: 168), indeed 'there is no such thing as society, there are individual men and women and their families' (Thatcher quoted in Keay 1987), who 'have a natural instinct for ownership and possession, and private enterprise provides an incentive, other than force for work. But Conservatives value private property and private enterprise primarily as the protectors of the family and of freedom' (Gilmour 1978: 148).

In this defence of the individual against socialism and excessive state power the family and private property are inextricably intertwined. Scruton (1984) argues that property is the primary relationship through which man lives socially, morally and economically, that it is the family that is the site of accumulation and inheritance, not merely of capital wealth, but also of key Christian values and attitudes. The family thus stands not only at the intersection of moral and material spheres; '[it] has its life in the home, and the home needs property for its establishment' (Scruton 1984: 101), but also signifies the importance of both to national survival:

> Religious decline and the collapse of family life are the root causes of man's belief that he has only himself to save, and only one life in which to do so. Why sacrifice that life, in defence of an order whose only meaning lies in its capacity to provide the pap of welfare? Why not abandon national loyalty if our enemies still offer us the nationalised breast?
>
> (Scruton 1987, quoted in Phillips 1988: 24)

Thus the nation's wealth and well-being are the family's wealth and well-being for 'Let us remember we are a nation, and a nation is an extended family' (Thatcher quoted in Campbell 1987a: 170), and 'a nation of free people will only continue to be great if family life continues and the structure of the nation is a family one' (Thatcher quoted in Keay 1987).

Small wonder, therefore, that this representation of the beleaguered family emanating 'from that well-heeled section of the community which segregates its own children away from the family in private schools and preparatory schools as soon as it is decently possible to do so' (Pearson 1983: 210) has become a central motif in contemporary Britain where the family is not simply a given subject but increasingly an instrument of social policy.

That homosexuality stands in opposition to New Right conceptions of sex, gender and sexuality as anomaly and hence threat, requires little further elaboration here. In a general gender sense the homosexual 'refutes the conception of the world dichotomised into two discrete sexes with their peculiar sets of characteristics' (Garfinkel 1967: 122–3), whilst with specific reference to sexuality:

> In a repressive order, which enforces the equation between normal, socially useful and good the manifestation of pleasure for its own sake must appear as 'fleurs de mal'. Against a society which employs sexuality itself as means for a useful end, the perversions uphold sexuality as an end in itself; they place themselves outside the dominion of the performance principle and challenge its very foundation.
>
> (Marcuse 1974: 46)

This challenge from the homosexual 'pervert' has been within the capitalist epoch resisted as we know by successive and persistent dramatisations of otherness; (s)he is unnatural, sick, godless, unstable, criminal, immoral, unproductive (other than in, for example, artistic fields), hedonistic and predatory; a pathological condition manifest in the collective, animalistic pursuit of anonymous random and thus ultimately unfulfilling sexual pleasure. Neo-conservative ideologues such as Scruton have maintained this attack. Scruton (1986) identifies all sexual licence as an 'assault on the self' and more importantly as an assault on the social order which produces the self, thus his concern for the survival of capitalism and the family as its central institution leads to the expected polemic against promiscuity and homosexuality, significantly dealt with together; 'The first [promiscuity] destroys the sacral character of the body, and, therefore, loosens the connection between desire and love. The second [homosexuality] severs desire from its generative tendency' (Scruton quoted in Marshall 1986).

Scruton's opposition to homosexuality is specifically because it encourages a new promiscuity:

... unsubdued by the awesome mystery of another sex, driven always to unite with flesh of his own all-too-familiar kind, the homosexual has no use for hesitation, except that which society imposes. He knows with too great a certainty, too great a familiarity what his partner feels, and has no need for the tiresome strategems of courtesy, courtship and shame. The gateway to desire, which hides its course in mystery, and diverts it to the path of love, has been burst open, and a short path to pleasure revealed.

(Scruton quoted in Marshall 1986)

Much of the symbolic force of homosexuality rests with its extreme representation of all non-procreative and thus institutionally unconstrained sexualities. In the post-war period there has been a considerable sexualisation of Western culture (the 'rutting revolution' (Amis 1985)), much of it accomplished by apparently open and explicit commoditisation, but sexuality has remained an illegitimate subject for open and explicit everyday social intercourse. Nowhere is this more manifest than in the government's refusal to countenance sexually explicit official anti-AIDS advertising, typified by Thatcher's reputed response to the initial draft of the first advertising campaign in

1986 which she vetoed for being 'like writings on a lavatory wall' (reported in Weeks 1988: 17). For all the prurience-raising temptations of the media and popular culture, sexuality remains conventionally sacred as, literally, the essence of life, obscured from rational attention by such private and individual mysteries as 'attraction', 'emotion', 'love'; its transient temptations offset against the greater spiritual and nurturing needs of marriage and warnings of the just rewards of profligacy. It is of course precisely because sex in our culture is believed to speak the truth about ourselves and expresses the essence of our being that it is the focus of such intense debate. Prior to the formulation of Section 28, AIDS had already been ideologically 'captured for the reconstruction of moral imperatives which seek to privilege above all other forms of sexual expression, those that are narrowly focused on procreative and penetrative vaginal intercourse ... within the context of exclusive and life-long monogamous relationships' (Aggleton and Homans 1988: 7). Constructed as a disease of 'lifestyle' and thus of 'choice' for promiscuous homosexuals and drug abusers, AIDS has been used to reaffirm the family, through the deserved fate of those 'guilty' victims set alongside, for example, the corrupted innocence of the duplicitous bisexual male's wife, and the child born to infected parents. With specific reference to homosexuality AIDS has been constructed as 'the viral personification of unorthodox deregulative desire' (Watney 1988: 60), as the triumphant rejection of the promiscuous homosexual; a passionate defence of long-term monogamous heterosexuality.

Section 28 declares that the homosexual responsible for the promiscuity 'which rampages through the barriers of shame' (Scruton quoted in Marshall 1986) cannot expect to find refuge in unconvincing copies of 'real' and 'normal' family relationships.

As we have seen, for the New Right the economic travails of the 1960s are inextricably linked to moral decline through 'permissiveness' wrought primarily by the bureaucratised intelligentsia: 'lecturers, teachers, NHS bureaucrats, directors of leisure, health education officers, adventure playground leaders, advisers, abortion counsellors, environmental health officers, and gay bereavement counsellors' (Anderson 1982: 6). It is hardly surprising, therefore, that Section 28 identifies as purveyors of homosexual propaganda, key representatives of this 'new class', teachers and local authority workers, all of whom have superior access to public services such as education where their influence can seriously threaten the authority of both state and family. Parents cannot safely trust their children to such dangerous others:

> The great majority of families recognise that the traditional way with very young children brought up at their mother's knee does have advantages – that's the way one gets transmission of culture, the best education for our children. *The safest way.*
> (Jenkin quoted in *Cosmopolitan* May 1983, my emphasis)

For the New Right parenthood is about protecting and even extending parents' rights against the interests of:

> the professional, with his claim to unique understanding of his area of practice, [which] when incorporated in state bureaucracy can lead to service provision being driven by producers' (i.e. professionals') views of what ought to be provided (e.g. in council housing) rather than consumers' views of what they want.
> (Family Policy Group quoted in *Guardian* 17 Feb. 1983)

Substitute sex education here for 'council housing' and all is more or less said. The *Longford Report on Pornography* (1972) had warned that a sound sex education could not come from the amoral context of the school but only from a familial environment, a warning apparently now accepted by the young themselves for, we are assured, 'young people are crying out for a set of rules and standards to live by. It is up to us to restore them' (Thatcher quoted in Keay 1987).

Hence Section 28 and the so-called Love and Marriage Amendment (Section 46) to the Sex Education Act (No. 2) (1986) which it complements, but whereas the latter was a quiet policy response the former was a grand public display which employed mythic terms that contained more than a suggestion of paradox.

Section 28 is intended to defend a universal, traditional homogeneous, God-given and natural family that should thereby, one might suppose, require little or no defending. It seeks to do so by raising the spectre of homosexuality as a 'pretended family relationship' thus acknowledging both the existence of a real as opposed to an idealised world in which there exist diverse social and cultural formations, and that homosexuality can take, albeit only as a pretence, relational rather than solely individual psychopathological and promiscuous forms.

New Right theorists such as Mount (1983) might reject evidence of the diversity of contemporary family forms and of the 'normal' family's historical and cultural specificity, yet that evidence is considerable. Only an estimated 5 per cent of workers are men with dependent wives and children; only 32 per cent of households are made up of married couples with dependent children; at least 18 per cent of households (excluding pensioners) are substantially or completely dependent upon a woman's earnings or benefits; 10 per cent of the population is homosexual, and substantially more have experienced homosexual sexual encounters and/or relationships (Land 1980; Allen 1982; Phillips 1988).[31] Sheila Allen (1982) might have been correct to observe then that household formations are hidden and unresearched because of the ideological stranglehold that means we don't ask the right questions, but we certainly have sufficient answers now to know that the world being addressed by this government's ideologues and law-makers, is not the world of diversity experienced by the majority of people in Britain. It is a major paradox of Section 28 that through its crude superimposition of ideological motifs we are reminded that this is so.

A further paradox is that although clearly designed to inhibit gay politics it has clearly had the reverse effect. In *Coming Out* (1977), Weeks concluded, that:

> the days of a euphoric [gay] rally to arms are over and it is more likely that the most creative work of Gay Liberation in the immediate future will come from a multiplicity of relatively small groups burrowing through their specialised concerns than from a massive new national initiative.
>
> (Weeks 1977: 234)

Section 28's appearance on the statute book is for some commentators a sign that these burrowings have been extremely effective. It is the response of people under pressure, they argue, who 'perceive that people's attitudes are changing, that they are being more tolerant. . . . ' (Otitoju *et al.* 1988: 23), and it is a response that has succeeded in reviving mass gay politics in a way Weeks thought no longer possible. Section 28 does not represent, therefore, a simple assertion of extreme neo-conservative

140

homophobia, but rather the successful inroads made by gay activism in a wide range of loci. 'It's tempting to think fascism's just round the corner. But we are being attacked because we are making progress particularly in areas of local government' (Parker quoted in Smith 1987): 'politicians didn't decide to take this issue on, [rather it was] the [gay] community deciding to take on the politicians, and . . . we have chosen to target in particular those we thought would take us . . . Labour Councils' (Otitoju et al. 1988).

It is very doubtful whether these claims are justified in terms of gay political objectives achieved in Britain as a whole (yet another facet of the 'London effect'[32] perhaps?) and it must be reiterated that the gay 'we' being identified is but a fraction of what is anyway a highly fractionalised 'community' but, as the tabloid press has consistently demonstrated, indeed ensured, the inroads that have been made have been high profile and to that extent at least, highly successful.

These same commentators argue that Section 28 has had many positive gay political consequences[33] amongst which are the following: there has been a strengthening of links, previously seriously strained, between gay male and lesbian 'communities'; 'it has given us a common enemy – something worse than each other to fight' (Cooper 1988); it has shocked and exposed the complacency of many gay males and lesbians who, through private relationships and lifestyles, have managed to avoid the political implications of being gay; and it has brought a considerable number onto the streets to demonstrate, which in a sense too has shown that only in extra-parliamentary arenas can gay interests be adequately demonstrated and represented; it has served, albeit weakly and no doubt temporarily, to unite on a broad front a wide range of particular and not necessarily gay interest groups and individuals such as the Labour Campaign for Lesbian and Gay Rights, the Gay Christian Movement, the National Council for Civil Liberties, the Gay Business Association, the Writers Guild of Great Britain, OLGA (Organisation for Lesbian and Gay Action), etc.; it has also been claimed that support for gays amongst the non-gay population has strengthened: 'For the first time people who have been unprepared to accept that being lesbian and gay is to be oppressed or to get a raw deal, are actually recognising the strength of feeling that exists' (Otitoju et al. 1988).

There can be no doubt that if this latter claim is correct much of it has been due to the effects of the earlier feared threats of censorship which mobilised the arts and media lobbies (containing 'soap' stars from, for example, *Eastenders* and *Brookside*) which made the threats posed more tangible.

> The expression of homosexuality through art and drama has always been more tolerated . . . than it has in other ways, and people who can entertain very illiberal attitudes towards gay people can nevertheless lay claim to appreciating artists and playwrights who are gay and who even treat that subject in their work. It has, therefore, been easier for people in the arts to put their heads above the parapet and argument has been easier for them to advance without any sort of personal opprobrium or ignominy.
>
> (Parris in Otitoju *et al.* 1988)

But perhaps the most interesting political consequence of both Section 28 and of AIDS as ideological constructs has been the demise of the liberal conscience, which is maybe no bad thing. B. Marshall (1989: 12) has argued that the 'recent backlash against homosexuality has served to reaffirm the basic legal principles of 1967', and this has certainly been its most dramatic effect. But in one sense this is misleading in that the leading neo-conservative players are committed to a return to pre-1967 principles: the reunification of morality and criminality; the abolition of that 'private realm' above and beyond the law; the reassertion of the imperatives of public morality as opposed to the liberal causalist emphasis on individual consent, which were the heritage of that legislation. In the moral panic around AIDS as a 'gay plague', 'private' homosexual behaviour has represented a threat to 'the heterosexual community';[34] AIDS transmission and treatment being effectively countered by the public exposure of those hitherto permitted hidden behaviours which have repaid the legality granted to their exponents with contamination. Section 28 widens and extends this view by proposing that, contrary to the liberal credo, anything that anybody does or says or thinks about homosexuality will eventually affect the moral community in much the same way, i.e. will 'promote' homosexuality.

In a slightly different form this is an argument that has in the past been most usually heard around sexual politics of the Left ('the personal is political'), yet now it is representatives of the

New Right, albeit a minority, who promulgate this sentiment most forcefully, not consistently perhaps, but with sufficient persuasiveness to win new constituencies of support (that is, if a 'London effect' has been accurately identified). Section 28 thus marks a subtle drift in the neo-conservative treatment of homosexuality as a condition to homosexuality as culture and alternative morality which can be promoted. In the rhetoric of the New Right there is no consistent use of such arguments, as we have seen from the exemplary instance of Geoffrey Dickens MP whose final sentence in the extract quoted earlier (p. 127) was 'They entice and corrupt and bring others into their unnatural net', but there are less risible proponents. Here, for example, is Lord Boyd Carpenter addressing the Lords during a Clause 28 debate:

> It is a fact that young males at a certain stage in life – i.e. soon after puberty – in many cases have a homosexual element or tendency in them which the vast majority of them succeed in restraining, to their credit. But if attempts are made deliberately to emphasise that side of their nature and to suggest that the homosexual way of life is just as good as ordinary married life – indeed, perhaps better – it is fairly certain that some of those young people will be led to adopt a homosexual orientation which they would not otherwise have adopted. That is the basic problem.
>
> (Boyd-Carpenter reported in J. Marshall 1989)

Indeed it is, and it is one that is ultimately, even at the level of myth, not answered by Section 28. Symbolic kite-flying exercises of this kind have a force not because of what they say but rather through their collation of various ideological signifiers that serve to key into the store of dominant cultural meanings that exist around them, so deeply buried in common sense that they barely exist at the conscious level at all, unless that is, they are in some way contradicted, as they are in Section 28. By presenting homosexuality as a relational phenomenon, albeit in sheep's clothing, it contradicts the stockpile of cultural meanings which present homosexuality as 'a psychopathological perversion';[35] 'a state of being', a condition. This paradox, implicit within Section 28, has already been referred to as one of its several formal legal weaknesses; if homosexuality is a 'state of being' how can it be promoted or represented as a 'pretended family relationship'?

143

But this ambiguity at the formal legal level is compounded by comparable confusion at the level of ideology. Once this is recognised it becomes clear why 'pretended' is such a necessary part of the formulation for it signifies an attempt, albeit weak, to reconcile the irreconcilable by warning that whilst homosexuality is unnatural, just as the family is natural, it has the capacity to seduce and convert. In the circumstances Section 28 is not only a failure as law, it is also a failure as myth.[36]

It is additionally ironic that in all the debates that have attended the passing of Clause 28 into law, it has been the gay opponents of Section 28 who have most consistently retained biological determinist arguments, by asserting that it is precisely because homosexuality is a 'state of being' that there can be no threat to that other, by implication, discrete population of heterosexuals.

> Clause 28 aims to protect young people from being persuaded to do something they really don't want to do and which goes against all the laws of nature. . . . *Jenny Lives with Eric and Martin* could no more convert a heterosexual into a homosexual than a cabbage patch into an orchard.
>
> (Werge 1988: 5)

Similarly, 'Sexuality is not acquired through teaching, any attempt at proselytising in either direction is both cruel and doomed to failure' (Boulton quoted in *Gay Times* May 1988: 11). This is a view of homosexuality that is clearly contradicted by all social constructionist accounts – psychological (e.g. Freudian theses of innate human bisexuality), sociological (e.g. inter-actionist accounts of homosexual moral careers and the 'coming-out' process and studies of situational homosexualities) as well as historical evidence on the changing social constructions of all sexual forms including the homosexual – evidence that one expects neo-conservatives to reject but not sexual radicals. It might be a view that serves to reassure the moral community, thereby reducing pressure on the gay, but it is intellectually and politically untenable.

A defence of a 'positive images' curriculum and school structure monitored to prevent anti-gay discriminatory practices must surely be developed which accepts that the consequences will be not only greater tolerance for gay pupils and staff, and greater self-esteem amongst both but, to put it bluntly, more gays. That this is recognised by the Right, in a garbled sense at least, is testified by Section 28, but it rarely appears to be accepted by the Left. For example, in the otherwise valuable *School's Out* by the Gay Teachers Group (1983: 3–6) it is stated that 'Children cannot "catch" homosexuality from openly gay teachers any more than gay pupils "catch" heterosexuality from openly heterosexual teachers.' Well 'catch' in the germ or viral sense no, but 'catch' in the sense of 'influenced in the direction of' quite possibly, surely? Many students who do later become homosexual have 'caught' heterosexuality in their school years when presented with only models and performances of an idealised 'universal', 'natural', heterosexual kind to learn from, not infrequently presented by closeted gay or bisexual teachers and peers. For the majority of students sexual knowledge, understandings and identities are not fixed, their future developments determined by a range of possible social and interactional learning contents and contexts amongst which, one would have thought, the school figures rather prominently. To change the treatment of homosexuality within sex education classes; to reveal homosexual themes, personalities and insights in history, and English studies; to stock school libraries with literature that presents homosexuality in 'objective' and non-stereotypical ways, to monitor anti-gay behaviours and languages amongst staff and students; to train teachers to address issues concerning homosexuality, is surely to have an effect on all participants. However, within texts such as *School's Out* it is assumed that sexual identity exists prior to and above and beyond educational instruction, which makes one wonder why there should be any changes to the educational system at all.

Whilst Section 28 is legislation of a peculiarly impoverished kind vitiated by ambiguities and contradictions in formulation and potential application, as an exercise in neo-conservative normative fundamentalism it has proved rather more effective. As with all moral panics Section 28 succinctly encapsulates a host of generalised commonsense concerns in order to mobilise commitment to first principles, and as such it has been consistent with the Thatcher government's electorally successful deployment of authoritarian populism. But the very dramatic 'success' and attendant over-exposure of this particular moral panic could well prove to be, indeed has already been to some extent, its undoing. Its initial wording drew well-publicised attention to the general issues of censorship and the infringement of civil, political and social rights, rather than specifically to the promotion of homosexuality in schools, which seriously softened the crude blow intended, and its focus on the promotion of homosexuality stimulated a political revivalism of almost equal fervour amongst those it sought to constrain and exclude. In one sense the government could hardly have done more to promote homosexuality if it had set Haringey up as the model moral council. It is by no means certain anyway that homosexuality is an unambiguously appropriate vehicle for the heavy duty symbolic work expected of it, for whilst surveys of public opinion show a hardening of attitudes against homosexuality's immorality during the past decade, there has been continuing respect for the 'private' rights of homosexuals. Indeed the more one contemplates Section 28 the more one wonders why it was ever thought to be necessary. The Thatcher and Major governments have not exactly been short of moral crusade fodder for feeding the family myth, and have accomplished a great deal in media and educational control through a stealth that this particular rich meal has done much to expose. Not least amongst the accomplishments of Clause 28 has been its irrelevance to the world of diversity of which large sections of the population and their legal officers are increasingly aware.

To believe that Section 28 will prove to be little more than a typical example of the use of chimera in moral panics; initially a terrifying 'fabulous fire-spouting monster' to be subsequently exposed as little more than an 'idle . . . wild fancy' (*Chambers' Dictionary* 1990), is to be gravely complacent, but it is surely reassuring to know that the beast is not as awesomely fearsome as it, at first, seemed.

It is not possible to say that current state strategies concerning homosexuality are consistent with this particularly muddled piece of legislation. Indeed a detailed analysis of Section 28 demonstrates the primacy of *ad hoc* crisis management in state discourses on this, and all other forms of sexual citizenship.

6

DUAL CITIZENSHIP?
Bisexuality

To come out as bisexual is extremely difficult because you can incur the wrath of both groups – gay and straight. Men call us who don't want to break up their marriages but long to talk to someone about the attraction they feel for their own sex. They feel they have nowhere to turn. Bisexuality is really the last taboo.

(Sunday Correspondent 21 Oct. 1990)

The last taboo or the latest discourse? In 1963, in one of the spate of texts on the male homosexual following the Kinsey *et al.* (1948, 1953) revelations concerning those who, through overt experience and/or 'psychologic reactions', were neither exclusively hetero- nor homosexual, the following typical judgement on the bisexual was made:

> Without a group to belong to, the case of the . . . [bisexual] seems to be peculiarly pathetic. While appearing to encompass a wider choice of love objects, he actually becomes a product of abject confusion; his self-image is that of an overgrown adolescent whose ability to differentiate one form of sexuality from another has never developed. He lacks above all a sense of identity, a feeling of group identification. As James Baldwin has so poignantly demonstrated in *Giovanni's Room* he cannot answer the question: What am I?
>
> (Cory and LeRoy 1963: 61)

For a brief period in the 1950s the lone voice of the psychiatrist Albert Ellis would have answered 'psychologically healthy' (1956), and during the 1960s bi-, or ambisexuality as it was then more usually called, surfaced as a key 'alternative adaptation' within youth, especially hippie, subculture (Coons 1972: Kelly 1974: Gould 1979). By the mid-1970s the mass media on both sides of the Atlantic were referring to what they called 'the new bisexual' (Money 1974: 79–80); follower of 'the newest sex style' (*Cosmopolitan* June 1974); with 'Bisexual chic, anyone goes' (*Newsweek* 24 May 1974: 90) for the 'bisexual life-style appears to be spreading and not just amongst swingers' (*New York Times* March 1974), but amongst all in pursuit of 'the best of both worlds' (Allen 1973).[1] Fifteen years on and it seems more like the worst, for one of the many dramatic effects of AIDS has been the emergence of especially, but not exclusively, male bisexuals as 'carriers of disease'; members of what is presented as a particularly threatening 'bridging group' between homosexual contamination and heterosexual purity (Staver 1987; Heller 1987). As a result the label has become very much more familiar as populations have been forced to consider forms of bisexual status, roles and lifestyles as well as behaviours amongst those who nevertheless eschew bisexual self-identities. The fundamental problem remains, however; does the bisexual have a culturally recognisable and thus legitimate social status and social identity? Is the bisexual not merely marginal to conventional sexual categories but, as some commentators aver, as a social and cultural being non-existent? Valverde (1985) is certain that

Bisexuality does not exist as either a social institution or a psychological 'truth'. It exists only as a catch-all term for different erotic and social patterns whose common ground is an attempt to combine homo- and heterosexuality in a variety of ways. The term 'bisexual' then merely tells us that someone can or does eroticize both men and women. It does not tell us anything about the morality or politics of that person.

(Valverde 1985: 119)

Within our culture, dominated by the essential exclusivities of hetero- and homosexuality consistent with the affirmed pre-eminence of biological sex (Birke 1982; de Cecco and Shively 1984), there would appear to be still no social space for bisexual forms, which have been effectively explained away by sexological and medical discourses despite their fundamental commitment

148

to bisexual essence as some form of sexual dimorphism. Freud was convinced that

> Since I have become acquainted with the notion of bisexuality I have regarded it as the decisive factor and without taking bisexuality into account I think it would scarcely be possible to arrive at an understanding of the sexual manifestations that are actually to be observed in men and women.

(Freud 1905/1977: 142)

Freud claims that bisexuality was first used as an explanation for sexual inversion (homosexuality) by Gley (1884, see Freud 1905/1977: 54) and that another early and crude account emerged from Ulrichs who presented it in a form which subsequently became more familiarly ascribed to the transsexual; 'a feminine brain in a masculine body'. It was, however, in the work of Moll (1897/1953) and Krafft-Ebing (1891/1965) that the condition became firmly established. Moll argued that the sexual instinct evolved through asexuality (marked by undifferentiated sex organs), and bisexuality (in which both male and female sex organs were present), to monosexuality within which 'the heterosexual reaction capacity' emerged, bisexual adults being, as commonly found in such essentialist literature, the product of either congenital weakness or childhood inhibition. Krafft-Ebing posited an initial bisexual state from which monosexual heterosexuality normally emerged as 'the organs of one sex vanquished those of the other' (see de Cecco and Shively 1984: 7), these organs being brain centres as well as the somatic organs of sex, and comparable explanations were developed by Arduin (1900), Havelock Ellis (1897), Hirschfeld (1903), Herman (1903), Fliess (1906), Moebius (1900), Bloch (1902–3), etc. More significantly, and drawing upon most of these sources, in 1905 Freud (1905: 45–87) proposed his more sophisticated theory of constitutional bisexuality initially via reference to Aristophanes' theory in Plato's *Symposium* that 'the original human beings were cut up into two halves – man and woman – and . . . are always striving to unite again in love' (Freud 1905: 45–6). The different qualities of these 'halves' were not, however, presented in clear and unequivocal ways by Freud (Murphy 1984: 66). Rather, he employed bisexuality to explain homosexual and heterosexual post-pubertal outcomes rather than allowing for a third discrete adult option. Puberty normally brings suppression of the 'other' as identified in the opposite sexed parent (Freud 1905: 143), innate bisexual essence in interaction with experimental factors in childhood enabling the subsequent expression of one choice or the other (Rosen 1979: 246). Freud identified amongst those men and women with 'contrary sexual feelings' (1905: 46) 'amphigenic inverts',[2] i.e. 'psychosexual hermaphrodites' for whom sexual objects could be of either sex, and amongst these he further distinguished 'contingent inverts' who 'under certain external conditions only' (p. 48) may make same-sex object choices, thereby elaborating distinctions which have subsequently been further developed within sociological as well as psycho-sexual literature.[3]

Freud (1905/1977: 52, 57) referred to both technical and psychical hermaphroditism, arguing that whilst for men 'the most complete mental masculinity can be combined with inversion', in women a tendency for inversion seemed always to be accompanied by psychical masculinity. In support of his advocacy of the bisexual ambiguities of male inversion as set against the less ambiguous female variant, Freud referred to ancient Greece, but not to males' love of other males, but rather of boys who

> combine the characters of both sexes . . . there is as it were a compromise between an impulse that seeks for a man and one that seeks for a woman while it remains a paramount condition that the object's body (i.e. genitals) shall be masculine. Thus the sexual object is a kind of reflection of the subject's own bisexual nature.
>
> (Freud 1905: 56)

This bisexual nature manifests itself in and is thus used by Freud to explain all manner of neuroses and psychoses: hysteria, Oedipal conflicts, paranoia, masochism, sadism, sexual 'activity' and 'passivity', latent homosexuality, etc. (p. 72), but in all of these accounts it 'appears only to signify that a human being can be attracted to a person of either sex' (Murphy 1984: 76) and not both, that 'all human beings are capable of making a homosexual object-choice and have in fact made one in their unconscious' (Freud 1905: 145).

On the basis of Freud's deliberations there have developed several popular, 'expert'-initiated, discourses on bisexual identity largely in terms of comparable negative qualities. As an identifiable fundamental biological presence in all animals from rats to lionesses, even cows in heat (Beach and Rasquin 1942; Cooper 1942; Rosen 1979) it becomes within humanoids correctly sublimated into adult heterosexual forms.[4] If established and persistent within adults, bisexual behavioural patterns are of course symptomatic of pathology (Klein 1978; MacDonald 1981). Transient bisexuality, however, could be due to temporary negotiation between exclusive hetero- and homosexuality,[5] possibly situationally induced, within 'heterosexuals' in same-sex institutions such as prisons, schools, prostitution or the armed services,[6] or within 'homosexuals' keen to conceal their sexual status behind the conventional facade of marriage, etc.[7]

All four explanations proclaim bisexuality as an illegitimate socio-sexual identity, a myth,[8] and those willing to so label themselves merely 'defence bisexuals', concealing their 'true' homosexuality behind a bisexual facade.[9] Clinically, therefore, bisexual behavioural patterns and self-identification are only manifest by default: in those 'searching for new experiences', 'overgrown adolescents' (Cory and LeRoy 1963: 61) unable to decide their sexual preferences, the confused, the psychopathically disturbed, 'out and out frauds' (Bergler 1956) and those 'unable to choose between a heterosexual and a homosexual object' (Rosen 1979: 449).

Lacking socio-cultural substance and legitimacy bisexuals thus become, in popular heterosexual discourse, the object of scepticism and suspicion, ambivalent and promiscuous opportunists who if openly adopting the label do so for unconvincing reasons of fad or avoidance of homosexual stigma. Comparably, within gay subcultures they are 'tourists' (Hart 1984), 'fencesitters, traitors, cop-outs, closet cases . . . who use and discard their same-sex lovers like so many kleenex' (Orlando 1984: 8).

Within such accounts bisexuality is given wide-ranging and inconsistent meanings from constitutional eunochoidism (Freud 1905) to sexual behaviour with both sexes (Kinsey *et al.* 1948, 1953; Ford and Beach 1952; Churchill 1967), the broader criterion of bisexual orientation and possibly self-labelling (Blumstein and Schwartz 1976a; 1976b; Klein 1978) and even to non-specifically or necessarily sexual (i.e. genital) dual 'affectional preference' (MacInnes 1973; Bode 1976; Klein 1978;

Scott 1978), but whichever the sense employed 'bisexual' signifies deviance, and a deviance with further temporal complications. The expression of dual sentiments and experiences may be simultaneous (i.e. bisexual troilism); concurrent (i.e. separate but within which the same period of time); serial (alternate male and female during successive periods) or life-history bisexuality within the whole span of which hetero- and homosexuality may be recorded. Inevitably, given the origins and subsequent sources of such discourses, bisexuality has been predominantly treated as an individual condition, detached from any clearly identifiable subcultural setting.[10]

That bisexuality can and has existed in elaborate and varied conventional social forms has been demonstrated by numerous cross-cultural and historical analyses, although given the lack of any clear contemporary social construct both sources tend to reinforce Valverde's (1985: 119) 'catch-all' observation by largely addressing the issue through the recorded co-incidence of identifiable heterosexual and homosexual forms rather than providing time and place specific accounts of bisexuality as such (Herdt 1981, 1982, 1984; Devereux 1937; Carrier 1980; Whitehead 1981; Mead 1935, 1975; Ford and Beach 1952, etc.).

An exception, as one might expect, is provided by Foucault (1987: 187) in his description of the sexual ethics of fourth-century Greece wherein the love of one's own and of the other sex were not understood as opposite, exclusive and radically different choices and types of behaviour. Of more importance was the distinction between 'a moderate, self-possessed man [and] one given to pleasures'. There was contempt for the latter, e.g. young men deemed to be too 'easy', effeminate and self-interested (pp. 190–1) and generally it was considered that to have loose morals was to be subjected to the rule of pleasure, to be incapable of resisting women or boys.

> When Alcibiades was censured for his debauchery, it was not for the former kind in contradistinction to the latter, it was, as Bion the Borysthenite put it, 'that in his adolescence he drew away the husbands from the wives, and as a young man the wives from their husbands'.
>
> (Foucault 1987: 188)

Were the Greeks bisexual then? Foucault replies as follows:

Yes, if we mean by this that a Greek could, simultaneously or in turn, be enamoured of a boy or a girl; that a married man could have *paedika*; that it was common for a male to change to a preference for women after 'boy loving' inclinations in his youth. But if we wish to turn our attention to the way in which they conceived of this dual practice, we need to take note of the fact that they did not recognise two kinds of 'desire', two different or competing 'drives', each claiming a share of men's hearts or appetites. We can talk about their 'bisexuality', thinking of the free choice they allowed themselves between the two sexes, but for them this option was not referred to a dual ambivalent and 'bisexual' structure of desire. To their way of thinking what made it possible to desire a man or woman was simply the appetite that nature had implanted in man's heart for 'beautiful' human beings, whatever their sex might be.

(Foucault 1987: 188)[11]

Thus within classical Greece the sexual enjoyment of both boys and women did not constitute two classificatory categories between which individuals could be distributed and men who preferred the former, *paedika*, were not considered to be essentially different from those who pursued women (p. 190). Within these terms, which could clearly not be replicated within modern cultures, bisexuality 'enjoyed the prestige of a whole literature that sang of it and a body of reflection that vouched for its excellence' (p. 190).

In late twentieth-century terms, if bisexuality does exist as more than 'a statistical combination of heterosexual and homosexual acts' (p. 190) it clearly has to somehow transcend the two entrenched classificatory categories of hetero- and homosexuality.

That it *is* a behavioural statistic cannot be doubted and before examining the possibility of its socio-cultural existence perhaps we had better consider the behavioural evidence. As with so much of late twentieth-century sexual discourse, it is to the Kinsey *et al.* (1948) research findings that one must look in order to understand how fact-finding has given considerable impetus to bisexual discursive elaboration (Gagnon 1977: 260).

Employing the (in)famous 7-point continuum of sexual orientation and behavioural 'outlets' from point 0 (completely heterosexual) to point 6 (completely homosexual) with between

5 degrees of bisexuality from point 1 denoting the overwhelming preponderance of heterosexuality and only incidental homosexuality to the reverse balance at point 5 with mid-point 3 being closest to what, in commonsense and statistical terms alone, might be called 'pure' bisexuality, 'rare in practice' (MacInnes 1973; Money 1980), manifesting roughly equal amounts of homo- and heterosexual behaviours and/or stimulation, considerable bisexuality was located and conventional understandings thereby undermined.

> It would encourage clearer thinking on these matters if persons were not characterised as heterosexual or homosexual but as individuals who have had certain amounts of heterosexual ... [and] ... homosexual experience. Instead of using these terms as substantives which stand for persons, they may be better used to describe the nature of the overt sexual relations, or of the stimuli to which an individual erotically responds.
>
> (Kinsey *et al.* 1948: 617)

A brief appraisal of Kinsey *et al.*'s findings clearly demonstrates the scale of the behavioural bisexual puzzle posed. 'A considerable portion of the population, perhaps the major portion of the male population, has at least some homosexual experience between adolescence and old age' (Kinsey *et al.* quoted in McCaffrey 1972: 4). About 60 per cent of pre-adolescent boys engaged in homosexual activities, and an additional group of adult males who avoided overt contacts were aware of their potential for sexually reacting to other males (p. 4). 'At least 37 per cent of the male population has some homosexual experience between the beginning of adolescence and old age' (p. 9) and approximately 13 per cent of males were found to 'react erotically to other males without having overt homosexual contacts after the onset of adolescence' (p. 25). Of all males 30 per cent had at least incidental homosexual experience and/or reactions (i.e. rated 1–6 on the continuum) over at least a three-year period between the ages of 16 and 55 (p. 25). One-quarter of males had more than incidental homosexual experiences and/or reactions (i.e. 2–6 on the scale) for at least three years between ages 16 and 55, whilst 18 per cent of adult males had at least as much homosexual as heterosexual experience (i.e. points 3–6 on the scale). Thirteen per cent were more homosexual than heterosexual (i.e. 4–6); 10 per cent more or less exclusively homosexual (i.e. 5–6) through three years and 8 per cent were exclusively so for at least three years between the ages of 16 and 55 (p. 25). The findings for women showed a similar ratio of 'bisexuals' to homosexuals but the general incidence of homosexual behaviours or reactions was significantly lower than for males.

As the authors observed:

> Concerning patterns of sexual behaviour, a great deal of the thinking done by scientists and laymen alike stems from the assumption that there are persons who are 'heterosexual' and persons who are 'homosexual', that these two types represent antitheses in the sexual world, and that there is only an insignificant class of 'bisexuals' who occupy an intermediate position between the other groups. . . . the histories which have been available in the present study make it apparent that the heterosexuality and homosexuality of many individuals is not an all or none proposition . . . there is a considerable portion of the population whose members have combined, within their individual histories, both homosexual and heterosexual experience and/or psychic responses.
>
> (Kinsey *et al.* quoted in McCaffrey 1972: 17–19)

Despite these strictures modern societies have continued to stylise and channel sexual practice in a linear reified developmental sense, into rigid norms by focusing on genital sex and thus the convention of heterosexual practice.

Specifically on bisexuality Kinsey *et al.* point out that as 50 per cent of the population was exclusively heterosexual throughout its adult life, and since only 4 per cent of the population was exclusively homosexual for the same term, it followed that 46 per cent of the population engaged in both heterosexual and homosexual activities or reacted erotically to persons of both sexes in the course of their adult lives. The authors expressed doubts as to whether location on all 1–5 placements exhibited bisexuality though they were prepared to accept that the term bisexual could be applied to at least *some portion* of this group:

> Unfortunately the term as it has been used has never been strictly delimited and consequently it is impossible to know

whether it refers to all individuals who rate anything between 1–5 or whether it is being limited to some smaller number of categories, perhaps centring around group 3. If the latter is intended, it should be emphasised that the 1s, 2s, 4s and 5s have not yet been accounted for, and they constitute a considerable portion of the population.
(Kinsey *et al.* quoted in McCaffrey 1972: 20)

Kinsey *et al.* continue that anyway such a scheme would only leave a 3-category scale which would not 'adequately describe' the continuum which 'is the reality in nature'. 'A seven-point scale comes nearer to showing the many gradations that actually exist . . . ' (pp. 26–7), gradations which infect hetero- and homosexual forms as well as bisexual. Psycho-sexual relations between same sex individuals were not rare, unnatural or abnormal and, without the considerable social stigma attached to homosexuality, their incidence would no doubt, they claimed, be considerably higher.

Kinsey *et al.* are normally characterised as 'outlets' obsessed and thus treat sexuality as a male masculinist construct (Faraday 1981), nor do they attend to the interpretations of such experiences by those experiencing them, or to the effects they might or might not have on self-identification as hetero-, homo- or bisexual, but within their brief and somewhat hesitant discussion of bisexuality the recognition of such complexities is implied, for example, through reference to sequential, parallel coincidental, group sex simultaneous and transitional forms.

Subsequent studies, though by no means as comprehensive, have replicated levels and varieties of 'bisexual' behavioural and orientation incidence, and combinations of both (Klein 1978; Mead 1975; Gagnon 1977; Gebhard 1972).[12] Fritz Klein *et al.* (1985) have proposed the awesomely titled Klein Sexual Orientation Grid (KSOG) which enables sexual orientation in seven facets, (sexual attraction, behaviour, fantasies, emotional preference, social preference, self-identification and straight/gay lifestyle), to be measured against strength of sex-object choice, also on 7-point Kinsey inspired continuums ranging from 'other sex only' to 'same sex only'. Their detailed findings, drawn from volunteers amongst the readership of *Forum* magazine clearly need not detain us, but the general conclusion to which they lead, that sexual orientation is not static, not fixed during early childhood or adolescence, that heterosexuals and homosexuals may negotiate with the other and bisexuality in adult life, suggest that, just as Bell and Weinberg have argued, we cannot talk of homosexuality, only of homosexualities, so too we should talk of heterosexualities and most crucially of all bisexualities (Bell and Weinberg 1978).[13]

Within such schema bisexual variations are analytically established, if only *faute de mieux*, and thus some scientific legitimacy is given, but once again the bisexualities arrived at are not social in form but merely reiterated evidence of the behavioural potential for the emergence of such social forms. As such we would appear to be no nearer to being able to convincingly counter Valverde's (1985) 'catch-all' 'non-existent' dictum. To properly examine its veracity we clearly need to move on to consider whether, despite the enormous inhibiting pressures outlined, we may detect a construction process underway. We need to move beyond the behavioural fixation that dominates the literature and try to locate bisexuality in terms of its possible scripting and interactional status.

Interactionist Gagnon (1977), after asserting that 'physiological events are no more (and often less) important as indicators of what people are experiencing than the statements people make about what they (others) feel or think' (pp. 260–1) and reiterating his paradigm's credo; ('people have different ways of being sexual . . . different relations require different scripts', etc. (p. 259)), disappointingly fails to examine the possibility of genuinely 'bisexual' scripts. Instead he reiterates the various familiar situational contexts within which homosexual behaviour may not be scripted as such by at least some of the participants who retain committed heterosexual self-identities; i.e. same-sex institutions, adolescent sexual learning and experimentation and adolescent 'hustling'.[14] Certainly he accepts that those 'who have sex with both women and men rarely simply do (or feel) the same things with both women and men' (p. 259). The lack of a clearly defined and distinct bisexual alternative inevitably means that negotiated and emergent references and thoughts will be inclined to the elliptical, i.e. mainly following the culturally dominant heterosexual and homosexual signposts rather than through straightforward reference to bisexuality. However, Gagnon seems to deny that there are any scripts with even minimally genuine bisexual implications. Disparagingly he

157

claims that 'true bisexuals', 'people emotionally and sexually attracted to both men and women and [who] have relations with them accompanied by all the *"correct"* emotions' (p. 272), are only clearly identified by those whom he calls 'ideological bisexuals' (p. 272, my emphasis). Indeed the only 'bisexual' script seriously considered by him is one that is literally not bisexual at all, being the rationalisations of those who have sex with both men and women regardless of any specific gender or sexual interests in either. Rather all they require is 'just another body' and Gagnon gives as example the case of a man 'so entranced by his larger than average penis that he described his sex simply as "sticking his good old thing in and touching bottom" ' (p. 272). To this type Gagnon gives the label 'monosexual' bisexual though it seems that Masters and Johnson's preferred term of 'ambisexual' might be better (1979: 145–6).

Whatever else may be unclear it is apparent that bisexuality is not a singular, coherent, readily perceptible phenomenon and that given the cultural dominance of heterosexuality and of homosexual stigma the identification of bisexuality via either behavioural patterns or self-labelling is bound to be fraught with difficulties. That this is so has been demonstrated by many who have been forced to acknowledge the considerable discrepancy between behavioural experiences, psycho-sexual orientations and self-labelling. Blumstein and Schwartz (1976a) found 'little coherent relationship between the amount and "mix" of homosexual behaviour in a person's biography and that person's choice to label themselves as bisexual, homosexual or heterosexual' (p. 358). Homosexual experiences are likely to be rationalised away so that even individuals with a significant mix of homo- in with the heterosexual experiences and responses in a lifetime, are unlikely to adopt lasting homosexual identification, for cultural constraints consistently force the rejection or slowing down of negotiations with homosexual status and, although some autobiographical accounts suggest otherwise, to eventually label oneself as bisexual must surely require initial negotiation with and ultimate rejection of homosexual identity as well as heterosexual.

Blumstein and Schwartz claim that homosexual behaviour is thus 'a less potent life-organising force than common stereotypes would lead us to believe' (1976a: 81) but this potency is dependent upon the strength and form of the homosexual alternative so, even fifty years ago, as McIntosh (1968) has demonstrated, despite the relatively undeveloped homosexual role, the Kinsey *et al.* data show clear polarising effects, though not of course of equal strength towards both ends of the heterosexual–homosexual continuum.

The potency of the homosexual option has grown considerably during the subsequent decades following Gay Liberation, legalisation and commercialisation of a predominantly leisure/lifestyle subculture. Some have argued that one result has been to further undermine the socio-cultural viability of bisexuality, by producing added 'pressure to identify with one or other "side". As a result it is unlikely that a bisexual will be willing to identify *quickly* with (or propound) yet a "third front" in this political struggle' (Hansen and Evans 1985, my emphasis). Such arguments are unconvincing, however, for despite polarising pressures, it would appear that both 'on the back' of this more elaborate and established private gay subculture, and in clear reaction against at least certain aspects of it, distinct bisexual subculture(s) are emerging. In order to explain how and why we need to briefly return to the homosexual subculture, and especially the ideological characteristics of the 'gay community'.

Within earlier chapters the consolidation of homosexual citizenship has been detailed. In the initial radical context of the Gay Liberation Front being homosexual was largely a deconstruction and rejection of hostile conventional judgements built on the social fiction of the hetero-homosexual distinction; being 'gay' was not to be confined to rigid sex-role conformity but signified being able to experiment with all manner of sexual and gender forms and to make personal sexual, gender (and political) choices. Being 'gay' was, in these terms, a capability rather than a restriction (Weinberg 1973; Clark 1977). However, out of such relatively unstructured reverse discourses there emerged the new restrictions of leisure, lifestyle, commodity and citizenship forms within the legitimate, but rigorously policed privacy of the 'gay community' (Altman 1982). Drawing on the black civil rights movement this 'community' defined itself as an ethnic minority, as emphatically differentiated from the heterosexual majority as any late nineteenth-century sexologist might wish, deserting its fleeting constructionist emphasis on self-determination and falling back on rigid and reassuring essentialism. As Udis-Kessler (1990) has observed

159

Constructionism challenged the 'oppressed ethnic minority' approach by arguing that sexuality could not be compared to skin colour as a natural phenomenon. To many lesbians and gay men, constructionism took away their greatest asset, the ethnic self-conception, and did not offer a sound replacement. It could too easily be utilised by homophobic leaders as an argument that lesbians and gay men could change and should, therefore, be forced to do so.

(Udis-Kessler 1990: 56)

As Udis-Kessler notes, constructionist philosophy undermines community, and by implication those few ambivalent characteristics which currently and embryonically define bisexuality; rejection of labels, fluidity and individual choice threaten the increasingly 'ethnic' essentialism of the modern 'gay community'. As the latter has become preoccupied 'in everyday life and in political action, busy hardening the categories' (Epstein 1987: 12), resilient constructionist elements have been forced out to colonise and occupy and discursively lay claim to alternative independent organisational and institutional sites. For Udis-Kessler, therefore, bisexuality has become a construct out of the bifurcation of the homosexual category around inherent essentialist and constructionist conflicts. She is, however, surely mistaken in believing that bisexuality will always be marked by such constructionism and resistant to essentialist pressures. She asks 'How does one reify fluidity?' (1990: 59) to which one can simply reply 'through routinisation, discursive elaboration, the market and the organised pursuit of civil rights', so that fluidity becomes an essence. Even so her analysis intriguingly suggests how the bisexual subculture has been promoted by inhospitable tendencies in the gay community, where hitherto bisexuals found at least some subcultural support.

Recent bisexual autobiographical accounts from both sides of the Atlantic repeatedly stress this equal hostility and distrust or 'biphobia', experienced from gay and straight others alike, and demand the development of supportive specifically bisexual organisations, newsletters, etc. (Geller 1990).

As one might expect, such 'biphobia' from the 'gay community', and AIDS inspired hostility from the straight, affect 'bisexual' men in different ways from women. The former's relatively greater economic social and legal power, combined with their more explicitly genital/'outlets' sexual focus contrasts clearly with women's relatively lower socioeconomic power and more diffuse sexuality. One must be careful not to over-stress these differences but they are certainly perceived by activists, the 'ideological bisexuals' about whom Gagnon was so scathing, as significant determinants of male and female bisexual, sexual, associational and political differences. For example, Robyn Ochs of the Boston Bisexual Women's and the East Coast Bisexual networks observes that

> If you look at the gay male community, it's much better funded, it's much more based on being consumers. There are a lot of bars and clothing stores, a lot of stuff that caters to gay men . . . the gay male culture was, because I think it's changing now with AIDS . . . a 'party' culture . . . [but] if you look at women's culture it's tied very closely with feminism . . . I see so much more a kind of non-profit orientation in the women's community. . . . Another part of it is that it is in this day and age very scary to be a gay or bi man . . . [both] being scapegoated as . . . somehow responsible for spreading AIDS. So if you are a bisexual man and you are going to get involved in a relationship with a woman, and if you're honest and open about who you are, there's a good chance that women won't get involved with you. And at the very least you'd have a whole lot of processing to do about it, whereas if you're a bisexual woman, bisexual women are not a high risk group.

(Ochs 1988)

AIDS adds a further imponderable to any calculation of the likely form and extent of bisexual development within modern societies. It might of course simply be thought of as being yet another discouragement, but negative stereotypy of sexual deviations has always been formally discouraging whilst at the same time informally raising the profile and presence of the forbidden phenomena.

As has become all too apparent, government and privately sponsored anti-AIDS educational campaigns, and especially media coverage, have tended to target 'risk' groups rather than behaviours, with those deemed to be at 'high risk' to themselves and others depicted in an exclusive either/or sense as 'innocent' or 'guilty'.[15] Together with the more immediately recognisable of the latter – intravenous drug abusers and homosexual men – appear bisexuals. Sometimes euphemistically designated as 'promiscuous men', lest we have any doubts that these include bisexuals, the familiar litany of 'innocents' includes haemophiliacs, 'children of the guilty' and 'female partners of bisexual men'.

In most medical accounts this bisexual male has been treated solely as a significant link in the chain of viral contamination, as an unfortunate but necessary staging post statistic in the epidemiological trek of HIV strains from their predominantly heterosexual incidence in central Africa[16] to being the 'gay plague' of North America and Europe, and within the latter as a major means of contamination of the heterosexual community.[17] Any attempt to establish the aetiology of AIDS inevitably implicates the bisexual; for example, 'by the middle of 1984 it was . . . suggested that Haitians working in Africa . . . had taken back with them an originally heterosexual disease which had then spread to the population of gay American holiday makers in Haiti' (Wellings 1988: 86). Unless the virus is airborne, such accounts clearly implicate bisexuality.

Popular discourses have been somewhat caught, as a result, between the need to maintain clear, simple, orderly, representations of 'pure' and 'impure' worlds whilst simultaneously seeking to dramatise, in similarly summary terms, warnings of possible insidious and nebulous sources of pollution. Being clinically and politically identified as 'high risk' means the bisexual cannot safely be ignored by the popular media but if his presence is too pronounced then clearly the conventional simplicity and unity of the 'pure' heterosexual community is thrown into doubt.

Despite the obvious ambiguity of the term 'bisexual', mass media reference points predominantly remain exclusive either/or sexual categories, with 'bisexuals' almost casually lumped together with other outsiders especially homosexuals. For example, under the banner headline 'Straight Sex Cannot Give You AIDS – Official', the *Sun* (17 Nov. 1989) nevertheless reported that 'the killer disease AIDS can only be caught by homosexuals, bisexuals, junkies, and anyone who has received a tainted blood transfusion. . . . The risk of catching AIDS if you are heterosexual is "statistically invisible".' Not only do all junkies and haemophiliacs thereby become either homosexual or sexless, so too bisexuals, despite their label, become a discrete category outside normal society. There is not necessarily any consistency to such accounts, of course, for it is as likely to be assumed that all injecting drug users are heterosexual and that all bisexuals are male (Watney 1989: 40).

Just as subcultural communities tend to cohere through the reification of their essential difference from mainstream culture, so too popular discursive representations within the latter necessarily depend upon simple, natural and absolute standards with key roles assigned to easily identifiable heroes, fools and villains (Klapp 1958), and in the media treatment of AIDS bisexuals have served their term amongst the last of these. More than other culpable 'bridging groups' – intravenous drug abusers and prostitutes – the bisexual male's lack of social and cultural substance gives him the potential to act as an ideal generalised controlling and inhibiting mechanism; his lack of identity, his innate irresponsibility and disloyalty, his almost miasmatic presence, proclaiming him doubly guilty for being through his own actions deservedly diseased, whilst duplicitously being knowingly responsible for 'leakage' into the heterosexual community. He could be anyone and anywhere; be warned, 'carelessness kills' (Prentice 1990).

However, to deploy the bisexual as such a 'folk devil' is to subvert the moral community's simple clarity and absolute certainty. The more powerfully the bisexual male is used to warn of his extensive presence and possible source of contamination, the more effectively he dilutes the 'ideology of patriotic heterosexuality' (Watney 1989: 15). One is reminded of Hocquenghem's (1978) comparable observation on the status of the homosexual: 'Homosexuality exists and does not exist, at one and the same time: indeed, its very mode of existence questions again and again the certainty of existence' (p. 39).

As Watney (1987) states 'AIDS is not only a medical crisis on an unparalleled scale, it involves a crisis of representation itself, a crisis over the entire framing of knowledge about the human body and its capacities for sexual pleasure' (p. 9), but it is a crisis which has been largely faced by denying the 'facts' of sexual pleasure in order to sustain a simple lie. If, from the purely epidemiological point of view, the most effective means of AIDS containment requires the dissemination of well-established evidence on the widespread incidence and situational contexts of bisexual behaviours amongst sizeable percentages of populations, as in prisons within which, it has, therefore, been proposed, free condoms should be available, then absolutist certainties are bound to be called into question.

Throughout the AIDS crisis, however, it has become clear that ethical expediency has been subordinated to the simpler requirement for sustained moral certainty. However, AIDS dictates the pace of this particular game and whilst there is a 'cacophony of voices which sounds through every institution of our society' (Watney 1987: 8), the forms and extents of AIDS-related illnesses themselves inevitably produce cracks in the fabric. They are no doubt not symptoms of structural damage, soon plastered over, but their unpredictable appearance is, if only momentarily, disconcerting, and of unknown eventual consequence. The male bisexual is one such crack. His conventional characteristics of elusive, shady ambivalence have been put to good moral panic use, but out of such ambiguousness it is doubtful whether he can be more elaborately constructed from this particular source.

However, his reiterated presence in such persistently negative terms has given added momentum to those committed to counter such stigma, whose task will presumably become easier as AIDS as an epidemiology and as a social construct develops further. There are already signs that the threat of AIDS to the heterosexual community has passed the bisexual stage as currently great efforts are made to portray AIDS as potentially a greater heterosexual than homosexual or drug abuser danger. For example, the very considerable publicity given to the 95 per cent British increase in AIDS cases caused by proven heterosexual transmission in the year up to 1 October 1990 suggested that what was required to effectively warn a clearly as yet unconvinced public was a retreat to exclusive absolute sexual categories and that new anti-AIDS propaganda should emphasise the increasingly heterosexual cluster of HIV infection and AIDS deaths (Prentice 1990). The male bisexual's implied presence at least remains a necessary part of this scenario but with his culpability somewhat reduced.

It is presumably at least as an indirect result of this higher profile of bisexuality constructed around AIDS that elsewhere in the media there have been increasingly sympathetic accounts of his presence and very particular problems.

Insurance manager Brian Evans had been married for five years when he met a man at a party. 'I'd known gay men before, but I'd always considered myself straight. Then I got drunk and started kissing this guy. We didn't do anything further, but my sexual feelings tormented me. I didn't know what to do about it. I still love my wife and she would find it impossible if I slept with someone else – particularly another man. Yet it is something that I want desperately.' Brian is *probably* bisexual, one of an unknown number who admit privately that their sexuality does not fall into the either/or categories of homosexual and straight.
(George in *Observer* 9 Sept. 1990: 30)

The author of the above proceeds to explain how, because most people don't know anyone who is openly bisexual, ignorant myths are born; that bisexuals are interested in group sex; that they are married and that this is one way of acquiring 'a bit on the side'; that they are evil predators spreading AIDS; 'that they don't have the courage to step completely away from hetero-sexuality' (p. 30). This journalist claims that such misinformation discourages many people who have sexual feelings for men and women from calling themselves bisexual and so 'the invisibility associated with bisexuality is perpetuated [and yet] in spite of the price of honesty, the number of bisexuals disclosing their sexuality appears to be increasing' (p. 30). Eager to overcome this dearth of understanding and knowledge, the author hesitantly provides a definition: being 'open to sexual and emotional feelings for both sexes – without necessarily fulfilling them' (p. 30).

In another recent similar journalistic piece psychologist Eleanor Stephens, editor of the Channel 4 series *Sex Talk*, implied that bisexuals exist as a group marked by its inability to exercise its rightful moral and sexual choices. She asks

. . . shouldn't a society obsessed with consumer choice also defend choice in the area of sexuality? What's wrong with consenting adults having their cake and eating it? Shouldn't we be fighting against the tyranny of sexual categorisation and be promoting exploration and choice on the basis of self-knowledge? Bisexuality is about choosing your partners for qualities other than gender. Far from denoting indiscriminate sexuality, it should allow us to take into account a wider range of human characteristics. Many heterosexuals find it easier to communicate with members of their own sex, so why rule out the possibility of sexual communication too?

(Stephens in *Sunday Correspondent* 21 Oct. 1990: 57)

The consumption language here speaks for itself, especially as so succinctly allied to claims on enhanced rights for those denied them in respect of bisexual choices and purchase. The right to have and to exercise 'self-knowledge' is most pertinent too, especially as implied here as that mythic inalienable 'truth' which, when not publicly permissible, inevitably calls into operation the intervention of the clinician, not merely as counsellor and therapist but also clearly as apologist. The condition exists, we are assured here, and its open recognition will reduce 'the tyranny of sexual categorisation'. On the contrary its further discursive elaboration can only increase that tyranny.

Generally, as we have seen, 'Psychiatry has not ... been hospitable to the notion of true bisexuality, usually maintaining that anyone who describes bisexual activity is basically homosexual, with heterosexual behaviour superimposed' (Gould 1979: 38). Ross (1983: 79) concludes his study of married homosexual males by noting that no distinction could be made between 'genuine' bisexuals and reaction or 'defence' bisexuals and that, therefore, 'the label of bisexual reveals either defence or guilt of an individual's homosexuality, or possibly in some cases, a slow adaptation to one's homosexuality by first defining oneself as bisexual then as homosexual' (p. 79). On the other hand the bisexual experience as recounted in media treatments such as Ms Stephens' would now seem to be no longer a calling-off point on the way to some other bigger and better-known destination; clearly it too can be home, as recent evangelical texts vouchsafe.

Given bisexuality's lack of social and political substance it is not surprising that these are redolent of GLF proselytising pamphlet culture of the late 1960s and early 1970s.[18] They assert the legitimacy of bisexuality which 'accurately reflects ... [for some] ... their individuality and we must learn to respect it' (Burns 1983: 228); they lay claim to the 'freedom to be ourselves and to be attracted without qualms to both women and men ... i.e. people for themselves regardless of sex' (Off Pink Collective

1988: 87). They challenge negative stereotypy and assert the need to resist the limitation of bisexual lifestyles through adaptation 'to others' norms which has made it more difficult for many people with heterosexual, lesbian or gay self-identity to be open to bisexuality in others and possibly themselves' (p. 87).

There is especial concern for 'young people . . . first exploring their sexualities' (p. 87). Legitimacy is drawn from Kinseyan behaviouralist, cross-cultural and trans-historical evidence, especially through claims made to prominent historical (e.g. Virginia Woolf, Alexander the Great) and contemporary (e.g. Janis Joplin, Dusty Springfield, David Bowie, etc.) personalities, regardless of cultural specifics and varieties of form and content (Klein 1978). Inevitably there is the tendency to universalise and thus normalise the status: 'A bisexual potential exists in the human race' (Himmelhoch 1990: 47) and the stressed determination to rectify the denial of bisexual integrity in contemporary culture, to develop alternative subcultural sites to those only partially sympathetic within gay male and lesbian communities, as part of an international movement. These sites are marked out as multi-expressionist, informal and communal qualities; therapy techniques, games, co-counselling, massage, dance, drama. 'Let us be relaxed, lighthearted and proud in being bisexual' (Off Pink Collective 1988: 90). Occasionally this fervency accompanies the claim that true bisexuality is transsexualism. The former term should, therefore, be rejected in favour of the latter, '. . . we call "transsexuals" those adults who consciously live out their own hermaphroditism, and who recognise in themselves, in their body and mind, the presence of the "opposite" sex' (Mieli 1980: 27).

Explicit manifestos serve mythic needs by being evangelically utopian. That of the Off Pink Collective (1988) contains the following goals:

1 To enable bisexuals to achieve a positive identity.
2 To work to replace society's prejudices against bisexuality with an understanding and acceptance of it.
3 To work for an education in all schools which properly presents the range of sexual orientations.
4 To challenge in the media negative representations of different sexualities.
5 To support the elimination of sexism in all its forms.

167

6 To support other sexual liberation movements whose aims are consistent with our own.

7 To foster links between bisexual individuals and groups, nationally and internationally, to encourage the formation of further groups and to support the publication and broadcasting of material which contributes towards these aims.

(Off Pink Collective 1988: 91)

Alternatively the Manifesto of the Radical Lesbian and Gay Identified Bisexual Network stresses the need for bisexuals to attain a strong and valid identity within the Lesbian and Gay Liberation Movement, the need to remove parental power over children 'so that children and young people have the opportunity to define their own lives and sexuality' (p. 92).

It hardly needs to be stated that such radical manifesto goals as these and the associations organised around their realisation are necessarily of minority appeal and that the numbers of individuals supporting the mushrooming parties small. The same was true of the Gay Liberation Movement of course, which was paralleled by the emergence of more reformist political and support groups. So, too, bisexual organisations of the latter kind are developing: the *Bi-Monthly* magazine; the *Men's Anti-Sexist Newsletter*; the London Bisexual Group; the London Bisexual Women's Group; Bisexual and Married Gays Group; SIGMA the support group for the partners of the gay or bisexual; Bisexuals in NALGO and various other similar groups throughout Britain. Even more highly organised are comparable groups in the USA and Canada. In the USA the National Bisexual Network serves as an umbrella organisation for all bisexual groups and bodies on the continent.[19] Its goals include alignment with the National Gay and Lesbian Task Force; creating a bibliography and computerised resource lists and arranging for representation at gay, lesbian and straight conferences (Geller 1990: 111). The professionally staffed and privately funded non-profit-making Bisexual Information and Counselling Service disseminates positive information on all manner of matters relevant to bisexuals, including the keeping of local resource lists of sympathetic business and associational bodies such as religious groups, amenable to the open bisexual and partners. Despite their fractured and sometimes short-lived existence, problems of funding and client support, a core bisexual infrastructure clearly does exist and, especially in America, it is one that already interacts with, perhaps even interpenetrates, sympathetic institutions within mainstream society.

Such initial reverse discourses are inevitably preoccupied with the autobiographical declaration of bisexual credentials through which common group and personal identities are increasingly delineated, as with such mutual problems as the 'double trouble' of bisexual coming-out (*Guardian* 20 Feb. 1986). These autobiographies serve as affirmations of faith which formulate the beginnings of distinct bisexual scripts. Of necessity, repetitive and highly personalised, they do not easily permit confident and convincing analysis especially as in order to reach such a stage of self-labelling the authors will have undergone, atypically, considerable script renegotiation to retrospectively impose clarity and certainty. However, a perusal of such accounts suggests certain persistent elements, some positive and rather more negative, around which bisexual commitments are formulated, and perhaps the most pronounced of these elements is the stressed frequency with which bisexual negotiations are addressed in terms of the claimed conscious individual assessment of costs and benefits being explicitly balanced.

Though a case study rather than an autobiographical account Richardson and Hart's (1981: 79–87) 'Stuart' reaches his chosen self-identity of 'monogamous bisexual' by attempting to balance the benefits of being homosexually interested in men, having access to unconventional social networks, being 'different' and thus 'interesting', and the costs of instability and stigma, against the heterosexual benefits of respectability and marital stability. Being able to function bisexually enables such cost–benefit calculations to be made.

Another core script element is the inability to take on either a homosexual identity and/or an unwillingness to continue or increase participation in homosexual lifestyles and the 'gay community'. Despite a sexual and/or emotional interest in same-sex others, there is a resistance to becoming homosexual whether because of the strength of conventional negative stereotypy (i.e. 'sick', 'lonely', 'transient and unstable relationships' (Richardson and Hart 1981: 82)) or because of the experience of hostility from gay peers unwilling to tolerate the 'cop out', 'phase' of 'utopian' 'freeloaders, trendies, fence sitters, hedonists (and,

169

vis-à-vis bisexual women, unpolitical) pseudo-feminists giving all their energy to men' (Off Pink Collective 1988: 13–14).

To consciously reject the homosexual identity presupposes a felt sexual interest in, and perhaps experience with both sexes during sexual learning. As has been noted Gagnon tends to suggest that homosexual experiences are explained away by the rejection of homosexual meanings and the adoption of 'defence' rationales. Within many autobiographies, however, early familiarity with and enjoyment of such encounters provided positive scripts difficult to dislodge once conventional correctional scripting is encountered via the strategies of parents and teachers later in adolescent development (Gagnon and Simon 1969), through e.g. being unable to reconcile pleasurable homosexual experiences with negative stereotypy (Off Pink Collective 1988: 20). First sexual experiences, whatever their form and their extent, are generally recognised as major determinants of sexual socialisation and their largely informal, hidden peer group occurrence enables the normalisation of unacceptable behaviours and experiences prior to encountering specific instruction into what is acceptable. The remembrance of and reluctance to forgo early bisexual experiences, therefore, forms the focus of another cluster of genuinely bisexual adult discourses, no matter how they are resolved (Richardson and Hart 1981).

Given the relative informality and lack of specificity of sexual socialisation compared with that which maps out gender difference (e.g. Gagnon and Simon (1969) describe sexual learning as being partially accomplished in negotiation with parental 'systematic misinformation' and 'application of judgements without naming'), it is not surprising that the former are frequently experienced through and organised by knowledge of the latter. Thus being labelled as a child, 'sensitive' if a boy or 'tomboyish' if a girl, is recounted by many adult 'sexual deviants', not only those self-labelled as bisexuals, as a key element in determining subsequent sexual development. Of course adult learned reasoning may be being retrospectively applied here, but in a sense this is irrelevant for what is important is how adults give meaning and order to their bisexuality and, as such, interpretations based on childhood gender non-conformity are clearly of some significance.

This especially seems to be the case for those who, having been so labelled as gender deviants, then seek to negotiate a possible compromised peer acceptance by adopting exaggerated 'fool' performances. For example, a 'sensitive' boy acting out a role as camp effeminate jester, requires the conscious monitoring of situational performances and leads to perhaps the enjoyment of being 'risqué and daring . . . [having] . . . a certain cachet' ('Kate' in Off Pink Collective 1988: 13); 'enjoying being different' and shocking people ('Stuart', p. 14). In several accounts of mid-teen and adolescent experiences 'cost–benefit' reasoning emerges in these terms, as with 'Kate' who states that being bisexual may not have been 'as daring as being a lesbian which was what I felt I was, but much more trendy and less likely to get me written off' (p. 13).

To be recognised as 'trendy' for being bisexual clearly presupposes prior knowledge that this is a legitimate social definition of a recognisable behaviour and identity. Recent autobiographical accounts suggest that both 'bisexual' and 'bisexuality' have now passed into sufficient currency for adolescents and teenagers to have at least a basic awareness of the category and that for some embracing it is a positive solution.

> I've always seen myself identified as loving both sexes. Until I came across the term bisexual I was a long time without a label. I've very ambiguous feelings about labels but despite the misconceptions about bisexuality saying I'm bisexual seems less of a non statement than saying I'm neither straight nor a lesbian.
>
> (Off Pink Collective 1988: 11)

The bisexual label is not merely encountered out of the blue, by casual reading or through television, although these sources of information may also be significant in making bisexuality more visible, more relevant, deprivatised along with sexualities in general. Formal medical and counselling bodies provide expert guidance too. For example, 'David B' (p. 22) recounts how with his marriage in difficulty he and his wife were referred to London's Tavistock Centre Institute of Marital Studies where they were given psycho-dynamic therapy, following which both moved on to their relatively appropriate subcultural support groups, the Married Gays Group and Anti-Sexist Men's Conference for him and SIGMA for her.

As this last point makes clear, for many men and women bisexuality is a political as well as sexual identity, indeed it may be more political than genital or emotional, and many accounts suggest a rejection of heterosexist sexuality; e.g. of 'penis penetration of the vagina' ('Clare' in Off Pink Collective 1988: 29), 'monogamy' (p. 30), 'the hatred of being possessed' (p. 35), 'I have always seen female contraceptives as another form of male control of women' ('Brian': p. 37), and an advocacy of non-sexist alternatives such as mutual masturbation (p. 38). The adoption of bisexual identity being consonant with committed feminism in women and 'feminism' in men, 'David B' refers to his awareness of how women and gay men are all oppressed by straight men and that his anti-sexism was a key aspect of his commitment to bisexuality. Bisexual women are especially likely to make such claims in contemporary radical bisexual pamphlets at least. 'I think that being a lesbian is a lot more than who you sleep with. It implies a whole cultural component of "where do you put your priorities", what are your politics, what kind of concerts do you like to go to?' (Ochs 1988: 41).

Being bisexual is also, despite the communal and group trappings that apparently accrue to the more radical of bisexual parties, very much an assertion of individuality through the exercise of personal sexual/political choice. The autobiographical form clearly encourages this heightened individualism but current scripting of bisexuality fundamentally concerns a commitment to the construction of one's own sexual self. In some accounts it is a matter of uncovering that which is innate in us all, but for others this will to knowledge is not effected by the peeling away of layers but by deciding which layers to don. It is, in its pure form, the rejection of labels and the assertion of the unique self. For some this means rejection of all labels; 'Labels are really stifling; I'm not pigeon-holeable and I don't like feeling that I have to be. I'm attracted to people as people, not for their genitals' (Wittstock 1987). For others it means inventing your own and constantly changing them:

> I've been a bisexual-transvestite, a quadrisexual, a male lesbian, an androgyne, a 'Don't label me'/postmodern sexual being. . . . Last night I came to the realisation that as of my 37th birthday, August 31st 1988, I'm a Bi-Bi Sexual.
>
> (Plumb 1990: 18)

by which is meant the bisexuality of the author's two personae, Andy and Selena Anne.

Such beliefs are characteristic of the early political stirrings of minority groups where there is of necessity rejection of the imposition of oppressive negative essentialism combined with fervently expressed faith that one can define one's unique self from out of oneself, and if the socio-cultural environment is hostile then that is of course the only possible alternative source. In practice, however, it is nothing of the sort; it is the beginnings of a process which can only, inevitably, lead to discursive entrapment. Again one is reminded of Hocquenghem's observation on the discursive status of homosexuality and it could with reason be argued that bisexuality is the most potent of all sexual discourses given its extreme emphasis on sexual self-sufficiency within a world typified by the colonising force of sexual citizenship.

7

TRANS-CITIZENSHIP
Transvestism and transsexualism

Have you seen all the divas of Sheridan Square?
Kroozin' down to the river by Morton St. Pier.
Some are all tough and taki
But some are flawlessly fair
And we ain't dishin'
   just wishin'.
We could be standing there.
(Love Jimmy and Hot Peaches,
   Rob Baker 1988: 335)

The emergence of radical gay politics in the late 1960s and early 1970s was perhaps more remarkable, not for the attempts to theorise gay oppression into mainstream Marxist class and capitalism analysis, but for the eruption of what became known as 'gender fuck' tactics. Watney (1980: 67) has described the early GLF in Britain as split 'between the organised leninist party supporters and the diffused forces of the alternative society . . . between "actionists" and "life-stylers" '. The latter emphasised 'role play' personal liberation through, at its most extreme, an anarchic challenge to conventional sex and gender roles. In reaction to 'Gay men who would not attempt to destroy their male privilege, their sexism' (*Come Together* 15 quoted in Walter 1980: 204) other men adopted political drag, 'the ultimate rejection of the male role in society' (p. 205), by wearing clothes that society permits only women to wear. 'There is more to be learned from wearing a dress for a day than there is from wearing a suit for life' (Mieli 1980: 193). Such 'queens [men who wear make-up and dresses] are rejected by society because they destroy the myth about men' (p. 205).

174

By wearing drag, I feel that I am helping to destroy the male myth as well as the female myth. I enjoy, when wearing a dress, many of the traits that men used to be allowed to enjoy, but which are now buried under the male myth. Make-up when used as a way of putting women down, is effective as it creates objects of them – mere beautified possessions; but when used by men, it turns this on its head . . . it is a demonstration, in society's terms, of a man externalising his femininity.

(*Come Together* 15 quoted in Walter 1980: 205)

The clothing androgyny of hippiedom helped:

It started with jellabas and kaftans and long hair and flowers . . . then we discovered glitter . . . and then nail varnish. Later, some of us – a quarter of the men I'd say, at some time or another – would get a nice new frock for the next Gay Lib dance. Then a few people began wearing it to meetings. It just evolved.

(James 1984: 96)

Drag in street theatre and drag demos followed, the latter perhaps most famously effected in the 'Miss Trial' held outside London's Bow Street Magistrate's Court as feminists were tried inside for disrupting the 1971 Miss World Contest. Outside Miss Trial, Miss Used and other hirsute 'queens' paraded in sympathy. In the United States this somewhat attenuated tradition has been perpetuated by the infamous Sisters of Perpetual Indulgence, equally hirsute nuns Sister Boom-Boom, Sister Missionary Position and others of their order. This 'radical drag' divided radical opinion as well as offended straight; for example, during the 1973 New York Gay Pride Rally it was

rumoured that if any drag queens appear on the rally stage, the lesbian feminists will trash the place, as they feel drag's insulting to women, and that the gay genital-male leather jacket and boots contingent will also riot, because they feel drag insulting to men.

(Burke 1973: 58)

. . . and apparently only after a fist fight with the lesbians were the transvestites allowed to speak.

(O'Sullivan 1979: 147–53)

The 'drag' here is but one of several cross-gendered performances acted out within the rigid confines of conventional sex and gender roles, and the only one intentionally radical, although it is a customary claim by all that 'the effect of the drag system is to wrench the sex roles loose from that which supposedly determines them . . . genital sex' (Newton 1972: 103). Brake (1976: 174–98) discusses this particular form under the label 'radical queens':[1] ' "street transvestites" [who] . . . take care to look like men dressed as women. Dramaturgically they present a piece of street theatre aimed at attacking fixed gender roles [and thereby] a kind of Agitprop guerrilla attack is made on the straight world' (pp. 189–90).

By contrast the medicalised 'gross aberrations of masculinity and femininity' (Stoller 1979: 109), transvestism and transsexualism, which dominate medical, legal and commonsense discourses of cross-gendered behaviours, or 'gender dysphoria' (Fisk 1973: Meyer and Hooper 1974) are, despite their elaborately 'deviant' performance props, seriously committed to narrowly idealised coventional gender standards. Theatrical drag artistes commonly 'minstrelize' (Brake 1976: 188) women in order to voice audience and cultural sexism; 'drag queens' perform the aggressive 'camp' humour of the gay subculture, both deploying exaggerated surface sex and gender role signs, the former to reinforce the normative order before a supportively conservative audience, the latter to mildly chastise that order to an audience mutually rebuked by and excluded from it, but 'conventional transvestites' (p. 188) and transsexuals acknowledge the rectitude of cultural norms and their respective desperate needs to adapt in order to achieve a tolerable social space and settlement within them. The latter, by definition, require medical assistance to aid career progress, the former do not unless they are unsuccessful. The unsuccessful transvestite thus becomes the representative of the pathological condition; 'the majority do not seek treatment precisely because they derive a great deal of pleasure from their activities' (Woodhouse 1989: 75).

The medical literature on both psychological 'dysfunctions' is elaborate (King 1981) and, despite the constant refinement of categorisations, diagnoses and treatments, relatively straightforward and uncontentious.[2] However, the social ambiguities as framed within liberal legal judgements are anything but.

176

The now given distinction between biological sex (male, female), learned and negotiated gender (masculine, feminine) and sexual orientation and expression, has enabled considerable refinement of psychological and sociological analyses of the social construction of gender variety and sexualities. As one of the earliest theoreticians to adopt these distinctions claimed (Stoller 1979: 109), 'If sex and gender were in a direct relationship, if masculinity and femininity were simply the result of one's sex – i.e. of biological factors – then the differentiation would be pedantic.' Assaying biological sex in terms of chromosomes, gonads, hormonal states, internal subsidiary reproductive mechanisms and external genitalia can lead to the identification of various conditions of intersexuality or hermaphroditism,[3] but the relationship between these as well as 'normal' sex biologies and gender expressions and performances is minimal. There need be little connection between one's biological sex and masculine and feminine behavioural traits. The weight of construction is socio-cultural as case studies such as those of Stoller (1968) and Garfinkel (1967) testify.[4] Those within the psychoanalytic stable inevitably place great emphasis on the establishment of the 'primeval stage in the development of "core gender identity" ' (Stoller 1979: 110–11)[5] by the age of three and the intervention of 'intrapsychic effects' on determining subsequent divergence between sex and gender, whilst the sociological emphasis, dependent upon the encountering, interpretation and negotiation of culturally and historically specific sex, gender and sexual scripts, emphasises the possibilities of ongoing careers in terms of all three. As with all other aspects of the sexual however, and particularly the more esoteric, the scripts are primarily clinical in origin and dissemination, and thereby are in the front line of constructionist versus essentialist or 'discovery' debates (Bury 1986; King 1987; Nicholson and McLaughlin 1987). Negotiated settlements therefore, though varied, are also likely to be primarily framed within parameters established by these discourses although it is increasingly apparent that legal and state policy interventions combined with emergent reverse discourses from transvestite associations and the embryonic effects of TV/TS commodification have begun to undermine the singular coherence of the medical explanatory models.

First, however, transvestism and transsexualism need to be distinguished. The major divergence within accounts of transvestism occurs over the presence or absence of a specifically sexual component, motivation or release. Literally and originally the term means the desire and practice of some individuals, more men than women, to dress in the clothes of the opposite sex.[6] Its identification and definition as a distinct condition (Hirschfeld 1911, 1948; Havelock Ellis 1936),[7] differentiated cross-dressing from its earlier assumed attachment to and presence within the then composite category of homosexual, but the present-day condition of transvestism has itself subsequently shed the quite distinct symptoms, aetiologies and manifestations of trans-sexualism. Clinically the latter is made manifest by 'complete' identification with the opposite sex (Kockott 1976), the key diagnostic symptoms of which are the desire to resemble the preferred sex in all respects, and to be accepted within the community as a member of that sex (Benjamin 1966) to the extent of possessing the urge for a sex change operation to rectify the believed discrepancy between biological and psychological self. Transsexualism was first employed in this modern sense by Cauldwell (1949a)[8] and elaborated in the clinical literature shortly thereafter by Benjamin (1966).[9]

The medical condition of transvestism is quite different in that those concerned are presented as having distinct definitions of self and gender-sexual ambitions. To the literal 'cross-dressing' (King 1981: 163)[10] is specifically added by most analysts the latter's fetishistic character: 'the use of clothes of the opposite sex to produce sexual excitement' (Stoller 1979;[11] Randell 1973; Allen 1969). Associations for 'conventional transvestites' (Brake 1976: 188), seeking a relatively respectable *locus* in the hierarchy of gender and sexual deviants, forcefully disclaim sexual motivations, certainly of a homosexual kind. Virginia Prince's Foundation for Full Personality Expression (latterly the Sorority for the Second Self) and its house magazine *Transvestia* depict male transvestites as almost perfect examples of androgynous humankind in general gender, or as Prince prefers 'femiphilian' love of the feminine gender role. On a more downbeat but comparable level the British Beaumont Society exists to serve the interests of the ' "true transvestite" . . . [and] does not admit persons seeking partners for homosexual or similar reasons' (quoted in Brake 1976: 189) but such disclaimers cut little ice with most medical Mandarins ('. . . to take sex out of transvestism is like taking music out of the opera' (Benjamin 1966: 37)), nor do they tally with the autobiographical accounts contained in clinical as well as non-clinical research samples (Evans 1988), which consistently testify that the music that must be faced is predominantly heterosexual (Docter 1988)[12] and given the cultural context concerning both dress codes for males and females, and of male masculine 'outlet'-focused sexuality, male. As the above reference to the Beaumont Society suggests, researched non-clinical groups of transvestites located within associations[13] oriented towards acceptance and wider recognition emphasise transvestism as a general gender rather than a fetishistic sexual anomaly, an understandable subcultural attempt at deviancy disavowal or at least stigma reduction (Brierley quoted in King 1981: 165). Clinicians, however, do not agree; Green (1987) notes that male cross-dressing, sexual arousal and masturbation form 'the behavioural triad' that is the hallmark of transvestism (p. 388).

As with so much else within the broader sphere of 'gender dysphoria' and sexual deviance, the female presence is distinctly low key in all accounts of transvestism and transsexualism, the female relationship to the former most usually being dismissed in medical literature dominated by male/masculinist understandings of sexuality: 'Fetishistic cross-dressing is essentially unheard of in women. While women cross-dress, they do not do so because clothes excite them erotically. In all the literature there is only one account of a woman so excited' (Rosen 1979: 127).[14] Elsewhere female transvestism is described as the understandable and modish acceptance of male/masculine dominance, although 'butch' lesbian styles excite much physical and verbal hostility from many men, 'straight' and 'gay'. But, compared to male transvestite styles, all forms of the female are, in public territories, more easily managed and/or concealed. 'Butch drag is less obvious than it was, and because of its very nature is less flamboyant' (Brake 1976: 196).

Feminist hostility to the transvestite is obviously a matter of the gender directions of both, respectively, away and towards the conventionally feminine. O'Sullivan's (1979) argument is that both are liberation tactics, or at least were so before both became incorporated into fashion design and marketing.

. . . the transvestite separates [feminine] symbols from the woman and incorporates them into his personality. Thus the transvestite uses feminine symbols to liberate himself from his sex-role stereotype just as the feminist uses masculine symbols to liberate herself. To argue against transvestites by saying they are imitating women, and thus downgrading them, is to deny that men are soft, vain, emotional and frivolous, and that means furthering the stereotype of men.

(O'Sullivan 1979: 149)

O'Sullivan argues that in effect feminist women who wear jeans, T-shirts and boots are 'male impersonators', they decry men who affect femininity, and yet deny that they themselves are attempting through their dress styles to demean men.

Kirk and Heath (1984) explain the differences between male and female cross-dressing as follows:

Clothes are either functional or decorative or a mixture of the two. . . . when women have transvested in the past they have generally done so in order to be taken seriously in a man's world. 'Passing women' like the 19th-century American politician Murray Hall, who masqueraded as a man for three decades, did so because otherwise she would never have had the opportunity to do the job of which she was so obviously capable. In a very diffuse way women began transvesting in fairly large numbers during the war, by donning trousers . . . most . . . in an entirely unself-conscious manner because this was useful, functional wear for fire-fighting or working in the munitions factory. A man can only put on a skirt self-consciously; however he does it it always seems like a gesture. She moves from decorative to functional, he from functional to decorative. She cross-dresses because she wants to be taken seriously; he generally cross-dresses because he doesn't.

(Kirk and Heath 1984: 9)

There are, however, female transvestites and transsexuals, and neither should be so easily dismissed. Certainly transvestism cannot be written off as but part of the overall propensity for male sexuality to be fantasy fixated and pornography obsessed, as simply 'another "phallocentric need" ' (Penelope 1980: 103).

From their appearances as seperate conditions in 1910 and 1949 respectively,[15] transvestism (on occasion transvestitism) and

180

transsexualism have provided the beginnings of any number of variations subsequently 'constructed' by medical experts armed to discover, cure, solve and relieve, not to say punish. We have recently been told that 'the knowledge base necessary to support a system of classification [of transvestism and transsexualism] is only now beginning to take shape' (Docter 1988: 9) but this inhibition has not restrained the classificatory zeal of the clinician. Docter (p. 9) talks of primary transsexualism, secondary transsexualism, 'so-called drag queens' and female impersonators as four versions of 'homosexual behaviours involving cross-dressing', as well as five heterosexual: fetishism, fetishistic transvestism, marginal transvestism, transgenderism and secondary transsexualism. These distinctions are not merely distinctions of degree, nor is there necessarily an escalation of cross-gender behaviours built into them, although inevitably they do tend to be presented in a rank order of seriousness. For example, the fetishist is described by Docter as being 'content' with the use of a particular component or series of components of the feminine gender array as heterosexual stimuli, whilst the fetishistic transvestite cross-dresses to impersonate a woman, not to *be* a woman, for the understanding is that the man's maleness is not in doubt and hence on occasion, as though to demonstrate this, a not totally convincing impersonation is intended.

This last point, along with the emphasised sexual release goal of transvestite behaviours, is perhaps also contentious. For example, Woodhouse (1989) claims that the transvestites in her sample were concerned with 'creating a feminine appearance' (p. ix),'the goal being the perfection of a feminine guise' (p. xii) and Kirk and Heath (1984: 73) agree that the transvestite 'wants to "pass" as a woman and not be "read" (identified by others) as a man; he likes to be treated in the way he thinks a woman should be treated'. Such explanations hardly tally, however, with the photographed examples they provide where, with the exception of transsexual individuals, maleness beneath the drag is hardly in doubt. One of the most glaring elements of transvestite performances in relatively relaxed club gatherings as found in my own research has been the accompaniment of forms of feminine garb with emphatic signs of fundamental maleness. Voices are modified not at all, walk and movements remain masculine, and where transformations into 'glamorous' feminine selves are apparently more effective, other key props in the performance such as wigs, are blatantly omitted. In these terms the intention is not to perfect a feminine guise before other transvestites but to emphasise mutual male *en travesti* status. This is not to deny the seriousness with which the transvestite performance is pursued in 'straight' contexts, but merely to underline the fact that transvestites are 'men with two gender identities' who need to enact both, and in autobiographical accounts of 'public' transvestite behaviours the unquestionable thrill experienced is seemingly enhanced by the few passers-by who 'read' the performing woman as a man:

> I spent a most enjoyable day in Stirling, only being spotted once (I didn't know the word 'read' in those days) by some schoolgirls who did a lot of giggling but I didn't let on I had noticed them and gave them their money's worth by studiously ignoring them and they soon gave up. I quite enjoyed the experience.
>
> ('Jane' in Evans 1988: 11)

Kirk and Heath (1984), and the medical Mandarins, represent the feminine self of male transvestites as an 'escape' from the pressures of being masculine, thus the chosen 'alter-ego is as far removed from the male model as is possible' (Cohen *et al.* 1978: 81), explaining or excusing the chosen often stereotypical cross-gendered personae, suggesting uncritical mimicry and satire rather than emulation. Certainly the 'escape' hypothesis is borne out by several transvestite accounts, including 'Jane's'. For example, following three years of less than successful sexual relations with his wife after marriage, the death of a child and both his and his wife's fathers, plus accusations that he was having an affair with another woman, he writes

> This was all too much for me and I decided I had to dress again even though it was just partly. I was pretty friendly with a girl in our general office so I gave her money and asked her to get bra, suspender belt, knickers, half slip and stockings . . . making the excuse that they were a present for my wife to cheer her up after the death of the child. My friend . . . did as I asked her although I think she was a little astonished at the sizes I asked for. That night I had a glorious session dressing in the underwear and mastur-

bating which relieved me for the time being at least of all the tensions and frustrations of the past few months.

('Jane' in Evans 1988: 12)

Interestingly 'Jane', beyond indicating the clothing items mentioned, does not describe the 'woman' she wanted or believed herself to be. 'Janice' from the same sample, however, does, in terms of Showtime Blondie or Dreamboat Showgirl: 'blonde hair à la Kathy Kirby, heavy black eye make-up, black stage leotard, fishnet tights and stiletto-heeled shoes' (Evans 1988: 13). Typically the image inspires masturbation but the image and the imaginer become one 'I rubbed myself right through an image to become part of it and Showtime Blondie and I were engulfed together in satin and nylon and silk and leather. . . ' (p. 13).

Although within the criminal law there is no specific offence involving transvestism, the wearing of clothes of the opposite sex in public can lead to many problems with residual laws. Indeed, even private transvestite behaviours may be viable evidence in determining some legal judgements, as with spouses of transvestites who can sue for divorce on the grounds of 'unreasonable behaviour', but generally it is the public presentation of transvestism which brings the law into operation.

Under Section 5 of the Public Order Act (1936) it is an offence for anyone to engage in a public place in 'insulting behaviour likely to cause a breach of the peace'. Originally introduced to deal with fascist street fighting in the 1930s, this statute has served as an ideal generalised legal weapon against any behaviours interpreted by law officers as 'insulting'. In addition, several towns and cities in Britain have local bye-laws phrased in similar language but with lesser penalties. For example, the Liverpool Corporation Act of 1921 (Section 416) states that it is an offence to behave in a public place in a 'manner . . . whereby a breach of the peace may be occasioned'.

The 1956 Sexual Offences Act, which states that it is an offence for a man to 'persistently solicit or importune in a public place for immoral purposes' (Section 32), has also been used against transvestites, especially in the use of public lavatories. Using a public toilet designated for women can lead to charges of breach of the peace, using one for men to charges of soliciting. However, transvestites in public territories are in effect open to prosecution just for being there, for interaction with others is inevitable (i.e.

even if it is in the form of looking at passers-by) and evidence suggests that even the slightest hint of response or interest provides the police with adequate grounds for arrest.

That the police can be seemingly uninterested in male transvestites in public is attested by the account of Rastan (1989) of the 14th Beaumont Society organised annual spring weekend which in 1989 took 80 members to Weston-super-Mare where in hotels, bars, cafes and on the promenade they were able 'to go to town with their female alter-egos which in many cases have been struggling to get out for years'.

A further offence formerly particularly common amongst transvestites, but perhaps less so now that there are specialist catalogues selling women's clothes, shoes, wigs, etc. (usually advertised in national newspapers under seemingly gentle headings such as 'Larger Sizes', etc.), is shoplifting. 'Jane's' account above (Evans 1988), of how she persuaded a female friend to purchase the required items of clothing for his cross-dressing is but one example of the ingenuity many transvestites employ to obtain performance props. Elsewhere 'Jane' describes how during the war when working in an armaments factory he, like most female workers, re-stitched the clothing rags used to pack armament parts, unsold lines from shops ripped to prevent re-sale (p. 11). Today many transvestites claim that a brass neck and confident manner enable the purchase of, for example, women's shoes, even by trying them on in some shops. Buying dresses can also be managed without too much difficulty with an experienced eye, using shop mirrors to judge length and size when held up. Through the Beaumont Society, at special events such as weekend holidays, much activity is organised around the purchase of clothes, the wearing of them to generally disport the feminine selves which, given the expenses involved, invariably tend to be emphatically middle class in aspiration at least, if not accomplishment. For example, one guest at the Weston weekend describes her planned outfit for the social event, the final dinner, as 'a black pleated skirt and high-necked blouse with Harrods gold bracelet and earrings'. In contrast 'Josie', 'who works nights at a Nottingham bakery' was reported as upset by comments about her 'short leather-look skirt' (Rastan 1989).

Transvestites with the necessary confidence and right geographical location can also visit specialist shops such as

Transformation in London's Euston Road, one of five shops catering exclusively for the transvestite and transsexual, also serving as the centre of mail-order companies and of a private gender identity clinic (Rouse 1990).[16] One of the owners has been quoted as claiming that Transformation's biggest competitor is the Marks and Spencer chain 'but they don't realise it'. Apart from clothes these shops also sell padded knickers 'that give them the right shape'; 'hour-glass corsets (£95) which provide all in one false breasts and built in hip and bum pads – or you can go the whole hog with silicone prostheses (£99.99)', arrange for electrolysis to remove facial hair, etc. The shops also stock oestrogen breast-development cream, penis-reducing cream and 'bizarre pills such as Female Fantasies which promise feminine dreams. "Look at all the stuff women buy that falls into this bracket. It is all about fulfilling fantasies" ', says the owner (Rouse 1990). More complete fantasies are facilitated by the provision of the Change Away service which, for a charge of £55, enables those without privacy or facilities at home to cross-dress completely in a 'private lounge'. Transformation employs women in its very private shops, a practice which is criticised by rival Yvonne St Claire of Charades: 'No woman knows what it is like to be a TV' she claims, which of course begs the retort, 'and no TV or TS knows what it is like to be a woman' (Rouse 1990).

Given that there are still few specialist shops, social groups and associations, and the stigma/discouragement of career movement towards contact with them, most transvestite men will have to either purchase, through mail-order firms, or steal women's clothes, if not from shops then from launderettes, washing lines ('Jane' (in Evans 1988) when young scoured rubbish tips) or 'borrow' clothes from others living in close proximity: sisters, mothers, wives and friends. Subcultural scripting in such circumstances will be limited, perhaps to the seemingly abundant fictions with transvestism as themes, within which is emphasised the innocence of the protagonist, exonerated from blame, who fights and eventually becomes reconciled to his status, thereby overcoming guilt whilst achieving fantastic success as a cross-dresser; 'many have a frankly incestuous happy ending between the hero and the hero's mother' (Beigel and Feldman 1963: 201).

Inevitably transvestites fall foul of the law and advice given to enable them to deal with police arrest includes the possession of 'something that looks like an official document which shows that you are acknowledged by someone in the medical and/or legal field as being in a particular situation which is harmless to everyone and good for you' (p. 204). Also, the possession of a Statutory Declaration, which shows a legitimate change of name, has been known to ward off some police prosecutions, as has the presentation of membership cards for such organisations as the Beaumont Society. Such documentation is not likely to be of any use, however, in cases of divorce and child custody, where transvestite status is virtually certain to be a disqualifying handicap. The Guardianship of Minors Act (1971) established that custody cases should primarily be determined on the 'paramount consideration' of 'the welfare of the minor', and according to the Divorce Reform Act (1969) the question of party responsibility for marriage breakdown is supposedly irrelevant when it comes to deciding custody. In practice transvestite status, along with lesbian status, is consistently employed to refuse custody rights.

Medical treatments of transvestism are not required by transvestites themselves, but transsexuals, suffering from a disease 'tailor-made for our surgical-technological age' (Szasz 1980: 86) clearly cannot realise their goals without being formally labelled as such by convincing medical opinion to ensure their appropriate candidature for gender therapy and surgery. Inevitably such performance strategies tend towards stereotypy. 'Without [medicine's] sovereign intervention transsexualism would not be a reality' (Raymond 1979: xv) is the supportive medical opinion, but it is still majority legal opinion in Britain and elsewhere that transsexualism is not a reality for chromosomal sex cannot be altered, a view echoed by most feminist and many other critics: 'Physicians perform cosmetic surgery yet certify that their patients have undergone a change of sex' (Urban and Billings 1982: 266).

Medical Mandarins – urologists, gynaecologists, endocrinologists, plastic surgeons, etc. – are largely male too which has not exactly endeared their gender judgements and practices to critics Greer (1986) and Raymond (1979). The former has asserted:

If . . . normal men who eat pills and have themselves castrated are to be admitted to the female sex (needless to

say by *men* who have not consulted the members of the sex
so honoured) then the situation had better be made public.

(Greer 1986: 191)

Raymond (1979: xvi) contextualises transsexualism as but one
manifestation of the male empire concerned with fabrication of
the 'she-male' along with 'male fashion designers who prescribe
female apparel; men who train women in beauty techniques,
finishing school manners, and charm . . . who portray the female
"form" in pornography and "great art" '.

Thus gender identity clinics treating transsexuals are
presented as monitoring the efficacy of their patients' script-
learning and pre-performance skills in the presentation of
uncontentious stereotypical cross-gender styles which are
ultimately fake because of the biological anomaly. Walking,
speaking, dressing skills are rigorously rehearsed; 'Dr Reid . . .
asks pre-operative transsexuals to try and live in the opposite role
for at least a year before embarking on any irreversible procedures' (Hodgkinson 1990: 17). Whether transsexuals are
'discovered' or 'constructed' by the clinicians they approach or to
whom they are referred is a moot point (King 1981, 1984, 1987),
but in a sense it is also irrelevant in that transsexualism as a social
construct establishes its existence for those who develop an
extensive negotiation with the category as the category for them,
as a means of giving themselves a sex/gender/sexual identity.
Thus, as with transvestites, it is Kirk and Heath's (1984) view that
male-to-female transsexual gender exaggerations emerge in
part because those concerned establish a 'need' for a radically
different *alter ego* as refuge from the exigencies of maleness and
masculinity. These male transsexual *alter egos*, or as most
transsexuals would argue 'real' egos, are restricted to a few
idealised female/feminine forms whilst this 'need' for male-to-
female transsexuals is not manifest in the choice of the female to
be, as with male transvestites, but rather the 'need' to enable that
'real' female self to emerge, releasing rather than constructing it.
Whether discovered or constructed the dilemma of those
socialised into the transsexual condition is real enough and its
resolution in the widest sense some claim is inevitable, in that the
goal of transsexualism unlike transvestism and homosexuality is
normality, 'ridding themselves of the suffering entailed in their
condition' (King 1984: 46). One should, therefore, expect

187

emphatically normal female/feminine *alter egos*, and that is what
one generally though not always finds, certainly amongst the
more notorious. However, we are also told by medical
practitioners of complex outcomes which suggest that for many
transsexual subjects, the escape to exaggerated normality is not
the main motivation. Dr Russell Reid again reports 'I've seen
many male-to-female transsexuals who have been married to
women, and whose sexual orientation seems to change after the
operation. But at least 25% become lesbians and remain attracted
to women' (quoted in Hodgkinson 1990: 17).

Recent accounts of transsexual medicine have suggested that
apart from their one common conviction, that against all the
physical evidence they are 'really' members of the opposite sex,
transsexuals 'have little in common with each other' (p. 17) and
that 'many modern male transsexuals' visit their doctors 'wearing
jeans and T-shirts' (p. 17), but researched treatment programmes as well as transsexual autobiographical accounts 'written in
the form of the religious confessional' (Jeffreys 1990: 178) are
replete with exaggerations of conventional gender roles.[17]

For example, Jan Morris, in her 'embarrassing book' (Riddell
1980: 6) *Conundrum* (1974) written in post-operative euphoria,
satisfied with 'a tinsel notion of women's existence' (Riddell 1980:
12), describes womanhood thus:

> ... her frailty is her strength ... her inferiority her
> privilege ... I like being a woman, but I mean a woman, I
> like having my suitcase carried, I like gossiping with the
> lady upstairs ... and yes I like to be liked by men. ... If I
> could live my life all over again, I suppose I would have
> been happiest being someone's second in command –
> Lieutenant to a really great man – that's my idea of
> happiness.
>
> (Morris 1974: 167–8)

And her new experiences as a 'woman' have taught her to
enjoy 'the small courtesies men now pay to me, the standing up
or the opening of doors, which really do give one a cherished or
protected feeling' (p. 169). As several female critics observed,
Morris sounds not like a woman, but like a middle-class male's
view of a woman.

... Once able to pass for a woman, she proceeds to reinforce the bars of the woman's cage. Though she mentions her growing awareness of women as second class citizens, by her behaviour she bolsters that discrimination, acting helpless, coy with waiters, passive with male friends . . . crying easily, making frivolous remarks on cue. . . .

(Tweedie 1974)

Jeffreys (1990) quotes an extract from ex-racing driver and car engineer Robert(a) Cowell's story which, she argues, illustrates this acquired 'sense' of what being a woman means.

A definite change in the functioning of my mentality began to become apparent. . . . My mental processes . . . slightly slowed up, and I also showed signs of greatly increased powers of intuition. . . . For the first time in my life I found I could read stories and novels with sustained interest. . . . My nature was becoming milder and less aggressive, and I found it much more difficult to summon up will-power when required.

(Jeffreys 1990: 178)

Given such criticism it is hard to question Raymond's (1979) view that 'Uniquely restricted by patriarchy's definition of masculinity and femininity the transsexual becomes body-bound by them and merely rejects one and gravitates towards the other' (p. 7). The one problem with this sweeping assessment is that the process follows such a tortuous path from individual self-identification to post-surgery, with so many gate-keepers having to be convinced *en route*, that cases inconsistent with established qualifying criteria are unlikely to emerge. It is quite possible that there are a number of proto-transsexuals from whom the label is withheld by experts because their cross-gender performances are unconvincing or perplexing, after all Raymond attacked *The Transsexual Empire* partly because a proportion of post-operative male-to-female transsexuals adopted a lesbian feminist identity and became actively involved in feminist politics where, through their retained 'real' maleness, they were able to dominate.

The most notorious transsexuals, however, do seem to safely fit the idealised patriarchal sex-role bill. For example, Ms Caroline (née Barry) Cossey's transformation has generally convinced, or at least tantalised the British media because of her photogenically convincing feminine attractiveness:

189

In 1973 Caroline confirmed her new name by deed poll. She began hormone treatment and had a breast construction operation. In December 1974 she had a sex change operation. . . . Eight years later . . . a medical examination by a consultant plastic surgeon showed her to be 'female in all respects'. She was 'a pleasant young woman with a gracefully female attitude to life'. Armed with her new persona, stunning good looks and a new business name, Tula, she had become a successful model.

(*Sun* 28 Sept. 1990)

Retrospective autobiographies of transsexuals inevitably replicate clinical discourses in grossly simplified form; indeed it has been reported that many patients have known the medical literature better than the clinicians consulted (Urban and Billings 1982), leading to 'complex collusion between patient and doctor (Szasz 1980: 81). For example, the latter demand 'an inborn predisposition toward gender non-conformity' (Bell *et al.* 1981: 188), an *idée fixe* (Money and Gaskin 1970–1) or an 'intensive desire' (Forester and Swiller 1972), whilst the former claim exactly these feelings; 'it is a form of classic schizophrenia, the body inhabited by two personalities, only resolvable by the expulsion of the alien, conditioned to existence by a false biology' (Riddell 1980: 21). Since the widely publicised Jorgensen case (Sagarin and Kelly 1975), and her claim that she always knew she had the wrong body, this has become a transsexual *credo* as 'nature's cruellest quirk' (*Independent* 20 April 1990: 3); 'I was born with my chromosomes out of synch. . . . I couldn't help that [but was forced] to live a lie. . . . I was always a woman trapped in a man's body' (Cossey quoted in *Sun* 28 Sept. 1990: 21); 'I had to search my inner spirit to find my true identity' (p. 21), 'I would always swop my copy of *Valiant* or *Hurricane* for . . . *Judy*s or *Bunty*s' (Grant 1980: 9) and 'almost never went out to play with other boys in the area' (pp. 16–17). Above all else, biology is destiny in these accounts: 'to assert freedom of choice . . . would trivialise . . . a central part of self-identity' (King 1984: 44). The 'true' transsexual has no choice. Journalistic reports invariably reinforce such scripts, reducing them to outline forms which unproblematically establish the condition, its causes and effects. Thus Cossey was:

taunted as a cissy at school and secretly dressed in his mother's clothes. By 15 or 16 he realised that, despite his male genitalia, psychologically he was a female. In 1972 living in London, he abandoned his male Christian names, began wearing women's clothes and adopted a role of a woman.

(*Independent* 20 April 1990: 3)

This kind of sympathetic reportage inevitably emphasises essentialist criteria; the 'victim's' biology and biographical development portray a singular type *en route* to the necessary tidying of nature's lapse in concentration: 'I gave nature the helping hand that it denied me at birth' (*Sun* 28 Sept. 1990: 21). So being taunted as a 'cissy' at school is interpreted confidently as a rare childhood experience with peers possessed of precocious psychic powers, and indicative of pathological proto-transsexualism. Similarly Barry's decision that he was 'really' (i.e. psychologically) a female is treated as the discovery of an inalienable truth rather than one possible negotiated response. As such a truth the desire for 'total sex change' (p. 21) is accepted as unproblematic and as immediate as the adoption of the role of a woman. Transsexualism is, however, fundamentally a condition of two conflicting inalienable truths increasingly in prominent institutional discursive conflict; in medical discourses the psychological reality of the transsexual transcends the physiological and biological realities, whereas in legal judgements the reverse is the case.

It is revealing that in all these accounts the neat and tidy world of either/or gender, sex and sexuality of journalistic common sense is maintained by 'a woman' being an archetype and more interesting questions than 'Why, or how do you feel you are a woman?' are passed over, such as 'Why do you feel you are the particular "woman" you believe yourself to be?' 'Have you been other "women"?' 'Why the physical/cosmetic form chosen for that woman, and how has it been realised?' 'What form of cross-gendered presentation of self is sought, scripted, learned and performed?' 'And why the particular new name chosen?'

As with other transsexuals, not all as glamorous as her, Caroline Cossey, or Tula, attempts to normalise transsexual status by making claims against other sexual and gender minorities with whom she might damagingly be confused, claims

justified precisely because these lesser others don't have the
excuse of biological anomaly (Townes *et al.* 1976; Ross *et al.* 1978).

> Transsexuals are not like transvestites who get a sexual kick
> out of simply dressing up as women. We are women in
> everything but name. No man I met has ever doubted that
> I am a woman in every way – physically, emotionally and
> sexually. I am highly sexed and feel pleasure the same as
> any woman. I satisfy my men as any woman does. The only
> thing I could not do for a man was bear his children.
>
> (Cossey quoted in *Sun* 28 Sept. 1990: 20–1)

The validity of this claim is tantalisingly presented in the *Sun*
by showing Caroline in swimsuit and shirtless 'hunky' male
model quoted as describing her as 'the perfect woman' agreeing
with her assertion that '. . . nothing can change the fact that I
really am a woman. Look at me' (p. 20).

It is clearly impossible to extricate alternative interpretations
of their condition from medicalised transsexuals; by definition
the only accounts we can have are from the medicalised. In a
sense this does not matter for clearly it is the forms of negotiation
with the constellations of power/knowledge around this and
related themes which are of importance. Many critics, however,
despite their advocacy of the constructionist position elsewhere,
exhibit inconsistencies in their responses to transsexualism and
transvestism. Altman, for example, states that 'it may well be true
that those transvestites and transsexuals who are behaviourally
heterosexual are, in fact, repressing their homosexuality'
(Altman 1982: 57). This was an argument much favoured by
clinical critics at the time of transsexualism's initial promotion by
Benjamin (1966), claiming that the pathological transsexual is
deluded for his or hers is 'a psychic illness' (Socarides 1979:
1424), the 'mental disturbance of guilt-ridden homosexuality or
transvestism' (Allen 1969) and thus no amount of hormonal
realignment or surgery could eradicate such a basic psychic
disturbance (Meyer and Hooper 1974).

Views such as Altman's (1982) assume that transvestism and
homosexuality have 'real', i.e. biological, prior significance and
come as quite a shock from someone of his pedigree. He argues
that in a culture where homosexuality is so stigmatised the ways
of enacting it are bound to be many and varied, and transvestism
and transsexualism can both thus be considered alternative

192

homosexual forms. Indeed their origins could overlap on this particular scripting difficulty but the solutions which each represents are clearly sufficiently distinct to make this a less than useful line of enquiry. Even so he quotes the following account by the clearly influential Jan Morris in support:

> I was walking along Jermyn Street one day when I saw, for the first time in twenty years, a member of the Everest team of 1953. My goodness, I said to myself, what a handsome man. I knew he had been handsome all along, but I had allowed myself to like him only for his gentle manners, and it was only now that I permitted myself the indulgence of thinking him desirable.
>
> (Morris quoted in Altman 1982: 58)

Jeffreys (1990: 185) also suggests that homosexuality is the main 'if not the only' motivation of transsexuals, arguing that once recognised in the clinical literature (e.g. by Hamburger *et al.* 1953)[18] this factor has become submerged by the empire-building of subsequent transsexual practitioners. This is as may be, but that zeal has effected a differentiation between the two conditions to such an extent that there is no justification, or point, in pursuing the primacy of homosexual orientation as the major cause of transsexualism.

Transsexualism clearly involves a claim, in all perceived senses, to being of the gender and sex opposite to that assigned at birth and thus 'is the claim to a state of being [the opposite sex] which would ordinarily be denied' (King 1984: 44). Within medicine, psychology and, therefore, the law transsexualism is generally regarded as a state of essential being but not unambiguously so, for whilst this 'gender dysphoria' exhibits an untenable conflict between gender identity and biological and physiological sex which medicine can alleviate if not correct, 'hormones and surgery are like insulin for the diabetic. They enable the patient to live comfortably and normally' (p. 45); clearing a legal and social space for male-to-female and female-to-male transsexuals is less easily managed, as test-cases are beginning to demonstrate with some force. Transsexual operations are accepted in medicine and law as bona fide medical treatments but once completed the transsexual is not generally legally recognised as such. Transsexual rights, however, commence with their medical realisation and so it is perhaps at this point that a brief history of transsexualism and summaries of the ideal career progress of male-to-female 'medicalised females' (Raymond 1979) and female-to-male transsexuals be given.

As King (1981: 175) reports, 'Up to probably the late 1950s at least, the category of transvestism was apparently vague enough to cover those who sought to change their bodies to resemble the opposite sex', although surgical methods were initially only available to those exhibiting evidence of hermaphroditism (Hamburger *et al.* 1953). Indeed it was medical attempts to 'correct' varieties of hermaphroditism which established a medical acceptance of the relative independence of gender from biological sex, and developed surgical techniques later to become important in the treatment of transsexuals. Following Cauldwell's (1949a) somewhat muted identification of the 'condition', it was Benjamin's (1966) discussions of diagnoses, aetiologies and treatments which contributed much to transsexualism's subsequent construction. Opposition from within medicine and the law (Hastings 1966; Holloway 1974) inhibited full recognition of transsexualism as a disease for many years but in 1966 Johns Hopkins University physicians admitted performing experimental sex reassignment surgery on 'true' transsexuals (Green and Money 1969), employing techniques previously used in the treatment of hermaphroditism (Money *et al.* 1957). By 1973 transsexualism had emerged from being an 'exceedingly rare syndrome' (Hamburger *et al.* 1953: 391) and become a 'serious and not uncommon gender disorder of humans' (Edgerton 1973: 74), aided by the reduction of diagnostic restraints following its redefinition as 'gender dysphoria' (Fisk 1973) affecting an estimated one in 40,000 males (Freedman *et al.* 1976). In 1979, however, Johns Hopkins University announced that it would no longer be carrying out such operations because transsexual patients were showing no objective benefits; transsexualism was a psychiatric disturbance which could not be alleviated by surgery. As Szasz says drily (1980: 90) this is 'what philosophers call an analytical truth'. The research findings which guided the Johns Hopkins decision, then, have subsequently been forcefully challenged, not least on the grounds that, whatever the problems, transsexual treatments 'save lives'.

The 'ideal' therapy and surgical transsexual career progress of males to 'females', passes through a number of identifiable stages of which the following, not necessarily in this order, are the most important. Private as opposed to public health treatment is also likely to affect their relative importance and order in that the latter tend to extend pre-operative treatments, whereas the most unscrupulous of those working in the private sector may attenuate it considerably.

1 Cross-gender performances monitored, most usually under the guidance of gender identity clinics in terms of dress, speech, movement. For some this is not a stage proper but a pre-stage phase that with persistence leads on to

2 Hormonal castration, the administering of oestrogen and progesterone to suppress existing physiological sex characteristics and to develop and maintain those of the 'female', to develop breasts, soften skin, reduce body hair, diminish erections, reduce testicular androgen production. Testes atrophy, body fat distribution is altered and muscular strength diminished, the latter as much through behavioural changes.

3 Because hair growth tends to be left relatively unchanged electrolysis is employed at a third stage.

4 Speech therapy is a quite distinct stage in transsexual progress because of the relative lack of hormonal and surgical impressions made on voice levels, thus therapy seeks to raise and soften the voice.

5 The fifth and major stage of surgery contains several 'treatments': penectomy, castration, reconstruction and vaginoplasty. The latter is the major construction, the creation of a cavity between the prostate and the rectum employing skin grafts from elsewhere on the body 'lined with penile and scrotal skin enabling some orgasmic sensation' (Raymond 1979: 32). This artificial vagina is maintained by the regular use of a mould or speculum (worn continuously for several weeks after surgery) to prevent contraction of scar tissue.

6 The enlargement of the breasts using artificial implants may precede or follow stage 5.

7 The next phase involves increased oestrogen therapy, without which post-operatives would experience persistent 'menopausal' symptoms ('hot flushes' and deterioration of general body tone. For Raymond (1979: 34) it is at this stage that male-to-female transsexuals are effectively 'medically managed' to the point of being superficially female.

8 Cosmetic surgery may well be pursued and usually is in order to facilitate the particular female shape required, in terms of nose and chin shapes, perhaps even limb surgery, etc. Pauley (1969: 47) has described transsexuals developing a 'poly-surgical attitude' i.e. demanding repeated forms of cosmetic surgery to improve chins, noses, legs, feet, etc.

9 The male-to-female transsexual is never fully finished as a construction, however, for constant medical monitoring is necessary to maintain hormone treatments and to correct physical complications such as damage to thin breast tissue, breast cancer, the surgical reduction of bloated limbs induced by hormone therapies, infections of urinary and rectal tracts, haemorrhaging, blood clotting, narrowing of the 'vagina' and of the 'urethra', etc. (Norburg and Laub 1977: 273).

It does not need to be stressed that this is both a very expensive and traumatic 'solution' to the rigidities of conventional gender and sex, though perhaps less so now than when proto-transsexuals had to seek treatments abroad privately as was the case with April Ashley (Ashley and Fallowell 1982). The latter's *Odyssey* took her, as a him, to Casablanca where the not immediately reassuring Dr Burou ('Do you realise I haven't done many of these operations, that you are a guinea pig?' (p. 84)) showed explicit photographs of surgery to test the patient's resolve. There were no psychiatric tests and one day's warning that the surgery was to be carried out. The generally gossipy tone of this autobiography is punctuated by undoubtedly fierce feelings of post-operative pain: '. . . the fact that there is pain connected with surgery takes some patients rather by surprise' (Hastings 1974: 337), recovery and lack of self-doubt '. . . I've just been born . . . I am a woman in Casablanca and I'm in agony but my spirit is soaring. . . .' (Ashley and Fallowell 1982: 88).

Stages in female-to-male transsexualism, described by Lothstein (1983: 14) in the most comprehensive account so far as 'primarily a disorder of self-esteem', are as far as possible the complement to those of male to female;[19] monitored cross-gender performances, hormone therapy, the injection of androgen to stimulate body hair growth, lower voice pitch, reduce breast tissue, and alter muscle and physiology (by widening shoulders, etc.). Long-term use of testosterone enlarges the clitoris. Menstruation is particularly likely not to respond to hormone treatment and thus radiation therapy (the 'radiation menopause' (Hoenig *et al.* 1971)) is used to eradicate it.[20]

The surgical stage involves mastectomy, hysterectomy, oophorectomy (removal of the ovaries) and 'phallus' construction. 'It is technically possible to create a penis by rotating a tube of flat skin from the lower left quadrant of the abdomen and closing the vaginal orifice' (Raymond 1979: 36). A urinary conduit may be inserted into this 'phallus' but being prone to complications it is also possible to retain the urethra beneath the 'penis'. The latter lacks sensitivity and can only become erect through the insertion of a stiffening material, either left in the 'penis' all the time or inserted and withdrawn as and when the 'male' likes. Stanford University gender clinic in 1977 reported that the female-to-male conversion required on average 3.5 surgical operations (Norburg and Laub 1977), and clinicians also claim that 'nobody ever mistakes a female-to-male transsexual for a woman . . . when women take male hormones hair appears on the face and the voice deepens very quickly. The outline also becomes more muscular' (Reid quoted in Hodgkinson 1990: 17).

The idea 'that human beings – especially women – are improperly made sexual machines' (Szasz 1980: 92) who can be corrected by surgery has become a dominant medical ideology, so that in particular medical knowledge of cosmetic surgery is now extensive and financially rewarding, and so much transsexual medical know-how exists to accomplish more than solely bringing extreme 'gender deviants' back into the rigidities of patriarchal sex stereotypy, a point which transsexuals understandably emphasise in their defence.

> However horrific their gender conformity programmes are to transsexuals, I think they are quite insignificant when compared to the thousands of gynaecologists, with equally sexist opinions, who are mutilating women with breast inserts . . . hysterectomies . . . caesarian sections and performing other atrocities on women's personhood.
>
> (Riddell 1980: 10–11)

The question of proto-transsexual rights is particularly tricky. From the time of the condition's first clinical recognition and the claim by the first notorious post-war transsexual, Christine Jorgensen (see Pauley 1969), that she had been a woman trapped in a man's body, transsexual rights have been inextricably bound up with the complexities of medical duties and ethics and their relationship to legal referents.

As we have briefly seen there are now clinically very precise diagnostic criteria for proceeding with transsexual therapy and especially surgery. In one important sense these strict criteria have been developed to protect practitioners from accusations that they are unprincipled, that they are guilty of 'collaboration with psychosis' (Meerloo 1967: 263), by simply accepting the proto-transsexual's right to medical treatment as he or she wishes. Stoller (1968), for example, has suggested that only 'males who are the most feminine' and who have manifested this extreme femininity since earliest childhood, who have not lived for long periods as and been accepted as males, who 'have not enjoyed their penises' and have not advertised themselves as males (e.g. through female impersonation) demonstrate valid prerequisites. In effect this means that anyone commencing his negotiation towards such a solution through late adolescence and adulthood is ruled out, except that proof of meeting these criteria is clinically somewhat dubiously attested by retrospective auto-biographical accounts as well as by medical records. Patients have the opportunity to carefully manage their performances to obtain clinical approval, but they have no automatic right to therapy or surgery. Instead a set of stringent duties is placed upon both them and their doctors to exhibit, monitor and relieve scientifically identified symptoms. At least this would be the seemingly very ethical picture if commodification principles had not been allowed to intervene.

Benjamin's (1966) ready advocacy of the transsexual condition provoked considerable opposition precisely because of his acceptance of the validity of patient self-diagnosis, and that human rights begin with the right to self-ownership. Hostility to these claims was vociferous:

> Although our subjects share certain needs, wishes and personality characteristics, it would be completely erroneous to conclude from these similarities that they represent an homogeneous group. The need for surgery that these persons share does not itself represent a disease entity but rather a symptomatic expression of many complex and diverse factors.
>
> (Worden and Marsh 1955: 1297)

Transsexuals of course have the right to approach the medical profession for help but, under the formal ethics of transsexual medicine, no right to demand treatment. However, there is no doubt that medical institutions have worked hard to promote specific transsexual as well as general cosmetic surgical expertise. The formal face of medicine as represented in the pages of clinical literature suggests that it is not a market-orientated and governed profession, but rather preoccupied with research to advance medical knowledge to alleviate and cure patient suffering. But, as with medicine's response to AIDS, where market ethics are inextricably realised in the sale of expertise to advance careers and drug companies' control over experimentation, the limited release and high cost of treatments have been so evident, so too commercial considerations have developed in the sphere of transsexualism.

Urban and Billings (1982: 277) explain the emergence of the transsexual medical condition quite explicitly as a discursive reflection and development of 'late capitalist logics of reification and commodification'. They argue that, with little or no prior knowledge, transsexual medicine by the late 1960s was extolling the benefits of sex role reassignment through books, articles, lecture tours as well as through non-medical journals and newspapers. Specifically, in the United States they identify the Erikson Educational Foundation, its National Transsexual Counselling Unit and the Harry Benjamin Foundation also under its auspices, as key developers, disseminators and providers of the transsexual commodity (pp. 271–2), advocating positive effects and success rates whilst minimising post-surgical and post-operative problems so effectively that doctors reported young patients saying 'I want to be a transsexual' (Person and Ovesey 1974: 17).

Thus 'the legitimation, rationalisation and commodification of sex-change operations have produced an identity category – transsexual – for a diverse group of sexual deviants and victims of severe gender role distress' (Urban and Billings 1982: 266). The medical establishment's concern and pre-eminent control over correcting gender deviance as a force for public good thus becomes a non-market justification for its pursuit of profit from it. As King observes (1987: 357), for Urban and Billings transsexualism's 'construction' is directly linked to the 'selling of it' through the whole package of personality and performance training as well as the surgical core. Transsexual specialists within medical institutions may have the desire to respond to patients' expressed needs for help because of their suffering, but this acknowledgement is somewhat swamped by their ability to obtain career and financial kudos from them.

King (1987: 367) is sceptical of Billings and Urban's claims because he argues with some conviction that this is a sphere of medical research and specialisation with relatively low status within the profession and, therefore, 'a profit minded surgeon could find easier and less professionally damaging ways of material gain than operating on transsexuals'. Rather less persuasively, however, King claims (p. 369) that whilst their account of commodification might fit the private financially sensitive organisation of health care in the United States, in Britain provision of sex-reassignment treatment and surgery is 'uncertain and unstable'. However, recent newspaper reports in Britain suggest otherwise. The *Independent* (28 Sept. 1990: 3) has reported that the gender identity clinic at Charing Cross Hospital in London, the only NHS centre where operations are carried out, sees about fifty people a week and performs an operation every fortnight and that it has a four- to five-month waiting list. This report also claimed that 'An estimated 10 to 15 private operations, costing more than £5000, are carried out each week.' Other newspapers have also picked up on the exposed practices of private gender identity clinics 'because of growing concern that teenagers, some with psychological problems and in council care, are able to obtain sex change operations' (*Sunday Correspondent* 7 Oct. 1990: 32). Here the claim was that private clinics are charging up to £15,000 for the entire treatment and that they are 'offering hormone treatment without any rules governing how they should be preparing patients for life as the opposite sex'.

Featured prominently in these reports was 17-year-old 'Toni', or 'Chantelle' or 'Ayesha', adopted names of one Jason Brown who had been, it was claimed, confused about his sexual identity from the age of 10 when he was taken into care by his local authority's social services department. At 17 he decided on a sex change operation at a National Health Service clinic but, on learning that he wouldn't be surgically treated for at least a year, arranged for treatment at a private clinic at '£80 a three monthly visit' (p. 32). The doctor reponsible accepted that it was unusual to commence treatment on individuals as young as 17 or 18 but was quoted as claiming that 'if someone is obviously transsexual it is unkind to put him on the back burner and wait until he becomes masculinised' (p. 32) adding that he once gave hormone treatment to a 13-year-old girl in the United States. The total cost of the transsexual treatment is given as £10,000, a sum found by Jason largely through prostitution.[21] A spokesperson for the Department of Health said that there were no legal restrictions on people of 16 years and over seeking 'whatever medical care they like' (p. 32). However, NHS clinics follow accepted diagnostic guidelines and expect proto-transsexuals to live in cross-gender style for at least a year prior to hormone treatment. It would seem that following such exposés the Royal College of Psychiatrists is being pressured to establish national guidelines. 'It is over 30 years since the first transsexual operation was conducted . . . but the treatment still has a hole in the corner flavour' (p. 32).

So proto-transsexuals have the right to request medical help once past the age of 16, and there would seem to be no formally established principles as yet to protect those inevitably very few who, despite their inability to qualify under National Health Service guidelines, are able to obtain sufficient money to buy the cosmetic body of the sex they believe themselves to be. The complex issue of transsexual rights does not stop here however.

Transvestism and transsexualism as designer chic are of course, like anything else, ripe for commodification. For example, the *Sunday Correspondent* (26 Nov. 1989: 43) under the headline ' "I'm Josephine and I'm chasing a rainbow" . . . he said', carried a report on couture designers deliberately flirting with 'the dark imagery of decadence'. It continued: 'Designer decadence takes many forms from glam kitsch (Katherine Hamnett) to designer bondage (Jean Paul Gaultier). But its most powerful expression is transvestism.' The London club, Kinky Gerlinky, was described in terms of 'theatrical eyelashes', 'flashing smiles', 'everyone is beautiful (well, the boys anyway)'. And what did it feel like? 'fun, fun, fun', and unthreatening: 'The most aggressive thing that happens here is a high decibel shriek' (p. 43).

'Cruellest quirk' transsexualism may be, but it is one that is not only played on the individuals concerned. Entire bureaucracies have been thrown into confusion as gradually transsexuals have become more openly recognised and legally accommodated, inevitably so, for if the clinical response to the transsexual condition is a positive therapeutic and surgical one, then the transsexual subject and the law itself must presumably find an appropriate social space. As Riddell argues (1980: 12) 'Do we deny the limbless artificial limbs . . . ? Should one not wear glasses because one is born with defective vision, in order to preserve bodily integrity?' Here the transsexual's claim on rights begins with medical treatment, and once conceded, all else is to be fought for.

For example in Britain, a 1983 Court of Appeal decision on prostitution adjudged a male-to-female transsexual as male (see O'Donovan 1985: 70); in two social security cases in 1980, male-to-female transsexuals were treated as men for the purposes of retirement age (p. 72); a 1977 case involving a female-to-male transsexual's claim of unfair dismissal from employment reserved in law solely for men, decreed that as she had become 'female' she had no rights. These may now be considered early and isolated examples of what, as very recent evidence has shown, will inevitably be an ongoing and increasingly forceful pursuit of rights by transsexuals themselves.

The sexual, civil, political and social rights of transsexuals have been recently thrown into relief as a result of the case of 'one of Britain's best known beauties . . . former Bond girl' (*Sun* 28 Sept. 1990: 1) Caroline Cossey who in 1984 lodged a challenge before the European Commission on Human Rights in Strasbourg against British marriage law's acceptance of the irrevocability of her birth certificate status as a man. The European Court's ruling on this case can now be added to an earlier European Court ruling: van Oosterwijck v Belgium (see O'Donovan 1985: 68) and two earlier British rulings: Corbett v Corbett involving the earlier mentioned April Ashley, Corbett being her married name (1970), and E.A. White v British Sugar Corporation (p. 71) as providing the clearest statements on the legal status of transsexuals, although the results are by no means unambiguous.

Under British law a transsexual is permitted perhaps a surprising degree of bureaucratic freedom to obtain officially documented recognition of new and chosen gender/sex status through change of name either by Deed Poll or by Statutory Declaration,[22] and as recorded in passport,[23] car log book, driver's licence, income tax forms and national insurance card, but is not permitted to obtain comparable formal recognition of change of sex, i.e. as recorded on the birth certificate (Corbett *v* Corbett).

The Corbett *v* Corbett case was one of marriage nullification and a judgement had to be made on the contradictions in formal state responses to transsexual status. In this instance what was required was a resolution of implications of transsexualism for the legal status of marital partners, and the conclusion was that 'Marriage is a relationship which depends upon sex and not on gender' (O'Donovan 1985: 64–5). A marriage between a transsexual and a person of the transsexual's former sex was not, therefore, a marriage between chromosomal male and female for the law required one partner to be 'naturally capable of performing the essential role of a woman in marriage' (p. 69). This phrase poses several problems, what can the 'essential role of a woman in marriage' be? The explanation was ambiguous:

> sex is clearly an essential determinant of the relationship called marriage because it is and always has been recognised as the union of man and woman. It is the institution on which the family is built, and in which the capacity for natural heterosexual intercourse is an essential element.
> (Corbett *v* Corbett 83 at 105 quoted in O'Donovan 1985)

However, the 'essential role of woman in marriage' as O'Donovan (p. 67) points out, cannot be the biological reproduction of children as the inability to procreate doesn't nullify marriage nor does the unwillingness to have children, and thus if procreation is not the purpose of marriage but even so the law requires the parties to be of different biological categories, 'then it seems that marriage is not a private matter for the individuals concerned, but a public institution for heterosexual intercourse'.

This Corbett *v* Corbett ruling was formally incorporated into the 1973 Matrimonial Causes Act which specifically forbade transsexuals from marrying a person of the transsexual's original sex, stating that a marriage is null and void if the parties are not respectively male and female. The biological bases for determining male and female sex, however, as the Corbett *v* Corbett linguistic ambiguities imply, have varied by legal judgement, largely concentrating on sex as a biological fact (congruent chromosomal, gonadal and genital status) but also drifting in marriage law judgements towards sex as a form of heterosexual intercourse.

Perhaps strangely, birth certificates are not required on entry into marriage, but the marriage ceremony requires parties to swear that they know of no 'lawful hindrance' to their legal union and thus the Corbett *v* Corbett judgement formalised transsexual status as just such a hindrance, i.e. at the time the marriage was entered into. There are also recorded cases where both transsexual and partner have been charged with 'knowingly' making a false statement for the purpose of obtaining a marriage certificate under the Perjury Act (1911) Section 2, although this is again highly problematic for it is 'perhaps ... a defence to argue that you do not "knowingly" make a false statement, if you put yourself down as the sex you consider yourself to be' (Cohen *et al.* 1978: 76). The termination of legally valid marriages (i.e. between biological male and female) is now more or less in accordance with the law affecting transvestism, although it is interesting that, in a case reported in 1958, it was held that although one partner was a transsexual under medical supervision awaiting a sex change operation, this did not amount to cruelty against the other partner because there was no proven intent to be cruel (*Daily Telegraph* 14 Nov. 1958). However, it is now no longer necessary to prove 'intention' to be cruel.

Caroline Cossey's challenge to British law, although stimulated by her suffering from precisely this marriage law judgement, necessarily also challenged the British law's refusal to allow transsexuals to officially alter their birth certificated sex, for the former judgement depends upon the latter. So Ms Cossey claimed that the failure of the British authorities to re-issue her with a birth certificate as a female was a violation of her privacy to the extent that whenever birth certificate authentication was required she had to explain the apparent sex and gender discrepancy. Her legal advisers were also presumably encouraged to pursue her case because of the earlier van Oosterwijck *v* Belgium ruling by the European Court, which had judged that it was a violation of private life to require transsexuals to carry documents of identity manifestly incompatible with personal appearance so that the transsexual is treated as 'an ambiguous being, an "appearance", disregarding in particular the effects of a lawful medical treatment aimed at bringing the physical and the psychical sex into accord with each other' (van Oosterwijck *v*

Belgium 1980 at 584 quoted in O'Donovan 1985: 68–9). Also an important support for Ms Cossey's claim was that whilst illegal under British law, transsexual marriage is permitted in other countries, some of them members of the EC, e.g. in Italy, West Germany, Denmark, Sweden and the Netherlands, and that it is also legally permitted for birth certificates to be changed in various countries such as Belgium, Luxembourg, Spain, the United States and Turkey.

Cossey's legal challenge was based on her claim that her inability to marry legally and have her birth certificate altered broke the European Convention on Human Rights (Articles 12 and 8 respectively). The former Article gives men and women the right to marry and found a family, the latter guarantees the right to respect for private life. Both claims were initially accepted by the Commission (by 10 votes to 6), which, therefore, encouraged the pursuit of the case for the six years it took to reach the judgement stage. However, the verdict of the European Court of Human Rights on 27 September 1990, against which no appeal is permitted, was that the challenge to British law was unwarranted. The panel of sixteen men and two women voted by 10 votes to 8 against Ms Cossey's right to have her birth certificate changed claiming that she did not have all the biological characteristics of the opposite sex. The Court also voted by 14 votes to 4 against her right to marry a man because it would result in 'the general abandonment of the traditional concept of marriage' (*Independent* 20 April 1990: 3). As these voting figures suggest, the former decision was very close indeed and whilst the Court concluded that United Kingdom law represented a ' "fair balance" between community and individual interests' (p. 3) it also recommended that the law preventing changes to birth certificates should be kept under review.

The European Court's response to the transsexual legal challenge has in most instances been as ambiguous as the British, although it is possible to see in the Cossey case voting an implied tendency to retreat. Inevitably the legal dilemmma here is comparable to that already touched on *vis à vis* gay marriages, how to legally defend the family institution when more and more attempts are being made by those who do not meet, indeed who seemingly challenge, its traditional and basic requisites are seeking to obtain entry to it. Thus legal judgements on transsexual status reveal crucial changes in the social forms of marriage where procreation is clearly no longer as fundamental a defining criterion as set against it being a public declaration and formalisation of social, emotional and sexual union and commitment, which clearly need not be heterosexual.

So marital union and the presumed purpose of marriage is being constantly reassessed by legal judgements on the transsexual. For example, in 1986 the European Court turned down the claim by female-to-male transsexual Mark Rees that he should be allowed to marry a woman, on the grounds that Article 12 of the Human Rights charter applied only to 'traditional' marriage between people of opposite biological sexes; the implications here being as elusive as that of the Corbett *v* Corbett insistence on the 'essential role of a woman in marriage'. It *could* be taken to mean that the couple had to be able to procreate; however, European Commission support for the Cossey case has tended to withdraw from this seemingly strong, though obliquely stated, stance by arguing that 'Men or women who are unable to have children enjoy the right to marry just as other persons',[24] whilst reiterating the precedent set in 1986 with its Mark Rees judgement. In effect it has declared that sex-change operations are a misnomer, because it is impossible to change chromosomal sex. Transsexual treatment then, which is within the law, is legally deemed to do no more than alter the physical expression of those chromosomes.

On the other hand, the van Oosterwijck case elicited the more tantalising response from the European Court that Article 8 of the Human Rights Convention 'comprises *to a certain degree* the right to establish and to develop relationships with other human beings, especially in the emotional field for the development and fulfilment of one's own personality' (21 at 584 quoted in O'Donovan 1985: 69). As O'Donovan records, the majority opinion within this judgement also concluded that in its opinion 'domestic law cannot authorise states completely to deprive a person or category of person of the right to marry' (quoted in O'Donovan 1985: 69). Marriage law as implied via transsexual judgements suggests interesting complications to the established legal boundaries most elaborately recognised by the *Wolfenden Report* (1957) between public and private territories and discrepant boundaries of illegality and immorality. In an ideal, formal sense family life is private: protected but not interefered with by law. However, access to this private family life demands the public meeting of specific legally verifiable criteria, biological as well as social. Thus, as the form of the heterosexual family unit has gradually lost its earlier 'alliance' emphasis on procreativity, others (lesbians, gay men, transsexuals) have claimed comparable rights in terms of social, sexual and economic mutual commitment and respect. The law has thus become directly involved in adjudicating on such cases, and others which tarnish traditional imagery and practice such as incestuous child abuse, invading the family to protect it.

The transsexual challenge to the law does not only emerge in and around marriage law, for other goals include changed birth certificate status and further changes in employment law where, as the Corbett *v* Corbett decision demonstrated in accepting transsexuals' right to changed national insurance status, transsexual rights are already partially recognised.[25] For example, the National Insurance Commissioner, who hears appeals from local tribunals which in turn hear appeals from insurance officers, has decided that a female-to-male transsexual cannot claim retirement pension at 60, only at 65 (C/P 6/76). Also the legal department of the former Department of Health and Social Security have suggested that a woman 'married' to a female-to-male transsexual cannot qualify for a wife's retirement pension based on the transsexual's contributions (quoted in Cohen *et al.* 1978: 72–3).

Undergoing transsexual treatment whilst employed can lead to dismissal. Cohen *et al.* report on one case, but give no dates, of a male-to-female transsexual teacher losing her job on 'educational grounds'. Under Section 68 of the Education Act (1944) the Minister of Education can reverse such a decision, but in this instance refused to do so, and as the teacher did not wish to gain unnecessary publicity by taking the matter to the High Court to get the Ministerial order quashed (a process called Certiorari), the case was simply dropped.

The Edwynn A. White *v* British Sugar Corporation case concerned a female-to-male transsexual, believed by the employers to have been male when employed and who had been dismissed following the discovery, reported by other male employees, that he was a transsexual. A claim of sex discrimination was made under the 1975 Sex Discrimination Act,[26] but the Industrial Tribunal adopted a biological test 'the applicant, whatever her physiological make-up does not have male reproductive organs and there is no evidence that she could not bear children' (1977, IRLR 121 at 123, quoted in O'Donovan

1985: 71). The complainant had been employed as an electrician's mate which included Sunday work but the 1961 Factories Act prohibits women working in factories on a Sunday without an Exemption Order from the Health and Safety Executive, and so sex determination was necessary and the complainant having been defined as a woman, was, therefore, deemed not to have been unjustly dismissed.

The Sex Discrimination Act (1975) contains the notorious GOQ (general occupational qualification) clause which pertains where the job needs to be held by a man 'because of the laws regulating the employment of women'. But the Tribunal also judged that the complainant had 'deceived' his employers, and that the other male employees were justified in objecting to 'his' presence in locker rooms and toilets. There was another twist in this judgement for the management also argued that even if E.A. White was a man he could not argue that he was discriminated against *as a man* because everyone who worked there was a man and they had not been dismissed. As with similar work and employment discrimination against male gay and lesbian employees this judgement reiterated that the prejudices of others, though perhaps in themselves regrettable, can nevertheless provide justifiable grounds for management actions. Thus under legislation formally designed to reduce or even to remove sex discrimination in work, a transsexual complainant is judged against on the essentialist grounds that biological status is irrevocable.

Transsexuals theoretically run the same public order risks as do transvestites and Cohen *et al.* (1978) add that 'presumably since Corbett *v* Corbett a heterosexual male-to-female transsexual can, even after a sex change operation, be convicted of "gross indecency with another male". . . . Conversely a gay female-to-male transsexual cannot be convicted of this offence' (p. 76). Whatever else all of these judgements may mean in terms of the legal context within which transsexuals may go about their business, they demonstrate a considerable degree of ambiguity but also the gradual retreat of the law from absolute essentialist principles. The Cossey judgement was conservative but the voting in support of it was far short of a consensus, the transsexual citizen most certainly exists in terms of some official medical and legal criteria within a peculiar complex of material rights and freedoms.

8

EMBRYONIC SEXUAL CITIZENSHIP

Children as sexual objects and subjects

> Piano keys don't lock doors.
> Footballs don't have toes.
> And, of course, cabbage heads
> Don't have a mouth or a nose.
> And kids don't go with strangers
> They never go with strangers.
> (quoted in Amis 1986: 13)

Can children in modern societies be legitimately regarded in any sense as sexual citizens? Do they have sexual rights? Do they consume, or are they merely consumed, sexual commodities? One of the most dramatic and increasingly dramatised aspects of the sexualisation of modern societies has been the construction of children as grave objects of concern, sexual innocents vulnerable to all manner of seductions. This pedagogisation of childhood, initially as a distinct idyllic and asexual stage in pre-adult personal development (Krafft-Ebing 1891/1965), and later as a period of undirected latent sexual energy under siege from innumerable exploitative others, became broadly established with the bourgeois elevation of the domestic realm to one of privacy, serenity, health, comfort and cleanliness, within which this precarious innocence could, it was believed, be safely ensconced (Donzelot 1980).[1] No longer is the inner family world the moral superior to potential external corruptions, however, but is itself the home of sexual abuse.[2]

Embellished negatively through facts on abuse incidence (Baker and Duncan 1986; NSPCC 1989; Finkelhor 1984; la Fontaine 1988)[3] innumerable clinical studies of 'victims' (Gagnon 1965; Fitch 1962; Finkelhor 1979; Burgess *et al.* 1978; Rush

209

1980; Weiss *et al.* 1955, etc.)[4] and their abusers (Peters 1976; Groth *et al.* 1982, etc.)[5]; feminist and professional welfare critiques and manuals to instruct the abused and aid those employed to save them (e.g. Blagg *et al.* 1989; Blagg and Stubbs 1988; Bentovim *et al.* 1988; Butler-Sloss 1988; Creigton 1984; MacFarlane 1986; Miner and Blythe 1988);[6] and prominent media panics about external and most recently parental abuse (Summit 1986; Finkelhor 1980, etc.), childhood sexuality itself has largely been a taken-for-granted 'paradigm of the natural' (Jordonova 1989).[7] However, the escalation of abuse scripts; pleas on behalf of children's rights and liberation in general (Cohen 1980; Holt 1975; Farson 1974a, b), and more controversially on behalf of their capacity for self-determined sexual relations, has meant that it is no longer possible to confidently claim that children and childhood are unambiguously pre-social, a-social, pre- or a-sexual (Jordonova 1989).

Cross-cultural and historical evidence demonstrates clearly that the customary separation of childhood and sexuality and the protraction of childhood well beyond adolescence is socially constructed. For example, as the cross-cultural data collated by Ford and Beach (1952) demonstrated in even the most 'primitive' and restrictive societies, some children engage in secret sex play, and where cultural values are less restrictive children are found to freely engage in various sexual practices in some instances beginning coitus by the age of 6 to 8 and where there are few virgins amongst those over the age of 10–11.

Kinsey *et al.* (1953) reminded us that earlier civilisations were well aware of the sexual capacities of at least teenaged youth. The Greeks and Romans had virtually no interest in childhood as something to be praised or as something free of sexual being:

> Achilles' intrigue with Deidamia, by whom a son was born, had occurred some time before he was fifteen. Acis had just passed sixteen at the time of his love affair with Galatea. Chione was reputed to have had a thousand suitors when she reached the marriageable age of fourteen. . . . Helen was twelve years old when Paris carried her off from Sparta. . . . Daphnis was fifteen and Chloe was thirteen.
>
> (Kinsey *et al.* 1953: 13)

Historians have presented extensive evidence that protected innocent childhood is a relatively modern construct within Judeo-Christian culture (Ariès 1962; de Mause 1979; Hunt 1970; Money 1977; Currier 1981; Franklin 1986; Plumb 1972; Boas 1966),[8] and that sexuality once marked the end of childhood:

> . . . the impatience of Juliet's family and of Romeo to make a woman of her will continue to seem acceptable to modern audiences until a convincing twelve-year-old actress comes along. Juliet did not cause the *frisson* in Shakespeare's age that Lolita provokes in our own.
>
> (Elias 1967: 454)

Most famously Ariès has argued that within the sociability of the pre-capitalist 'machinery of alliance' children were integral participants in adult life: 'as soon as the child could live without the constant solicitude of his mother, his nanny or his cradle-rocker, he belonged to adult society' (Ariès 1962: 331), likewise 'by the age of ten girls were already little women' (p. 332), both with their corresponding rights and responsibilities. Others have disagreed, arguing that such definitions of the non-child were restricted to the nobility and that for the great majority 'a space did exist for the type of childhood which would be recognisable in the 20th Century' (Ennew 1986: 13).[9] Anthropological evidence too suggests that universally children are regarded as weak, helpless and in need of protection, cultural variations being limited to the exact setting of childhood's boundaries, its particular weaknesses and the appropriate forms that the required protection should take (Mead 1955).

What cannot be disputed, however, is that within the capitalist epoch concern over and surveillance of the sexual, emotional, social and physiological immaturity and lack of autonomy of those defined as within childhood, has been progressive. In eighteenth-century Britain there was little regulation by institutional authority, no compulsory registration of births or controls on age of marriage and little formal education. Childhood emerged as incorrupt but corruptible thus requiring the family and educational institutions to preserve its innocence and purity *en route* to adulthood. Through emergent concerns about the prostitution of young girls linked to the spread of VD (see Jordonova 1989), and over the dangers to boys of masturbation (see Macdonald 1967; Hare 1962; Neumann 1975; Taylor 1953), childhood and sexuality became separated, their boundaries rigorously policed, so that by the mid-nineteenth century the removal of children from the social world of production and the gradual extension of formal schooling established their status as uniquely familial creatures with distinct non-adult identities. By the beginning of the present century it was possible to observe that:

> . . . the child has in our own day entered into his rights. For the first time in the history of the race, he has become an entity in himself; his physical needs, his mental requirements, his moral training as considerations to be studied entirely apart from adults.[10]
>
> (Simeral 1916 quoted in Ennew 1986: 1)

These rights were not, however, the rights of independent beings but the imposed paternalist recognition of the legitimate needs of dependent young for affection, protection and security within that source of enrichment, love, companionship and solidarity, the patriarchal nuclear family. However, contradictory demands were thereby placed on the family; simultaneously required to protect its children's natural asexuality within a culture which defines sexuality as integral to the natural, and to nurture in children maturity and autonomy within a context of stifling emotional demands. Inevitably, therefore, the increased sexual demands of modern cultures have imposed pressures on the private family space, casting doubt on both the sexual innocence of the children and the ability of parents to provide the requisite protection for them, through crises over 'child sex abuse', paedophilia, age of sexual consent, sex education in schools, the medical provision of contraceptive advice to those under the age of consent without parental knowledge while the surveillance roles of external agencies continue to erode the family's boundaries.

It was mainly in the latter half of the nineteenth century that childhood as something to be protected and carefully nurtured was formally acknowledged in British law, although by 1840 it had been established that courts had the right, if it was deemed in the children's interests, to remove them from the custody of parents guilty of felonies,[11] Poor Law legislation further strengthened the courts' powers to monitor and curtail parental authority.[12] The Industrial Schools Amendment Act (1880)

212

enabled courts to remove children shown to be living in the society of depraved and disorderly persons and to place them in industrial schools[13] (see Mort 1987: 124–5) and 1889 saw the first Cruelty to Children Act (Martin 1989).

With specific regard to the sexual, purity campaigners thrived on panics over the reputed 'white-slave' trading of juvenile girls into prostitution, eventually succeeding in raising the age of consent from 13 to 16 through the 1885 Criminal Law Amendment Act. There was understandably greater reluctance to legally acknowledge the incestuous threat within the virtuous Victorian family, no doubt in part due to the perceived difficulties of effectively policing this private space, but considerable doubts were also expressed about the deleterious impact of widespread public discourses on such a sensitive matter (O'Donovan 1985: 102–4). Even so, by 1908 the legal parameters of an innocent childhood to be protected from inter- and intra-familial sexual exploitation had been established,[14] and despite the many subsequent tensions surrounding it this core myth persists, though not unscathed. Psychoanalytic stress on innate and extensive infantile sexuality, the commodification of the leisure and lifestyles of all age groups, and the persistent extension of analyses of citizenship rights and duties, has inevitably resulted in children and childhood becoming, in very particular ways, sexualised. By both design and default the elaboration of childhood as something to be protected, reclaimed, remembered, reinterpreted and eventually 'liberated', has been central to the obsessive pursuit of our innermost sexual selves, enabling us to become our own and ultimate confessors.

That children are either asexual or sexually latent, innocent but violable is formally acknowleged with considerable variations in the legal machineries and practices of all modern societies,[15] and at least alluded to in the major modern international rights declarations.[16] In British law childhood sexual innocence is demarcated negatively by various protective legal statutes, there being no single offence of child sexual abuse. The most important of these are laws governing age of consent,[17] incest,[18] rape,[19] indecent assault,[20] unlawful sexual intercourse,[21] unlawful homosexual acts[22] and pornographic representations,[23] etc.

Consent permeates all of these statutes, though ambiguously. British law[24] deems females to be insufficiently mature to give consent to heterosexual acts if under the age of 16. Those under

16 requiring *some*, those under 13 *severe*, protection. There is no age of consent legislation covering male heterosexual involvement although current English law states that boys under 14 are incapable of sexual intercourse.[25] However, any male over the age of 10 can be charged with 'gross indecency', and boys over the age of 14 can be charged with 'rape'.[26]

The male homosexual age of consent is 21, by which one might reasonably assume that the law's intention is to protect those under this age from those above it. Even so, males under 21 can be charged with 'gross indecency' and those between 14 and 21 even 'passively' involved with buggery according to Section 8 of the Sexual Offences Act (1967).[27] Whilst lesbian sexual behaviours are not illegal, any female over the age of 10 could be charged with an 'indecent assault' on a woman,[28] and as no female under 16 can give consent to an 'assault', any woman older than 16 having a lesbian relationship with someone younger than 16, can be charged with 'assault'. Charges may be brought against women as well as men under the Indecency With Children Act (1960) for being sexually involved with a male or female under the age of 14, although in practice such distinctions can be irrelevant, as 'care' rather than criminal proceedings are preferred for most under-aged offenders.

Current legal commentaries on childhood and sexuality thus not only aver that the two should be formally separated until such time as notional composite sexual maturity (Freeman 1977) can be safely assumed to have occurred, they also imply that this separation is *not* natural, children, especially boys, being regarded as capable of sexual behaviours, feelings and emotions at least from the age of 10 onwards. Comparisons with other modern legal systems demonstrate the same preoccupations but with widely varying solutions. In 1990, for example, the Netherlands parliament decided to permit heterosexual and homosexual intercourse between those over the age of 12;[29] two years earlier France set the age of male homosexual consent at 15;[30] and current English and Welsh law recognises that boys are capable of rape four years later, at 14 instead of 10, than in Scotland.

'Consent' legislation recognises male masculine sexuality as the main threat not only to children, but also to parental, in effect paternal, authority. The 1956 Sexual Offences Act, for example, established that apart from it being illegal for a man to have sexual intercourse with a female under the age of 16, it is also an

214

offence for a man to take a girl under the age of 18 out of the 'possession' of her parents in order to have sexual intercourse with her, where the taking is against the wishes of the parents – irrespective of the wishes of the female – these wishes of the parents being effectively those of the male household head.

Inevitably legal judgements on age of maturity, consent and parental and state responsibilities, no matter how painstakingly arrived at, can be little more than token gestures, bound to vary between and even within modern societies. However, Britain, as the passing of such statutes as Section 28 amply shows, is amongst the most conservative and intransigent even when repeatedly recommended to facilitate changes by legal and policy review bodies.[31]

The widely publicised decision by the Dutch Parliament in November 1990 to legalise heterosexual and homosexual intercourse for those over the age of 12 if without complaint from either participants or their parents, caused dismay in Britain.[32] The age of consent was not reduced to 12, but made sexual intercourse for those between the ages of 12 and 16 legal under effectively flexible consent conditions, granting the 12 to 16-year-olds and their parents the legal right to resort to the retained statutory consent age of 16 in cases of dispute over parental authority or perhaps the exploitation of children, at the same time freed but also possibly more vulnerable. Parental authority could attempt to over-rule 12 to 16-year-old's wishes, but not without providing a convincing case to a Council for the Protection of Children. Through this legislation, therefore, Dutch children of 12 to 16 years accrued conditional rights of consent to sexual behaviours, and parental authority was conditionally reduced. Simultaneously it was recognised that all under 16 remained open to, and thus had the right to protection from, exploitation and abuse, and to that end the period within which charges of abuse may now be brought has been extended from three months to twelve years. Overall the legal message here is that children over the age of 12 are sexual and potentially self-determining, and they remain weaker than adults, and should be protected accordingly, but not under the autonomous authority of parents.

In Holland defence of these reforms has been formulated on grounds which find little favour in Britain: effective early explicit sex education of children in the home 'where they tell them sex is not a bad thing' (*Independent* 18 Nov. 1990: 13) and in the school, as measured by fewer teenage pregnancies, recorded cases of abuse, and Dutch children who have sexual relations under the age of 14 at least.[33] In Britain difficulties with sex education in schools are manifest not merely through such spectacular measures as Section 28, but also through the ongoing and everyday resistance by some parents and teachers alike. Mort (1987: 155–63) provides a fascinating account of one such battle in Dronfield, Derbyshire in 1913 where parental opposition to one teacher's attempts at basic instruction in matters sexual was directed against the dissemination of 'disgusting and abominable information' undermining the sacredness and authority of the home. Nearly eighty years later, in October 1990, the publication in Britain of a new manual for the teaching of sexual information to children aged 5 to 11, covering such issues as contraception, masturbation, homosexuality and the transmission of AIDS was attacked by the head of the Professional Association of Teachers as 'a corrupting influence . . . a form of indoctrination' (*The Times* 31 Oct. 1990). The authors' defence was akin to the causalist justifications so persuasive in Holland; 'lower rates of abortion and sexually transmitted diseases among the young in those countries where sex education is *properly* taught'.[34] Opponents, however, despite their occasional lapse into causalist language, remained entrenched in their Dronfield moralist stance:

> They have had 20 years of this kind of sex education in secondary schools, and we have the highest rate of promiscuity in our history. Now the same perversity is being introduced to little children. God help us if they don't stop now.
>
> (Gillick quoted in *The Times* 31 Oct. 1990)

Two versions of protection, one of sexual beings from harm because of their immaturity and ignorance, the other of the non-sexual from the 'perversity' of sexual indoctrination; two versions of the engrossing contemporary conjunction of childhood and sexuality; two versions of competing claims on the rights of children and parents and two of the state's bounden duty. At the beginning of this chapter questions were asked about the sexual status of children, about whether sexual discourses were transforming them in ways consistent with adult developments in sexual citizenship. Clearly the dynamics of current developments are pointing in that direction but in order to examine their particular parameters it is necessary first to consider how children are scripted into sexuality.

The major discursive channels through which the young learn about sexuality are: through infancy (i.e. prior to language) onwards through childhood and adolescence,[35] the exploration and experience of somatic sensations and the attachment of meanings to them; indirect learning of sexual knowledge within general gender socialisation; specific largely negative and non-labelling parental instruction; sex education in schools largely of a technical character; informal interactions with peers; gossip, innuendo, sex play and jokes; and media instruction.

On the bedrock of innate 'polymorphous perversity' and the measured capacity for specific (i.e. orgasmic) sexual responses within the first four months of life the foundations of sexual knowledge are laid (Kinsey et al. 1948). In infancy, although the child does not have an appropriate language to describe touch, pleasure, discomfort, hurt, etc., experience of such sensations provides a structuring context for the acquisition of all subsequent sexual knowledge. Children may not be fixated on particular sensations in the longer term but, following Freud's (1905: 125–69) scripting ('so far as I know not a single author has [hitherto] clearly recognised the regular existence of a sexual instinct during childhood' (p. 128)), there is the Mandarin and widespread common-sense expectation that at least oral, anal and genital fixations will be experienced during this psycho-sexual development. In the more general sense of somatic pleasures Martinson (1976: 252) has noted, 'it seems safe to assert that the human child prior to puberty is capable of enjoying the same range of physiological activities as the adult', and yet of course we know little of the child's subjective scripting of this enjoyment. However, from the observer's point of view the child certainly exhibits sexual potential or, as Simon and Gagnon (1969: 10) prefer, 'potentiation' for 'this groundwork for the potential complexity of the sexual' forged not only from this generalised experience of somatic sensations but also from the experience of general gender modelling.

Gagnon (1967: 26) notes that 'the fact that the parents are clear in their belief that the infant is either male or female has permanent consequences for the child', including those of a specifically sexual kind, by encouraging the acquisition of appropriate general gender traits through mimicry of adult styles with implicit sexual meanings. Small girls in particular are encouraged to be coyly seductive through early play with make-up and jewellery, several studies describing how many girls appear to actively solicit and enjoy the sexual attentions of adults (Mohr *et al.* 1964). Also mother/father to son/daughter inter-actions such as cuddling, washing and bathing, or punishment practices are likely to be negotiated by the adults to minimise sexual meanings, tactics which even so convey sexual signs through avoidance norms and taboos (Wollen 1979). That parents are now highly sensitised to the possible sexual implications of close parent/child contacts is amply demonstrated by the following attempt by the National Society for the Prevention of Cruelty to Children to allay fears. Parents are informed that it is perfectly natural for them to:

cuddle, hug, kiss and stroke children when showing love and affection. All these activities are normal and acceptable and ... to deny a child love and affection constitutes neglect. Children can enjoy physical play but if your child feels uncomfortable it is time to stop. It is not normal for any adult to become sexually excited or aroused by their own children.

(NSPCC quoted in Search 1988: 7)

Perhaps such instructions are not so reassuring after all given the self-surveillance advocated. Parent/child interactions which elaborate generalised gender traits such as aggression and genitality in boys, and non-genital lability in girls provide crucial gender, and thus sexually, differentiated forms of 'potentiation'.

Thus the child early in life does not develop a fully articulated sexual structure, but rather there are limits and parameters set, within and around which the growing child will operate. Thus the experiences of the child with nurturance and ... toilet training define to a greater or lesser degree his (and her) capacities to deal in the future with situations which are homologous or analogous to the early experience.

(Gagnon 1967: 27)

Parental instruction of children into the specifically sexual is marked by a number of avoidance strategies which distract

218

attention and withhold appropriate language and knowledge. Despite recommendations by some contemporary experts that children should receive from parents positive and explicit encouragement in their sexual learning (Yates 1978), parental strategies are generally of a negative kind: condemning behaviours as sexual but without explanations as to why; mis-labelling behaviours to remove possible sexual connotations; and, most ambiguously, sanctioning behaviours deemed to be sexual by parents but without accompanying explanations given to children as to why. Through these parental strategies those under instruction are left with fragmentary understandings, only uncertainly and incoherently recognised as sexual. Sexuality is thus constructed not through knowledge but through feelings of shame and guilt in a private world, which gives full rein to the 'fantasy proneness of children [and] the tendency for [their] . . . unsatisfied curiosity . . . to lead them [regardless] directly into sexual play' (Gagnon 1967: 33). To deny children sexuality, in this way is possibly to enable some adults who recognise this to abuse it (Blagg *et al.* 1989: 7).

To the extent that it is now possible for the very young to be taught technical knowledge about the body and its functions through the plethora of picture books and comic style guides (e.g. Rayner 1978; Stones 1989; Berenstein and Berenstein 1987), it is unlikely that even the most unwilling and bashful of parents can entirely avoid at least being passively tolerant of such basic sex instruction, but precisely how such information is managed in the context of somatic learning, isolated self-interaction (Plummer 1975: 58–9), general gender instruction and peer group relations, is difficult to assess, especially as shame, guilt and ignorance remain important enforcers of sexual innocence and purity – especially guilt perhaps for as Simon and Gagnon (1969) have observed:

> Although we talk a lot about sexuality, as though trying to exorcise the demon of shame, learning about sex in our culture is in large part learning about guilt: learning how to manage sexuality commonly involves learning how to manage guilt.
>
> (Simon and Gagnon 1969: 11)

Parents find it all too easy, perhaps, to underestimate the sexual capabilities of children, interpreting their effective concealment of the child's sexual feelings and interests as latency (Donaldson 1978).[36] However, perhaps it is the parents who are unsettled by their children's honesty which leads them to so determinedly obliterate it through misinformation. Germaine Greer (1991: 18) asks 'Why do we lie so to children? Why do we foist upon them nonsense about Santa Claus and Easter Bunnies and Tooth Fairies if not in some way to revenge ourselves for their blazing candour.'

Unambiguous negative training is common to all aspects of infant socialisation, but whereas in most, subsequent learning qualifies and expands knowledge through the 'naming' of ever more specific and explicit parts, sexual knowledge normally receives little such help. During the 1980s, however, concern over sexual 'abuse' and other consequences of childhood sexual ignorance such as pregnancies, VD and AIDS, has produced a forceful lobby demanding that children should be made more sexually aware (Jackson 1982). Inevitably such demands reflect upon highly contentious issues such as the precise form and content of such knowledge, how to impart it whilst retaining a respect for the child's innate innocence, and whether the reponsibility to teach it should be the parents' or the state's.

Article 2 Protocol 1 to the European Convention on Human Rights requires societies to respect the right of parents to ensure that the education of their children conforms to their own religious and philosophical convictions. As has been noted the classic objection to sex education in schools is that it is a corrupting influence, encouraging high levels of promiscuity. Following a ruling by the European Court in 1976 (Kjeldsen, Busk Madsen and Pedersen 1976 discussed by Bainham 1988), the parameters of sex education in schools were established. The Court decided that the setting and planning of the curriculum is within the competence of state authorities but that it was incumbent on them to 'take care that the ... knowledge included ... was conveyed in an objective, critical and pluralistic manner. It was not open to states to pursue a policy of indoctrination' (p. 182). Thus as long as it can be shown that sex education in schools presents knowledge more correctly, precisely, objectively and scientifically than informal or other sources, it is justified. Since September 1967 in England and Wales, sex education in schools has been under the collective consideration of Local Education Authorities, governing bodies and head teachers. The Education

(No 2) Act (1986) directed that sex education must be given 'in such a manner as to encourage those pupils to have regard to moral considerations and the value of family life' (Section 46), whilst other directives require that sex education be 'appropriate and responsible' (Children's Legal Centre 1987: 42.4), 'complementary and supportive' to the primary responsibility of parents for educating children in sexual matters.[37] Regard for 'the considerations of family life' has effectively meant the avoidance of such issues as homosexuality ('teaching which advocates homosexual behaviour, which presents it as a "norm", or which encourages homosexual experimentation by pupils' is strictly forbidden (DES 11/1987: para 22)) and reluctance to go beyond the narrow biological dimensions, thereby serving to maintain the school as a non-sexual environment, as parental non-labelling does likewise for the family home. Furthermore, and in direct reference to the influential Gillick case (1986) teachers are advised that

> the general rule must be that giving an individual pupil advice on such matters without parental knowledge or consent would be an inappropriate exercise of a teacher's professional responsibilities, and could, depending on the circumstances, amount to a criminal offence.
> (DES 11/1987: para 26)

The results are, where measured, predictably unsatisfactory as the urgent need to give information to children about AIDS has shown all too clearly. A late 1990 survey of sex education policy and teaching in schools in the South East Thames Health Authority region found that only a third of teachers had specific training to prepare them for teaching about AIDS/HIV, that a fifth had no resources (videos, etc.) with which to teach, most did not share the 'restraint and celibacy' line emphasised by the DES, but nor were they willing, perhaps because of the strictures referred to above, to discuss safer sex techniques. Most damagingly of all, one-fifth of the schools within this survey had no sex education policy at all (AVERT 1990).

It is possible within these circumstances to argue that strategies of non- and negative labelling have been extended to public agencies. Strictly speaking this is not true in that there has been a steady encroachment within schools of technical knowledge on the body and reproduction, but all else does appear to

221

be dealt with through euphemism and avoidance. This is especially so with dire child sex-abuse warnings such as 'Do not talk to strangers', 'Never get into a car or go off with a strange man', which are broadcast throughout the child's social worlds, at home, on television, in school, etc., and where it will also be learned that the sanctity and moral superiority of the family is itself in doubt 'Have you been bathed in a way that made you feel uneasy? . . . cuddled or kissed in a way that left you feeling uncomfortable? . . . [have] . . . other less obvious things . . . been done or said to you?' (Bain and Sanders 1990: 13). Sexual learning within the family remains largely governed by non- and negative labelling but it is questionable whether heightened dramatisations of abuse in the public domain have employed strategies less negative.

The bulk of any children's sexual socialisation, given these circumstances, will be most effectively and meaningfully accomplished, albeit haphazardly, within the clandestine and subversive context of play, games, jokes, innuendo and gossip (Babuscio 1976; Lees 1986; etc.). 'The children's world resembles a secret society keeping information from parents' (Gagnon 1967: 36); and all too accurately preparing children for the adult world of personal, private and pruriently fascinating sexualities. In addition to learning sexual scripts through the negotiation of guilt and shame, children have to learn secrecy and guile, to learn that the sexual is private almost before discovering what it is (Lees 1986; McRobbie 1981). The child's 'blazing candour' may well inadvertently pass sexual information to parents, but given normal avoidance strategies it is unlikely that parents will respond. The child's secret sexual world is of course very difficult to research, except within atypical institutional contexts such as in communes (Johnston and Deisher 1973: Rothchild and Wolf 1976), or in remand schools, hospitals, etc., as was the case with Mitchell's (1966) study of the sexual 'contraculture'[38] of a group of boys between the ages of 5 and 11 in an American psychiatric hospital. Adults care about such things as modesty, respect for elders and other 'proprieties' against which children develop corresponding 'improprieties' through language and actions (Elkin and Handel 1978). It would, therefore, be a mistake to see Mitchell's study as furnishing evidence in support of the oft heard clinical claim that only deviant, maladjusted or delinquent children are openly sexual (Bowlby 1972: 141), although the closed all-male setting clearly encouraged certain distortions. Mitchell (1966: 71) found an intense preoccupation with genitalia, bodies and bodily functions, managed through a range of general gender references. Phallic-shaped guns, swords and other toys were used as symbolic penises variously called Big Bertha, 'secret weapon', 'spear' or 'mickey' usually to the accompaniment of self-boasting about having the 'largest spear' or 'biggest gun' or to claims that they were 'plugging the nurse' (p. 72). The boys occasionally attempted anal intercourse with each other in the showers, in line for meals they would rub up against each other, frequently they would joke about fellatio and repeatedly drew images of the penis. Fights invariably led to assaults on the genitals, urination and defecation. These boys, freed temporarily from the normal constraints of 'play innocent' for the grown-ups, demonstrated the extent to which sexual behaviour can be integral to the experience of play.

Given that children's sexuality is secret, hidden and normally unspoken to adults, there is a clear potential for scripting disjuncture between their respective understandings as to what might or might not be sexual. Some adults may well impose meanings to justify cross-generational sexual acts and relationships, others to uncover 'abuse' and to train the child in abuse scripts. Reference has already been made to basic texts which provide children with crash courses in 'abuse' (Bain and Sanders 1990; Nelson 1988). These texts challenge conventional scripting by claiming that childhood innocence cannot be effectively protected through the constraints of ignorance and shame, which merely serve to conceal and facilitate abuse. Rather, the highest priority is to reveal abuse, through detailed explication to enable victims to transcend it.

> We have learned . . . that being locked in isolation and kept in ignorance breeds guilt, fear and helplessness. So we feel that it is important that you have knowledge that will give you some control over the effects of your experiences.
> (Bain and Sanders 1990: 10)

In this particular text sexual abuse is not clearly defined however, and the few references to being touched on the breasts and genitals and being made to have oral sex appear shocking intrusions. Rather veiled references dominate: to 'touching and using a child in a sexual way' (p. 12), (distinguished from 'good touches' (p. 13)) by adults who can 'trap, lure, force or bribe' (p. 13) children into sexual activity. 'Abuse' is wrong, even though the child cannot know exactly why or indeed what *it* is because it 'hurts the *victim*', causing 'confusion, fear, anger, self-blame and serious problems later in life' (p. 14).[39] Everyone, we are told, should decide for themselves what they do with their own bodies, but not children for they cannot understand or say 'no' to adults. Some sex play is okay however, such as the kisses and cuddles 'which express affection, reassurance and caring' (pp. 13–14).

Such inventories of generalised feelings: 'confusion, fear, guilt, shame, anger, feeling different, worthlessness, sadness and depression' (p. 54), memories, acts and sensations may explicitly construct the child who can say 'no', but they do much else besides. In instructing what they should say 'no' to, they also instruct, admittedly in coded terms, in what not to say 'no' to, thereby suggesting that under certain circumstances it might be interesting to say 'yes' to a fascinating list of possible adventures. They also suffuse the child's entire world of feelings with sexual implications once the 'victim' has learned to recognise them and to administer self-cleansing therapies; e.g. 'target your anger, punch cushions, hit the bed with your tennis racquet, make models of the abuser in clay, stick pins in them, squash them, break them into little pieces' (pp. 71–3). But most importantly it is demanded that there is public exculpation too: 'Child sex abuse thrives on silence' (p. 46), so *tell*: 'It is your right to tell' (p. 47).

Children's sexual innocence may well be protected by such methods, but their sexuality discursively rockets into a stratosphere of individual mental, physical and emotional angst, especially as the threat of abuse is emphatically not restricted to strangers external to the protective family. These texts assert the rights of professionals to intervene, and to question the parents' monopoly of control of child care under the primary aim of heightened welfare of children. The primary right of the modern child is welfare protection from extra-familial sources when parents fall down on their duties.

These pro-interventionist discourses have met with some stern resistance. Most notably in Britain Victoria Gillick, 'one of the three populist heroines of the right' (Campbell 1987a: 4) campaigned effectively, though ultimately without success, against the medical provision of contraceptive advice to girls' under 16 years of age without parental consent, by laying charges against the Department of Health and Social Security for sanctioning such provision.[40] Variously described as having 'called up the social purity movement of the 19th century and thus appeared to connect with a pro-woman culture of sexual dissent' (p. 182) and as representative of the populist wing of the parental autonomy ideology championed by several academic works (e.g. Goldstein *et al.* 1987), Gillick pursued the conflict of interests between the 'natural rights' of, especially female, parents and experts. Mrs Gillick lost her initial case that the provision of medical advice on contraception to a daughter of hers under 16 infringed her parental rights, but won in the Court of Appeal, only to lose the House of Lords judgement by a majority of three to two. It is these majority opinions which established the first formal parameters of parental powers.

The Court of Appeal had decided unanimously that parents possessed prima facie, the right and duty to control completely their children (Gillick *v* Norfolk and Wisbech Health Authority and DHSS AC 112, 1986). The Law Lords, however, ruled somewhat differently, rejecting absolute parental authority over children, arguing that parental rights could only be conditional on that authority being used to the benefit of the child. It must, therefore, yield to the child's right when s(he) reaches 'a sufficient understanding and intelligence' (Campbell 1987a: 186) to make up his or her own mind. So while it was recognised that parents did have the right to authorise medical treatment, it was not a sovereign right but one qualified by what amounted to the legal recognition that, under the age of consent, children may still be accounted to reliably and maturely know their own minds. In this sense the Gillick ruling enshrines the kind of increasingly flexible approach to childhood sexuality that we have already encountered in the instance of the Dutch review of the age of consent. The Gillick ruling was possibly the most significant link thus far in the chain of parental custody rights as 'dwindling rights' (Hewer *v* Bryant 1970 1QB357: 369); of children's rights to independence from parental authority and possibly self-determination, and of the necessarily enlarged role for a monitoring state. This issue will be returned to at the end of this chapter.

Children's sexual innocence is also negotiated through a

225

further and distinctly modern source of sexual socialisation; media instruction from computer games, comics, magazines, videos, cinema and of course television. There is certainly no space to adequately indicate the breadth and depth of such scripts but, just as adults have become infused with sexual commodified meanings, so too children have been subjected to what has been called 'media child abuse' (Macmillan 1989: 7). Wertham's (1953) study, *Seduction of the Innocent*, written forty years ago, emphasised the sexual fetishism of comic books with the *de rigueur* admixture of cruelty by men against women. Wertham's observations were broad and, with hindsight, broadly familiar from the homo-eroticism of the 'dynamic duo' Batman and Robin to a Tom Mix cowboy comic with

> no less than sixteen consecutive pictures of a girl tied up with ropes, her hands of course tied behind her back! She is shown in all kinds of poses, each more sexually suggestive than the other, and her facial expression shows that she seems to enjoy this treatment.
>
> (Wertham 1953: 185)

Wertham deplored the early commercialisation of children and childhood in tones redolent of Gummer (1971); 'Advertisements in comic books have caused decent boys and girls many tears' and 'hypochondriasis' (p. 197)[41] through their stress on the buying of solutions for various physical, physiological, psychological and sexual 'problems' related to height, weight, muscular strength, complexion, hair, etc. All can be solved through the purchase of therapies, medicines and cosmetic accoutrements. Even when comics and magazines say nothing explicit about sex, they still instruct negatively. From *Roy of the Rovers*, *The Eagle Picture Library*, *The War Picture Library* through to *Computer Games Week* boys' literature, aggressiveness, competitiveness and commodification are addressed through the virtual absence of female referents. Studies of comparable materials for girls have shown in some abundance the extent to which, forty years on, Wertham's acknowledgement of what we might now call 'bio-power' discourses, many if not most commercial, have permeated feminine childhood sexuality (McRobbie 1991) to the possibly ultimate extent of marketing and producing what have recently been described as the dread threat of 'teenage plastic mutants':

Listen to teenage America: this is the voice of the bubblegum generation, and they're talking of breast implants, tummy tucks and lip injections. Here is a 14 year old from Beverley Hills: 'Boys go for physical appearance, so I might as well look best to get the guys I want'. . . . An astonishing number of American teenagers are coming of age by undergoing cosmetic surgery.

(*Sunday Correspondent* 29 Oct. 1990: 34)

In the modern age physical defects which cause mental distress and depression can be simply snipped and tucked away through 'aesthetic surgery', ear-pinning, chin augmentation, breast implants, hair replacement, dermabrasion, rhinoplasty ('Match the nose to the doctor is a frequently played game on Rodeo Drive and at the Polo Lounge . . . [as] a matter of status' (p. 34)), and whilst in Britain parental consent is required for the under 16s to have cosmetic therapy, their money may not be, for serious psychological traumas arising from physical defects are now treatable under the National Health Service (*The Times* 25 Oct. 1990).[42]

Children, despite being drawn so comprehensively into the wider implications of 'bio-power' are still not meant to be sexual in the narrow sense. They are expected to be health, appearance and clothes conscious and to vicariously buy them through their parents, but sexual precocity is still frowned upon, so that when media representations have crossed this very finely drawn line they are dealt with swiftly, especially those televised into the home. *Minipops* was one such: appearing in 1983 on Channel 4 it showed children as young as 4 miming to adult pop records whilst mimicking the original performer's dress, behaviour and actions, ('here were all the attributes paedophiles . . . often look for in children – crisp white shorts, bare knees, skimpy skirts, tight trousers' (Moody 1983: 4)). But as with the penetration of women's magazines by more sophisticated codes of sexual meanings, so too 'media child abuse' has become similarly displaced, and in both instances the displacement and codes are firmly attached to and facilitated by the sale and purchase of commodities. Childhood innocence has in major part now become the pursuit of happiness realised through parental provision of consumer artefacts commensurate with their status and lifestyle (Ennew 1986). These artefacts are marketed as crucial affirmations of parental love and childhood happiness, and in the displaying of them the children themselves take on commodified and 'proto-sexual' forms, 'innocent' embodiments of parental love and expenditure.

Millett (1981: 80) has noted that 'Children have virtually no rights guaranteed by law in our society and besides, they have no money which, in a money economy, is one of the most important sources of their oppression'. Whilst rightly recognising this inextricable relationship between consumption and citizenship, she fails to realise that inevitably, therefore, children will acquire both rights and access to the market, albeit under particular conditions of qualified maturity, dependence and protection. Increased attention is being given to children's rights, childhood is now big business and tied to both is the reconstruction of a compatible sexual 'innocence'.

Whenever childhood sexuality is directly addressed or championed in ways which short circuit such codes, whether by advocates of paedophilia or by child liberationists the response has been both dramatic and hostile.

Paedophilia and korephilia,[43] respectively adult male and female 'sexual love directed towards children . . . in pre-puberty and early adolescence' (PIE 1978), have been openly championed by various organisations in the recent past such as NAMBLA (North American Man/Boy Love Association), the René Guyon Society, the Boston-Boise Committee (see Mitzel 1980) and, in Britain, by PIE (Paedophile Information Exchange) and on occasion by others on the radical left. PIE, following its inception in October 1974, eventually fell victim to several major waves of sex abuse panics ten years later, but not before its alternative ideology on childhood sexuality had received considerable publicity.[44]

PIE was overtly concerned to justify paedophile relationships through the liberation of 'the *positive* [sexual] potential that resides in everyone' (O'Carroll 1980: 248) including children. Contemporary childhood innocence, it argued, is a myth constructed out of erroneous essentialist reasoning and repressive practice in the denial of inalienable rights. In past cultures 'quite young children coped with responsibilities now regarded as the province of adults, and in some cultures they still do' (p. 248). Childhood 'chastity is an invention of puritans . . . truly innocent children simply enjoy sex and are interested in it' (p. 7).[45]

Pre-pubertal children may be incapable of reproductive sexuality but innately they have the capacity for sexual, genital pleasure. So too the paedophile's sexuality is 'natural, harmless and an integral part of their personality' (PIE 1978: 5), their 'furtiveness, guilt and repression, forced on them by society' (O'Carroll 1980: 47).

The fundamental paradox here is clear for it crops up in other contemporary sexual political manifestos, such as with the radical/cultural feminist stance on pornography (Dworkin 1981; Griffin 1981; etc.) Socio-cultural forces construct 'the problem', in this instance the innocence of children and the deviant paedophile, thereby corrupting the natural essence, proponents claiming extra-social knowledge that this is so.

The main thrust for PIE was, therefore, to normalise both deviations. For example, much is made of the ways in which adult women are permitted to realise their sexual interest in children because modern cultures expect that 'a woman, close to a child's body does this by right of law and nature' (Sebbar 1981).

> women can express their sexual feelings towards children in a far less obvious way than men. Mothers can be extremely sensual with their children . . . without attracting untoward attention, as indeed can women in such professions as social work, child nursing and teaching.
>
> (PIE 1978: 4)

Nor are paedophiles' sexual interests restricted to children, they are sometimes married and parents. Indeed it is claimed some parents who do not define themselves as paedophile have sexual feelings for their own children. Paedophiles are not 'mentally ill' but are labelled so because they are political dissidents opposed to the state and, as with homosexuals before them, it is claimed that the future will contain the gaining of a comparable degree of legality and acceptance. Nor is there a paedophile clinical type of personality, physiognomy or physique, which medical treatments can cure, rather the latter merely serve to incapacitate (Sebbar 1981: 2).

Normalisation of the paedophile extends to the bases of their attraction to children which is due to

> the same range of factors that dete mine other people's sexual and emotional preferences. For some it is mostly a

physical or aesthetic matter (the charm of smallness and lightness), for some it may be psychological (identification, nostalgia, the need to protect), while for some it could have moral significance (a love of directness, innocence, emotional honesty . . . qualities adults tend to lose). For most, probably a mixture of these things. There are as many answers as there are paedophiles.

(PIE 1978: 3)

Being innately loving, paedophiles rarely 'assault' children, who are mostly the willing partners of adults 'gentle, fond of children and benevolent' (Virkunnen 1975: 179). 'Indecent assault' is a misnomer for 'tender . . . mutually satisfying acts' (PIE 1978: 3). Throughout, academic support is garnered to demonstrate that from infancy children sexually enjoy 'physical exhilaration'[46] and are capable of initiating sexual encounters with adults. Within this discourse it is, therefore, accepted that paedophile relationships surprise with their 'naturalness and innocence' (p. 3) expressed through 'fondling, kissing and mutual masturbation' (p. 4). This discursive tack, therefore, sexualises the child and de-sexualises the interested adult (Howells 1977).

Dismissed as 'folklore' are fears about the physical damage caused by such relationships. The *Wolfenden Report* (1957) is quoted to reassure that 'cases in which physical injury result from the act of buggery are very rare' (PIE 1978: 4) to which are added other reassurances, for example, 'in vaginal intercourse with girls, as with women, there is the possibility that the hymen will rupture, but *real* damage to the vagina is extremely uncommon' (p. 4). Psychological damage however, if it occurs, arises from the reactions of sanctioning others rather than the relationships themselves.

> The emotional placidity of most of the children would seem to indicate that they derived some fundamental satisfaction from the relationship. The children rarely acted as injured parties and often did not show any evidence of guilt, anxiety or shame. Any emotional disturbance they presented could be attributed to external restraint rather than internal guilt.
> (Bender and Blau 1937: 516)

It is 'abuse scripting' and the involvement of 'experts', police,

230

courts and press, which leads to trauma, transforming the natural, pleasurable and loving into the confusing, frightening and guilt-laden, encouraging feelings of hatred and retribution, a situation which early enlightened sex education would help to avoid (Finkelhor 1986).[47]

> Children can be seductive towards adults, can participate fully in and enjoy sexual acts with them, and can suffer greatly when the acts are discovered and there is a family scene followed by police investigation and court proceedings.
>
> (Ingram 1977: 512)

Within this alternative critique the issue of the child's ability to 'consent' is central. Conventional criticisms of the paedophile position stress that, even if children are innately sexual and paedophiles innately benign, the power imbalance can only mean that there is 'an abuse of the very thing that makes a child a child; its unquestioning trust in the benevolence of the world around it' (de Courcy in *Evening Standard* 19 Aug. 1983: 14). If children are socialised to trust, respect and obey adults, social, moral and sexual power imbalances are inherent, it being adults' responsibility not to abuse such power (Wilson 1983). If childhood innocence and paedophile sexual interest in children's innocence, trust, respect and willingness to obey regardless of the child's own wishes are social constructs, then surely paedophilia is scripted to exploit this power imbalance? Not so, PIE responds, because the age of 'consent' is irrelevant to the proven sexual needs and awareness of children,[48] and paedophiles are mostly responsible people.

> One could study a child's intellectual development, his growing awareness of moral concepts, in an attempt to pinpoint some age, or stage, at which he is capable of considering moral questions. But this would assume that the child needs to make some difficult decision. If we believe that sexual activity is morally neutral, neither 'right' nor 'wrong', there is no need for the child (or anyone else) to worry over complicated questions. All that matters is whether the act is pleasurable. Some children will withold consent because they have learned their parents' code. No one ever asks whether they understand that.
>
> (PIE 1978: 7)

Instead of informed 'consent' we should rather assess 'willingness', protected by children being taught that there are reliable ways out of such situations and that it is proper to say 'no' sometimes to adults, and by an improved civil rather than criminal legal machinery in which parents would be able to intervene to make claims on behalf of their children (O'Carroll 1980).

The normalisation intent of such tracts entails a lack of regard for scripted gender differences, adults and children being treated as unitary categories (*Minor Problems* 15 April 1983: 4). However, girls clearly grow up with very different understandings of freedom and pleasure to those of boys. It is males who sexually assault, beat up and rape, women and children who demur. Masculine desire is scripted to overcome equivocation and hesitation by persuasion, moral as well as, within somewhat ambivalent bounds, physical. Even if one concedes that young boys can demonstrate clearly their wishes, young girls are in a weaker position to do so and in no position to rebel (Jackson 1984; Walkerdine 1991).[49]

> brought up from birth to please men and to repress sexual desire until marriage [they] are not going to find it easy to say no to a cajoling adult. . . . To vocalise no is to both admit to the possibility of forbidden sexual feelings *and* to displease a powerful adult.
>
> (Roberts 1980: 48)

PIE's typical riposte was to claim that such objections are fraught with hypocritical double-thinking. Children don't choose school but are still made to go. It is normal for adults to dominate children as parents, teachers, social workers, etc. (O'Carroll 1980). Even babies have ways of expressing their wishes, the only language needed to do so being 'yes', 'no', 'nice' and 'nasty', but it is up to the adult to identify in the child's demeanour whether 'consent' is being given. Pestering, force, assault, child prostitution and commercialised pornography should all be more strictly penalised, especially the first two which are mainly perpetrated in the repressive family where 'parental control is hard for a child to evade or challenge . . . [truly] loving parents . . . allow their children room to learn from new experiences and so be more independent' (PIE 1978: 8).

Set alongside recent legal changes such as those in Holland commented upon earlier, the PIE manifesto seems, *pace* its proselytising and provocative goals and language, not dissimilar, indeed, in many ways indicative of many subsequent develop- ments and tensions around childhood: the 'freeing' of children from 'consent' laws; the questioning of parental autonomy and reified notions of family; the requirement for increased state intervention and the need to gradually incorporate children into rights machinery.

In the 1970s, however, PIE and the many child abuse scandals it was invariably associated with served to mobilise what later would be recognised as New Right conservatism. The abuse of childhood sexual innocence has been a permanent feature of the 1980s but within this period there has been a subtle gear change in its depiction and treatment. Until roughly the demise of PIE in 1984, childhood sexuality was mainly addressed in utopian essentialist terms, threatened by the legacy of the permissive 1960s which had weakened parental authority through the increased interventions of the 'enemy within', professionals of a morally moribund state. Whether screamed through the panicked headlines of the tabloids or more calmly considered through the musings of New Right ideologues such as Scruton (1983), the message was a crude reification of the sanctity of traditional family life threatened by a range of forces without, symbolised most perfectly by PIE.[50]

By the decade's close, however, state moral authority had been reasserted through a range of measures which, despite New Right rhetoric, required increased rather than more restricted state intervention, escalating concern over parental abuse being the culprit. Research evidence had long shown that most child/adult sexual experience occurred within the family, but it appears that widespread popular panics over the paedophile external threat drew attention to the structure of 'abuse' itself, its incidence, effects and its most common perpetrators (*Sun* 26 Aug. 1983). By 1990 child sex abuse had become a prominent subject of popular television campaigning, ironically so given earlier conservative fears of this medium's ability to corrupt the private home space with sexual messages. This *has* now been accomplished but by aggressive defensive discourses which cast grave doubts on the home's moral superiority. By contrast, and equally ironically, the New Right's 'rolled back' state has been forced to respond by heightened bureaucratisation and professionalisation of interventionist child care.

Let us consider each of these phases in a little more detail. Popular media panics around child sex abuse and PIE produced predictable responses. PIE ('You Scum' (*Sun* 26 Aug. 1983)) was said to be dominated by 'enemy within' functionaries: 'teachers lawyers and civil servants' (*Daily Express* 22 Aug. 1983: 1) ideally placed to throw 'a mantle of decency and normality over sexual relations with children of six or seven or even younger'. Childhood innocence was mourned as a thing of the past: 'Once upon a time, less than 25 years ago most children were sheltered and fully protected from the adult world' (Dame Jill Knight quoted in *Daily Express* 22 Aug. 1988: 1).[51] Protected by their parents' 'caring authoritarianism', few sniffed glue, were alcoholic, addicted to drugs or gambled, and teenage venereal disease, pregnancy and marriage were relatively rare. 'There was . . . less rowdyism, vandalism and more respect for both property and person' (p. 1). No more, however; children 'from the age of 8' were dressing like adults, had access to adult pastimes, sport and, most threatening of all, television, an erosion of childhood 'ignored by professionals such as teachers, social workers and doctors' (p. 1).

PIE readily served as the stalking horse for these concerns pursued under sensationalist headlines: 'Terror of New Fiend' (*Sun* 26 Aug. 1983); 'New Beast on the Loose' (*Daily Express* 22 Aug. 1983: 1); 'They Even Snare Kids of Four' (*Daily Mail* 23 Aug. 1983). Of necessity there was a talking up of recorded cases, though rarely conveying the full incestuous abuse message within them.[52] Stories broke of sex romps in children's homes,[53] hints dropped of the involvement of 'leading public figures': 'One of these people is a friend of mine but you have to be merciless protecting the young' (G. Dickens MP quoted in *Daily Express* 22 Aug. 1983: 1)); gays inevitably implicated ('Gays are so upset' (p. 1)) and 'Gay caller knows attacker' (*Daily Mail* 24 Aug. 1983); and the government harangued for its inaction: 'On a remote Scottish island Leon Brittan [Home Secretary] is disporting among the heather with his family' (*Sun* 26 Aug. 1983: 1). Past spectres were also wheeled out to serve their turn:

> Myra Hindley has a different hair style. She has had her nose fixed. She says she is a changed person and a suitable candidate for probation. But we – and we imagine decent caring people everywhere – cannot erase the ghastly

memory of the helpless little children she and her vile
partner Ian Brady, tortured and killed for pleasure.

(*Sun* 26 Aug. 1983: 1)

New Right analysts at this stage held to the broad
characteristics of these populist appeals. Scruton (1983: 14)
argued: 'we should be thankful to paedophilia because it vividly
reminds us that sexual acts between consenting partners are
sometimes wrong. Not just wrong but evil and despicable', and
he attacked the 'easy sympathy' of the tolerant which leads to a
moral insensibility threatening to society itself. Rights rhetoric in
defence of freedom of speech for 'deviants' was emphatically
rejected, Scruton arguing that it was the rights of the intolerant
which had to be defended in order to protect 'common decency'.
Such a homily depended upon a utopian vision of proper
childhood innocence with a purpose; inhibition through shame,
threatened not only by PIE but also by 'sex education that
insidious propaganda devoted to freeing the sexual act from its
moral overtones, [and] to liberating our children from guilt'
(p. 14). Without such a childhood we would lose our adult
respect for the:

> act of love, not as something which happens to us – like
> hunger or thirst – but something we choose with our full
> personality. This is the true meaning of modesty, that we
> withhold ourselves except from that to which we give
> ourselves entirely. Only the modest person is capable of
> passion. For only by so damming up the sexual impulse do
> we ensure that, in surrendering to it, we surrender
> ourselves. Modesty is, therefore, the virtue which frees us to
> commitment and its highest form – virginity – rightly prized
> as a component, in the unpolluted readiness for love.
>
> (Scruton 1983: 14)

Out of such hostility PIE's 'precarious discourse' (Derbyshire
in *City Limits* 16 Sept. 1983) was effectively closed down, and with
little opposition from sexual minority parties. CHE (the
Campaign for Homosexual Equality) and SHRG (Scottish
Homosexual Rights Group) gave their support, but in doing so
opened themselves to criticism from within their own ranks ('this
chicken PIE is deadly poison and . . . we want no part of it'
(Stewart in *Gay Scotland* Jan. 1983)). More general issues of rights

and their infringement were picked up by the NCCL (National Council for Civil Liberties) and the quality press. The former, then campaigning to lower the age of consent to 14, defended its affiliated member PIE on the grounds that unless something is unlawful people should not be prosecuted for the views they hold, and this issue of freedom of speech was also stressed by many journalists. 'Freedom of speech is not a uniformly benign condition. It permits cacophony, vulgarity, cruelty, injustice and the exploitation of human passions and human miseries for money' (Conor Cruise O'Brien in *Observer* 22 March 1983), but it is even so a condition to be defended. 'They [PIE] have to be free to say these things, and say them the way they want to say them, or we are all less free' (O'Brien 1983). Similar debates followed the imprisonment of Tom O'Carroll of PIE under a 'judge invented version of lynch law' (Watkins in *Observer* 22 March 1981); the charge of 'conspiracy to corrupt public morals',[54] the only evidence for which being circulated lists of interested paedophiles and a campaign to lower the age of consent, in themselves legitimate entitlements within democracies.

Despite research findings on levels of parental abuse there was at this time simply no climate of belief for the fact that children were substantially at risk of sexual abuse from their parents. A watershed was possibly the widely reported 1984 MORI poll findings that more than 10 per cent of adults had been sexually abused as children, more than 80 per cent of them by members of the immediate family (*The Times* 30 Oct. 1986) for it was within the following two years that the parental abuse bandwagon gathered speed.

On television Esther Rantzen's Childline campaign elicited a reported 60,000 calls in three days after the first *Childwatch* programme on 30 October 1986;[55] 'single handedly Esther Rantzen thrust child abuse into the popular consciousness' (Amiel 1986), detailing the horrors of exchanging sexual favours for 'cigarettes, 50p, a cup of coffee' (*Observer* 19 Nov. 1988: 51); symptoms and descriptions of forms of abuse;[56] identification of the most likely perpetrators,[57] 'whilst young children are dependent upon their fathers and mothers these are their most likely abusers' (p. 56), all of which left Scruton's romantic notion of blissful childhood guilt in the protective family somewhat tarnished. He had expressed his belief that:

CHILDREN AS SEXUAL OBJECTS AND SUBJECTS

We ardently believe – although we seldom declare it – that our lives as sexual beings are divided into two distinct periods. There is a line between the sexuality of the child and that of the adult which we cross never to return. Everything which happens to us before we cross that line is crucial to our subsequent development. So too is the existence of the line

(Scruton 1983: 14)

By 1990 if that line was holding at all it was only because of the surveillance of 'expensive highly trained experts from . . . multi-disciplinary teams of professionals' (*Observer* 19 Nov. 1988: 56), striving to overcome their resistance to looking at a subject so painful, distasteful and unacceptable; 'training in child sexual abuse must be recognised as an essential part in the education of teachers, social workers, residential care workers, child and mental health professionals, and will have to be adequately resourced' (p. 56). The legal system has been told that it must adapt to facilitate the collection and extraction of convincing complainant evidence,[58] and we have been warned that unless there is a more constructive attitude towards perpetrators we should be 'pessimistic about rehabilitation of the family unit. . . . Children have the right to say no, but will society empower them to do so?' (p. 56). Childhood has lurched from privacy, non-regulation and minimal legal protection into public regulation by a phalanx of specialist agencies. Thus a

paradoxical result of the liberalisation of the family, of the emergence of children's rights, of the rebalancing of the man–woman relationship: the more these rights are proclaimed, the more the stranglehold of a tutelary authority tightens around the poor family. In this system family patriarchalism is destroyed only at the cost of the patriarchy of the state.

(Donzelot 1980: 103)

Childwatch (1986), which included a children's anthem: 'My body's nobody's body but mine/You run your own body let me run mine', saturated childhood with sexualised messages, telephone calls detailing a whole range of childhood fears and worries. Rantzen claimed 'I think that child abuse is anything that puts a child through pain, makes them feel uncomfortable and unhappy' and young callers responded in kind so that 'belea-guered parents . . . [were] under siege for a whole range of private parenting concerns' (Amiel 1986) from children trained to com-plain and denounce and to be proud of doing so. Can anything be more destructive to the family as a unit, or more effectively bring sexualised childhood into the public realm of rights, where children's right to say 'no' to any physical contact that doesn't feel right extends to their parents, who should never force physical affection upon them 'be it a kiss, cuddle or hug, on a child. Let them decide on the boundaries of affection' (Elliott 1990).

Within classic analyses of rights and liberties children have been consigned to non-adult status, their immaturity and ignorance demanding the paternalist protection of father and state. Mill's famous Liberty Principle (1910: 13) establishes the pre- or proto-citizenship status of the child:

> the only purpose for which power can be rightfully exercised over any member of a civilised community against his will, is to prevent harm to others. His own good whether physical or moral is not a sufficient warrant. In the part [of his conduct] which merely concerns himself, his independence is, of right, absolute. Over himself, over his own body and mind, the individual is sovereign.
>
> (Mill 1910: 13)

Children, however, cannot be sovereign because they have not reached:

> the maturity of their faculties. We are not speaking of children or young persons below the age which the law may fix as that of manhood or womanhood. Those who are still in a state to require being taken care of by others must be protected against their own actions as well as against external injury.
>
> (Mill 1910: 13)

The past twenty years have not shown a desertion of such principles but a severe questioning of them so that the quality of innocence to be protected, of parental ability to protect it, an acceptable age of maturity, and formal state protections have become elaborate issues of concern, stimulated not only by battles over paedophilia and abuse, but also by the considered arguments of the so-called child liberationists (Farson 1974a, b;

Holt 1975; Cohen 1980). The children's rights 'crusade' (*Time* 1974) has generated a considerable literature although much of it is little more than 'traditional conservative concern with protecting battered children' (Constantine 1977).[59]

Child liberationists' objections to liberal machineries argue broadly that 'age of consent' laws are arbitrary and, therefore, unjust to those under any age specified. Also they claim that 'because you are a child' is not an adequate explanation for denying basic rights (e.g. to travel, work, purchase on credit, etc.) because many children clearly do have competence to do many if not all the things denied them whilst many adults do not. As Lindley (1989) has argued perhaps, therefore, universal competence tests are what is required. Such arguments clearly attract little support despite their perhaps overly self-conscious playing down of sexual rights; e.g. only one of Holt's (1975: 15–16) eleven principles being so concerned and that eliptically.[60] However, Holt and Farson (1974a, b), amongst others, put on the agenda the possibility of political, legal and financial independence of children, the 'open family' (Constantine 1977, 1979), as a general context within which, by implication, pro-paedophile discourses on the sexual self-determination of children may be lodged (Foster and Freed 1972; Farson 1974a, b); 'the liberation of young people, so that they are empowered to make their own decisions regarding all aspects of their lives including their sexuality' (T'Sang 1981: 10).

It is interesting that rights discourses for children, despite the passions raised on all sides, have crystallised around the conjunction of sexual, economic and political independence in ways usually concealed when the dimensions of adult sexual citizenship are discussed, and rights themselves, directly linked to the child's proto-roles as consumer and earner as well as sexual citizen, elaborated within instructive texts for children themselves who may now read up on the complexities of their rights (Wright 1990).[61] In all these respects children are learning not only to say 'no', but what there is to say 'yes' to, and to recognise that both answers involve economic, political as well as sexual judgements, and whilst Rantzen-type crusades have tended to claim a monopoly of child opinion, alternative sources suggest that many children do say 'yes' and have said 'yes', that many more would say 'yes' if they thought they could. 'You can be desperate for sex at 13' (Moffett quoted in T'Sang 1981).

9

PUBLIC *AND* PRIVATE
The parameters of female sexual citizenship

> Marriage and the family are two of the most important
> institutions on which society is based. Particularly at this
> time of rapid social change and accompanying stresses
> marriage has never been more important in preserving a
> stable and responsible society.
>
> (Thatcher quoted in Phillips 1988: 40)

References to female as well as male sexualities have been made
throughout this text but the decision to conclude with a specific
discussion of female sexual citizenship in general is in recognition
of the still predominantly private and patriarchal subjection of
women and the largely reflective, interpellated, female presence
within the sexualisation of modern societies. If, as has been
argued, forms of sexual citizenship are forged out of the
conjunction of 'liberalising', amoral, material discourses, which
propound the right to privately purchase unique individual
sexual selves, with those, inhibitive and conservative, which
emanate from the state's guardianship of absolute public
morality and essential sexual truths, then women's relative lack
of power to realise the former, and crucial structural and
symbolic role in the fulfilment of the latter, renders their advance
into sexual citizenship altogether more ambivalent, diffuse and
tardy than that of men. Female sexual citizenship depends upon
the effective mystification of a different set of contradictory
ideologies, those that differentiate conditions which permit
women to participate in public spheres and as sexual consumers,
and those which reify the absolute primacy of their innately
fecund, private domesticity.

In *On the Subjection of Women* (1929) J.S. Mill explored the

240

dichotomy between public and private, the former objective, rational, reasoned through knowledge, constrained through laws, contracts and customs, the latter passionate, emotional and irrational. Although Mill advocated the equality of women with men in the public sphere he could not contemplate any challenge to women's prior, because innate, commitment and suitability to maternity and domesticity; women's qualities were and in large part remain private qualities, and the contradictions between public and private, masculine and feminine, continue to define the complex ambiguities of women's participation in public life, especially those which attend sexual identities and performances.

The second half of this century has witnessed rapid and widespread changes in the structural location of women in modern Western societies, with the qualified movement of increasing numbers from the home into waged labour and leisure, coterminous with the 'relaxation in the social and legal control of selected aspects of female sexual practice' (Hall 1979; Gerson 1983; Masnick and Barie 1980). Abortion law reform, the availability of the Pill, other forms of contraception and reproductive technologies, whatever their contentious other effects, have combined to loosen female sexuality from 'alliance' constraints of marital procreativity, and enabled the elaboration of alternative 'independence' discourses and varieties of non-reproductive and non-marital sexual pleasure.

Whatever their class, ethnicity or religion, etc., all women have experienced to some degree new social and economic 'opportunities': for financial independence, waged careers,[1] state and welfare support,[2] leisure,[3] and alternative forms of interpersonal relationships,[4] offset by the erosion of traditional female securities through the greater instability of marriage,[5] decline in the male 'family wage',[6] and increased state 'policing of families'.[7] These 'opportunities' originate in women's increasingly ambiguous structural and ideological loci, required to more efficiently produce domestic use values,[8] to relinquish inefficient facets of traditional domestic labour and consumption to market and state agencies (Castells 1978) which have in turn become 'feminised' zones of waged labour (Oakley 1982), whilst simultaneously carrying the increased symbolic weight of traditional family and female qualities. As women have moved into public spheres the state has made inroads into the private family, treated as virtually its adjunct to safeguard its 'privacy'

241

(Gerson 1986/7: Barrett and McIntosh 1982) and to minimise the costs to the state of its casualties.[9] Given that 'the relationship of capitalism to the family is contradictory . . . [tending] both to destroy it and maintain it' (Bruegel 1978), the state has been active in constructing a fetishised family, one increasingly divorced from the complex varieties of the actual forms it has to sustain, and from the equally diverse roles of women within and outwith them.[10] So discrepant are the ideology and reality of the modern family and the status of modern womanhood, that political rhetoric has not always met the challenge of coherence and consistency, although this in itself has perhaps significantly contributed to effective mystification.

It is inevitable that, once more, the most effective examples surround the sayings and deeds of Margaret Thatcher. Having devoted a political lifetime to reifying an ideal monogamous heterosexist family form, Thatcher during her 1990 Pankhurst Lecture proclaimed 'Of course there's never been a golden age of universal marital bliss', humbly admitting that she had spent her life in an 'ordinary married family' (*Guardian* 19 July 1990: 3). Such commonplace homilies were, however, the prelude to familiar expressions of 'deepest unease' at Britain having

> one of the highest proportions of lone-parent families in Europe, that 800,000 of them now receive income support, and that only one child in three of these families actually benefits from regular maintenance payments from the absent parent to which it is entitled.
>
> (*The Times* editorial 19 July 1990)

For women in modern first world economies, material, political and moral pressures are deeply ambiguous, devaluing procreation though enhancing motherhood (Stanworth 1987; Oakley 1982), encouraging cheaper feminised forms of labour whilst also encouraging families (i.e. women) to re-assume responsibility for members in need of special care (Family Policy Group 1983 quoted in Phillips 1988: 19), seeking to maximise private domestic commodification whilst developing women's access to public leisure and lifestyle consumption, all the while asserting traditional family values and the crucial role of the female in maintaining and retaining them. Thatcher showed typical audacity when she mobilised the icon of the housewife against organised labour in 1975: 'Perhaps it takes a housewife to see that Britain's national housekeeping is appalling' (quoted in Campbell 1990: 234). As Campbell comments, 'There was an exquisite irony in this, for her claims to domesticity transformed it from a condition of subordination to one of supremacy. It placed the housewife at the centre of the Conservatives' project for citizenship – citizen as consumer' (p. 234).

However, Campbell continues, by 1990 at the Conservative Party Conference Thatcher contemptuously turned on the housewife by likening Neil Kinnock to 'people queuing up for the winter sales' (p. 235). With his warming woollies, camp bed and Thermos flask he bolted into the store only to find that 'that woman was ahead of him' (p. 236). The housewife *manqué* thwarted by the career woman.

Formal institutional and juridical discourses on the ambivalence of such polemics over the family and the housewife swivel in a sort of zero-sum logic between assessments of the economic and moral costs and merits of female dependency on a male partner (preferably spouse), set against 'independence' through legal, social and economic dependency upon the state. Despite emphatic moral blandishments, financial considerations also emerge as of major practical political significance. If the male partner absents himself, and the female with small children is not able to provide the missing income, the state must pick up the tab. 'As Mrs Thatcher said "Parenthood is for life." So are the consequences for the Exchequer' (*The Times* 19 July 1990).

In this same Pankhurst Lecture (18 July 1990) Margaret Thatcher amply, though unintentionally, demonstrated the uneven class effects of these ambivalent pressures. Taking her text from the Book of Proverbs and the qualities of a capable woman whose 'worth is far beyond rubies' she praised the increased participation of women in public life, aided by 'legislation and tax reforms to stamp out discrimination'. She noted:

> But let me say this: it is wrong to describe the choice as between working and not working. Anybody who has tried to bring up children knows that there is no more demanding – and fulfilling – work. And if we do not make enough time to be with our children we should regret it forever.

I've always found that to get the most out of life you have

243

to work really hard. And the more effort you put in the more satisfaction you get out. . . . Yet no matter how hard you work or how capable you are, you can't do it all yourself. You have to seek reliable help – a relative, or what my mother would have called 'a treasure': someone who brought not only her work but her affections to the family.

(reported *Guardian* 19 July 1990: 3)

Two months earlier in an interview on BBC Radio 4's *Woman's Hour* she had warned against crèches as not in the best interests of children, whilst her government continued to freeze child benefit payments and made tax concessions for child care to working mothers (*The Times* 17 May 1990).[11] In her inaugural George Thomas Lecture for the National Children's Home later the same year she maintained that the breakdown in the family unit is 'a new kind of threat to our whole way of life', but state practice as opposed to state ideology has increasingly formalised this 'breakdown' through policy compensations, tying the broken into new forms of public dependency, and encouraging women, professional women at least, presumably because of their greater access to 'treasures', to pursue waged careers around the exigencies of maternity and motherhood.

As these and other examples demonstrate, over such actual and potential policy issues as incentives to encourage marriage, depriving single mothers of 'fast-track' access to council housing (Family Policy Group quoted in Phillips 1988: 19), the ease and expense of divorce, whether cohabiting couples should be covered by family law,[12] the provision of benefits or tax concessions for help with child care, child benefit,[13] maternity leave[14] and overall the forms and extents of dependency on state welfare that the withdrawal or absence of a husband's support brings, the ambivalent pressures on women reflect the 'dense', 'distanced', 'impossible to unravel' (Riley 1981), 'muddled' (Challis quoted in Rowbotham 1989: 151) and 'contradictory' (Smart 1981) state practices behind the facade of the idealised natural, private family.

Nowhere is this more apparent than in the main proposals of the government White Paper, Children Come First (29 Oct. 1990). These include the setting up of a child support agency to chase absent parents for maintenance payments; fathers having to pay up to 50 per cent of their disposable income on such

244

maintenance; lone working mothers possibly losing 20 per cent of benefit if they fail to reveal fathers' whereabouts and also having to contribute to maintenance; single parents being given incentives to work; £15 maintenance disregard on family credit; and eligibility to family credit reduced from 24 hours per week to 16. Thus the respectability of the family is to be 'maintained' through elaborate intervention, the Exchequer financially less embarrassed, whilst women, i.e. primarily working-class women caring for children, will be encouraged to obtain waged work, typically of the cheaper, part-time 'two-phase bi-modal' kinds (Hakim 1979: Siltanen 1986), by modest tax concessions to finance child care in crèches which, if available, are bad for the children placed in them anyway. Ideologically family behaviour may remain 'the most private and personal of all areas of behaviour, almost totally free from external supervision and control' (Anderson 1979: 67), in practice it is anything but, and it is out of this discrepancy between ideal and real families, the one with simple natural rights, the other propped up by a mass of civil, political and social sealing wax, that modern female sexual citizenship emerges.

Mount (1982) has observed that defenders of the family always assert its biological individuality and hence independence, privacy and right to live according to its natural instincts, and that for this reason, even in societies where male supremacy is officially total, the family asserts its maternal values. Accordingly it remains in a sense true that:

> . . . the state intervenes less conspicuously in the lives of women than of men, when it does so it appears to be done more benevolently. The relation of women to state agents is much more often indirect than that of men.
>
> (McIntosh 1978b: 256)

Certainly measures to legally enforce maintenance commitments on 'errant fathers' (*Guardian* 19 July 1990: 1)[15] appear beneficent but, as women have become increasingly socialised into public life, state–women relations have of necessity become more conspicuous and formally direct. As 'the family . . . [has got] smaller and smaller in order to make itself "one", in a desperate struggle against the disparity of its members in the outside world' (Mitchell 1971: 157), so the proportion of women directly experiencing this disparity, materially and sexually, has grown. Female waged labour confronts the male family wage; 'equal' formal citizenship in public faces not only unequal public citizenship practice but also private patriarchal dominance; independence versus dependence; sexual self-control in the cosmetic pursuit of pleasure set against motherliness and homeliness; throughout, material 'freedoms' indubitably, though not mechanically, signify women's transition into the discursive machinery of 'sexuality' set alongside the reconstruction of 'alliance' traditions. That the latter retain their dominance is demonstrated not merely by persistent ideologies of maternity and motherhood but also by the law's continued denial of women as sexually responsible individuals. Despite women's entry into civil, political and social rights in British law women's sexualities are still deemed passive and responsive, only men are still deemed capable of committing sexual crimes.

For these reasons it is clear that the judgements of some earlier commentators that equal pay and anti-discrimination legislation are simply token concessions to feminist claims by a state otherwise actively defending the family by discouraging women from moving into waged labour (Wilson 1977) aided by a culture steeped in patriarchal traditionalism outwith juridical control, were misplaced. Smart and Smart, for example, argued that:

> the extent to which the primary sources of women's oppression are outside, or even beyond judicial influence, that is to say rest within, or arise from, prevailing material conditions, cultural values, customs and social practices, such as the differential socialisation of male and female children within the family, schooling, forms of speech and language, media propagated stereotypes and numerous seemingly innocuous social processes.
>
> (Smart and Smart 1978: 1)

All true of course, but only part of the truth, for in response to the combined impact of existing and new 'liberalising' social relations of consumerism, first world states have been forced to act altogether more ambivalently to manage to least damaging effect the fundamental confrontation between private 'alliance' and public 'sexual' demands on women (Rowbotham 1989: 153). Hence the advance of specifically female 'freedoms' and 'rights'.

McIntosh (1978b: 257) has argued that 'Women are now full citizens in most purely legal respects; they have the right to vote,

246

to own and dispose of property, to make contracts, to go to law, to hold passports.' She goes on to argue that even so the state relates to married women differently, still through their husbands, 'especially in income tax and the social security system . . .' (p. 257), but here too, in line with the British trend away from the couple and towards the individual as taxation units (e.g. as with Poll Tax), the trend has subsequently been towards further 'liberalisation', i.e. independent income tax for women (Pahl 1990).[16] The trend is clearly continuing towards drawing all women, married and unmarried into material citizenship in 'purely legal respects'. It is not 'equal' citizenship of course: civil and social rights have tended away from formal equalities, stressing instead the unique position of women as mothers and workers and thus reifying sex difference; formal recognition of the full sexual independence of women has been withheld, and whatever the formal legal equalities, grave inequalities persist in legal and social practice.

Whilst all women have experienced the equivocal mixture of increased opportunities and insecurities, of perhaps greater importance has been their uneven and fragmenting impact in especially class, but also ethnic and religious terms. Women have been placed 'in increasingly divergent but equally precarious social positions' (Gerson 1986/7: 214).[17] As Gerson explains, whether domestic with children and largely dependent upon a man's wage, or non-domestic and supported by their own income, women 'face precarious and uncertain circumstances, each . . . motivated to defend its position vigorously through political action. The stage . . . [thereby] . . . set for deep political conflict'.[18]

Given their condensed symbolic power, it is not surprising that sexual issues such as abortion, contraception, surrogacy, sex education, child sex abuse, marital violence and rape, pornography and erotica, all revolving in some way around the central issue of sexual self-determination, have featured prominently in these emerging conflicts, for in different ways they all powerfully short-circuit the general structural and material upheavals to which they are ultimately tied. These conflicts arise out of general insecurities and reactions to structural changes, more specifically about 'what type of family the state should support' (Gerson 1986/7: 214), and what types women might, should and can be. 'We know what we are but not what we may be or what we might have been' (Greer 1970 quoted in Shearer 1987: 86); they emerge from tentative responses to uncertain, material changes which escalate into spectacularly dramatised panics around the public exposure of the sexual implications of women's weakened ties with their 'natural' locus, the family home. The sexual is inextricably, though in a complex and not necessarily obvious way, tied to the material.

> Because sexuality in Western societies is so mystified, the wars over it are often fought at oblique angles, aimed at phony targets, conducted with misplaced passions, and are highly and intensely symbolic. Sexual activities often function as signifiers for personal and social apprehensions . . .
>
> (Rubin 1984: 297)

But Rubin goes on to add '. . . to which they have no intrinsic connection', which is surely incorrect. Sexual relations have an economic base. The majority dispense their sexuality in monogamous heterosexual coupledom, and social conventions and their emotional trappings convey the fundamental economic consequences of the relationships between men and women and, by default, for those who diverge from them. The correlation of male sex needs with female attractiveness is material (McIntosh 1978b). Wars over sexual issues, if they signify anything, denote the ability of populations to almost subconsciously recognise that, despite all the fragmenting and mystifying cultural scenarios, sexual and material worlds are indeed intricately related. It is precisely because sexuality in Western societies is considered as a discrete essence that wars over widespread social changes may be fought confidently in its name.

Equal Pay (1970, 1975) and Sex Discrimination (1975) legislation, are usually judged in terms of their specific practical consequences, in which terms the verdict correctly being that both are weak and wanting (Robarts et al. 1981; Snell et al. 1981; Beechey 1986a, b; etc.),[19] but their wider implications are surely rather more substantial. They mark the formal movement of women into forms of 'independent' public life and acknowledge that, having less power and lower status than men, it is the state's responsibility to provide the required legal protection. In so doing these statutes draw women into broader, female-specific dependent relationships with what is for them a newly benign state, seemingly hostile to domestic patriarchal traditions. By establishing the base rights of 'public' women they also make women public sexual beings, differentiated by the individualising and fragmenting consequences of their relations to both state and market, albeit always under the ultimate qualification of reified 'alliance' conditions. Women have become publicly sexualised and superficially sexual, but ultimately still as passive and responsive sexual citizens who displace their sexualities onto 'attitude' (Coward 1984: 21), [20] 'the ideal perfect body' (p. 39),[21] onto being reconstituted Madonnas, like virgins, shiny and new as if 'touched for the very first time'.

Ehrenreich (1981: 98–9) has observed that 'the economic stresses of the seventies split women into two camps: those who went out to fight for some measure of economic security . . . and those who stayed home to hold on to what they had' and that for both the intermediary role of the state became crucial, for the former to aid liberation from domestic patriarchal dominance, for the latter to defend conventional heterosexual practice from immorality, 'permissiveness', un-Christian forces. To talk in terms of two camps is clearly to simplify the complex inconsistencies which structurally divide women in their relations with the state, especially over sexual issues, culturally apolitical, immanently unsocial and explicitly experienced only through piecemeal and single-issue legislative changes and campaigns. These inconsistencies are mirrored in reverse feminist discourses. Many fighting for state protection of economic independence and committed to the 'personal is political' ('. . . feminist consciousness has exploded the private. . . . To see the personal as political means to see the private as public' (MacKinnon 1983: 655)), tend to oppose state interference in their sexual lives, claiming rights of privacy over sexual self-determination, whilst those demanding state action to protect traditional family forms, to censor and to police around the family, are understandably nervous at the extent to which this leads to state invasion of privacy, providing sex education, monitoring sexual abuse of children and wives, etc.

These twin objectives of the state underline the particular qualities of female as opposed to male sexual citizenship. Certainly general criteria of citizenship apply: as women have moved in increased numbers into public life their incorporation into civil, political and social rights has been assured and has 'freed' their entry into complex formal and informal relations with state and market. But in so doing women have neither structurally nor ideologically been allowed to leave the family, they are not sexually responsible citizens as men are; on the contrary through the fetishisation of the family and state practice in 'liberalising' family law and statutes dealing with sex crime, essential gender and sexual differences have been reconstituted rather than questioned, dominant discourses recycling anew old influential icons which triumph over the temptations and confusions of rapid social change. As expounded in the Official Programme for the wedding between Prince Charles and Lady Diana Spencer:

> At the centre of a nation's life, there is a bewildering kaleidoscope of events, peopled by a huge and ever changing cast of politicians and personalities. We are fortunate in having at the heart of our national life another ingredient, the presence of a family, providing a sense of continuity and pointing to the most profound themes of human life which do not change from century to century.
>
> (quoted in Coward 1984: 165)

Once past the wedding, Diana, 'La Princesse Sexy' (*Paris Match* quoted in Shearer 1987: 104), whose picture on any British magazine cover we are told adds up to 40,000 additional sales (p. 104), became the New Housewife: 'the housewife stereotype of the fifties, revived, and rejuvenated and elevated: a captive indulged wife who dominates by being dominated ... a reinvention to keep the female classes in order' (Lowry 1985).

Rejuvenated housewife and revitalised mother: 'Guess who's made motherhood OK again?', why Princess Di of course:

> Young marriage and early motherhood are not just permitted again ... they have become a perfectly reasonable choice for the intelligent educated young woman to make. ... By being what she is, young and in love with life in all its aspects and proud of her parenthood, she has given women back to themselves
>
> (Rayner in *Women's Own* quoted in Shearer 1987: 105)

In the wake of such 'gush' the Windsor's well-publicised marriage breakdowns and 'Diana-gate' scandals have provided an ironic symbol of the strains of sexual citizenship negotiated by 'ordinary' women.

As Stanworth (1987: 15) notes, the ideology that motherhood is '. . . the natural, desired and ultimate goal of all "normal women", so that those who deny their ' "maternal instincts" are selfish, peculiar or disturbed', is as prevalent as ever. In illustration she reports top obstetrician Patrick Steptoe's claim that 'It is a fact that there is a biological drive to reproduce. Women who deny this drive, or in whom it is frustrated, show disturbances in other ways' (p. 15).[22]

The state's task, here exercised through one particular professional institution and over one particular issue, is to continuously construct and reconstruct 'respected areas of privacy requiring decisions over regulation or non-regulation' (O'Donovan 1985: 99), respected because they conciliate contradictory 'alliance' and 'sexuality' modes. Furthermore, by being 'freed' to have independent access to the market, women become exposed to material individualisation through the commodification of both traditional and modern gender and sexual differences. Again staying with this example, women's access to abortion and reproductive technologies is not simply or even mainly a matter of law but depends upon ability to pay, knowledge of what one is choosing to purchase, particular ethnic and religious inhibitions, regional variations in market access, etc.

Alternatively, female sexual citizenship is forged out of the uneasy conjunction of supposedly innate private qualities: emotionalism, irrationality, passion, attractiveness and dependency with those required in many public performances: rationality, reason, independence, etc. They apparently coalesce with the 'New Woman', filtered through various state and market channels as 'independent' women in consumer pursuit of both their individual nurturing domestic and public career and sexual selves. Thus commodification reinforces female sexual difference and secondary citizenship, traditional diffuseness enabling satisfaction via an array of displaced commodity forms including those of the newly sexualised woman despite formal changes which imply the contrary.

That it is an uneasy conjunction is due in no small measure to the eruption of the women's liberation movement in the late 1960s and the subsequent explosion of 'reverse' discourses on all aspects of the woman question, initially perhaps concentrating on family issues; confinement, 'ghettoised "private life" ' (O'Sullivan 1987: 42), dependence and lack of identity, but subsequently

251

opening out onto the wider implications and consequences of woman's raised public profile for general gender and specifically sexual issues.

Movement into public spaces has made the female body in all its ideal and imperfect forms a major site of 'bio-power' in modern societies, with the emergence of, for example, 'new' largely sex-specific illnesses of public space and performance under unfamiliar public scrutiny, such as claustrophobia, agoraphobia and anorexia. Orbach singled out the last of these as the key physical and psychological metaphor of these new public performance pressures on women.

> . . . women entering the world beyond the home do so as guests not as principals; the necessary shifts, adjustments and negotiations are contingent on women making them. Women are required to accommodate themselves to the public sphere much as they accommodate others in private.
>
> (Orbach 1986 quoted in Shearer 1987: 130)

For Orbach anorexia, 'the starvation amidst plenty, denial set against desire, the striving for invisibility versus the wish to be seen', frequently leading to cessation of menstruation, is 'at once an embodiment of stereotyped femininity and its very opposite' (p. 130).

That all women *have* become increasingly subjected to sexualising discourses in the post-war period cannot be seriously doubted. Whether explicitly with regard to such issues as frigidity, contraception, abortion, orgasm, masturbation, child sex abuse, pornography, lesbianism, prostitution, etc., or implicitly through wider 'bio-power' channels of fashion, cosmetics, entertainment, fitness, health and dietary styles, this sexualisation has established the conditional, contentious, sexual 'independence' of women lodged in legal rights and practices, and the legitimate commodification of its realisation. Any account of such matters is bound to be selective but two issues exemplify this sexualisation process: abortion and the marketing of the New and even Newer Woman.

The relevance of abortion to the modern female sexual condition is obviously paramount for numerous reasons: it is directly linked to claims for women's rights of bodily self-control set against those of men and medicine. It demonstrates how in diffuse ways the state penetrates civil society via intermediary neutral professional bodies and it exemplifies the possibilities of popular politicisation of sexual issues and how they might be transformed in the process. Abortion also demonstrates how materially and discursively women have been successfully divided between and amongst themselves.

The paramount importance of abortion emerges out of fundamental feminist slogans and ambitions of the late 1960s through which 'women's liberation brought the body into politics' (Rowbotham 1989: 61): 'the personal is political'; 'power over our bodies, power over our lives' (Rakusen 1976). Kinsey *et al.* (1953) and Masters and Johnson's (1966) popularised revelations of clitoral sexual potential underlined the considerable gap between women's biology and experience, and the Pill transformed the mode of reproduction, enabling child-bearing to be, theoretically at least, voluntary. 'It need no longer be the sole or ultimate vocation of women: it becomes an option among others . . . easily available contraception . . . threatens to dissociate sexual from reproductive experience . . .' (Mitchell 1966). It has, however, been abortion rather than the Pill which has carried the symbolic confrontation, through the emotive presence and status of the foetus.

> . . . in a world where men and women have traditionally had different roles to play and where male roles have traditionally been the more socially prestigious and financially rewarded, abortion has become a symbolic marker between those who wish to maintain this divison and those who wish to challenge it.
>
> (Luker 1984: 201)

Abortion also underlines the transition from medical knowledge imposed in an insulated world of abstract universal standards,[23] to knowledge and treatments open, at least in part, to popular and women's demands. As such abortion marks the emergence out of Mandarin control of doctrines of decriminal-ised self-regulation and the open politicisation of the issues themselves.[24] Smith-Rosenberg (1985: 218) identifies two nineteenth-century anti-abortion ideologies – one male (professional, medical, which stressed the self-indulgence of bourgeois women unwilling to undergo the inconvenience of childrearing), the other female (akin to the then feminist attitudes to prostitution, abortions being seen not as the responsibility of aborting women but of the lustful men who had forced them into pregnancy). During the 1950s abortion 'escaped' the confines of both, especially the former (Skocpol 1986–7: 191), Luker (1984) claims with the connivance of medical professionals themselves, seeking to rationalise laws and practices in circumstances of increasing obstetric and gynae-cological health care. Initially, as a medically inspired political issue, it was relatively low-key but during the late 1960s and the 1970s, feminist advocacy of women's right to absolute control of their own bodies and fertility, both necessary to the realisation of waged careers and other public involvements, turned abortion into *the* basic female civil right, at the centre of a broadly publicised popular discursive battle (Harvey 1984: 204).[25]

The 1967 Abortion Act set British late twentieth-century abortion law standards. O'Donovan (1985: 91) argues that it also moved abortion from prohibition in criminal law to being 'a mainly private matter', although in practice it became an even more elaborate public matter, addressed in detail through all media channels and establishing even greater medical control, putative abortees having to resort to hierarchies of 'experts' or else pay exorbitant market rates to avoid them. Certainly this appears even more so given subsequent developments in wider reproductive technologies. As Stanworth argues, on the one hand women have a greater technical control over decisions to have children whilst 'on the other, the domination of so much repro-ductive technology by the medical profession and by the state has enabled others to have an even greater capacity to exert control over women's lives' (Stanworth 1987: 15–16), a control qualified by the differential ability of women to pay for what they want.

Women's right to decide is still ambiguously recognised, married women's rights of independent choice increasingly so. In this sense abortion also illustrates both the lack of clarity of legal distinctions between public and private and ambivalence over women's formal citizenship rights. The US Supreme Court has pronounced that 'the right of personal privacy includes the abortion decision' (O'Donovan 1985: 91) and also asserted women's right to privacy as an important constitutional right which has to be kept in balance with other interests (Barnett 1982), but stopped short of endorsing the principle that the *only* person qualified to make a decision about abortion is the woman herself (Petchesky 1984). Possibly most women believed that the battle had been won but by 1977 the Supreme Court had decided to allow individual states to withhold Medicaid funds from poor women for abortions which turned out to be the opening salvo in an all out attack on abortion rights for all women. In 1980 Reagan was elected on an anti-abortion platform and in 1981 Congress was debating a Human Life Statute which declared a foetus a person and defined abortion as murder.

British law has no such formal recognition of rights of privacy over abortion decisions, although out of the Paton *v* Trustees of the BPAS case (O'Donovan 1985: 91), following appeal to the European Court (Article 8), it was ruled that a husband does not have the right to be consulted in respect to termination of the wife's pregnancy. The European Court's judgment emphasised the crucial issues of legal concern as: the wife's state of health and her rights to respect for her private life which takes precedence over that father's right.

This lack of clarity affects not only legal statutory but also as briefly mentioned earlier, the arguments of pro-choice discourses which defend women's rights of privacy over sexual self-determination, contraception and abortion, but happily cede such rights over intra-familial economic and political matters, and in a sense depoliticise all aspects of sexuality including abortion in the process. For example, in response to the pro-life movement in the USA, NARAL (National Abortion Rights League) claimed 'Abortion is something personal. Not political' (*New York Times* 26 April 1981); 'The real issue is not abortion. The issue is the right of individuals to live free of government intrusion' (Caldwell 1981: 59). On the other hand, feminist discourses demand state intervention to overcome the economic and political inequalities of domestic patriarchy. Not surprisingly, as a result of such contradictions the 'exact nature of the right to privacy has remained elusive' (Back 1986–7: 201). In any case it is always bound to be a matter of relative boundary drawing.

Liberal democratic, as well as many feminist critics, chose to interpret abortion law reform as almost entirely a triumph of popular feminist politics and it was in this sense that *Newsweek* (8 Oct. 1979: 47) described the pro-abortion movement as 'one of the few genuine social movements of the 1970s', and Back (1986–7: 204) argued that 'abortion is the medical question that – taken from professional control – has permeated public opinion'. However, the value of effective birth control to the advanced world economies, the devaluation of the first sexual commodity, reproduced labour, and the 'freeing' of cheap female labour, were structurally of greater importance, leading to a classic case of late twentieth-century ambiguous pressure on the state, to defend traditional standards whilst enabling capitalism's 'liberalising' needs. There could eventually only be the one solution, piecemeal *ad hoc*ery, reforms of traditional strictures behind mystifying consensus about the latter's absolute and essential inviolability, especially to mollify pro-lifers.

Linked to medical professionalism but on a more general level the abortion issue also demonstrates, as does that of child sex abuse, how the state successfully penetrates sexual issues through not merely the law, but also via medical and other professional 'expert' semi-autonomous institutions stranded somewhere between public and private spheres, public to the individual and the family but private, or at least less public, to the law makers and the state. In a sense all 'experts' who socially police individuals and families are so located, their 'public' personae offensively intrusive to their 'clients', their 'private' personae economically inefficient to a suspicious state keen to distance itself from them and to query the sense of their actions. Ultimately all such 'experts' are concerned to encourage clients to live respectable, normal lives, on behalf of a benign state which, to retain its neutrality, cannot afford to be too closely associated with them.[26]

Abortion has also served as a specific instance in the 'culmination of a development in which the interpersonal aspect of sexual relationships has become a major political issue' (Back 1986–7: 198). Its incendiary qualities are due to the general politicisation and commodification of sexuality, but more than any other it is the issue which most dramatically questions the 'alliance' link between female sexuality and procreation and challenges the simplicities of given discourses around the sexual double standard (McIntosh 1978a; Adams and Laurikietis 1976; Lakoff 1975; Lees 1986). For these reasons it is the issue in which women can be the only front-line protagonists.

For Caldwell (1981) abortion allows being in control of one's own body, having choice, not having to submit to one's husband or the inevitability of male sexuality, whilst Harvey (1984) goes further: 'women's autonomy must include the right to express ourselves as sexual beings . . . with the fundamental right to define our own sexuality . . . [our] right to *enjoy* sex without fear of pregnancy' (p. 205). Abortion doesn't imply forethought as most methods of contraception do, it accommodates women who do not think of themselves as active sexually, and enables the retention, albeit tenuously, of 'alliance' definitions of sexualities and sexual difference. Caldwell (1981) claims that abortion also allows the retention of a punitive attitude to women's bodies, which exercises 'our speciality', guilt; 'pleasure may be sacrosanct but guilt is remorseless' (Coward 1984: 14), and is, therefore, a perfect focus for the imposition of contemporary sexual discourses (Caldwell 1981). Willis (1981: 217) agrees, arguing that even the most forceful opponents of the right to life movement can be emotionally intimidated by the latter's ability to 'tap the vast store of sexual guilt and anxiety that lies just below this society's veneer of sexual liberalism'.

> The abortion debate has become a debate among women, with different values in the social world, different experiences of it, and different resources with which to cope with it. . . . While on the surface it is the embryo's fate that seems at stake, the abortion debate is actually about the meanings of women's lives. The debate is a referendum on the place and meaning of motherhood.
>
> (Luker 1984: 193–4)

That abortion as a political and moral issue, probably more forcefully than any other issue, exemplifies the structured differentiation of women as they have become increasingly socialised into public life has understandably not gone without comment. Ginsburg (1984) for one asks 'How is it that women living in what appears to be the same society have come to such radically opposing views concerning the shape and control of reproduction and sexuality?' (p. 173). Grassroots supporters of both sides are predominantly white, middle-class females, but they have totally different ideologies and verdicts on each other: most pro-choice women believe that 'pro-lifers' are dupes of, or 'a battering ram' for, a number of religious and New Right causes including many explicitly anti-feminist ones, using abortion as a 'condensation symbol' (Joffe 1986/7; Edelman 1964: 6) and attacking pro-choicers as promiscuous and immoral. Being pro-life also questions the meaning of feminism for both Ehrenreich (1983) and Luker (1984) reported respondents against abortion for fear that it would facilitate male sexual irresponsibility. Perceived as alternative moral choices however, abortion manifests the usual cultural segregation of sexual issues from their material source.

General popular attitudes to abortion are similarly afflicted though, as reported earlier, exceptionally it has attracted increasing liberal support during the 1980s. This can only be because it has become redefined and dissociated from other issues of sexual permissiveness with which it was formerly associated, desexualised, no longer linked primarily to sexual freedom or contraception but rather to the general principle of women's rights. However, as several critics insist, abortion remains a last resort birth control measure for most women who abort (Rossi 1972). Rossi argues that the fact that most abortions are due to women not wanting an unwanted child is simply not faced because it contradicts 'alliance' definitions of women as nurturant, loving creatures who welcome every new possibility of adding a member to the human race, even though other cultures regard as normal these 'deviant' definitions. The conflict over abortion as contraception has become a major rights issue in the newly unified Germany. Prior to unification, since 1972, birth control via free abortion during the first twelve weeks of pregnancy has been a basic right for all East German women. In the West however, under a Bismarckian statute, abortions remain illegal unless approved by a doctor on medical and social grounds, a law enacted with particular stringency in Catholic Bavaria, setting up a quite unforeseen and ironic consequence of the re-birth of a unified Germany (Murray 1991: 11). It is no surprise either to note that in other Catholic countries where access to alternative forms of birth control is difficult or illegal because 'the primary aim of sexual encounters – the possibility of procreation – means that any form of contraception other than a "natural one": i.e. the rhythm method or abstinence, is forbidden', abortion is also the main means of contraception (Caldwell 1981: 50). In Catholic countries with considerable taboos on women's active sexuality, enjoyment and pleasure, 'abortion keeps ideas of sexuality and reproduction inextricably linked' (p. 52).

In the USA and Britain this link still lingers with some force behind the facade of liberalisation, for popular support for abortion is not support for women's right to choose, but rather for women's right to a choice when the circumstances of the pregnancy are exceptional or unnatural. Popular support declines through a hierarchy of qualifying criteria from rape and foetal abnormality, but with little support for abortion as last resort birth control for women who most seek them, still as described by Kinsey forty years ago, women who are in poverty, or who, whether unmarried or married, simply do not want the child (Rossi 1972). In practice, of course, women with sufficient finances can obtain abortions on demand, whilst those without are constrained by National Health provisions in accordance with popular values and rhetoric.

As far as the second of the dominant female sexualising discursive channels is concerned, the commodification of female 'public' sexuality, Coward (1984) has observed:

> To be a woman is to be constantly addressed ... [and] ... scrutinised, to have our desire constantly courted – in the kitchen, on the streets, in the world of fashion, in films and fiction. ... Desire is endlessly defined and stimulated. Everywhere female desire is sought, bought, packaged and consumed ... with the promise of future perfection ... dissatisfaction displaced into desire for the ideal.
>
> (Coward 1984: 13)

As Coward implies, the commodification of women commences in the home as 'shoppers in chief', and where the parameters of feminine desire are forged: desire articulated through the market where women may feel 'abandoned', 'oblivious to everything', 'out of control', 'lost to the earth', through all manner of accoutrements that express their individuality, be they washing machines, microwaves, nose reconstructions, designer aerobics, body stockings or perfumes.

> There is a mode of individualisation specific to women, it operates above all through the field of sexuality. (Whole sectors of industry devote themselves to offers of individ-ualization: a perfume which is one woman's own, the exclusive scent of a certain soap, that 'certain something' of a cigarette made for women only.) In the first instance it is through exhortations to acquire 'exclusivity' that the ordering of sexuality takes effect for women; these domains arise as an effect of, and are instrumental in producing, that order.
>
> (Haug 1987: 202)

From out of such assemblages of norms there emerge particular types of women across the full expanse of bio-power; 'elegant', 'sexy', 'alluring', 'sporty', 'warm', 'cold', 'free', 'independent', 'fun loving', 'loose', 'smart and attractive', the 'having it all' (Brown 1984) *Cosmopolitan* Woman, *Marie Claire* Woman, etc., which have to be reconciled with reconstituted versions of women as highly commodified 'domestic clearing houses' (Haug 1987) with scientific domestic expertise (Oakley 1976) who now also have sexual needs, the fulfillment of which enhances maternal, housewifely performances. As with fashion and cosmetic styles, homes encourage a narcissistic identification between women's bodies and their 'style'. 'Houses like women are after all called, stylish, elegant and beautiful' (Coward 1984: 64). The technicalities of domestic consumption are matched by the cosmetic; women are urged to make the most of the natural qualities they have, their skin type, hair, facial features, legs, bathrooms, curtains, kitchens, distracting attention from the means and forms of their material construction. The 'implicit reference . . . is that a given type is what we *are* – and not . . . that there are long processes at work through which that type is *made*' (Haug 1987: 203). Women who claim to be a particular type, claim to have a particular essence, what Haug calls a relation of cause and effect from the inside outwards or 'auto-naturalisation', the subjective subordination (ideological subjection) of individuals to the ordering of the sexual as a *process* (p. 203).

So for Haug the sexualisation of a woman's body – a process equivalent to her individualisation – represents an inclusion of the female subject in the ordering of the sexual, which by extension, through the adaptation of traditional scripts of diffuse feminine sexuality, becomes displaced onto all manner of female related objects and commodities. 'In girls, the process of individual socialisation is synonymous with the sexualisation of the body and its parts' (p. 203). Feminist resistances to such ideologies may have been forthcoming and relatively popular (Munter 1984) but dominant ideology, in all senses, it has remained.

The widespread popular commodification of female bodies and beauty can possibly be set in Britain at the birth of the Page 3 nude in the *Sun* on 17 November 1970 above the caption:

From time to time some self-appointed critic stamps his tiny foot and declares that the *Sun* is obsessed with sex. It is not the *Sun* but the critics who are obsessed. the *Sun* like most of its readers likes pretty girls. . . . Who cares whether they are dressed or not?

(*Sun* 17 Nov. 1970: 3)

By 1990, apparently very many fewer, for topless 'girls' are likely to be encountered elsewhere, 'Now you can see 200 on Brighton beach' (editor of the *Sunday Sport* quoted in *Independent on Sunday* 18 March 1990: 8). The tabloids claim that the populace has become more demanding: 'People are fed up, they want a bit more personality' (organiser of Miss World Contest quoted: 8) hence the move in press pictures for more of a 'cover-up and less bimbo-type image – more sophisticated and upmarket. The days of the great Samantha Fox making thousands by taking her clothes off are over, there are women in business now' (photographer for Pirelli calendars quoted: 8). So commerce and commodification are tasteful and/or prurient? Well other branches of the media are not so certain for many erstwhile non-sexist 'quality' male oriented magazines, *GQ*, *Arena* and *Esquire*, have rediscovered 'that sexuality is a large part of life' (Isobel Koprowski managing editor of *Penthouse* quoted in *Independent on Sunday* 9 Dec. 1990) and reintroduced the proof back into their pages. Such hesitancy in popular imagery has understandably pushed the New Woman beyond anorexia, to new heights of performance panic, e.g. into the arms of 'dysmorphobia'.[27]

The relationship between advertisers, advertising agencies and consumers is of course rife with claims and counter-claims 'Advertising is not in the business of evangelism. It does not set up trends but reflects them. . . ' (Gail Camp of *Campaign* quoted in Root 1984: 60). and certainly most marketing imagery is conservative and traditional. But evangelism, in the guise of responding immediately to predicted changes in style, provides vital practical and voyeuristic momentum. In a 1988 article in *Campaign* Peter York, 'inventor' of the Sloane Ranger, established the profile of the New Man in television advertising: 'an uncomplicated soul, with a penchant for mobile phones and 'absolutely huge windows' who lives according to a 'mean chic' morality based on 'greed, competition and treachery" (*The Times* 16 March 1988). This New Man was an advertising success.

By contrast the New Woman 'breed of affluent "post-feminists" who have grown up to take sexual equality as read and assume that life consists of a happy, if complex, balance of work, home, personal relationships and self-indulgence is a much trickier prospect for advertising' (*The Times* 16 March 1988).

In theory she should be an advertiser's dream: 'She's easy to deal with, relishes being a woman, she can flirt, tell jokes, and won't bite your head off. She's great to sell to' (Sue Phipps of *RIVA* quoted in *The Times* 16 March 1988). Indeed, given that most advertisers are male she *is* an advertiser's fantasy in that the proportion of women materially able to respond remains relatively small, which is perhaps why she has been slower to success than her male counterpart. For television advertisers in particular the challenge is dauntingly twofold; on the one hand, to prove the lie that 'dressing to succeed in business and . . . dressing to be sexually attractive are *almost* mutually exclusive' (Molloy 1980 quoted in Shearer 1987: 108), and then to convey within 60 seconds 'the right balance between femininity and assertiveness, professional success and emotional depth' (p. 108). Unlike the New Man, the New Woman is never shown at work, but clearly has a successful career, is confident but sufficiently relaxed about life to be feminine and to not have to compete with the New Man. Amongst the more popular TV adverts propounding this thesis have been those for the Renault 5 and Black Magic.

> In the Renault 5 example his car won't start on the way to work, so they go in her Renault 5. He drives, she ribs him about his car, and sprays herself with scent as they go. 'The power broking woman would have been driving the car, this one doesn't have to.'
>
> (Kitty O'Hagen, Planning Director GGK
> in *The Times* 16 March 1988)

This New Woman doesn't reject 'alliance' virtues but transforms them into high gloss exchangeable accoutrements which become indistinguishable from the process of exchange regardless of the commodities involved. For example, the New Woman has recently made a vast impact on the sale of classical records with Cecilia Bartoli selling Rossini arias via black leather biker's jacket and gloves; Ute Lemper marketing Weill songs through Garboesque soft focus; violin virtuoso (perhaps it should be virtuosette), Anne Sophie Mutter being dubbed 'The Strapless Violinist' by *Vanity Fair*; and Ofra Harnoy sultrily promoting

Vivaldi Cello Concerti by reclining poutily full length on a chaise-longue: 'she likes the idea of reaching out' (Marketing Manager RCA quoted in *Independent on Sunday* 4 March 1990: 3). For the managing editor of *The Gramophone* this can only mean one thing: 'classical music is joining the real world' (p. 3).

Predictably, on the cusp of the new decade there are energetic predictions of even newer women, whilst the same old social-isation of the young continues. The transformation of adolescent girls from 'slags or drags' (Cowie and Lees 1987) and their US equivalents into Madison Avenue's 'Societally Conscious Achievers': 'inner directed rather than conforming to external standards, combining the best of home life and work as well as being ecologically responsible in a health-aware way' (Shearer 1987: 109), who, we are told, now account for more than 50 per cent of adult US female consumers, is one of the discursive miracles of our age, remarkable if it were not little more than marketing sleight of hand. Women's pages in the 'quality' press maintain the tension and test the confidence of their readers by an onslaught of new styles of the 1990s, often ostensibly not serious, but even so loaded with sufficient deadly serious cynicism to make one wonder. The following, passing under the crudely eupeptic labels of Cosmic Connie, Mrs Green and Sapphic Susie, may invite mirth but the reasoning exposed is not too far from marketing practice. Cosmic Connie:

> positively sparkling in her Persil-white outfit and sequinned back pack, in which baby Thursday is carried from working appointments to dinner parties: Connies love Rifat Ozbek. They gasped when the designer visualised their karma with his all white cat-walk spring collection. No one has told them that hidden backstage were other, perhaps more commercial colours.
>
> Mrs Green ... who is divorced [is] currently sporting a designer duffle coat – in the Nineties anti-fashion garments cost a packet – and badges with worthy slogans ... 'I'll be wearing strictly casual ensembles this year. . . . I think its the whole global thing, I mean look what happened in Eastern Europe.' They can never be specific, even if challenged, because they are not quite sure of the relationship between world peace/social rights and a hooded sweatshirt with 'Nirvana' emblazoned across the chest.

Sapphic Susies or 'bra-crossed lovers' . . . [are] a curious phenomenon of the New Age: part-time lesbians, who still live with their boyfriends but are temporarily experimenting with safer sex.

(*Observer* 14 Jan. 1990: 37)

From the beginning of the 'permissive' era's feminist revival, the dominance of traditional over modern sexual discourses has been amply recognised, several initial key texts claiming that the subjection of women is rooted in sexuality itself rather than capitalism, some eliding the two into a simple and simply misleading unity.

In the wake of Kinsey *et al.* (1953) and Masters and Johnson's (1966) revelations concerning multiple clitoral orgasmic women: 'MOMS – multi orgasmic monsters' (Coveney *et al.* 1984: 97), an, if not *the*, imperative of the sexualising age has been the harnessing of this potential, rather more successfully by Madison Avenue it has to be said than by feminist counter-claims, many elements of which the former has safely incorporated. Confined to procreative routine, suddenly women were faced with 'fulfillment', 'pleasure', and 'orgasmic potential'. Perhaps most famously Koedt (1974) claimed that the clitoral disclosure had truly revolutionary possibilities, it threatened heterosexism and demanded redefinitions of female sexualities 'which take into account mutual sexual enjoyment' so that penetration and The Sexual Act ceased to be the core of heterosexual experience, and heterosexual experience ceased to be the only option (Coote and Campbell 1982: 220–1), although as Campbell (1987b) notes 'what the feminist movement may have thought it invented in Anna Koedt's essay . . . had a long pre-feminist history' (p. 29).

Kinsey *et al.* (1953) and Masters and Johnson (1966), although influential popularising oracles, provided the official con-firmation of a gradually emergent discourse of 'active' female sexuality earlier promoted by gynaecologists and sex counsellors, and other, mostly self-appointed, 'experts'. In the first decades of this century Marie Stopes, Dora Russell and Stella Browne were some of the many female writers to assert women's right to sexual pleasure, free from unwanted pregnancies. 'There has grown up a masculine mythology suppressing and distorting all the facts of women's sexual and maternal emotions' opined Stella Browne (1917 quoted in Coote and Campbell 1982: 216). One year later,

THE PARAMETERS OF FEMALE SEXUAL CITIZENSHIP

in *Married Love*, Marie Stopes explained how a man might stimulate his wife during pregnancy without penetration (p. 216). Unsurprisingly, these campaigners still saw female sexuality as inextricably tied to maternity, but the inevitability of this link was at least implicitly questioned. 'Their ideal was the sexually satisfied earth mother: their ideas . . . anchored more in eugenics than eroticism' (p. 217). They perceived women's sexuality insofar as it could match men's, not propounding an active female sexuality as such, but one equally responsive to men in a mutual pursuit of satisfaction (Heath 1982).

However, with the popularisation of the separation of reproduction from female sexual pleasure in the 1950s and 1960s, as indicated by the critical reaction to Koedt, momentarily at least there appeared the possibility of a truly radical feminist sexual politics. Indeed, there has subsequently been deep, and deeply divisive, soul-searching over many specific issues of female and feminist sexualities. Pornography (Brown 1981; Dworkin 1981; Griffin 1981; Coward 1987; Kappeler 1987; Burstyn 1985), sex work (Delacoste and Alexander 1988), rape and other forms of male sexual violence (Griffin 1971; Findlay 1974; Brownmiller 1975; Hall 1981; Ellis and Beattie 1983), lesbianism (Ardill and Neumark 1982; Clark 1987; Nava 1987), S/M (Bellos 1984; France 1984; Califia 1988; Ardill and O'Sullivan 1987), and of course abortion have been the most significant, but no convincing truly oppositional and perhaps more importantly, potentially popular feminist sexual discourse has emerged to challenge either the reconstructed female of dominant political ideologies or the ersatz feminism of the market's New Woman. Resistance to dominant hype there has certainly been and not only from narrowly feminist tracts. Shere Hite (1976), for example, asked pertinent questions. She argued that the question should not be 'Why aren't women having orgasms from intercourse?', but why have women found it necessary to try everything from exercise to psycho-analysis and sex therapy, to make it happen?

But the problems commence once women are ideologically removed from this commodified incorporation into the cult of the 'Big O', for if women's sexuality is neither reducible to giving birth, breast feeding and menstruation nor to being MOMS, then what can it be?

Feminist Review (1987), despite overstated claims: 'at the beginning the feminist protest survived only because the challenge was supported by the mass of women' (p. 2), confronts the problem as the 'masculinisation' of women's sexualities into active, objectified and objectifying, alienated and alienating performance-led, orgasm-centred forms. 'A major concern of feminists over the past decade has been to make *visible* the extent to which sexuality has been defined by men and is experienced by women as coercive and objectifying' (p. 2). But as the *Hite Report* made clear it isn't experienced by most women as anything of the kind; being effectively scripted to pursue, through direct experience and displaced consumption, versions of 'the zipless fuck' (Jong 1973), the more so if the zips cost some. Of course there is heightened concern about formal injustices over sexual violence, prostitution and abortion, but informally the female embrace of mammon is pretty comprehensive. Just as male homosexuals could not be effectively commodified or politically incorporated as long as they remained illegal, passive non-objectifying subjects, consumed rather than consuming, so too actively consuming public women need to be reconstituted in commensurate sexually active forms, and this indeed is what they have become. Subjects they remain of course, but active 'feminine' subjects distracted and incorporated by their ability to buy, so that, being women, they may in turn be consumed. To define contemporary female sex norms and values as 'masculinised' is, therefore, to avoid the unappetising truth of reconstituted femininity, and to be distracted by the search for an obliterated essence, a female sexuality free of coercion, objectification, alienation, monogamy, 'jealousy and romantic longings' (p. 3).

Rubin (1984: 301) has identified in US feminist sexual politics two distinct perspectives which find comparable though not identical replication within British feminism: First, that which confronts restrictions on women's sexual behaviour, denounces the high costs imposed on women for being sexually active, and seeks the liberation of a female sexuality through material and institutional changes that would work for men as well as women. The second perspective of radical or cultural feminism[28] condemns almost all forms of sexual expression as anti-feminist and considers institutional and cultural liberalisation to be inherently an extension of male privilege. This 'demonology . . . resonates with conservative anti-sexual discourse' (p. 302), and leaves monogamous long-term lesbian relationships not involving polarised role play as the sexual form with the greatest status. In British feminism, the socialist presence has been altogether stronger, but it too has ceded to radical feminism over sexual matters. It is a cliché to say that the former's economism has inhibited its ability to address sexual issues, even so this relative weakness has enabled radical feminism to achieve virtual hegemonic control of sexuality in feminism and to atrophying effect. Feminism's peeling back of the layers of sexual false consciousness, its clearing of 'a personal space to fight back'[29] has thus become a retreat into self, a 'natural' state of being beyond patriarchal discourse, indeed beyond discourse altogether if this term is interpreted as systematic, objective, i.e. male/masculine knowledge and dominance (Rowbotham quoted in Shearer 1987: 18), a retreat into unconstructed, introspective, unspoken, mysterious, intuitively 'true' and unassailable knowledge of essential and universal female difference (Dworkin 1981; Griffin 1981, etc.). Against this logically consistent, forceful but highly exclusive and politically disengaging 'sentimentalisation of femaleness ... based on a cult of women-are-wonderful' (Campbell 1987b: 35), it is not surprising that alternative scripts of comparable clarity addressing female sexuality in the material worlds in which most women live have been unforthcoming, or that this uncompromising counter-ideology has done little more than further fragment feminism and alienate proto-feminists.

The fundamental problem with the radical feminist paradigm is that it subverts the articulation of a requisite counter-discourse 'simultaneously affirmative of nonprocreative sexuality yet critical of contemporary sexual culture' (Joffe 1986/7: 211), for it attempts to drag female sexuality outside discourse by presupposing innate knowledge of innate being.

We must say that we want sex and set our own terms. We must build a movement that validates the right to yes instead of no: a movement that thinks we haven't heard enough about sex rather than too much, and which reclaims an eroticism not defined by a simple political perspective or narrow vision which insists on excluding women to sustain its standards. We are searching for ways to examine sexuality, consent and power. We want to expand what we understand about sexuality so that more of us can live the desires we envision. We must start from where we are right now, from the real bodies we live in, the real desires we feel.

(Hollibaugh 1984: 408)

But is the 'real' here natural or a social construct? Either way the task is a daunting one which some have felt unequal to: 'The responsibility of creating a sexual life congruent with our often mute desires seems awesome and very likely impossible' (Webster 1984: 387–8), indeed, if it is believed that bodies are outside discourse, that desire transcends culture, and that the trek to find 'mute desires' doesn't bring the whole exercise back into the scripted world where 'not even one's sexuality is one's own' (*Feminist Review* 1987: 2), it clearly is impossible.

For Foucault no one's sexuality is ever their own, the belief that it *is* being but a crucial part and sign of immanent subjectivity, likewise the belief that asserting it is oppositional. Radical feminism's commitment to the discovery of female sexual essence has been born from the familiar confusion between oppression and repression: 'We live in such a strange transitional time that we bear the marks – we women – of extreme sex repression, total lack of images being motivated by sexual desire' (Wilson 1981; Gallop 1982). That such concerns have emerged during a 'transitional time' is not to be doubted but it is clearly analytically and politically naive to claim sexual repression and its consequences as here. Similarly to demand '. . . an account of sexuality which is about sexuality and its *discontents*. That is important for feminism . . . not an account of the conditioning of people into femininity' (Wilson 1987: 72), mistakenly suggests that the former can be reached without understanding the constructive force of the latter in creating discontents.

In *La Volonté de savoir* (1981) and elsewhere Foucault is himself of little help in this respect, being largely unconcerned with the ways in which sexual difference is constructed in patriarchal capitalism. However, in later interviews he did suggest how feminist responses to oppressive discourses could be, as with other minority groups such as male homosexuals, 'youth, blacks in America. . . ' (O'Higgins 1982–3), influentially oppositional. In Chapter 1 it was argued that Foucault ultimately allows no room for truly reverse dissent, a conclusion drawn from the polemical logic of *La Volonté de savoir* and other works, but later work demonstrates attempts to dilute if not disavow this interpretation through the making of typically elliptical references to feminist counter-discourses as, for example, 'surmountings'; defiant responses couched in the language of oppressive discourses (Foucault 1977b: 156).

> . . . for a long time they tried to pin women to their sex. For centuries they were told: 'You are nothing but your sex.' And this sex, doctors added, is fragile, almost always sick and always inducing illness. 'You are man's sickness.' And towards the eighteenth century this ancient movement ran wild, ending in a pathologisation of woman: the female body became a medical object *par excellence*. . . . But the feminist movement responded defiantly. Are we sex by nature? Well then, let us be so but in its singularity, in its irreducible specificity. Let us draw the consequences and reinvent our own type of existence, political, economic, and cultural. . . . Always the same movement: to use this sexuality as the starting point in an attempt to colonize them and to cross beyond it toward affirmation.
>
> (Foucault 1977b: 156)

But affirmation of what exactly? The radical feminist perspective reifies the essential criteria of dominant 'alliance' discourses to the extent of *con*firmation and, with interest, takes oppositional feminism out of the mainstream political arena by positing the enemy as male rather than capital or the state, proposes solutions which reject heterosexism and isolates feminism outside newly erected barriers around normal, modern, public, politically responsible female citizens structurally differentiated and politically divided by this uncompromising paradigm. As Rubin (1984: 302) comments 'Whatever happened to the family, religion, education, child-rearing practices, the media, the state, psychiatry, job discrimination, and unequal pay?'

Latterly the search for a feminist sexual politics has become more fruitfully theorised through ambitious analyses of women's particular relationships to and experiences of power forms as well as effects and in this context inevitably Foucault has been given due regard. Clearly his emphasis on the body as the ever-intensified locus of power and resistance identifies a site that feminists recognise far more readily than men, being at the heart

269

of prostitution, abortion, rape, pornography and body imagery campaigns. Similarly Foucault's emphasis on immanent normative power is sympathetically attuned to women's more diffuse and oblique relationship to juridical forms (see Margolis 1989). All the more strange, therefore, that Foucault failed to exemplify his analysis through the female/feminine subject although, as we have noted, his deconstructed paradigm does not require the identification of class, state, patriarchal or other formal structures of domination. For Hartsock (1990) this failure is spiritual as well as analytical: 'Foucault's analysis is not for women because Foucault's imagination of power is "with" rather than "against" power' (p. 169). Even so, radical feminism deploys similar understandings of seemingly irresistible colonising immanent power/knowledge on female subjects, resolutely tied to a patriarchal source it is true, but a source it is not felt necessary to analyse closely, and thus in possession of a similarly abstract and inhuman dynamic. For example, Jeffreys (1990: 2) claims that all the post-'permissive' era has proved is that heterosexuality is 'the eroticisation of female subordination – of power difference – so that female subordination becomes sexy for men and for women'.

For Jeffreys the explanation is the assertion of sexologic discourse:

> The language of liberation was so loud in connection with the new sexual prescriptions for women that commentators have assumed some obvious relationship between the 'sexual revolution' and progress in women's condition. . . . As we shall see the rules of sexologic remained unaltered. Behind the baloney of liberation, the naked power politics of male supremacy were being acted out. The high priests of sexologic, helped by the pornographers, progressive novelists and sex radicals continued to orchestrate woman's joyful embrace of her oppression through the creation of her sexual response.
>
> (Jeffreys 1990: 2)

But why is female subordination sexy for women? Why the joyful, and financially draining, embrace of oppression? Subordination and oppression have certainly not been eased in the past generation but they have been dramatically deflected through the superficial improvements in women's material status. If sexologic has any momentum it is surely of and from the

270

market. Jeffreys' inability or unwillingness to accept as much leads her to the isolationist salvation of a lesbianism naively assumed to be outside of male sexologic and the 'lived reality of subjectivity' (*Feminist Review* 1987: 3).

As feminist and Foucauldian logic implies, though to disagreed prognoses, this 'lived reality of sexuality' is from whatever discursive source insistently homing in on the inner self, fulfillment of self by the self, so that whether masculine or feminine, sexual scripts inexorably draw us, as Greer (1990) argues, into an onanistic hell. Masters and Johnson (1966) reported that their women subjects achieved the most intense orgasms whilst masturbating, hence 'Masturbation became the symbol of autonomous feminist sexuality, a logical reconciliation of our bodies and our lives, and a necessary foundation for knowing what was erotically satisfying' (Webster 1984: 387–8), but masturbation has always been the main preoccupation of men defensively written off maybe as 'sex with someone I love' (Woody Allen), 'the good thing about masturbation is that you don't have to dress up for it', the ultimate sexual and personal commodity of 'me', realised through the fantasy constructs of pornography or 'dick-speak'. Clitoral sexuality behaviourally and symbolically opens up female sexuality to commodification and to the constructs of erotica:

Not only were the fingers, tongues and toes of either sex sufficient for the attainment of clitoral ecstasy, but dildos and a host of electrically vibrating devices purchased by mail order or in a local drug store could provide women with sexual gratification at a far cheaper price than the traditional path of life-long enslavement to marriage and man.

(Delfini 1986: 24)

Thus for Greer (1990) women have taken up their place in 'the masturbating society. Our heads are crammed with glittering, bulging fantasies that have drained the colour out of real life. Our libido is tightly wound in media symbolism, packaged music, disco grind and bounce', charmed by the market's provision of variety, impersonality and free self-exploration. This is under-lined by the appearance in Britain since 1988 of three volumes of female erotica (Reynolds 1990). As one critic commented 'This sudden flowering of female erotica is rather disturbing: should we deplore it as indication of women taking control or deplore it as yet another example of big business cashing in on women's sexuality?' (Allen 1990).

The only escape for some has been to deny the sexual in sexuality altogether, as with Rich's notions of 'lesbian continuum' and 'lesbian existence', the latter being lesbian identity defined not by sexual practice but by the communality of women independent of men, the former encompassing this range of female communality at any one time or over time in all women's lives (Rich 1980). But even here there is no escape, there is speech, values, emotion, experiences, scripts and bodies infused with culture which has constructed this particular lesbianism and sisterhood in ways that clearly impose self-policing into dominant essential rigidities. It is commonly claimed that 'To politicize sexuality has been one of the most important achievements of the Women's Liberation Movement . . . [creating] . . . the space in which women can refuse sexual exploitation and begin to reflect on our own desires' (*Feminist Review* 1987: 1).

Weeks echoes this view

> The rupture that feminism proposes both with traditional ways of thought and with well-established political practices – the assertion of the power of female desire in all its forms against masculinist assumptions and practices – has had a profoundly disturbing effect on the politics of sex. . . .
>
> (Weeks 1985: 9)

But although structural dissonance enabled the development of feminist popular demands, the politicisation of sexuality has not been solely or even primarily a feminist achievement, but a necessary concomitant to its commodification. Feminism did not create the space for sexual differentiation, or fragmentation into resistance and reflection, nor is feminism in opposition to a unitary, traditional unchanging structure. On the contrary it is precisely because of the major structural upheavals of the second half of this century that feminism has been spurred into action, always to an embryonically radical extent,[30] but effectively 'surmounting' into newly stabilising ideologies for the ambivalent experiences of modern 'independent' private/public womanhood. Even radical feminism's retreat into nature, into self, is an alternative route into individual obsession, style, constructed out of individual perquisites as effectively as if by market and citizenship, and contributing, albeit *in extremis*, to the reconstruction of modern women's status. There seems to be nothing awry with Jeffreys verdict that:

> . . . women caught up in the 'sexual revolution' struggled to survive. They advised each other on how to swallow semen in the same way in which they would advise each other on how to remove red wine stains from the carpet in another kind of women's magazine. Fellatio was a new kind of housework.
>
> (Jeffreys 1990: 114)

. . . what alternatives are there? Sanded floors and cunnilingus, every bit as commodifiable and exploitable as the gold-plated zipless fuck. Whilst the power relations inscribed on modern women and female bodies are, consonant with their structural schizophrenia, altogether more diverse and contradictory than those placed on men, the female subject in modern societies is as much a derivative product of 'certain contingent, historically specific linguistically infused social practices' (Foucault 1981) within which feminist 'surmountings' have played a superordinate stabilising role in the incorporation of women into sexual citizenship.

NOTES

1 SEXUALITY AS DISCOURSE AND SCRIPT

1 The English edition's title *The History of Sexuality: An Introduction* is weak. *The Will to Know* or *The Will to Knowledge* conveys better the intricate relationship between sexuality and power: power is knowledge, *pouvoir* = *savoir*. The title is clearly Nietzschean in inspiration, i.e. as set against the latter's *The Will to Power*: 'I am simply Nietzschean' (Foucault 1985: 8).

2 In his later work Foucault disputed earlier implications that power is knowledge in an equivalent sense. 'What I set out to show was how certain forms of power that were of the same type could give rise to bodies of knowledge that were extremely different both in their object and in their structure. Let us take the problem of the structure of the hospital: it gave rise to confinement of a psychiatric type, to which corresponded the formation of a body of psychiatric knowledge whose epistemological structure may leave one fairly skeptical. But in another book, *Naissance de la clinique*, I tried to show how, in that same hospital structure, there developed a body of anatomo-pathological knowledge that was the foundation of a medicine possessing a quite different potential for scientific development. We have, then, power structures, fairly closely related institutional forms – psychiatric confinement, medical hospitalisation – that are bound up with different forms of knowledge, between which it is possible to draw up a system of relations based not on cause and effect, still less on identity, but on conditions' (1984a: 264–5).

3 We are on guard in public, whereas our private preoccupations with self mean that we tend not to perceive external or penetrating power. E.g. 'In our public mode of being we speak the common language of reason and live under the laws of the state, the constraints of the market, and the customs of the different social bodies to which we belong. In our private incarnation, however, we are at the mercy of our own sense, impressions and desires' (Unger 1975: 59).

4 '. . . the only part of the conduct of anyone for which he is amenable

274

to society is that which concerns others. In the part which concerns himself, his independence is of right absolute. Over himself, over his own body and mind and the individual is sovereign. . . . [This] appropriate reform of human liberty covers matters of conscience, thought, opinion, expression. It also covers liberty of taste and pursuits; of framing the plan of our life to suit our own character, as doing as we like subject to such consequences as may follow' (Mill 1910: 9).

5 For a more conventional view: 'Human actions appear here compulsive as their subjects belong to earlier historical formations (e.g. with unbroken religious faith). The capacity to subject instinctual reactions to moral criticism and to change them on the basis of individual consideration could only develop with the growing differentiation of society' (Horkheimer 1986: 87).

6 Juliet Mitchell (1971: 157) observes: 'It is almost as though the family has got smaller and smaller in order for it to make itself "one" in a desperate struggle against the disparity of its members in the outside world.'

7 On a contemporary, popular media level Peter Conrad has noted of The Oprah Winfrey Show 'combining roles of earth mother and sob sister, investigative muckraker and New Age Evangelist, she talks through the diurnal miseries of the 20 million Americans who watch her each afternoon and healingly exhorts them to "turn their lives around".' Conrad describes this show as 'hour-long life sessions' (1990).

8 Cohen (1968: 116) defines norms as 'that which regularly occurs . . . what members of a society have a right to expect'.

9 '. . . conventional practice accepted as appropriate but not insisted on' (Sumner quoted in Chinoy 1962: 17).

10 '. . . normative patterns which define what are felt to be . . . proper, legitimate, or expected modes of action or social relationships' (Parsons 1949: 203).

11 See Althusser (1971).

12 'Social systems are those constituted by states and processes of social interaction among acting units. If the properties of interaction were derivable from properties of the acting units, social systems would be epiphenomenal, as much "individualistic" social theory has contended. Our position is sharply in disagreement' (Parsons 1971: 7).

13 Foucault (1987: 16) describes the 'aesthetic approach to life'/'aesthetic existence': 'What I mean by this phrase are those intentional and voluntary actions by which men not only set themselves rules of conduct but also seek to transform themselves to change themselves in their singular being, and to make their life into an oeuvre that carries certain stylish criteria.'

14 'Sexism is . . . a belief that the human sexes have a distinctive make-up that determines their respective lives, usually involving the idea that (a) one sex is superior and has the right to rule the other and (b) a policy of enforcing such a right and (c) a system of society and government based on it' (Frazier and Sadker 1973: 5).

275

15 Symbolic interactionism (Blumer 1962) lay in comparative obscurity until 'brought to prominence by the spirit of the times' (i.e. 1960s) (Joas 1987).
16 'Labelling' or 'social reaction' theory is well discussed by Taylor *et al.* (1973: 140–71).
17 For a useful discussion of sexual socialisation see Plummer (1975: 56–60, 131–53).

2 SEXUAL RIGHTS AND COMMODITIES: THE MATERIAL CONSTRUCTION OF SEXUAL CITIZENSHIP

1 For a detailed account of women's employment in contemporary Britain (including horizontal and vertical segregation, feminisation, etc., see Beechey (1986a, b) as well as Hakim (1979, 1981).
2 Oakley (1982: 134) observes that women's prior responsibility to the family serves to characterise them as 'deficient labourers'. For a discussion of capitalism's creation of 'housework' see Middleton (1975).
3 On the domestic labour debate Molyneux (1980) notes: 'The political economy of women is a crucially important area of research but the terms of the debate have to be broadened . . . to analyse the complex combination of material relations through which women's subordination is mediated' (p. 22).
4 Engels (1968) argues that once the wife fulfils her duties in the private service of her family she remains excluded from public production and cannot earn anything; and when she wishes to take part in public industry and earn her living independently, she is not in a position to fulfil her family duties. For a feminist critique of Engels see Delmar (1976).
5 See McIntosh (1978b, 1984) who in the latter explores state–family relations through child care policy and care for the aged and disabled. Both K. Marshall (1986) and Phillips (1988) address succinctly Thatcherism's ideological use of women and the family.
6 '. . . in the family role of women "mothering" is . . . seen as an essential ingredient, its absence pathogenic, threatening the whole purpose of the family – the production of healthy children' (Oakley 1976: 69).
7 Not only through private home ownership, but also through the expansion of consumer durables and technologies of modern domestic labour.
8 McIntosh (1984) discusses in some detail the competing perspectives on state–family relations in contemporary Britain.
9 Also in McIntosh (1984) the state's formal intervention to secure continuous adequate child care (the Children's Act 1975) is part of the overall theme of an increasingly interventionist state into welfare and education institutions replacing the family 'in providing for the functional needs of the society' (p. 214).
10 Women's work is often 'deemed inferior simply because women do

it' (Phillips and Taylor 1986) not least by male-dominated trades-unions (Cockburn 1986), alternatively gender differentiated skills culture inhibits and prohibits at all levels of educational and work experience (see Stanworth 1984; Deem 1978, 1980; Spender and Sarah 1980; Snell 1986). The last named concludes; 'Most women are still concentrated in low-grade, low-paid women's jobs with little prospect of better paid jobs or promotion' (p. 34).

11 Beechey (1982) argues that a Marxist-feminist variant of Marxist deskilling theory should include the family within its terms of reference.

12 Approximately 40 per cent of female employees work less than 30 hours a week, compared to 5 per cent of men: 25 per cent of women work less than 16 hours, 90 per cent of women working less than 30 hours are married and 65 per cent have dependent children. . . . Almost twice as many men as women work overtime. (See Coote and Campbell 1982: 63.)

13 Charles (1986) notes that whilst in recent years the TUC (Trades Union Congress) has adopted policies 'progressive in terms of women's equality within the trade-union movement' (p. 160), they are little more than token commitments masking sexist practices and ideologies of familialism. Menstruation and child care are thus generally excluded from the agendas of trade unions, union meetings are held outside working hours, and do not have crèche provision, making it very difficult for most women to attend. To say, therefore, that female wage labour is 'politically less well organised' than that of men is to observe that it is so structured.

14 See Bland et al. (1978), Adamson et al. (1976), Bruegel (1986).

15 As Beechey warns (1986a, b) dual labour market theory (e.g. Barron and Norris 1976) may explain why women are a secondary sector work-force, lacking the characteristics which would make them a preferred primary sector work-force (i.e. not being men), but it ignores the positive advantages to employers when they hire female labour (p. 156).

16 These terms are of course not in themselves clichés, but they have all been employed as such.

17 Whilst in Britain the wealthiest 1 per cent's share of total wealth has gently declined during this century figures on shares of total wealth contain an 'optical illusion' (Rentoul 1987: 41) for as total personal wealth has increased and the share of the rich, especially the top 10 per cent, has remained the same, the latter have seen large increases in their holdings – many times larger than the increases enjoyed by those at the average level of increased wealth. The richest 10 per cent own 52 per cent of the personal wealth in Britain, whilst throughout this century there has been a drift towards 'impersonal' capital. For Coakley and Harris (1983) the City of clearing banks, building societies and insurance companies, pension funds and foreign based banks remains the centre around which the whole financial system revolves.

18 In 1956 the proportion of the work-force employed in

manufacturing was 38 per cent, in 1983 it was 26 per cent and it continues to fall. Between 1960 and 1982 Britain's share of OECD manufacturing output fell from 9.6 per cent to 4.1 per cent. Between 1960 and 1982 the proportion of the work-force employed in the service sector rose from 47 per cent to 62 per cent (Harris 1985: 9).

19 Between 1911 and 1981 the proportion of manual workers in Britain's total occupied population fell from 74.6 per cent to 47.7 per cent and that of non-manual workers increased from 18.7 per cent to 52.3 per cent.

20 Perhaps 'non-work' time would be more appropriate.

21 There are doubts as to whether Thatcherism 'rolled back' the state, or reconstructed it. (See Thompson 1984 and Jessop et al. 1988.)

22 The 'free' here should be read as parenthetic.

23 'False needs' as opposed to 'true needs' essential to human survival and well-being.

24 D'Emilio (1983a: 144) notes that during the 1960s in the US, in particular in the legal profession, the role of the state, the right to privacy, 'violations of due process and arbitrary and capricious enforcement practices,' were addressed in ways broadly comparable to those being pursued in post-*Wolfenden Report* (1957) Britain. See e.g. Schwartz (1963).

25 Parsons (1965: 1009–10) defines citizenship as 'full membership of the societal community' i.e. 'that aspect of the total society as a system which forms a Gemeinschaft, which is the focus of solidarity or mutual loyalty of its members and which constitutes the consensual base underlying its political integration'.

26 However, as Dworkin (1990: 1) has pointed out, whilst such ideals may be approximately met in practice, there is no formal machinery to prevent a decline in 'the culture of liberty, the culture of freedom'.

27 One purpose of a Bill of Rights is to place certain subjects beyond the reach of majorities and officials: 'One's right to life, liberty and property, to free speech, a free press, freedom of worship and assembly and other fundamental rights may not be submitted to vote: they depend on the outcome of no elections' (Pannick in *The Independent* 20 April 1990: 17 referring to a 1943 statement by Justice Jackson on behalf of the US Supreme Court).

28 'Both the letter and the spirit of the American Constitution seem to many citizens to be violated by governmental methods of electronic surveillance, police actions against non-violent protesters, and disregard for individual minority and women's rights' (Duchacek 1973: 3).

29 Charter 88 is committed to just such an incorporation and prior to the 1992 General Election the Labour Party was also flirting with such a commitment: 'if Labour is to reach beyond class interests it must emphasise a sense of common citizenship by defining a set of common rights' (Plant 1988: 12).

30 E.g. in 1981 Dudgeon won the European Court of Human Rights verdict that the unrepealed Northern Ireland law outlawing homosexuality was a violation of a person's privacy and thus

contrary to Article 8 of the Convention. The British Government brought Northern Ireland's law on homosexuality into line with that of England and Wales in 1982. Norris won a comparable verdict in 1990 on anti-homosexual law in Eire. Norris was described by the *Independent on Sunday* (28 Jan. 1990) thus '. . . devoted to James Joyce for his genius with words and his honesty, Mr Norris loves the way the Irish use English – "a free language" he calls it, that permits a housewife to say "since we got a new aerial the deception is wonderful".'

31 These two principles have a 'lexical order' (Rawls 1972: 42–4) both in order of consideration and satisfaction 'it suggests permissible trade-offs and impermissible ones. . . . We can e.g. sacrifice aggregate wealth or personal income at each of several levels to achieve greater liberty of all or to help level out some of the natural or social contingencies that work against "fair equality of opportunity". But we cannot trade off a lesser liberty to achieve a greater overall standard of wealth' (Martin 1985: 15).

32 T.H. Marshall's analysis is entirely British in reference but it serves as a convincing broad account of the development of citizenship rights in all modern societies. For discussions of different strategies of citizenship and in particular a comparison between citizenship developments in the US and Britain see Parsons (1971: 93), Mann (1987), and for a comparison of US/British sexual rights developments see Weeks (1985: 54–6).

33 Prior to both Acts political rights were qualified by material circumstance.

34 The 'such' here is meant to indicate an approximate watershed.

35 Whilst the *Beveridge Report* (1942) is generally credited with creating the foundations of the modern social security system Ginsburg (1979: 95) suggests that the bases for unemployment insurance and national assistance had been laid before the Second World War. 'Thus the reforms of the 1940s simply improved benefits and rationalised previous policies.'

36 There have been numerous 'spy' scandals involving homosexuals: e.g. Blunt, Burgess, etc. as well as exposés of men and women in the armed services discharged for misconduct. At the time of writing, however, reform of current law making homosexuality illegal in the latter has been proposed.

37 FROCS stands for Faggots Rooting Out Closeted Sexualities.

38 E.g. see *Changing the World: A London Charter for Gay and Lesbian Rights* (1985) produced by the GLC in co-operation with the GLC Gay Working Party.

3 THE 'PERMISSIVE' WATERSHED

1 D'Emilio (1983a: 140) talks of the Stonewall Riots as 'the event that ignited the gay liberation movement'. Bronski (1984: 87) describes them as a 'defiant, innately political act' which 'established a

homosexual militancy and identity in the public imagination that was startling and deeply threatening to Americans' (p. 3).

2 E.g. in the US the neo-conservative sponsored John M. Ohlin and Bradley Foundation's 'Second Thoughts' Conference of Autumn 1987.

3 The pill first appeared in Britain as a form of fertility control in 1964.

4 Since the Act became law in 1971 'the number of divorces doubled from 80,000 to 159,000 by 1984', but divorcees re-marry and 'overall the proportion entering marriage has declined only very slightly' (Elliott and McCrone 1987: 488).

5 Such laws are 'receptacle' or 'residual', their use against specific categories of offender is thus hard to monitor; they are deployed to clear public territories of degrees of nuisance and are also often fall-back laws when stronger specific others (e.g. concerning sexual indecency) fail through lack of sufficient police evidence.

6 Whilst all this legislation may be broadly described as 'liberalising', elsewhere strengthened legislation appeared specifying the state's right to intervene in order to protect the rights of particular categories of citizen: e.g. 1955 Children and Young Persons (Harmful Publications) Act and the Race Relations Act 1965 which both inhibited free speech by outlawing specific published and verbal expressions.

7 Hobsbawm (1968) demonstrates how the British economy's boom of the late 1950s and 1960s was strikingly restricted to the sphere of private, domestic consumption.

8 Between 1955 and 1969 average weekly earnings rose by 88 per cent, prices by 63 per cent. In 1950 car ownership was at 2.3 million, by 1970 it was 12 million. Refrigerators were owned by 8 per cent of households in 1956, by 70 per cent in 1970. By 1971 91 per cent of households owned a TV.

9 The first campus demonstrations in the US were at Berkeley University in 1964, where Nesbit was Professor of Sociology. For a broader discussion of student campaigns in Britain see Young (1972).

10 Critiques of the 'bourgeois' family were not confined to feminist writers, e.g. see Laing (1971) Cooper (1971), etc.

11 In the 1950s and 1960s there was consensus between Conservative and Labour parties on a wide range of policies, from provision and maintenance of the welfare state, and corporatist management of the economy, to Britain's role as a nuclear power and NATO membership. This consensus extended to socio-legal and moral reforms referred to by Hall (1979: 1) as 'legislation of consent' and by Greenwood and Young (1979: 172) as 'interventionist permissiveness'.

12 However, Rayside and Bowler (1988) warn that the general pattern of younger cohorts exhibiting more liberal attitudes to sexual and moral issues was broken in their 1985 findings which showed male teenagers less supportive of gay rights than men in their 20s.

13 Which is not to say that particular circumstances and campaigns may
    not reverse this trend, if only over short periods; e.g. a LWT
    (London Weekend Television) survey, of dubious methodology
    admittedly, carried out shortly after the introduction of Section 28
    of the Local Government Act 1988 found that support for
    legalisation of homosexual relations dropped from 61 per cent in
    1985 to 48 per cent in 1988, with over half of the sample believing
    homosexuality 'unnatural'. Broadly, it would appear that there is
    increasing tolerance of legalisation but simultaneously, no doubt
    due to such legislation, increased moral censoriousness and concern
    about contamination of 'pure' public spaces.

4 HOMOSEXUAL CITIZENSHIP: ECONOMIC RIGHTS . . .

1 For a recent British reappraisal see Scherker (1989).
2 E.g. 'San Francisco is a refugee camp for homosexuals. We have fled
   here from every part of the nation . . . not because it is so great here
   but because it was so bad there' (Wittman 1977: 330).
3 D'Emilio (1983a) on the link between the development of
   homosexual subcultures and the enabling base of free wage labour
   notes: 'Only when individuals began to make their living through
   wage labour instead of as parts of an independent family unit, was it
   possible for homosexual desire to coalesce into a personal identity –
   an identity based on the ability to remain outside the heterosexual
   family and construct a personal life based on attraction to one's own
   sex' (p. 144).
4 Witham (1977a) argues that homosexuality is an orientation and a
   'fundamental element of personality' (p. 8), 'emerging in childhood
   without a script' and 'not a homosexual role' (p. 96).
5 Weeks (1981b) considers in detail such specifically anti-homosexual
   statutes as the Labouchère Amendment to the 1885 Criminal Law
   Amendment Act and more general enabling statutes such as the
   1898 Vagrancy Act which sought to control importuning for
   immoral purposes, and included clauses against homosexual
   soliciting. See also Crane (1982) and the Report of the Howard
   League Working Party (1985).
6 In addition to these references on 'camp' see Baker (1968) and Kirk
   and Heath (1984) for interesting texts on 'drag'.
7 Dank (1971: 180) defines his influential study as being 'directed
   toward determining what conditions permit a person to say, "I am a
   homosexual" '. Various subsequent analysts together with Dank
   have sought to isolate possible key stages, settings and scripts
   including the following: (i) first awareness of desire or sexual feelings
   towards persons of the same sex; (ii) first homosexual experience;
   (iii) first participation in territories defined as being principally for
   homosexuals. Hooker (1967) defines 'coming-out' as occurring
   'when he identifies himself publicly for the first time as a homosexual

in the presence of homosexuals, by his appearance in a bar'; (iv) consciously labelling oneself as homosexual (this is the Dank usage: '. . . self-identification may or may not occur in a social context in which other gay people are present' (p. 182)); (v) accepting self as homosexual. Self-labelling does not necessarily entail self-acceptance; (vi) the learning of subcultural scripts and roles; (vii) and of positive definitions counter to those of stigma in general cultural use; and finally (viii) 'coming-out' in the fully political sense of open declaration in 'straight' territories. Of course any such 'deviant career' scheme is little more than a device to aid analysis of processes of considerable dynamic complexity.

8 Westwood (1952) talks of the pre-legalisation male homosexual British subculture as consisting of the street corner, the 'queer' bars, private and exclusive clubs, and outsiders. Cory (1953) includes 'drag' as a part of the subculture and Cory and LeRoy (1963) talk more loosely of 'bars for chance encounters'.

9 Houston (1978: 15) likens these new styles to 'the boy who laughs and jokes with the school bully, in the hope that by siding with him he'll go unmolested. But the boot licking doesn't save him when the school bully takes it into his head to beat him up'.

10 E.g. Netherlands receives 50 pages with Amsterdam accounting for 26 of them (573–623), the UK and Northern Ireland have 58 pages, London getting 16 (833–91), Spain 53 (702–55), etc.

11 'Clones' having short hair, moustaches, being denim or leather-dressed 'virilised' gay males.

5 . . . AND POLITICAL OBLIGATIONS

1 Jay and Young (1977) provide a few including Wittman's 'A Gay Manifesto' (330–42). Other sources on late 1960s and early 1970s gay activism in the US are Teal (1971); Tobin and Wicker (1972); Altman (1972); Jay and Young (1978). On GLF in Britain see Weeks (1977); Watney (1980); Walter (1980); Cant and Hemmings (1988); Mellors (1990).

2 Rowbotham (1979) has commented that the idea of oppression is both vague and static, fixing people in their role as victim rather than pointing to the contradictory aspects of relationships which *force* the emergence of new forms of consciousness.

3 The Stonewall Group was formed one year after the passing of Section 28 by a largely media/arts group to set up an all-party parliamentary working group on lesbian and gay rights and to lobby for legal reforms: lowering the age of homosexual consent to 16, abolition of crimes of gross indecency and soliciting; outlawing anti-gay discrimination in the provision of goods and services; legal recognition for same-sex couples; removal of anti-gay laws in the armed services; creation of a new offence of incitement to hatred on grounds of sexual orientation; outlawing discrimination at work, in the provision of hotel facilities, education, entertainment, banking,

etc.; ending prosecutions of under 16-year-olds engaging in consensual homosexual activities; the creation of a new offence of 'aggravated indecent assault' to cover male rape.

4 J. Marshall (1989: 21) describes 'outing' as ' "tabloid witch hunt" tactics adopted by gay activists to expose closeted gay celebrities. It began in the US magazine *Outweek* under the title "Peek-a-Boo". The justification was as follows: "Gay people in positions of power and influence ought to come out publicly and there are some who openly abuse their position of power by supporting homophobic measures." '

5 FROCS stands for Faggots Rooting Out Closeted Sexualities.

6 OutRage is 'a broad based group of lesbians and gay men committed to radical non-violent direct action and disobedience to (i) assert the dignity and pride and human rights of gay men and lesbians; (ii) to fight homophobia, discrimination and violence against lesbians and gay men and (iii) to affirm the rights of lesbians and gay men to sexual freedom, choice and self-determination. OutRage tactics are reminiscent of those of the early GLF such as 'zapping' the 16th International Congress of the Family in July 1990.

7 ActUp has notably organised mass demonstrations in various US cities against alleged US government ineptitude in handling AIDS research, e.g. at the National Institute of Health at Bethesda in May 1990 and outside the 6th International Conference on AIDS in San Francisco earlier that year. See *Gay Times* (21 May 1990). Also see catalogue for *Read My Lips: New York AIDS Polemics*. Tramway: Glasgow, November 1992.

8 Charter 88 is a broader based and reformist civil rights and liberties organisation.

9 Amongst them being Austria, Bulgaria, Czechoslovakia, Finland, Hungary and the UK. In Bulgaria, Czechoslovakia and Finland the higher discriminatory age of consent also applies to lesbians (Tatchell 1990, 1992).

10 Stonewall's reformist measures have sparked comment in British broadsheets such as the following *Times* editorial (13 Feb. 1990): 'The Church of England and the Labour Party are currently both suffering from sexual embarrassment. Both . . . have a constituency which actively lobbies for homosexual equality causing discomfort to their leaders who know that the issue is a pew emptier and a vote loser. . . .' This editorial argued against the lowering of the age of consent to 16 on the grounds that once changed it could never be reversed and that the current higher discriminatory age of 21 was a symbol of the moral difference between hetero- and homosexuality. Further, it was claimed that the sexual development of the male adolescent needs special protection, especially important as the current age of consent enables policing of male prostitution during the AIDS crisis.

The age of consent issue re-emerged in early December 1991 when Scotland's Lord Advocate was reported as considering new 'sensible guidance to procurators-fiscal', namely that charges against males between the ages of 16 and 21 engaging in homosexual acts should only be brought if there is evidence of 'seduction, corruption or breach of trust'. In the event intervention from Whitehall seemingly blocked any such change in legal practice. For a discussion of the issues involved see Evans (1991: 15). At the time of writing there would appear to be the outside possibility of a free vote on this issue in the forthcoming Parliamentary session.

11 Of the twenty-three, six were jailed for buggery, four for attempted buggery and thirteen for gross indecency. Eight were jailed for up to 1 year and seven were jailed for up to 2 years, six for up to 3 years and two for between 3 and 4 years. These figures were given by Home Office Minister John Patten in answer to a Commons question from MP Gavin Strang according to a report in *Gay Times* (March 1990: 5).

12 Although the Labour Party's 1988 Annual Conference voted to reduce the age of consent the Labour front bench was and remains less than enthusiastic.

13 GALOP (Gay London Policing Group) claims that the police deliberately charge gay men under local council bye-laws to deny them the right to trial by jury for which there is provision in national sexual offences legislation (*Gay Times* Aug. 1989); fabricate evidence; physically assault those charged with gay offences; and arrest gay men for 'attitudinal problems' such as 'looking at the police in a hostile manner' (*Gay Times* Jan. 1989: 9).

14 'The policeman was dressed in ripped, faded jeans, tight white t-shirt, black leather jacket and had black cropped hair and a moustache. He was acting in a manner that suggested that he was looking for sex' *Gay Times* (Aug. 1989: 7).

15 *Gay Times* (Dec. 1986) reported on a judge's summing up to the jury hearing the case of two men accused of an armed attack on a homosexual man: 'You must remember that Mr Stanley is a man of homosexual tendencies. He must be warped to be so.' *Gay Times* (June 1990) claimed that there were outstanding 15 unfinished police enquiries into murders of gay men.

16 E.g. *Independent on Sunday* (29 July 1990) reported *OutRage*'s issuing of '100s of whistles dangling from brightly coloured strings . . . in gay bars and clubs in London . . . the initiative is a copy of whistle patrols in New York, San Francisco and Sydney'.

17 *Gay Times* (Aug. 1990) referred to complaints by SHRG (Scottish Homosexual Rights Group) of such police harassment by Strathclyde Police during enquiries into the murder of David Nicholl in May 1990.

18 *Gay Times* (Dec. 1989; Feb. 1990) reported on 'Operation Mouthwash' in which British police raided eighteen houses, the addresses having been obtained from the Dutch contact magazine *ScatClub*. One man was fined £1000 for possessing indecent or obscene materials.

19 Gay's The Word were supported in their campaign by NCROPA (National Campaign to Reform the Obscene Publications Act) (*Gay Times* Dec. 1989: 7). Academics are also affected, *Gay Times* (Sep.

1988) reported that J. Dollimore and A. Sinfield had resigned as general editors of a series on cultural politics after a decision was taken by Manchester University Press to block publication of a book on gay politics. This is precisely the kind of self-censorship intended by Section 28.

20 However, the Press Council has since decided that it is not acceptable for the media to use the words 'poof' or 'poofter' as terms of abuse against gay men. 'Although the words "poof" and "poofter" are in common parlance they are so offensive to male homosexuals that publishing them is not a matter of taste or opinion within a newspaper editor's discretion', Press Council Ruling reported in *Gay Times* (June 1990: 6).

21 Leonard Matlovich, court-martialled in 1975 because of his homosexuality, fought to keep his position in the United States Air Force.

22 'Ban Gay Judges' (*Sun* 19 Jan. 1990) 'It would taint the whole administration of justice if a judge was suspected of a homosexual relationship.' The same edition included a Franklin cartoon showing a judge sitting cross-legged on the bench wearing suspenders and stockings, being addressed by the prisoner as follows 'I promise to tell the poof, the whole poof and nothing but the poof.' See also *Gay Times'* (Aug. 1988) report on the High Court's rejection of the appeal of GCHQ worker Andrew Hodges who had his security clearance removed after telling his employers he was gay. The gay and straight media are full of comparable cases clustering in particular employment areas such as education, security, law, etc.

23 ARC is the acronym for AIDS Related Complex; minor infections considered early signs of immune system depression, e.g. oral thrush.

24 *Gay Times* (Aug. 1989: 5) reported that the House of Commons Social Services Committee recommended that insurers should drop questions about HIV so that more people would be willing to test.

25 The London march (9 Jan. 1988) reportedly attracted 92,000; that in Manchester on 20 Feb. 20,000 and again in London (30 April) 50,000. All were organised by Stop the Clause Campaign. On 23 May BBC 1's evening news programme was 'zapped' by lesbian infiltrators: 'Dykes Penetrate Auntie' as one tabloid put it, lesbian demonstrators abseiled into the Lords chamber, numerous actors and media personnel used awards ceremonies such as the SWET Theatrical Awards and the Evening Standard Film Awards to appeal against the 'repressive measures within this clause' (see the *Pink Paper* 28 Jan. 1988), etc.

26 Sex education has become an obvious battleground. E.g. *Gay Times* (Dec. 1986: 7) reported the reprimand by BBC chiefs of a Radio Wales producer whose schools programme on AIDS (Manylu-Radio Cymru) contained 'earthy' and 'coarse' language.

27 The 1967 Sexual Offences Act applied to England and Wales. Scotland and Northern Ireland were brought into line later (see p. 279) but there are still some regions of the UK within which homosexuality remains illegal (e.g. Isle of Man and Jersey) although

at the time of writing both are under pressure from the European Court to repeal existing legislation.

28 Other European countries have legislation restricting the 'promotion' of homosexuality (e.g. Austria and Finland) and Turkey has brought charges against lesbians and gay men for 'spreading homosexual information'.

29 E.g. Hull City Council refused to allow the screening of Genet's *Un chant d'amour*; East Sussex County Council barred a Home Office backed guide to voluntary work opportunities for the young because it contained advertisements for the London Lesbian and Gay Centre; Kent County Council excluded Britten's *Death in Venice* from a school festival because it features a man's obsession with a boy; Aberystwyth University students had their exhibition on Clause 28 removed from the University Library; Brighton WEA (Worker's Education Authority) insisted on a change of name to their Lesbian Literature course; in Southampton the council dropped a lesbian chapter from their women's handbook; the London Boroughs Grant Scheme insisted on changes to the constitutions of the London Lesbian and Gay Centre and the Outcast Theatre Companies; the children's book at the heart of many of the tabloid press accounts of Haringey local authority's 'promotion of homosexuality' *Jenny Lives With Eric and Martin* was taken from the shelves of Wolverhampton's public libraries; Hereford and Worcester County Council refused to give the lesbian organisation Border Women a grant for printing materials, etc. See Evans (1989/90) for further discussion.

30 The London Borough of Ealing eventually allowed the lesbian Green Cross Code to be published; the ILEA (Inner London Education Authority) after a year's delay released two new teaching videos about lesbian and gay youth; Wolverhampton councillors lifted a ban on screening of gay videos; Strathclyde Regional Authority's threatened withholding of funds for student lesbian and gay groups was lifted after the intervention of the NUS (National Union of Students); Essex County Council lifted its ban on gay and lesbian socials at the Colchester Institute of Further Education, etc. However, there are as many and more examples of the Section's lasting inhibiting influence.

31 Leach (1972: 105) observes, 'The nuclear family is a most unusual kind of organisation and I would predict that it is only a transient phase in our society.'

32 E.g. 'The reported activities of some London gay and lesbian committees have not been a vote winner on many council estates' (*Guardian* 15 Dec. 1987).

33 'The issue of lesbian and gay rights is thought to have moved irreversibly into the mainstream of political debate in this country with extensive coverage in serious newspapers and magazines, on television and on the radio' *Gay Times* (July 1988).

34 With AIDS 'the moral community' appears to have become unequivocally 'the heterosexual community'.

35 Nicholas Fairbairn's contribution to a Commons debate reportedly

included the following: 'Male homosexuality is a perversion of human function . . . it is using the excretory organ and rectum with a reproductive organ' (*Pink Paper* 17 March 1988). By comparison M. Barnes QC (reported by Wolmar 1988) argued that the term 'homosexuality' is 'meaningless by comparison with homosexual relationship'.

36 *The Times* (9 July 1989) reported the following: 'New York – The USA has taken another step on the road to "post marital society" with a court ruling that a homosexual couple should be considered "a family". New York State's highest court ruled this week that a gay man who lived with his lover for a decade should be allowed to remain in the couple's rent-controlled Manhattan apartment after his partner died of AIDS. The decision was the first by a top court giving a long established gay relationship the status of family. It represents too the increasing recognition that unmarried partners should be allowed the same benefits as married couples. Lawyers said that the ruling could also apply to heterosexual couples.'

6 DUAL CITIZENSHIP? BISEXUALITY

1 Other journalistic pieces of this period include two in *New Yorker* magazine (April 1974: 31–6, 37–8), the former entitled 'Sexual Chic, Sexual Fascism and Sexual Confusion': *VIVA* (July 1974: 42–5): *The Village Voice* (15 Aug. 1974: 27) and the gay journal *The Advocate* (4 May 1977: 31–2), entitled 'Bosom Buddies'. All were descriptive in the context of expensive, commodified lifestyle chic.

2 Freud also referred to 'absolute' and 'contingent' inverts, the former having sexual objects exclusively of their own sex and incapable of carrying out the (normal) heterosexual act and of deriving any enjoyment from it. The latter are what would in modern sociological accounts be called 'situational homosexuals', i.e. for Freud those who because of inaccessibility of 'any normal sexual object' are capable of making a same-sex sexual object choice (1905: 47).

3 Freud was not responsible for creating such distinctions. They had, e.g., already been addressed by Tarnowsky (1898) who located them in very specific, and to us familiar, situational contexts of prisons, barracks, 'long voyages' and boarding schools ('perverted' boys contaminating boys' boarding schools).

4 E.g. 'the bisexual potential of the embryonic gonad' (Rosen 1979: 474); also 'bisexual potential may well be in the "diencephalic structures controlling both the pattern of sexual behaviours and . . . of gonad otrophim secretion" ' 170 (pp. 474–5).

5 E.g. Dannecker and Reiche (1974) use the term 'defence bisexuals'. Ross (1983) also uses 'defence bisexuals' in the discussion of his sample of married male homosexuals.

6 As note 3 states these contexts have been addressed by medical/psychoanalytic discourses since the late nineteenth century at least. Initially the emphasis was on pathological susceptibility

when exposed to such environments, by the late twentieth century the focus has shifted to the contamination potential of the environments themselves, an emphasis clearly central to symbolic interactionism's focus on 'negotiation' and 'emergence' (see Plummer 1975).

7 E.g., as argued most famously by Bieber *et al.* (1962). Alternatively MacDonald (1981) makes the point that all existing studies of homosexuals will have been based on 'homosexual' populations which contain many who are hidden bisexuals and so we not only know little about bisexuals and bisexuality, what we know about homosexuality is biased accordingly.

8 E.g. Limentani (1976: 205) states that bisexuality is primarily a means of concealment: 'Their bisexual involvement was largely illusory as the two objects male and female with whom they were involved were a cover up for splitting of the original love-object together with a severe pre-Oedipal disturbance.'

9 Perhaps in a sense, certainly at the time of their research, Weinberg and Williams' (1974) findings agree for they concluded that their self-identified homosexual respondents were much less inclined to conceal their homosexual experiences and behaviour, than were their self-identified bisexual respondents.

10 One possible exception is political lesbianism where the entire self is focused on women: 'while sexual energies are not discounted, alone they do not create the lesbian-feminist' (Faderman 1981: 86).

11 On this see also Dover (1978: 60–3).

12 E.g. Fred Klein (1978), on a post-Kinsey basis, estimated there to be between 30–40 million people in the US with either attraction to or behavioural experience with members of the same and the opposite sex, others have been content to quote Mead's belief (1975) that it is a 'normal capacity of persons to love members of both sexes'.

13 Bell and Weinberg (1978: 60–1) conclude that 'a fairly strong heterosexual element' is found in about one-third of the homosexual men likely to participate in surveys such as theirs and that 'large numbers of homosexual women . . . exhibit a "partial bisexual style". Homosexuals of both sexes have a history of sexual contact with persons of the opposite sex, and although they may not presently engage in such contact, sometimes they are aware of their continuing potential for heterosexual response.'

14 That this is familiar to non-academic anti-homosexual bureaucrats is wittily made clear by Davenport-Hines (1991) who quotes the Director of Public Prosecutions in 1944 bemoaning the increase in male homosexuality because the lives of adolescents had undergone 'complete change' as the result of the extended duration of education and National Service, creating an unprecedented atmosphere in which homosexuality 'can be easily acquired and become deeply ingrained' (pp. 298–9).

15 Numerous texts deal with the stigmatisation of 'guilty' AIDS sufferers, but see Plummer (1988).

16 E.g. in 1984 in Zaire for every 11 male AIDS cases there were 10

female compared to the 15 to 1 ratio in Europe, a ratio that has since fallen (see Wellings 1988).
17 'Gay plague' was for a while endemic in the media, e.g. see *Daily Telegraph* (2 May 1983); *Observer* (26 June 1983); *Sun* (2 May 1983); *Daily Mirror* (2 May 1983).
18 E.g. *Great Gay in the Morning* by the 25 to 6 Baking and Trucking Society (1972, New York: Times Change Press).
19 National Bisexual Network, see Geller (1990) for details.

7 TRANS-CITIZENSHIP: TRANSVESTISM AND TRANSSEXUALISM

1 The term employed by Brake (1976). His other transvestite types are: theatrical drag artistes for whom drag is a professional costume; 'closet' transvestites who dress up individually in secret; conventional transvestites 'out' in that they belong to organisations such as the Beaumont Society and on occasion go out cross-dressed in public; 'drag queens' who are camped in all senses at the centre of gay 'camp' culture; and lastly 'street transvestites' who openly live as 'females' whether of conservative or radical types (pp. 188–90).
2 See American Psychiatric Association's *Diagnostic and Statistical Manual of Mental and Physical Disorders* (1990).
3 There are 46 human chromosomes in the human cell with genetic variations in the number of sex chromosomes: XX = normal female, XY = normal male but X, XXX, XXY and XYY variations are also found. X = Turner's Syndrome, the female body is normal except the ovaries are non-functional, preventing normal pubertal development. This Syndrome is alleviated by oestrogen. XXX = female body, but diminished fertility and greater possibility of mental retardation. XYY = Klinefelter's Syndrome, males, abnormally tall, sterile with genital abnormalities (small penises, shrunken testes, low androgen output, possibly breast formation (Money and Erhardt 1972). Even with normal chromosomal patterns, if male gonads (testes) fail to secrete the Mullerian inhibiting substance between the sixth and twelfth weeks of birth, female Mullerian ducts (uterus, fallopian tubes) will develop, in addition to normal male internal and external organs. In all males and females testosterone (male hormone) and oestrogen (female hormone) balance affects development. Legal sex is usually established by midwives and obstetricians solely on visual evidence of external genitalia at birth, hence legal as well as biological and psychological complications ensue.
4 Garfinkel (1967) discusses the hermaphrodite Agnes's attempts to pass as a 'normal sexed person' to demonstrate the social construction of sex, gender and sexual meanings.
5 I.e. pre-verbal, rudimentary, but fixed as an unalterable conviction by the age of 3.
6 Hirschfeld by 1911 used the term to mean 'the desire of'. Earlier

comparable terms were 'contrary sexual feeling' (Westphal) 'psychic hermaphroditism' (Laurent) and 'metamorphosis sexualis paranoica' (Krafft-Ebing). However, these terms were employed variously to a basket of sex, gender and sexual abnormalities.

7 Ellis (1936) preferred Eonism (or 'sexo-aesthetic inversion') after the famous or rather infamous eighteenth-century Chevalier d'Eon de Beaumont who one presumes also inspired the name for the Beaumont Society.

8 Cauldwell was a prolific and proficient pamphleteer producing for the general reader such texts as *What's Wrong With Transvestism?* (1949b) and *Unconventional Modes of Sexual Expression* (1949c).

9 Benjamin erroneously believed that he had coined the word transsexual in a 1953 New York Academy of Medicine lecture. Benjamin's most detailed discussions of transsexualism may be found in two texts (1966, 1969). The American Psychiatric Association (1980: 261–2) defines transsexualism as a gender identity disorder involving a 'persistent sense of discomfort and inappropriateness about one's anatomic sex and a persistent wish to be rid of one's genitals and to live as a member of the other sex'.

10 King (1981: 163) notes that it was Edward Carpenter who was the first to employ the term 'cross-dressing' as a translation of Hirschfeld's term.

11 Stoller (1975) states 'The usual TV is a man who, however his gender, lives comfortably enough as a masculine person most of the time. He's however intermittently propelled into his masquerade of cross-dressing. He does this precisely on behalf of his penis . . . it is when he disguises his masculinity that he attains the height of maleness i.e. his potent erection.' Alternatively Ellis and Abarbanel (1961) emphasise the relaxation, pleasure and feelings of naturalness induced by cross-dressing.

12 Docter (1988: 6) states 'psychiatry texts gave prominence to the idea . . . that transvestism was often based on homosexual orientation. This is now known not to be the case.'

13 Rastan (1989: 14) claims 'There are 200,000 known transvestites who belong to societies alone.'

14 The one case referred to is to be found in Gutheil (1954).

15 Ellis (1936, Vol. 2: 36) distinguished between two types of eonist which is effectively a distinction between transvestism and transsexualism.

16 Rouse (1990) quotes the business as having an annual turnover of 10 million and over 150 customers a day at the Euston Road London shop.

17 Classifications of 'normal female/feminine' transsexual types have been provided by many analysts: e.g. Kando (1973) who refers to housewife, showbusiness (including prostitutes, strippers, dancers, models, etc.), and career woman types.

18 '. . . in women who feel like men the wish for a change of sex does not seem to manifest itself or become dominant until the person in question falls in love with another woman; this happens in the great majority of cases' (Benjamin 1966).

19 See Lothstein (1983: 14). Estimates of numbers of male-to-female and female-to-male transsexual cases vary because of the unknown number of 'private' cases and different organisations of health care in different countries, but Raymond (1979) estimates four male cases to every one female in the US. More recent British estimates suggest it is only two to one, and that now in the US it is one to one (Hodgkinson 1990).

20 Raymond (1979) suggests, however, that the greater medical management of male-to-female cases is due to many other social factors; male control of medicine and surgery, male-to-female operations are cheaper, easier and more successful, females have less access to medical treatment than males, females have less money to buy treatments. Alternatively some practitioners say that female-to-male transsexuals are less troublesome, their operations overall more successful.

21 One receptionist of a private clinic was quoted as follows 'a full medical examination and counselling costs £50. If everything is OK there is no reason why treatment should not start immediately.'

22 The latter is cheaper and completed via a solicitor. It is usually recommended that surnames are retained.

23 Local passport offices may require a medical letter (from surgeon or psychiatrist) and require evidence of change of name by Deed Poll or Statutory Declaration.

24 As mentioned in one case study (Fraser *et al.* 1966: 1006) where the husband was a genuine intersex, with an ovary and a fallopian tube internally on the right side, but with nothing internally on the left. He had been legally sexed at birth by his small penis and testicle on his left side.

25 However, the National Insurance Commission has decided that biological sex be held as the test for retirement rights and age of qualification for pension rights (see O'Donovan 1985: 72).

26 Which states that a person discriminates indirectly against a woman when on the grounds of her sex he treats her less favourably than he treats or would treat a man.

8 EMBRYONIC SEXUAL CITIZENSHIP: CHILDREN AS SEXUAL OBJECTS AND SUBJECTS

1 Here 'child' will be used to describe all those pre-adults otherwise distinguished as infants, children and adolescents. See Ruddick (1989).

2 One of the most commonly adopted definitions of which being '. . . the involvement of dependent developmentally immature children and adolescents in sexual activity they do not truly comprehend to which they are unable to give informed consent, or that violate the social taboos of family roles' Kempe and Kempe (1978).

3 Given the current reconstruction retrospectively of child sexual abuse, and inherent problems in measuring current incidence, estimates vary widely, but all agree that abuse has been and is more

widespread than official records show, and that it is on the increase in all socioeconomic groups (Finkelhor 1984). Baker and Duncan (1986) e.g. report 'substantial increases' in Europe the US and Australasia; the National Society for the Prevention of Cruelty to Children (quoted in Search 1988) claims incidence in England and Wales increased twelve-fold between 1983 and 1987; Blagg *et al.* (1989) estimate that one in ten children are sexually abused.

4 Studies of victims address the effects or consequences in terms of subsequent adult sexual dysfunctions: frigidity, neuroses, guilt, inhibitions, anxiety, etc., causing adolescent and adult prostitution (James and Meyerding 1977; Silbert and Pines 1981); disturbed personality development (Bender and Grugett 1951) which could recycle in abuse of previous victims' own children (Goodwin *et al.* 1981) and even suicide (e.g. Goodwin and Geil 1982).

5 Numerous studies include Mohr *et al.* (1964); Cook and Howells (1981); Groth and Birnbaum (1978); and Burgess *et al.* (1981) which focuses on 'sex rings'. Rossman (1976) identifies five types of organised paedophilia: acquaintance networks operating under cover as, e.g. sports clubs, etc.; pederast 'apologists' who collect information on paedophile subculture; photographers and pornographers who collect material substitutes for the 'real thing'; the pederast underworld proper and pederast rings. Taylor (1981) identifies eight types.

6 See also Conte and Smore (1982); Glaser and Frosh (1987); Jehu (1988).

7 Jordonova (1989: 13) refers to such expressions as 'pure', 'innocent' and 'plantlike'. Common-sense assumptions of children as in all ways 'incomplete' compared to adults has limited the study of children qua children.

8 E.g. Franklin (1986: 10) 'childhood is a fairly recent invention. . . . The first children were middle class and male'; Plumb (1972: 153) states 'The very idea of childhood is a European invention of the last 400 years.'

9 See Fuller 'Uncovering childhood', in Hoyles (1979) and Hughes (1989).

10 The beginnings of a children's rights movement can be traced at least back to an 1852 article by Slogvolk: 'The rights of children'. See Freeman (1983) for discussion.

11 Infant Felony Act (1840).

12 The Poor Law Amendment Act (1889) allowed guardians to resolve that parental rights should vest in them where the child was deserted or the parent imprisoned or where there had been an offence against the child. The Poor Law Amendment Act (1899) allowed for the testing of parental fitness and for detention under the Inebriates Act (1898). The 1891 Custody of Children Act allowed a court to refuse habeas corpus to a parent who had abandoned or deserted his/her child or otherwise behaved in a manner that required the court to remove custody. See Maidment (1983).

13 The Industrial Schools Amendment Act enabled courts to remove

children shown to be living in the society of depraved and disorderly persons and to place them in such schools. See Mort (1987: 124–5).

14 With the Prevention of Incest Act (1908). See Jeffreys (1985). Incest had been an offence in Scotland since 1567.

15 For a detailed discussion of incest legislation in the US see Herman and Hirschman (1981).

16 One of the earliest being the *Declaration of the Fifth Assembly of the League of Nations* 1924 regarding children's material needs following the First World War. The *Universal Declaration of Human Rights* (1948) Article 25 stated 'Motherhood and childhood are entitled to special care and assistance. All children whether born in or out of wedlock shall enjoy the same social protection.' The *Declaration of the Rights of the Child Resolution of the UN General Assembly* Article 9 states '. . . the child shall be protected against all forms of might, cruelty, and exploitation . . . shall not be the subject of traffic in any form . . . [nor] admitted to employment before an appropriate minimum age in any occupation . . . which would prejudice his [sic] health or education, or interfere with his physical, mental or moral development'.

17 The Criminal Law Amendment Act (1885) raised the age of consent to sexual intercourse for girls from 13 to 16. It became a felony to have sexual intercourse with a girl under the age of 13 – a misdemeanour if the girl is under 16. Consent by the girl was not a defence to a charge under the Act. Present law is contained in Sections 5 and 6 of the Sexual Offences Act (1956). Offences against females under 13 years of age have maximum punishment of life imprisonment, against those under 16 the maximum is 2 years in prison. A 1981 review recommended remaining with present law. Homosexual consent of males is covered by the 1967 Sexual Offences Act (England and Wales) to which other regions of the UK have been brought into line subsequently. The male homosexual age of consent is 21. See earlier chapters for discussions of attempts to change, and defences of present law.

18 The Punishment of Incest Act (1908) criminalised sexual behaviours between persons related by consanguinity; grandparent and grandchild; parent and child; brother and sister; half brother and half sister. Sexual acts of the under-16s had been banned by the 1885 Criminal Law Amendment Act. Contemporary incest laws are to be found in the Sexual Offences Act (1956) Sections 10 and 11. O'Donovan (1985: 104) reports a Criminal Law Review Committee consideration of a reduction in statutes to cover only cases where parties are under the ages of 18 or 21.

19 For a detailed discussion of rape law see the *Report of a Howard League Working Party* (1985). In the past two years, initially in Scotland and subsequently in England and Wales, it has been formally recognised that rape can occur within marriage.

20 'Indecent assault' covers a range of behaviours inflicted on people under the age of consent from gentle touching to forcible buggery, the term is also used to describe non-consensual sexual acts (short of

rape) with persons over the age of consent. Unlike 'gross indecency' indecent assault must involve physical contact.

21 I.e. coitus by a man with a female below the age of consent, sometimes referred to as 'statutory rape'.

22 For conditions of the 1967 Sexual Offences Act (England and Wales) see the *Report of a Howard League Working Party* (1985) and Crane (1982).

23 See Merck (1992).

24 Whilst Scots and English and Welsh legal systems vary there is much influence between the two as recently over marital rape, age of homosexual consent, age at which a male is capable of rape, etc.

25 Current proposals within the Criminal Justice Bill (1990–1) are to reduce this statutory age to 10 as is presently the case in Scots law.

26 See Cohen *et al.* (1978: 132).

27 Wherein 'indecent assault' may be no more than touching without consent.

28 Most relevant details are contained in the Children and Young Person's Act (1969). Under this legislation there does not need to be direct physical contact for this offence to have taken place e.g. 'indecent photographing' could be one such offence. It makes no difference if the 'victim' gave her consent or not, all that matters is her age and whether the jury or magistrates think there was indecency.

29 Although the age of consent formally remains at 16, those between 12 and 16 are permitted to have sexual relations unless parents of either party complained.

30 'Age of consent' legislation is changing all the time. For the latest information on Europe see Tatchell (1992).

31 See O'Donovan (1985) for many examples.

32 'Another telling argument for keeping British sovereignty' exclaimed one member of BBC TV's *Question Time* panel (15 Nov. 1990).

33 The Netherlands Institute for Social and Sexual Research questioned 11,500 schoolchildren. Of those under 14, 6 per cent claimed to have had sexual intercourse. Of those under 16, 17 per cent claimed likewise and by 17 over 50 per cent made this claim. In most cases sexual partners were contemporaries or one or two years older (*Independent* 20 Nov. 1990).

34 Eva de Lang, teacher in the Netherlands quoted in *Independent on Sunday* (18 Nov. 1990). Amongst the research evidence the authors had in mind or could have quoted is that provided by the Swedish National Board of Education (1986: 10–12) and Boethius (1984).

35 Ruddick's (1989) distinctions are that infants can move limbs, children can move about. Infants cannot understand any words whereas children can. Infants are demanding, children make demands. Adolescents progress towards adulthood.

36 However, Calderone (1977: 3) claims that 'true rights of children' include 'the right to know about sexuality, the right to be sexual, the right to have access to educational and literary sexual materials, the

... right to produce and distribute these materials ... [and] the right of the unwilling or inappropriate audience to have its privacy or peace of mind protected'.

37 Parents have no statutory right to withdraw their children from such classes, but appeals to Governors may be considered. Nor do children have the right to sex education in schools, rather emphasis is on parents' rights of choice of schools in which sex education varies widely.

38 By 'contraculture' Mitchell is not only recognising a culture set apart from that of adults, but in opposition. This use is derived from Yinger (1960).

39 Claims of sexual harm by 'victims'' own accounts have increased as 'abuse' scripts have become more widely available. E.g. in Kinsey *et al.* (1953) only 5 per cent of women claimed any such abuse and only one-fifth of these (i.e. 1 per cent of the total sample) attributed any subsequent difficulties to their early experiences.

40 Through a Health Notice issued by the Department of Health and Social Security HN (80) 46 which advised that 'in exceptional circumstances a doctor might lawfully provide advice or treatment on contraceptives to a girl under 16 without prior parental consultation or consent provided that s(he) acted in good faith to protect her against the harmful effects of sexual intercourse'.

41 In particular television has come in for criticism, see Liebert and Sprafkin (1988) and Palmer and Dorr (1980).

42 *The Times* (25 Oct. 1990) under 'Teenagers Sharpen their Image with Surgery' reported that plastic surgeons claim that 25 per cent of business is teenage. In 1988 117,000 teenagers under 18 (16 per cent of the total) had nose surgery, accounted for 16 per cent of ear pinning, 9 per cent of chin augmentation, 7 per cent of hair replacement and 7 per cent of dermabrasion.

43 Korephilia is adult females' love of young girls. See Catherine L. (1983: 4).

44 PIE produced *Paedophilia: Some Questions Answered* in 1978. PIE was established in 1975 and disbanded in 1984, it was the successor to PAL (Paedophile Action for Liberation). In 1979 six members of PIE were charged with conspiracy to corrupt public morals.

   In June 1984 Geoffrey Dickens MP brought a private member's bill to make it a criminal offence to belong to a group which discussed sex with children (other than to condemn it). The bill fell because of lack of time. See *Capital Gay Report* (19 Sept. 1984).

45 The PIE and O'Carroll argument is that once social barriers are removed some children enjoy sex with adults and actively seek it out.

46 Evidence is provided by Kinsey *et al.* (1948); Bender and Blau (1937).

47 Finkelhor's four traumagenic factors are the extent to which the victim's sexual development has been damaged, the extent of betrayal felt, of stigmatisation and powerlessness felt. All could of course be scripted through the intervention of welfare agencies Finkelhor (1986).

48 E.g. as argued by the *Evidence on the Law Relating to and Penalties for Certain Sexual Offences Affecting Children*, Speijer Committee of the Dutch Council of Health Affairs (1969) which refers (Section 3(1)) to the general freedom upheld by law for individuals to engage in such sexual activities as they have freely chosen, though subject to qualifying conditions.

49 Writers refer to the 'difficult doubleness' of female child scripting (i) considered as children girls are fitted into a naturalistic model of child development involving the gradual acquisition of the rationality of the adult whilst (ii) considered as girls they are future nurturers themselves, destined to remain on the passive propping side in relation to children and men.

50 The *Daily Express* (22 Aug. 1984) stated: 'People believe that such acts of perversion and wickedness must tell us something about our times and society. They do . . . in the last few decades we have witnessed a deliberate overturning of the values . . . which . . . form[ed] the cultural bedrock of our daily lives.' Numerous studies backed up such populist claims (Landis 1956; Gagnon 1965; Finkelhor 1979) whilst media coverage sensationalises, e.g. the *Observer* (12 Nov. 1989) reported on Leeds where Consultant Paediatricians were reported to have seen 800 suspected cases to the ratio of 2 boys to 3 girls: 'The youngest child we have seen was 4 months and one third of all sexually abused children are pre-school'.

51 Dame Jill Knight, a noted opponent of minority sexual status groups. Her idealisation of childhood's past was mirrored by others, e.g. Dr Adrian Rogers in the *Daily Telegraph*'s Viewpoint column (26 Aug. 1983) commented 'Once upon a time less than 25 years ago most children were sheltered and fully protected from the adult world.'

52 'According to recent studies in the US child sex abuse is increasingly prevalent. In the past 5 years reports of such incidents have increased more than 100 per cent. Nearly 1 parent in 10 said their children had suffered abuse or attempted abuse. Some of the parents had had 2 children abused. Many of the parents had themselves been sexually abused as children, of these one third had been abused before they were 9 years old' *Daily Express* (22 Aug. 1983 quoting National Centre of Child Abuse, Washington).

53 '. . . it was a mad house brothel' NUPE representative quoted describing New Hays Centre Liverpool, 22 Aug. 1983.

54 Revived from an offence invented by the Law Lords in the *Ladies Directory* case of 1961 in which a publisher had compiled a list of prostitutes: 'a judge invented version of the lynch law'.

55 Of these 60,000 only 4,000 got through and more than one-third were adults wishing to recount to counsellors what had happened to them as children.

56 'The main abuses are fondling, masturbation, oral sex, vaginal sex and buggery. The most common form disclosed is buggery. Vaginal intercourse is uncommon under the age of 10 years. Pornography and prostitution are abuses we have seen mostly in older children' (*Observer* 19 Nov. 1988).

Such accounts present the so called tell-tale signs of abuse such as (i) unwillingness to be left alone; (ii) references to sexual activities far beyond 'natural' understandings; (iii) bed wetting; (iv) sleep disturbance; (v) return to younger behaviour; (vi) unusual flirting or very obviously sexual behaviour 'too old' for the child's actual age; (vii) withdrawal into a fantasy world of his or her own; (viii) sudden drop in normal school performances; (ix) urinary infection; (x) chronic stomach pains or/and more frequent headaches than usual. Suffice to say all these 'symptoms' of possible sex abuse are also 'symptoms' of growing up.

57 According to the *Observer* article 'stepfathers, natural fathers and cohabitees . . . mothers . . . grandfathers, grandmothers, uncles and aunts older siblings, cousins, babysitters . . . all may abuse'.

58 Videoed evidence given by children not in court was also a central platform of *Childwatch*, a suggestion not welcomed on all sides for the assumption it carried that the accused was not, therefore, innocent until proved guilty but assumed guilty.

59 See e.g. Adams *et al.* (1971); Gottlieb (1973); Gross and Gross (1977); Keocher (1976); Constantine (1977).

60 Holt's tenth principle is 'the right to make and enter into on the basis of mutual consent, quasi-familial relationships outside of one's immediate family; i.e. the right to seek and choose guardians other than one's own parents and to be legally dependent upon them'. Holt's other principles ranged from the most general 'the right to be treated no worse than any adult' to the more specific, i.e. the right to take part in political affairs, to privacy, financial independence, to own, buy and sell property, to have credit, manage one's own education, travel, receive a minimum wage from the state: 'the right to do in any way what an adult may do'.

61 Wright's *Young People's Rights* (1990) contains information on babysitting; being left alone; changing name; drinking alcohol in private; ear piercing and hairstyles; fireworks; guns and other weapons; negligence; pets; physical punishment; pocket money; religious upbringing; schooling; divorce; remarriage; adoption; fostering; care; employment; travel; crime; business; health and, of course, sex. In October 1992 the British media reported on the first British child to seek a 'divorce' from her parents.

9 PUBLIC *AND* PRIVATE: THE PARAMETERS OF FEMALE SEXUAL CITIZENSHIP

1 The focus here is on structural changes but the impact of feminist politics and ideologies in effecting many of them is obvious. It is impossible to do more than provide here broad trends: e.g. by 1987 the number of women in employment in Britain had risen to 9,700,000 (7,200,000 in 1971), the increase mainly in part-time employment. The percentage of women economically active rose from 49.3 per cent (1984) to 53 per cent in 1989. Women continue

to form an increased percentage of the total British labour force (predicted as 43.7 per cent by 1995). However, vertical and horizontal gender segregation in waged work and the two-phase, bi-modal employment pattern of most married women has largely continued unchanged (Hakim 1979; 1981; Beechey 1986a, b). Still considerably lower than men's, full-time employed women's gross weekly earnings excluding overtime as a percentage of men's had risen to 66.3 per cent by 1987. By 'financial independence' I mean e.g. the increasing statutory recognition of married women's rights to independent income tax status. However, see Hewlett (1989) who estimates that in the US only 10 per cent of women have in any sense become 'better off', the rest have more difficult, pressurised and economically insecure lives than twenty years ago. For a discussion of the comparative position of men and women in Western democracies see Norris (1987).

2 'Support' and 'intervention' are double edges of the one sword. Structurally, as one would expect, most state intervention supports married women to fulfil domestic and mothering roles, and reluctantly provides support for single or married women outwith the family. E.g. the income of 'fatherless' families is much more dependent on state benefits than that of 'motherless' families, in part because it is harder for fathers to get benefits to stay at home. Pressures are also put on fathers to remain at work, but also it is much more difficult for lone mothers not to rely on benefits. 'A lone mother is often faced with the invidious choice of either raising her children at the low standard of living provided through the Supplementary Benefits system, or seeing very little of her children because she has to work long hours to achieve a reasonable wage. However, if she does rely on State benefits, she will lose benefit in her own right if she begins to cohabit, which will hinder the possibility of her forming a new heterosexual relationship. These factors impose real constraints on the control of her life and that of her children' (Leonard and Speakman 1986: 59–60).

3 See Rapoport and Rapoport (1975); Deem (1986); Green et al. (1986); Wimbush and Talbot (1988).

4 In 1989 25 per cent of UK births occurred outside wedlock (12.5 per cent in 1981), by 1991 the proportion in England and Wales was over one-third (The Times 17 June 1991: 5). Of mothers under 20 years of age in 1989 82 per cent of births were outwith wedlock (Guardian 19 July 1990: 3).

5 Of the population 13.5 per cent cohabit unmarried. Re-marriages account for one in four of all marriages. In the late 1980s there were 180,000 divorces a year in the UK, four out of every ten marriages ending in divorce, (Guardian 19 July 1990: 3). On US trends, see e.g. Weitzman (1985). Currently the Law Commission in Britain is recommending divorce law reforms, including the removal of 'fault'. Instead of parties having to prove irretrievable breakdown, divorce would become a 'process over time', settling the future of children, money and home over a period of

9–12 months. The couple would effectively be given 'divorce on demand' after that period (*The Times* 31 May 1990), particular attention being paid to child welfare.

6 Barrett and McIntosh (1980: 51) note 'The notion of a "family wage" has been in the past a divisive issue. . . . It is the idea that an adult man ought to earn enough to enable him to support a wife and children.'

7 As McIntosh (1984) demonstrates, state 'intervention' in the family is complex and problematic. 'It only means that the state is intervening in areas that it had hitherto defined as being private' (p. 235).

8 See e.g. Delphy (1977); Benston (1980); Malos (1980); Molyneux (1980); Walby (1988), etc.

9 'The interventions and abstentions of welfare states involve gender identities, family relations and sexual behaviour' Skocpol (1986–7). Even so during the 1980s in Britain the number of single parents receiving benefits has risen by 141 per cent to £1.2 million with the greatest increase among unmarried mothers. The cost of child support through income benefits rose from £1.2 billion in 1981–2 to £2.7 billion in 1988 (*The Times* 19 July 1990).

10 Williams' (1983) notion of 'mobile privatisation' is suggested by Jessop *et al.* (1988: 46–7) as an appropriate means by which to describe Thatcherism's ideological deployment around a more privatised family unit. 'Mobile privatisation' means the consequences of structural and technological changes, the dissolution of extended kinship networks, traditional communities and productive labour, increased mobility 'opportunities' and more privatised styles of family unit under increased structural threat.

11 See *The Times* (17 May 1990) report on Sir Keith Joseph's (1990) attack on the government.

12 At the time of writing the subject of a Scottish Law Commission (reported *The Times* 30 May 1990).

13 Child benefit costs in 1990 were £4.5 billion. Child benefits have a 98 per cent take-up rate with a quarter of the £4.5 billion paid out to families with incomes in excess of £20,000 per annum.

14 Britain has a higher percentage of women seeking waged work than any other EEC country except Holland. For maternity leave most EEC countries offer an average of 16 weeks with pay calculated as a proportion of former earnings. Britain provides leave related to pay levels for only 6 weeks, the shortest period in the EEC. Also eligibility for maternity leave in Britain depends upon being with the same employer for a minimum of two years. Britain has no provision for parental leave and has child care provision for fewer than 5 per cent of children of 3 years of age or less.

15 The White Paper published on 29 Oct. 1990, *Children Come First* dealt with the following issues: a child support agency should chase up absent parents for maintenance payments; fathers will have to pay up to half of their disposable income; lone working mothers caring for children might forfeit benefit qualification and supports; lone

mothers may lose 20 per cent of benefit if they fail to reveal the father's whereabouts; single parents will be given incentives to work e.g. £15 maintenance disregard on family credit; and eligibility for family credit to be lowered from 24 to 16 hours per week of paid work.

16 The Social Security (Pensions) Act 1975 made provision for people not in full-time work because of home commitments to qualify for pensions.

17 On such fragmentation in Britain see Women 2000 (1988) reported on in the *Independent* (24 March 1988).

18 Conflict which broadens out to include all manner of change *v* tradition disputes frequently via religious organisations and lobbies especially in the US. See Liebman and Winthrow (1983).

19 However, see O'Donovan (1985: 17) who claims that there have been a number of successful gender-based equal opportunities and equal pay challenges.

20 'Attitude is as good a place as any to begin. Because no creams or lotions or lists of information are going to make as big an impact on the way you look and feel as your attitude to your body' (*Honey* A–Z of your Body quoted in Coward 1984: 21).

21 'Brown, slim, lively and lovely . . . that's how we would all like to see ourselves on holiday. Here are a few tips on achieving this and maintaining it' (*Ideal Home* quoted in Coward 1984: 39).

22 See Stanworth (1987); Barrett and Roberts (1978); MacIntyre (1976).

23 In the nineteenth century the state was anti-public information, 'dirty, filthy knowledge', on abortion and contraception. For a detailed discussion of the background to abortion law reform see O'Donovan (1985).

24 Rossi (1972) describes the broadening out of knowledge from gynaecologists and obstetricians through to public health officials and legal experts and eventually to 'women themselves'. Mohr (1978) and Luker (1984) describe how nineteenth-century medical experts advanced their monopoly of information and control over abortion by supporting restrictive laws on women's rights to abortion. Back (1986–7) argues that professional control can keep emotionally charged issues out of the public arena and, therefore, their political and public discussion requires a curb on professional claims of expertise.

25 'In 1970 a group of New York area feminists distributed a copy of "A Model Abortion Law"; a blank piece of paper. Their position was unequivocal: a woman's right to abortion must be absolute, because her very personhood depends on her ability to control her own reproductive system' (Harvey 1984: 204).

26 Cambridge Women's Liberation Group (1978).

27 'Dysmorphobia', the morbid fear of deformity or of becoming deformed. 'The prognosis is not good at the moment for those with body dysmorphobic disorders. Not many get picked up for therapy and the therapy is often not successful. The closest parallel you can draw is with an anorexic. With neither of these cases does visual

feedback work: they can look at a video of themselves and still say "I'm ugly"' (*Independent on Sunday* 9 Dec. 1990).

28 'Cultural feminism ... equates women's liberation with the nurturance of a female counter culture which it is hoped will supersede the dominant culture ... cultural feminists are committed to preserving rather than challenging gender differences ... [and] ... some demonstrate a cavalier disinterest in whether these differences are biological or cultural in origin' (Echols 1984: 51).

29 'A truly radical feature of feminism has been the permission we have given each other to speak ... we spoke the unspeakable, we broke the taboo on silence' (Webster 1984: 386), who goes on to say, however, 'our discussions of sex were barely audible.'

30 E.g. the underlying task of peeling back the layers of 'false' female consciousness of femininity which defines vulnerability, submission and avoidance of conflict as natural has led to a feminist re-working of psychoanalytic method which in some ways confirms the inevitability of women's subordination. See Chodorow (1978); Mitchell (1975); Rose and Mitchell (1982); Mitchell and Rose (1982).

BIBLIOGRAPHY

Abrams, M., Gerard, D. and Timms, N. (eds) (1985) *Values and Social Change in Britain*, London: Macmillan.

Adams, C. and Laurikietis, R. (1976) *The Gender Trap*, New York: Harper & Row.

Adams, P. (ed.) (1971) *Children's Rights: Towards a Liberation of the Child*, New York: Praeger.

Adamson, O., Brown, C., Harrison, J. and Price, J. (1976) 'Women's oppression under capitalism', *Revolutionary Communist* No. 5.

Aggleton, P. and Homans, H. (1988) *Social Aspects of AIDS*, Lewes: Falmer.

Allen, C. (1969) *A Textbook of Psychosexual Disorders*, Oxford: Oxford University Press.

Allen, K. (1990) 'Women, pornography and erotica', *Independent* 6 November: 36.

Allen, S. (1973) 'Bisexuality: the best of both worlds', *Spare Rib* April: 4.

―― (1982) 'Gender inequality and class formation', in A. Giddens, and G. MacKenzie (eds) *Social Class and the Division of Labour*, Cambridge: Cambridge University Press.

Althusser, L. (1971) 'Ideology and ideological state apparatuses', in *Lenin and Philosophy and Other Essays*, London: NLB.

Altman, D. (1972) *Homosexual: Oppression and Liberation*, Sydney: Angus and Robertson, New Century Press.

―― (1981) *Coming Out in the Seventies*, Boston: Alyson.

―― (1982) *The Homosexualisation of America: The Americanisation of the Homosexual*, New York: St Martin's Press.

Altman, D. *et al.* (1988) *Which Homosexual? Essays from the International Scientific Conference on Lesbian and Gay Men's Studies*, London and Amsterdam: Gay Men's Press and Uitgeveri AN Dekker/Schorer.

American Psychiatric Association (1980) *Diagnostic and Statistical Manual of Mental and Physical Disorders*, Washington DC.

―― (1990) *Diagnostic and Statistical Manual of Mental and Physical Disorders*, Washington DC.

Amiel, B. (1986) *The Times* 5 November: 22.

Amis, M. (1985) 'Making sense of AIDS', *Observer* 23 June: 22.

302

—— (1986) 'The killings in Atlanta', in *The Moronic Inferno: And Other Visits to America*, London: Penguin.

Anderson, D. (1982) 'The Marxist myth about class', *Free Nation* 7 November: 5.

Anderson, M. (1979) 'The relevance of family history', in C. Harris (ed.) *The Sociology of the Family*, Keele: Sociological Review Monograph No. 28.

Ardill, S. and Neumark, N. (1982) 'Putting sex back into lesbianism', *Gay Information* No. 11.

Ardill, S. and O'Sullivan, S. (1987) 'Upsetting an applecart: difference, desire and lesbian sadomasochism', in *Feminist Review* (ed.) *Sexuality: A Reader*, London: Virago.

Arduin, Dr (1900) 'Die frauenfrage und die sexuellen Zwischenstufen', *Jahrbuch fur Sexuelle Zwischenstufen* 2: 211.

Ariès, P. (1962) *Centuries of Childhood*, London: Jonathan Cape.

Aristotle (1972) *Politics*, Harmondsworth: Penguin.

Armytage, W.G., Chester, R. and Peel, J. (1984) *Changing Patterns of Sexual Behaviour*, London: Academic Press.

Ashdown, P. (1989) *Citizen's Britain* quoted in D. Oliver (1991) 'Active citizenship in the 1990s', *Parliamentary Affairs: A Journal of Comparative Politics* 44, 2: 157–71.

Ashley, A. and Fallowell, D. (1982) *April's Odyssey*, London: Jonathan Cape.

Auden, W.H. (1977) *The English Auden: Poems, Essays and Dramatic Writings 1927–39*, London: Faber.

AVERT (1990) *A Survey of AIDS Education in Schools*, Horsham: Avert.

Babuscio, J. (1976) *We Speak for Ourselves: Experiences in Homosexual Counselling*, London: SPCK.

—— (1977) 'Camp and the gay sensibility', in R. Dyer (ed.) *Gays and the Film*, London: BFI.

—— (1988) 'Facing the backlash', *Gay Times* July: 28–31.

Back, K. (1986–7) 'Why is abortion a public issue? The role of professional control', *Politics and Society* 15, 2: 197–206.

Bailey, S. (1988) 'A comment on Alec McHoul's reading of Foucault and Garfinkel on the sexual', *Theory, Culture and Society* 5: 111–19.

Bain, O. and Sanders, M. (1990) *Out in the Open: A Guide for Young People Who Have Been Sexually Abused*, London: Virago Upstarts.

Bainham, A. (1988) *Children, Parents and the State*, London: Sweet & Maxwell.

Baker, A.W. and Duncan, S. (1986) 'Childhood sexual abuse', in R. Meadow (ed.) *Recent Advances in Paediatrics*, London: Churchill Livingstone.

Baker, R. (1968) *Drag: A History of Female Impersonation on the Stage*, London: Triton.

Baker, R. (1988) 'A time for schizophrenia: reflections on the transvestite threat to the (gay) macho mystique', in M. Dennemy, C. Ortleb and T. Steele (eds) *The View from Christopher Street*, London: Chatto & Windus/Hogarth Press.

Baldwin, J. (1956) *Giovanni's Room*, London: Corgi.

Barbalet, J.M. (1980) 'Principles of stratification in Max Weber: an interpretation and critique', *British Journal of Sociology* 31: 401–8.

Barker, D.L. and Allen, S. (eds) (1976) *Dependence and Exploitation in Work and Marriage*, Harlow: Longman.

Barnes, C. (1970) 'Special introduction' to the *Report of the Commission on Obscenity and Pornography*, New York: Bantam.
Barnett, L.D. (1982) *Population Policy and the U.S. Constitution*, Boston: Kluner-Nijhoff.
Barrett, M. (1989) *Women's Oppression Today*, London: Virago.
Barrett, M. and McIntosh, M. (1980) 'The family wage: some problems for socialists and feminists', *Capital and Class*, 11: 51–72.
—— (1982) *The Anti-Social Family*, London: Verso/NLB.
Barrett, M. and Roberts, H. (1978) 'Doctors and their patients. The social control of women in general practice', in C. Smart and B. Smart (eds) *Women, Sexuality and Social Control*, London: Routledge & Kegan Paul.
Barron, R.D. and Norris, E.R. (1976) 'Sexual divisions and the dual labour market', in D.L. Barker and S. Allen (eds) *Dependence and Exploitation in Work and Marriage*, Harlow: Longman.
Bartlett, N. (1988) *Who Was That Man? A Present for Mr. Oscar Wilde*, London: Serpent's Tail.
Bataille, G. (1988) *The Accursed Shore, Vol. 1.*, New York: Zone Books.
Bauman, Z. (1988) 'Sociology and postmodernity', *Sociological Review* 36: 790–813.
Beach, F.A. and Rasquin, P. (1942) 'Masculine copulatory behaviour in intact and castrated female rats', *Endocrinology* 31: 393–409.
Beauvoir, S. de (1972) *The Second Sex*, London: Allen Lane.
Becker, H.S. (1971) *Sociological Work*, London: Allen Lane.
Beechey, V. (1982) 'Some notes on female wage labour in capitalist production', in M. Evans (ed.) *The Woman Question*, Oxford: Fontana.
—— (1986a) 'Studies of women's employment', in *Feminist Review* (ed.) *Waged Labour: Reader*, London: Virago.
—— (1986b) 'Women's employment in contemporary Britain', in V. Beechey and E. Whitelegg *Women in Britain Today*, Milton Keynes: Open University Press.
Beigel, H.G. and Feldman, R. (1963) 'The male transvestite's motivation in fiction, research and reality', in H.G. Beigel *Advances in Sex Research*, London: Harper & Row.
Bell, A.P. and Weinberg, M.S. (1978) *Homosexualities: A Study of Human Diversity Among Men and Women*, London: Mitchell Beazley.
Bell, A.P., Weinberg, M.S. and Hammersmith, S.K. (1981) *Sexual Preference*, Indiana: Indiana University Press.
Bellos, L. (1984) 'For lesbian sex, against sadomasochism', in H. Kanter (ed.) *Sweeping Statements: Writings from the Women's Liberation Movement 1981–3*, London: Women's Press.
Bender, L. and Blau, A. (1937) 'The reaction of children to sexual relations with adults', *American Journal of Orthopsychiatry* 27: 500–18.
Bender, L. and Grugett, A. (1951) 'A follow-up report on children who had atypical sexual experiences', *American Journal of Orthopsychiatry* 22: 825–37.
Benjamin, H. (1966) *The Transsexual Phenomenon*, New York: Julian Press.
—— (1969) 'Introduction' to R. Green and J. Money (eds) *Transsexualism and Sex Reassignment*, Baltimore: Johns Hopkins Press.
Benston, M. (1980) 'The political economy of women's liberation', in E. Malos (ed.) *The Politics of Housework*, London: Allison & Busby.

Benton, R. and Newman, D. (1969) 'The new sentimentality', in H. Hayes, (ed.) *Smiling Through the Apocalypse: Esquire's History of the Sixties*, New York: McCall.

Bentovim, A., Elton, A., Hildebrand, J., Tranet, M. and Vizard, E. (1988) *Sexual Abuse in the Family: Assessment and Treatment*, London: J. Wright.

Berenstein, S. and Berenstein, J. (1987) *The Berenstein Bears*, London: William Collins.

Berger, P.L. and Luckmann, T. (1967) *The Social Construction of Reality* London: Allen Lane, Penguin.

Berger, R. (1977) *Government by Judiciary: The Transformation of the 4th. Amendment*, Cambridge, MA: Harvard University Press.

Bergler, E. (1956) *Homosexuality: Disease or Way of Life?*, New York: Hill and Wang.

Beveridge, Lord (1942) *Report on Social Insurance and the Allied Services* London: HMSO.

Bieber, I. *et al.* (1962) *Homosexuality: A Psychoanalytic Study of Male Homosexuality*, New York: Basic Books.

Birke, L. (1982) 'Clearing the mind, speculations on conceptual dichotomies', in S. Rose (ed.) *Against Biological Determinism*, London: Allison & Busby.

Biskind, P. and Ehrenreich, B. (1980) 'Machismo and the Hollywood working class', *Sociological Review* 50/51: 113.

Blachford, G. (1981) 'Male dominance and the gay world', in K. Plummer (ed.) *The Making of the Modern Homosexual*, London: Hutchinson.

Blackburn, R. (ed.) (1972) *Ideology in Social Science: Readings in Critical Social Theory*, London: Fontana/Collins.

Blagg, H., Hughes, J.A. and Wattam, C. (eds) (1989) *Child Sexual Abuse*, London: Longman.

Blagg, H. and Stubbs, P. (1988) 'A child centred practice? Multi-agency approaches to child sexual abuse', *Practice* 2, 1: 10–12.

Bland, L., Brunsden, C., Hobson, D. and Winship, J. (1978) 'Women "inside" and "outside" the relations of production', in Women's Studies Group, Centre for Contemporary Cultural Studies *Women Take Issue*, London: Hutchinson.

Bloch, I. (1902–3) *Beitrage zur Aetiologie der Psychopathia Sexualis* Vols I and II, Dresden: H.R. Dohm.

Blumer, H. (1962) 'Society as symbolic interaction', in A. Rose (ed.) *Human Behaviour and Social Processes*, London: Routledge & Kegan Paul.

—— 1969) *Symbolic Interactionism, Perspective and Method*, New Jersey: Prentice-Hall.

Blumstein, P.W. and Schwartz, P. (1976a) 'Bisexuality in women', *Archives of Sexual Behaviour* 5, 3: 171–8.

—— (1976b) 'Bisexuality in men', *Urban Life* 5, 3: 339–58.

Boas, G. (1966) *The Cult of Childhood*, Studies of the Warburg Institute 29.

Bode, J. (1976) *View From Another Closet: Exploring Bisexuality in Women*, New York: Hawthorn.

Boethius, C.G. (1984) 'Swedish sex education and its results', *Current Sweden* No. 315, March, Stockholm: Swedish Institute.

Bolick, C. (1988) *Civil Rights at the Crossroads*, New Brunswick: Transaction.

Boswell, J. (1989) 'Revolutions, universals, and sexual categories', in M.B. Duberman, M. Vicinus and G. Chauncey Jr. (eds) *Hidden from History: Reclaiming the Gay and Lesbian Past*, London: Penguin.

Bowlby, J. (1972) *Child Care and the Growth of Love*, Harmondsworth: Penguin.

Brake, M. (1976) 'I may be queer but at least I'm a man: male hegemony and ascribed versus achieved gender', in D.L. Barker, and S. Allen (eds) *Sexual Divisions and Society: Process and Change*, London: Tavistock.

—— (ed.) (1982) *Human Sexual Relations: Towards a Redefinition of Sexual Politics*, Harmondsworth: Penguin.

Bray, A. (1982) *Homosexuality in Renaissance England*, London: Gay Men's Press.

Breines, W. (1988) 'Whose New Left?' *Journal of American History* 75, September: 529.

Brierley, H. (1975) *Transvestism: Illness, Perversion or Choice?* New York: Pergamon.

Britton, A. (1979) 'For interpretation: notes against camp', *Gay Left* 7: 11–14.

Brogan, D.W. (1960) *Citizenship Today*, Chapel Hill: University of Carolina Press.

Bronski, M. (1984) *Culture Clash: The Making of Gay Sensibility*, Boston MA: South End Press.

Brown, B. (1981) 'A feminist interest in pornography', *m/f* 5–6: 5–18.

Brown, H. Gurley (1984) *Having It All*, London: New English Library.

Brown, J., Comber, M., Gibson, K. and Howard, S. (1985) 'Marriage and the family', in M. Abrams, D. Gerard and N. Timms (eds) *Values and Social Change in Britain*, London: Macmillan.

Brownmiller, S. (1975) *Against Our Will: Men, Women and Rape*, Harmondsworth: Penguin.

Bruegel, I. (1978) 'What keeps the family?' *International Socialism* 2, 1: 5–6.

—— (1986) 'The reserve army of labour: 1974–9', in *Feminist Review* (ed.) *Waged Work: A Reader*, London: Virago.

Bunzel, J. (1988) *Political Passages*, New York: Aldine.

Burdeau, G. (1949) *Traité de Science Politique, Vol. 2, L'Etat*, Paris Librairie Générale de Droit et de Jurisprudence.

Burgess, A., Groth, A.N., Groi, S.S. and Holmstrom, L.L. (1978) *Sexual Assault of Children and Adolescents*, Lexington MA: Lexington Books/ D.C. Heath.

Burgess, A., Groth, A.N. and McCausland, M. (1981) 'Child sex initiation rings', *American Journal of Orthopsychiatry* 51: 110–18.

Burke, T. (1973) 'Violet millennium or the invert comes of age', *Rolling Stone* 30 August: 58.

Burns, R. (1983) 'The fight for equality', in B. Galloway (ed.) *Prejudice and Pride*, London: Routledge & Kegan Paul.

Burstyn, V. (ed.) (1985) *Women Against Censorship*, Vancouver and Toronto: Douglas & McIntyre.

Bury, M.R. (1986) 'Social constructionism and the development of medical sociology', *Sociology of Health and Illness* 8, 2: 137–69.

BIBLIOGRAPHY

Butler-Sloss, E. (1988) *Report of the Enquiry into Child Abuse in Cleveland*, London: HMSO.
Calderone, M.S. (1977) *Sexual Rights*, London: SIECUS Report.
Caldwell, L. (1981) 'Abortion in Italy', *Feminist Review* 7: 49–64.
Califia, P. (1988) *The Lesbian S/M Safety Manual*, Denver: Lace Publications.
Califia, P. and Rubin, G. (1981) 'Sadomasochism: fears, facts and fantasies', *Gay Community News*, 9, 5: 7.
Callil, C. (1990) 'The eunuch's bequest', *Sunday Correspondent* 20 April: 19.
Campbell, B. (1987a) *Iron Ladies: Why do Women Vote Tory?* London: Virago.
—— (1987b) 'A feminist sexual politics: now you see it, now you don't', in *Feminist Review* (ed.) *Sexuality: A Reader*, London: Virago.
—— (1990) 'Model female or female role model?' *The Times* 23 November: 20.
Cant, B. and Hemmings, S. (1988) *Radical Records: Thirty Years of Lesbian and Gay History*, London: Routledge.
Carrier, J.M. (1980) 'Homosexual behaviour in a cross-cultural perspective', in J. Marmor (ed.) *Homosexual Behaviour: A Modern Reappraisal*, New York: Basic Books.
Castells, M. (1978) *City, Class and Power*, London: Macmillan.
Cauldwell, D.O. (1949a) 'Psychopathia trans sexualis', *Sexology* 16: 274.
—— (1949b) *What's Wrong With Transvestism?* New York: Haddemann-Julius.
—— (1949c) *Unconventional Modes of Sexual Expression*, New York: Haddemann-Julius.
Cavaan, S. (1966) *Liquor License: An Ethnography of Bar Behaviour*, Chicago: Aldine.
Cecco, J.P. de and Shively, M.G. (1984) 'From sexual identity to sexual relationships: a contextual shift', in J.P. de Cecco and M.G. Shively (eds) *Bisexual and Homosexual Identities: Critical Theoretical Issues*, New York: Haworth.
Challis, L. (1989) 'The great under fives muddle: options for day care policy', quoted in S. Rowbotham (1989) *The Past Before Us*, p. 151, London: Penguin.
Charles, N. (1986) 'Women and trade unions', in *Feminist Review* (ed.) *Waged Work: A Reader*, London: Virago.
Children Come First (1990) Government White Paper: 29 October, London: HMSO.
Children's Legal Centre (1987) *Childright*, London: Children's Legal Centre.
Chinoy, E. (1962) *Sociological Perspective*, New York: Random House.
Chodorow, N. (1978) *The Reproduction of Mothering: Psychoanalysis and the Sociology of Gender*, London: University of California.
Churchill, W. (1967) *Homosexuality in the Male Species – A Cross Cultural Approach*, New York: Hawthorn.
Citizen's Charter: Raising the Standard (1991) Cmnd. 1599, July, London: HMSO.
Clark, D. (1977) *Loving Someone Gay*, New York: Signet.

307

Clark, W. (1987) 'The dyke, the feminist and the devil', in *Feminist Review* (ed.) *Sexuality: A Reader*, London: Virago.

Coakley, J. and Harris, L. (1983) *The City of Capital*, Oxford: Basil Blackwell.

Cockburn, C. (1986) 'The material of male power', in *Feminist Review* (ed.) *Waged Work: A Reader*, London: Virago.

Cohen, H. (1980) *Equal Rights for Children*, Totowa, NJ: Littlefield Adams.

Cohen, P. (1968) *Modern Social Theory*, London: Heinemann.

Cohen, S., Green, S., Merryfinch, L., Jones, G., Slade, J. and Walker, M. (1978) *The Law and Sexuality: How to Cope with the Law if You're Not 100% Conventionally Heterosexual*, Manchester: Grass Roots.

Comay, R. (1986) 'Excavating the repressive hypothesis: aporias of liberation in Foucault', *Telos* 67: 111–19.

Conrad, P. (1990) 'Oprah Winfrey: the divine Miss Winfrey', *Observer Colour Supplement* 3 June.

Constantine, L.L. (1977) 'Open family: a lifestyle for kids and other people', *The Family Co-ordinator* 26: 113–80.

—— (1979) 'The sexual rights of children: implications of a radical perspective', in M. Cook and G. Wilson (eds) *Love and Attraction: An International Conference*, Oxford: Pergamon.

Conte, J. and Smore, D. (eds) (1982) *Social Work and Child Sex Abuse*, New York: Hawthorn.

Cook, M. and Howells, K. (1981) *Adult Sexual Interest in Children*, London: Academic Press.

Coons, F.W. (1972) 'Ambisexuality as an alternative adaptation', *Journal of American Collective Health Association* 21: 142–4.

Cooper, A. (1988) 'Clause and effect: is there gay life after Clause 28?' *Marxism Today* 32, June: 22–8.

Cooper, D. (1971) *The Death of the Family*, Harmondsworth: Penguin.

Cooper, J.B. (1942) *Comparative Psychology Monograph* 17: 1–48.

Coote, A. and Campbell, B. (eds) (1982) *Sweet Freedom: The Struggle for Women's Liberation*, London: Pan.

Cory, D.W. (1953) *The Homosexual Outlook: Subjective Appraisal*, London: Nevill.

Cory, D.W. and LeRoy, J.P. (1963) *The Homosexual and his Society: A View from Within*, New York: Citadel.

Cosmopolitan (1974) 'Bisexuality: the newest lifestyle', June: 189–92.

—— (1983) 'Maggie's family policy: a plot against women', May: 149–50.

Coveney, L., Jackson, M., Kaye, L. and Mahony, P. (1984) *The Sexuality Papers*, London: Hutchinson.

Coward, D.A. (1980) 'Attitudes to homosexuality in 18th-century France', *Journal of European Studies* 10: 231–55.

Coward, R. (1984) *Female Desire*, London: Granada.

—— (1987) 'Sexual violence and sexuality', in *Feminist Review* (ed.) *Sexuality: A Reader*, London: Virago.

Cowie, C. and Lees, S. (1987) 'Slags or drags', in *Feminist Review* (ed.) *Sexuality: A Reader*, London: Virago.

Crane, P. (1982) *Gays and the Law*, London: Pluto.

Creigton, S. (1984) *Trends in Child Abuse*, London: NSPCC.

Crompton, R. and Gubbay, J. (1977) *Economy and Class Structure*, London: Macmillan.

Crowley, M. (1968) *Boys in the Band*, Harmondsworth: Penguin.

Culler, J. (1981) 'The semiotics of tourism', *American Journal of Semiotics* 1: 127–40.

Currier, R.L. (1981) 'Juvenile sexuality in global perspective', in L.L. Constantine and F.M. Martinson (eds) *Children and Sex*, Boston: Little Brown.

Dank, B. (1971) 'Coming out in the gay world', *Psychiatry* 34: 180–97.

Danneker, M. and Reiche, R. (1974) *Der Gewohnliche Homosexuelle: Eine Speziologische Untersuchung über Mannliche Homosexuelle in der Bundesrepublik*, Frankfurt am Main: S. Fischer Verlag.

Daraki, M. (1986) 'Michel Foucault's Journey into Greece', *Telos* 67: 87–100.

Davenport-Hines, R. (1991) *Sex, Death and Punishment*, London: Fontana, Harper/Collins.

Davies, C. (1975) *Permissive Britain: Social Change in the Sixties and Seventies*, London: Pitman.

—— (1980) 'Moralists, causalists, sex, law, and morality', in W. Armytage, R. Chester and J. Peel (eds) *Changing Patterns of Sexual Behaviour*, London: Academic Press.

Davies, P. (1987) 'Dickensian dilemmas', *Gay Times* May: 12.

—— (1988) 'Sexuality: a new minefield in schools', *Independent* 26 May: 5.

Deem, R. (1978) *Women and Schooling*, London: Routledge & Kegan Paul.

—— (1980) *Schooling for Women's Work*, London: Routledge & Kegan Paul.

—— (1986) *All Work and No Play: The Sociology of Women and Leisure*, Milton Keynes: Open University.

Delacoste, F. and Alexander, P. (1988) *Sex Work: Writings in the Sex Industry*, London: Virago.

Delmar, R. (1976) 'Looking again at Engels', in J. Mitchell and A. Oakley (eds) *The Rights and Wrongs of Women*, Harmondsworth: Penguin.

Delph, E.W. (1978) *The Silent Community: Public Homosexual Encounters*, Beverly Hills, CA: Sage.

Delphy, C. (1977) *The Main Enemy: A Materialist Analysis of Women's Oppression*, London: Women's Research and Resources Centre, Explorations in Feminism.

D'Emilio, J. (1983a) 'Capitalism and the gay identity', in A. Snitow, C. Stansell and S. Thompson (eds) *Desire: The Politics of Sexuality*, London: Virago.

—— (1983b) *Sexual Politics, Sexual Communities*, Chicago: University of Chicago Press.

Denzin, N.K. (1971) 'Rules of conduct and the state of deviant behaviour: some notes on the social relationship', in G.J. McCall and J.D. Douglas (eds) *Social Relationships*, Chicago: Aldine.

Department of Education and Science (1987) 'Sex Education in Schools', London: HMSO.

Devereux, G. (1937) 'Institutional homosexuality of the Mohave Indians', *Human Biology* 9: 498–527.

Dicey, A.V. (1965) *Introduction to the Study of the Law of the Constitution*, London: Macmillan.

Dipboye, R.L., Fromkin, H.L. and Wiback, K. (1974) 'Relative importance of applicant sex, attractiveness and scholastic standing in evaluation of job application resumés', *Journal of Aplied Psychology* 60: 39–43.

Dipboye, R.L., Arvey, R.D. and Terpstra, D.E. (1977) 'Sex and physical attractiveness of raters and applicants as determinants of resumé evaluations', *Journal of Applied Psychology* 62: 288–94.

Docter, R.F. (1988) *Transvestites and Transsexuals: Towards a Theory of Cross-Gender Behaviours*, New York: Plenum.

Donaldson, M. (1978) *Children's Minds*, London: Fontana.

Donzelot, J. (1980) *Policing the Family*, London: Hutchinson.

Dover, K.J. (1978) *Greek Homosexuality*, London: Duckworth.

Dreyfus, H.L. and Rabinow, P. (1983) *Michel Foucault: Beyond Structuralism and Hermeneutics*, Chicago: Chicago University Press.

Duchacek, I.D. (1973) *Rights and Liberties in the World Today*, Santa Barbara, CA: ABC-Clio.

Dummett, A. and Nicol, A. (1991) *Subjects, Citizens and Others*, London: Weidenfeld & Nicolson.

Dworkin, A. (1981) *Pornography: Men Possessing Women*, London: Women's Press.

Dworkin, R. (1978) 'Liberalism', in S. Hampshire (ed.) *Public and Private Morality*, Oxford: Oxford University Press.

—— (1990) *A Bill of Rights for Britain*, London: Chatto & Windus, Counterblasts 16.

Dyer, R. (ed.) *Gays and the Film*, London: BFI.

Ebony (1988) 'The hidden fear: black women, bisexuals and the AIDS risk', January: .

Echols, A. (1984) 'The taming of the id: feminist sexual politics 1968–83', in C. Vance (ed.) *Pleasure and Danger*, London: Routledge & Kegan Paul.

Edelman, M. (1964) *The Symbolic Use of Politics*, Urbana: University of Illinois Press.

Edgerton, M. (1973) 'Transsexualism: a surgical problem?' *Plastic and Reconstructive Surgery* 52: 74–6.

Ehrenreich, B. (1981) 'The women's movements: feminist and anti-feminist', *Radical America* Spring: 98–9.

—— (1983) *The Hearts of Men: American Dreams and the Flight From Commitment*, New York: Anchor.

Elias, J.A. (1967) review of G. Boas, *The Cult of Childhood*, Studies of the Warburg Institute, Vol. 29. in *The History of Ideas* 28: 454.

Elkin, F. and Handel, G. (1978) *The Child and Society*, New York: Random House.

Elliott, B. and McCrone, D. (1987) 'Class, culture and morality: a sociological analysis of neo-conservatism', *Sociological Review* 35, 3: 485–511.

Elliott, M. (1990) *How to Help them Stay Safe: Parents' Pack*, London: Kidscope.

Ellis, A. (1956) 'The effectiveness of psychotherapy with individuals who have severe homosexual problems', *Journal of Consulting Psychology* 20: 191–5.

Ellis, A. and Abarbanel, A. (1961) *The Encyclopedia of Sexual Behaviour* (2 vols), New York: Hawthorn Books.
Ellis, H. (1897) *Studies in the Psychology of Sex, Vol. 2, Sexual Inversion*, Philadelphia: F.A. Davis.
—— (1936) *Studies in the Psychology of Sex* (7 vols), New York: Random House.
Ellis, L. and Beattie, C. (1983) 'The feminist explanations for rape', *Journal of Sex Research* 19: 74–93.
Elshtain, J.B. (1982/3) 'Homosexual politics: the paradox of gay liberation', *Salmagundi* 58–9: 252–80.
Engels, F. (1968) 'Origin of the family, private property and the state', in *Marx and Engels; Selected Works* Volume 1, London: Lawrence & Wishart.
Ennew, J. (1986) *The Sexual Exploitation of Children*, Cambridge: Polity.
Epstein, S. (1987) 'Gay politics, ethnic identity: the limits of social constructionism', *Sociological Review* 93/4: 12.
Ettore, E.M. (1980) *Lesbians, Women and Society*, London: Routledge & Kegan Paul.
Evans, D.T. (1988) *Transvestite Lives*, research paper (unpub.).
—— (1989/90) 'Section 28: law, myth and paradox', *Critical Social Policy* 27: 73–95.
—— (1991) 'Facing up to the real age of consent', *The Scotsman* 6 December: 15.
Ewing, K.D. and Gearty, J.D. (1990) *Freedom Under Thatcher: Civil Liberties in Modern Britain*, Oxford: Clarendon.
Faderman, L. (1981) *Surpassing the Love of Men: Romantic Friendship and Love Between Women from the Renaissance to the Present Day*, New York: William Morrow.
Faraday, A. (1981) 'Liberating lesbian research', in K. Plummer (ed.) *The Making of the Modern Homosexual*, London: Hutchinson.
Farson, R. (1974a) *Birthrights: A Bill of Rights for Children*, New York: Macmillan.
—— (1974b) 'A bill of rights for children', *M.S. Magazine*, March.
Featherstone, M. (1983) 'Body and consumer culture', *Theory, Culture and Society* 1, 2: 18–33.
Feminist Review (ed.) (1986) *Waged Work: A Reader*, London: Virago.
—— (1987) *Sexuality: A Reader*, London: Virago.
Fernbach, D. (1981) *The Spiral Path*, London: Gay Men's Press.
Findlay, B. (1974) 'The cultural context of rape', *Women's Law Review* 60: 199–207.
Finkelhor, D. (1979) *Sexually Victimised Children*, New York: Free Press.
—— (1980) 'Risk factors in the sexual victimisation of children', *Child Abuse and Neglect*, 4: 265–73.
—— (1984) *Child Sexual Abuse: New Theories and Research*, New York: Free Press.
—— (1986) *A Sourcebook on Child Sexual Abuse*, Beverly Hills, CA: Sage.
Fisk, N. (1973) 'Gender dysphoria syndrome. (The how, what and why of a disease)', in D. Lamb and P. Gandy (eds) *The Second International Symposium of Gender Dysphoria Syndrome*, Palo Alto: Stanford University Press.

311

Fitch, J.H. (1962) 'Men convicted of sexual offences against children', *British Journal of Criminology* 3: 18–37.

Fletcher, R. (1971) *The Making of Sociology: A Study of Sociological Theory, Volume One. Beginnings and Foundations*, London: Michael Joseph.

Fliess, W. (1906) *Der Ablauf des Lebens*, Vienna.

Ford, C.S. and Beach, F. (1952) *Patterns of Sexual Behaviour*, London: Methuen.

Forester, B.M. and Swiller, H. (1972) 'Transsexualism: a review of the syndrome and presentation of a possible successful therapeutic approach', *International Journal of Group Psychotherapy* 22: 343–51.

Foster, H.H. and Freed, D.J. (1972) 'A bill of rights for children', *Family Law Quarterly* 6: 343.

Foucault, M. (1965) *Madness and Civilisation*, New York: Vintage.

—— (1972) *The Archaeology of Knowledge*, London: Tavistock.

—— (1977a) *Discipline and Punish: The Birth of Prison*, London: Allen Lane.

—— (1977b) 'Power and sex', discussion between M. Foucault and B.H. Levy, *Telos* 32: 152–61.

—— (1978) 'Sexual morality and the law', in L.D. Kritzmann (ed.) *Michel Foucault: Politics, Philosophy, Culture. Interviews and other Writings 1977–84*, London: Routledge.

—— (1981) *The History of Sexuality, Volume One: An Introduction*, Harmondsworth: Allen Lane, Penguin.

—— (1983) 'Homosexuality: sacrilege, vision, politics', interview with J. O'Higgins in *Salmagundi* 58–9: 10–24.

—— (1984a) 'The concern of truth', in L.D. Kritzmann (ed.) (1988) *Michel Foucault: Politics, Philosophy, Culture: Interviews and other Writings 1977–84*, London: Routledge.

—— (1984b) 'Sex, power and the politics of identity', *The Advocate*, 400.

—— (1985) 'Final interview', *Raritan* Summer: 8–13.

—— (1986) *The Care of the Self. Volume Three, The History of Sexuality*, London: Allen Lane.

—— (1987) *The Use of Pleasure. Volume Two, The History of Sexuality*, Harmondsworth: Allen Lane, Penguin.

Foucault, M. and Sennett, R. (1981) 'Sexuality and solitude', *Humanities in Review* 1: 3–21.

France, M. (1984) 'Sadomasochism and feminism', *Feminist Reveiew* 11.

Frankel, B. (1987) *The Post-Industrial Utopians*, Cambridge: Polity in association with Blackwell.

Frankl, G. (1974) *The Failure of the Sexual Revolution*, Hove: Kahn & Averill.

Franklin, B. (ed.) (1986) *The Rights of Children*, Oxford: Basil Blackwell.

Fraser, K., O'Reilly, M.J.J. and Rintoul, J.R. (1966) 'Hermaphroditus Versus, with report of a case', *Medical Journal of Australia* 1: 1003–6.

Fraser, N. (1983) 'Foucault's body-language: a post-humanist political rhetoric', *Salmagundi* 61: 55–71.

Frazier, N. and Sadker, M. (1973) *Sexism in School and Society*, New York: Harper & Row.

Freedman, R., Green, R. and Spitzer, R. (1976) 'Reassessment of homosexuality and transsexualism', *Annual Review of Medicine* 27: 57–62.

Freeman, M.D.A. (1977) *Coming of Age*, London: Legal Action Group Bulletin.
—— (1983) 'The concept of children's rights', in H. Geach and E. Szwed (eds) *Providing Civil Justice for Children*, Sevenoaks: E. Arnold.
Freud, S. (1905) *Three Essays on the Theory of Sexuality*, in A. Richards (ed.) (1977) *Sigmund Freud: Volume 7: On Sexuality*, Harmondsworth: Penguin.
—— (1907) 'On the sexual theories of children', in A. Richards (ed.) *Sigmund Freud: Volume 7: On Sexuality*, Harmondsworth: Penguin.
—— (1950) *Totem and Taboo: Some Points of Agreement between the Mental Lives of Savages and Neurotics*, London: Routledge & Kegan Paul.
—— (1963) *Civilisation and its Discontents* (revised edn), London: Hogarth Press and the Institute of Psycho-Analysis.
Friedan, B (1965) *The Feminine Mystique*, Harmondsworth: Allen Lane, Penguin.
Fromm, E. (1942) *The Fear of Freedom*, London: Routledge & Kegan Paul.
—— (1955) *The Sane Society*, New York: Holt, Rinehart & Winston.
Fuller, P. (1979) 'Uncovering childhood', in M. Hoyles *Changing Childhood*, London: Writers and Readers Publishing Co-operative.
Gagnon, J.S. (1965) 'Female child victims of sex offenses', *Social Problems* 13: 176–92.
—— (1967) 'Sexuality and sexual learning in the child', in J.S. Gagnon and W.H. Simon (eds) *Sexual Deviance*, London: Harper & Row.
—— (1977) *Human Sexualities*, Illinois: Scott, Foreman & Co.
Gagnon, J.H. and Simon, W.S. (1967) *Sexual Deviance*, London: Harper & Row.
—— (1969) 'Psychosexual development', *Transaction* March: 9–17.
—— (1970) *The Sexual Scene*, Chicago: Aldine.
—— (1973a) *Sexual Conduct: The Social Sources of Human Sexuality*, Chicago: Aldine.
—— (1973b) 'Prospects for change in American sexual patterns', in G.F. Streib (ed.) *The Changing Family: Adaptation and Diversity*, New York: Addison Wesley.
—— (1986) 'Sexual scripts: permanence and change', *Archives of Sexual Behaviour* April: 97–121.
Gallop, J. (1982) *Feminism and Psychoanalysis: The Daughter's Seduction*, London: Macmillan.
Gandel, K. (1986) 'Michel Foucault: intellectual work and politics', *Telos* 67: 121–34.
Gardner, J.R. (1990) 'What lawyers mean by citizenship', in *Encouraging Citizenship: The Report of the Speaker's Commission on Citizenship*, London: HMSO.
Garfinkel, H. (1967) *Studies in Ethnomethodology*, New Jersey: Prentice-Hall.
Gassman, A. (1986) 'My life as a sex warden', *The Advocate* 23 December: 9.
Gebhard, P. (1972) 'The incidence of homosexuality in the US and W. Europe', in J.M. Livingwood (ed.) *NIMH: Task Force on Homosexuality. Final Report and Papers*, DHEW. pub. no. HSM 72–9116: US National Institute of Mental Health.

—— (1984) 'Sexuality in the post-Kinsey era', in W.G. Armytage, R. Chester and J. Peel (eds) *Changing Patterns of Sexual Behaviour*, London: Academic Press.

Geller, T. (ed.) (1990) *Bisexuality: A Reader and Source Book*, New York: Times Change Press.

Gerard, D. (1985) 'Religious attitudes and values', in M. Abrams, D. Gerard and N. Timms (eds) *Values and Social Change in Britain*, London: Macmillan.

Gerson, K. (1983) 'Changing family structure and the position of women', *Journal of the American Planning Association* 49, 2: 138–48.

—— (1986/7) 'Emerging social divisions among women: implications for welfare policies', *Politics and Society* 15, 2: 213–21.

Gilbert, A. (1974) 'The *Africaine* court martial: a study of buggery in the Royal Navy', *Journal of Homosexuality* 1: 111–23.

—— (1979) 'Review of M. Foucault *The History of Sexuality, Volume One: An Introduction*', *American Historical Review* 84: 1020–1.

—— (1981) 'Conceptions of homosexuality and sodomy', in S.J. Licata and R.B. Petersen (eds) *Historical Perspectives on Homosexuality*, New York: Haworth.

Gilmour, I. (1978) *Inside Right: A Study of Conservatism*, London: Quartet.

Ginsburg, F. (1984) 'The body politic: the defense of sexual restriction by anti-abortion activists', in C. Vance (ed.) *Pleasure and Danger: Exploring Female Sexuality*, London: Routledge & Kegan Paul.

Ginsburg, N. (1979) *Class, Capital and Social Policy*, London: Macmillan.

Glase, T. and Frosh, S. (1987) *Childhood Sexual Abuse*, London: Macmillan.

Glaser, B.G. and Strauss, A.L. (1971) *Status Passage: A Formal Theory*, London: Routledge & Kegan Paul.

Gley, E. (1884) 'Les aberrations de l'instinct sexuel', *Revue Philosophique*, January.

Goffman, I. (1976) *Gender Advertisements*, London: Macmillan.

Goldstein, J., Freud, A. and Solnit, A.J. (1987) *Before the Best Interests of the Child?*, London: Burnett Books.

Goldthorpe, J. and Payne, C. (1986) 'Trends in intergenerational class mobility in England and Wales 1972–1983', *Sociology* 20, 1: 1–24.

Goodwin, J. (1982) *Sexual Abuse: Incest Victims and their Families*, Boston: John Wright PSG.

Goodwin, J. and Geil, C. (1982) 'Why physicians should report child abuse: the example of sexual abuse', in J. Goodwin (ed.) *Sexual Abuse: Incest Victims and their Families*, Boston: John Wright PSG.

Goodwin, J., McCarthy, T. and DiVasto, P. (1981) 'Prior incest in mothers of abused children', *Child Abuse and Neglect* 5: 87–95.

Gordon, A.W. (1969) *Peter Howard: Life and Letters*, London: Hodder & Stoughton.

Gordon, D.M. (1976) 'Capitalist efficiency and socialist efficiency', *Monthly Review* 28, 3: 19–39.

Gottfried, P. (1988) 'Selectively remembering the 1960s', *Telos* 76: 127–31.

Gottlieb, D. (1973) *Children's Liberation*, New Jersey: Prentice-Hall.

Gough, J. and McNair, M. (1985) *Gay Liberation in the Eighties*, London: Pluto.

Gould, R.E. (1979) 'What we don't know about homosexuality', in M.P.

Levine (ed.) *Gay Men: The Sociology of Homosexuality*, New York: Colophon.

Grant, J. (1980) *George and Julie*, London: NEL Times/Mirroe.

Green, E., Hebron, S. and Woodward, D. (1986) *Leisure and Gender. A Study of Sheffield: Women's Leisure Experiences*, Sheffield: Sheffield City Polytechnic.

Green, J. (1989) *Days in the Life: Voices of the English Underground: 1961–71*, London: Heinemann.

Green, R. (1987) *The 'Sissy-Boy Syndrome' and the Development of Homosexuality*, New Haven: Yale University Press.

Green, R. and Money, J. (eds) (1969) *Transsexualism and Sex Reassignment*, Baltimore: Johns Hopkins Press.

Greenwood, V. and Young, J. (1979) 'Ghettos of freedom: an examination of permissiveness', in National Deviancy Conference (ed.) *Permissiveness and Control*, London: Macmillan.

Greer, G. (1970) *The Female Eunuch*, London: McGibbon & Kee.

—— (1984) *Sex and Destiny: The Politics of Human Fertility*, London: Secker & Warburg.

—— (1986) Review of J. Morris *Conundrum* (1974), in G. Greer *The Mad Woman's Underclothes*, London: Pan.

—— (1990) 'Self-love or self-abuse', *Marie Claire* October: 97–100.

—— (1991) 'Home thoughts: Germaine Greer *v.* the tooth fairy', *Independent Magazine* 26 January: 18.

Griffin, S. (1971) 'The all-American crime', *Ramparts* September: 26–35.

—— (1981) *Pornography and Silence*, London: Women's Press.

Gross, A.E. (1978) 'The male role and heterosexual behaviour', *Journal of Social Issues* 34, 1: 87–107.

Gross, B. and Gross, R. (1977) *The Children's Rights Movement*, Garden City, NY: Anchor Doubleday.

Grosz, E. (1990) 'Contemporary theories of power and subjectivity', in S. Gunew (ed.) *Feminist Knowledge: Critique and Construction*, New York: Routledge.

Groth, N. and Birnbaum, J. (1978) 'Adult sexual orientation and the attraction to underage persons', *Archives of Sexual Behaviour* 7: 175–81.

Groth, N.A., Hobson, W. and Gary, T. (1982) 'The child molester: clinical observations', in J. Conte and D. Shore (eds) *Social Work and Child Sexual Abuse*, New York: Haworth.

Guardian (1969) *The Permissive Society: The Guardian Enquiry*, London: Panther.

Gummer, J.S. (1971) *The Permissive Society*, London: Cassell.

Gutheil, E. (1954) 'The psychological background of transexualism and transvestism', *American Journal of Psychotherapy* 8: 231–9.

Hakim, C. (1979) *Occupational Segregation: A Comparative Study of the Degree and Pattern of the Differentiation Between Men and Women's Work in Britain, the United States and Other Countries*, Research Paper No. 9. Department of Employment, November.

—— (1981) 'Job segregation: trends in the 1970s', *Employment Gazette*, December.

315

Hall, R. (1981) 'Women against rape', in *No Turning Back: Writings from the Women's Liberation Movement: 1975–80*, London: Women's Press.

Hall, S. (1978) *Policing the Crisis*, London: Macmillan.

—— (1979) 'Reformism and the legislation of consent', in National Deviancy Conference (ed.) *Permissiveness and Control*, London: Macmillan.

—— (1983) 'The great moving right show', in S. Hall and M. Jacques (eds) *The Politics of Thatcherism*, London: Verso.

—— (1984) 'The rise of the representative/interventionist state', in G. McLennan, D. Held and S. Hall (eds) *State and Society in Contemporary Britain*, Cambridge: Polity.

—— (1985) 'Authoritarian populism: a reply', in B. Jessop *et al.* (1988) *Thatcherism*, Cambridge: Polity.

Hall, S., Clarke, J., Jefferson, T. and Roberts, B. (eds) (1976) *Resistance Through Rituals*, London: Hutchinson.

Halperin, D.M. (1991) 'Sex before sexuality: pederasty, politics, and power in classical Athens', in M.B. Duberman, M. Vicinus and G. Chauncey Jr (eds) *Hidden from History: Reclaiming the Gay and Lesbian Past*, London: Penguin.

Halsey, A.H. (1985) 'On methods and morals', in M. Abrams, D. Gerard and N. Timms (eds) *Values and Social Change in Britain*, London: Macmillan.

Hamburger, C., Sturup, G.K. and Dahl-Iversen, E. (1953) 'Transvestism, hormonal, psychiatric and surgical treatment', *Journal of the American Medical Association*, 152: 391–6.

Hansen, C.E. and Evans, A. (1985) 'Bisexuality reconsidered: an idea in pursuit of a definition', in F. Klein and T.J. Wolf (eds) *Bisexualities Theories and Research*, New York: Haworth.

Harding, S. (1988) 'Trends in permissiveness', in R. Jowell, S. Witherspoon and L. Brook (eds) *British Social Attitudes: 5th Report*, Aldershot: SCPR-Gower.

Harding, S., Philips, D. and Fogarty, M. (eds) (1986) *Contrasting Values in Western Europe*, London: Macmillan.

Hare, E.H. (1962) 'Masturbatory insanity: the history of an idea', *Journal of Mental Science* 108: 1–25.

Harris, J. (1987) 'The political status of children', in K. Graham (ed.) *Contemporary Political Philosophy*, Cambridge: Cambridge University Press.

Harris, L. (1985) 'British capital: manufacturing, finance and multi-national corporations', in D. Coates, G. Johnston and R. Bush (eds) *A Socialist Anatomy of Britain*, Cambridge: Polity.

Harrison, P.R. (1987) 'From bodies to ethics: the second and third volumes of Foucault's History of Sexuality', *Thesis Eleven* 16: 128–40.

Hart, J. (1984) *So You Think You're Attracted to the Same Sex?* Harmondsworth: Penguin.

Hartsock, N. (1990) 'Foucault on power: a theory for women?' in E.J. Nicholson (ed.) *Feminism/Postmodernism*, New York and London: Routledge.

Harvey, B. (1984) 'No more nice girls', in C. Vance (ed.) *Pleasure and Danger: Exploring Female Sexuality*, London: Routledge.

Hastings, D.W. (1966) 'Transsexualism and transvestism', *Journal of the American Medical Association* 197: 594–600.

—— (1974) 'Post-surgical adjustment of male transsexual patients', *Plastic Surgery* 1: 335–44.

Haug, F. (1987) *Female Sexualisation*, London: Verso.

Heater, D. (1990) 'Citizenship: the civic ideal', in D. Heater *World History, Politics and Education*, London: Longman.

—— (1991) 'Citizenship: a remarkable case of sudden interest', *Parliamentary Affairs: A Journal of Comparative Politics* 44, 2: 140–56.

Heath, S. (1982) *The Sexual Fix*, London: Macmillan.

Hebdige, D. (1979) *Subculture: The Meaning of Style*, London: Methuen.

Heller, A.C. (1987) 'Is there a man in your man's life? What every girl should know about the bisexual guy', *Mademoiselle* July.

Herdt, G.H. (1981) *Guardians of the Flutes: Idioms of Masculinity*, New York: McGraw-Hill.

—— (1982) *Rituals of Manhood: Male Initiation in New Guinea*, Berkeley: University of California Press.

—— (1984) *Ritualised Homosexuality in Melanesia*, Berkeley: University of California Press.

Herman, G. (1903) *'Genesis' das Gesetz der Zeugung*, Bd. Libido und Mania, Leipzig.

Herman, J.L. and Hirschman, L. (1981) *Father–Daughter Incest*, Harvard: Harvard University Press.

Hewison, R. (1990) 'Washes Whiter Getaway People', BBC 2 29 April.

Hewlett, B. (1989) *A Lesser Life: The Myth of Women's Liberation*, New York: Warner Books.

Hiley, D. (1984) 'Foucault and the analysis of power: political engagement without hope and comfort', *Praxis International* 4: 192–207.

Himmelhoch, B. (1990) 'The bisexual potential', in T. Geller (ed.) *Bisexuality: A Reader and Source Book*, New York: Times Change Press.

Himmelweit, S. and Mohun, S. (1977) 'Domestic labour and capital', *Cambridge Journal of Economics* 1: 15–31.

Hirschfeld, M. (1903) 'Die objective Diagnose der Homosexualität', *Jarbuch für Sexuelle Zwischenstufen* 1: 4.

—— (1911) *Die Transvestiten*, Berlin: Pulvermacher.

—— (1948) *Sexual Anomalies*, New York: Emerson.

Hite, S. (1976) *The Hite Report*, New York: Macmillan.

HMSO (1990) *Children Come First*, White Paper, 29 October.

Hobbes, T. (1963) *Leviathan*, London: Macpherson.

Hobsbawm, E. (1968) *Industry and Empire*, London: Weidenfeld & Nicolson.

—— (1981) 'The formal march of labour halted?: or observations on the debate', in M. Jacques and F. Mulhern (eds) *Observations on the Debate*, London: New Left Books.

Hocquenghem, G. (1978) *The Problem is not so much Homosexual Desire as the Fear of Homosexuality*, London: Allison & Busby.

Hodgkinson, L. (1990) 'Bridges across the divide to the opposite sex', *Independent* 9 October: 17.

Hoenig, J., Kenna, J. and Youd, A. (1971) 'Surgical treatment for transsexuals', *Acta Psychiatra Scandanavia* 47: 106–36.

Hollander, P. (ed.) (1988) *Survival of the Adversary Culture*, New York: Oxford University Press.

Hollibaugh, A. (1984) 'Desire for the future: radical hope in passion and pleasure', in C. Vance (ed.) *Pleasure and Danger: Exploring Female Sexuality*, London: Routledge.

Holloway, J.P. (1974) 'Transsexuals: legal considerations', *Archives of Sexual Behaviour* 3: 33–50.

Holt, J. (1975) *Escape from Childhood: The Needs and Rights of Children*, Harmondsworth: Allen Lane, Penguin.

Hooker, E. (1967) 'The homosexual community', in J.H. Gagnon and W.S. Simon (eds) *Sexual Deviance*, London: Harper & Row.

Horkheimer, M. (1986) 'Materialism and morality', *Telos* 69, Fall: 85–98.

Hotchner, B. (1979) 'Contemporary American sex shocks', in M. Cook and G. Wilson (eds) *Love and Attraction*, Oxford: Pergamon.

Houston, R. (1978) 'The way we wear', *Gay News* 131: 14–15.

Howard League for Penal Reform (1985) *Report of a Howard League Working Party: Unlawful Sex*, London: Waterlow.

Howells, K. (1977) 'Some meanings of children for paedophiles', in M. Cook and G. Wilson (eds) *Love and Attraction*, Oxford: Pergamon.

Hoyles, M. (ed.) (1979) *Changing Childhood*, London: Writers and Readers Publishing Co-operative.

Hughes, J. (1989) 'Thinking about children', in G. Scarre (ed.) *Children, Parents and Politics*, Cambridge: Cambridge University Press.

Humphreys, L. (1970) *The Tea-Room Trade*, London: Duckworth.

—— (1971) 'New styles in homosexual manliness', *Transaction* 8: March–April, and in J. McCaffrey (ed.) (1972) *The Homosexual Dialectic*, New Jersey: Prentice-Hall.

Hunt, D. (1970) *Parents and Children in History*, New York: Basic Books.

Hussain, A.H. (1981) 'Foucault's history of sexuality', *m/f* 7: 169–91.

Huussen Jr, A.H. (1991) 'Sodomy in the Dutch Republic in the eighteenth century', in M.B. Duberman, M. Vicinus and G. Chauncey Jr (eds) *Hidden from History: Reclaiming the Gay and Lesbian Past*, London: Penguin.

Hyde, H.M. (1970) *The Other Love: An Historical and Contemporary Survey of Homosexuality in Britain*, London: Heinemann.

Index to International Public Opinion (1979–80) Westport, CT: Greenwood.

Inglehart, I. (1977) *The Silent Revolution: Changing Values and Political Styles Amongst Western Publics*, Princeton: Princeton University Press.

—— (1978) *Culture Shifts in Advanced Industrial Culture*, Princeton: Princeton University Press.

Ingram, M. (1977) 'The participating victim: a study of sex offences against pre-pubertal boys', in M. Cook and G. Wilson (eds) *Love and Attraction*, Oxford: Pergamon.

International Gallup Polls (1979) Princeton, NJ.

Jackson, E. and Persky, S. (eds) (1982) *Flaunting It: A Decade of Gay Journalism*, Vancouver: Pink Triangle Books.

Jackson, M. (1984) 'Sexology and the social construction of male sexuality (Havelock Ellis)', in L. Coveney, M. Jackson, S. Jeffreys, L. Kaye and P. Mahoney (eds) *The Sexuality Papers*, London: Tavistock.

—— (1982) *Childhood and Sexuality*, Oxford: Basil Blackwell.

James, J. and Meyerding, J. (1977) 'Early sexual experiences as a factor in prostitution', *Archives of Sexual Behaviour* 7, 1: 31–42.

James, M. (1984) Interview in K. Kirk and E. Heath (eds) *Men in Frocks*, London: Gay Men's Press.

Jay, K. and Young, A. (eds) (1977) *Out of the Closets: Voices of Gay Liberation*, New York: Jove/HBJ.

—— (1978) *Lavender Culture*, New York: Jove/HBJ.

Jeffreys, S. (1985) *The Spinster and her Enemies*, London: Pandora.

—— (1990) *Anti-Climax*, London: Women's Press.

Jehu, D. (1988) *Beyond Sexual Abuse: Therapy and Women who were Childhood Victims*, Chichester: Wiley.

Jenkins, R. (1959) *The Labour Case*, Harmondsworth: Penguin.

Jessop, B., Bonnett, K., Bromley, S. and Ling, T. (1988) *Thatcherism*, Cambridge: Polity.

Joas, S.H. (1987) 'Symbolic interactionism', in A. Giddens and J.H. Turner (eds) *Sociological Theory Today*, Cambridge: Polity.

Joffe, C. (1985) 'The meaning of the abortion conflict', *Contemporary Society* 14, 1: 26–9.

—— (1986/7) 'Abortion and anti-feminism', *Politics and Society* 15, 2: 207–12.

Johnson, S. (1989) 'Clause 28 comes out of the closet', *Sunday Times* 23 July.

Johnston, C.M. and Deisher, R.W. (1973) 'Contemporary communal child rearing: a first analysis', *Paediatrics* 52: 319–26.

Jong, E. (1973) *Fear of Flying*, New York: Holt, Reinhart & Winston.

Jordonova, L. (1989) 'Children in history: concepts of nature and society', in G. Scarre (ed.) *Children, Parents and Politics*, Cambridge: Cambridge University Press.

Jowell, R. and Witherspoon, S. (eds) (1986) *British Social Attitudes: The 1986 Report*, Aldershot: Gower-SCPR.

Kando, T. (1973) *Sex Change: The Achievement of Identity Among Feminised Transsexuals*, Springfield, IL: Thomas.

Kanin, E. (1967) 'Reference group and sex conduct in norm violations', *Sociological Quarterly* 8: 495–505.

Kappeler, S. (1987) 'The white brothel: literary exoneration of the pornographic', in *Feminist Review* (ed.) *Sexuality: A Reader*, London: Virago.

Kavanagh, D. (1987) *Thatcherism and British Politics: The End of Consensus?* Oxford: Oxford University Press.

Keay, D. (1987) 'AIDS education and the year 2000', *Woman's Own* 31 October: 10.

Kellner, D. (1983) 'Critical theory, commodities and the consumer society', *Theory, Culture and Society* 1, 3: 66–84.

Kelly, G.A. (1979) 'Who needs a theory of citizenship?' *Daedalus* 108, Fall: 21–36.

Kelly, G.F. (1974) 'Asexuality and youth culture', *Homosexuality Counselling Journal* 2: 16–25.

Kempe, R.S. and Kempe, C.H. (1978) *Child Abuse*, London: Fontana/Open.

Keocher, G.P. (1976) *Childrens' Rights and the Mental Health Professionals*, New York: Wiley.

King, D. (1981) 'Gender confusions: psychological and psychiatric conceptions of transvestism and transsexualism', in K. Plummer (ed.) *The Making of the Modern Homosexual*, London: Hutchinson.

—— (1984) 'Condition, orientation, role or false consciousness? Models of homosexuality and transsexualism', *Sociological Review* 32, 1: 38–56.

—— (1987) 'Social constructionism and medical knowledge: the case of the transsexual', *Sociology of Health and Illness* 9: 351–77.

Kinsey, A.C., Pomeroy, W.B. and Martin, C.E. (1948) *Sexual Behaviour in the Human Male*, Philadelphia: W.B. Saunders.

Kinsey, A.C., Gebhard, P., Pomeroy, W.B. and Martin, C.E. (1953) *Sexual Behaviour in the Human Female*, Philadelphia: W.B. Saunders.

Kirk, K. and Heath, E. (1984) *Men in Frocks*, London: Gay Men's Press.

Klapp, O.E. (1958) 'Social types: process and structure', *American Sociological Review* 23, 1: 674–8.

Klein, F. (1978) *The Bisexual Option: A Concept of 100 Per Cent Intimacy*, New York: Arbor House.

Klein, Fritz, Sepekoff, B. and Wolf, T. (1985) 'Sexual orientation: a multivariable dynamic process', *Journal of Homosexuality* 11, 1–2: 35–49.

Kline, S. and Leiss, W. (1978) 'Advertising needs and commodity fetishism', *Canadian Journal of Political and Social Theory* 2: 5–30.

Kockott, G. (1976) 'Cerebral dysfunction in transsexualism', in *Nervenarzt* 47: 310–18.

Koedt, A. (1974) 'The myth of the vaginal orgasm', in The Radical Therapist Collective (ed.) *The Radical Therapist*, Harmondsworth: Penguin.

Krafft-Ebing, R. von (1891/1965) *Psychopathia Sexualis: A Medico-Economic Study*, transl. M. Wedeck, New York: Putnam's & Sons.

Kritzman, L.D. (ed.) (1988) *Michel Foucault: Poltics, Philosophy, Culture: Interviews and other Writings 1977–84*, London: Routledge.

Kumar, K. (1971) *Revolution*, London: Weidenfeld & Nicolson.

L., Catherine (1983) 'Women loving girls: yes they exist', *Minor Problems* 1, 15 April.

Lacan, J. (1968) *The Language of Self: The Function of Language and Psychoanalysis*, Baltimore: Johns Hopkins Press.

La Fontaine, J. (1988) *Childhood Sexual Abuse*, London: ESRC Research Briefing.

Laing, R.D. (1971) *The Politics of the Family and Other Essays*, Harmondsworth: Penguin.

Lakoff, R. (1975) *Language and Women's Place*, New York: Harper & Row.

Land, H. (1980) 'The family wage', *Feminist Review* 6: 55–78.

Landis, P. (1956) 'Experience of 500 children with adult sexual deviants', *Psychiatric Quarterly Supplement* 30: 69–91.

Lasch, C. (1979) *The Culture of Narcissism*, New York: Warner.

Lash, S. (1985) 'Post-modernity and desire', *Theory and Society* 14: 1–31.

Leach, E. (1972) *Environmental Solutions*, New York: Oxford University Press.

Lees, S. (1986) *Losing Out*, London: Hutchinson.

Leonard, D. and Speakman, M.A. (1986) 'Women in the family:

companions or caretakers?' in V. Beechey and E. Whitelegg (eds) *Women in Britain Today*, Milton Keynes: Open University Press.

Lester, A. (1970) 'Is there equality before the law?' in Lord Devlin *et al. What's Wrong With the Law*, London: BBC.

Levitt, E.E. and Klassen Jr, A.D. (1974) 'Public attitudes towards homosexuality', *Journal of Homosexuality* 1: 29–43.

Liebert, R.M. and Sprafkin, J. (1988) *The Early Window: The Effects of Television on Children and Youth*, Oxford: Pergamon.

Liebman, R.C. and Winthrow, R. (1983) *The New Christian Right*, New York: Aldine.

Limentani, A. (1976) 'Object choice and actual bisexuality', *American Journal of Psycho-analysis and Psychotherapy* V: 205.

Lindley, R. (1989) 'Teenagers and other children', in G. Scarre (ed.) *Children, Parents and Politics*, Cambridge: Cambridge University Press.

Longford Committee (1972) *Pornography: The Longford Report*, London: Coronet.

Lothstein, L.M. (1983) *Female to Male Transsexualism*, London: Routledge & Kegan Paul.

Lotringer, S. (1981) Interview with Mark Moffett in D. T'Sang (ed.) *The Age Taboo*, London: Gay Men's Press.

Lowry, S. (1985) *The Princess in the Mirror*, London: Chatto & Windus.

Luker, C. (1984) *Abortion and the Politics of Motherhood*, Berkeley: University of California Press.

Lukes, S. (1973) *Individualism*, London: Basil Blackwell.

—— (1984) 'The future of British socialism', in B. Pimlott (ed.) *Fabian Essays in Socialist Theory*, London: Heinemann.

McCaffrey, J. (1972) *The Homosexual Dialectic*, New Jersey: Prentice-Hall.

McCrone, D., Elliott, B. and Bechhofer, F. (1989) 'Corporatism and the New Right', in R. Scase (ed.) *Industrial Societies: Crisis and Division in Western Capitalism and State Socialism*, London: Unwin/Hyman.

MacDonald, A.P. (1981) 'Bisexuality: some comments on research and theory', *Journal of Homosexuality* 6: 21–35.

Macdonald, R.H. (1967) 'The frightful consequences of onanism: notes on the history of a delusion', *Journal of the History of Ideas* 28: 423–31.

MacFarlane, K. (ed.) (1986) *Sexual Abuse of Young Children*, New York: Holt Rinehart & Winston.

MacInnes, C. (1973) *Loving them Both: A Study of Bisexuality and Bisexuals*, London: Martin Byan.

McIntosh, M. (1968) 'The homosexual role', *Social Problems* 16, 2: 182–92.

—— (1978a) 'Who needs prostitutes? The ideology of male sex needs', in C. Smart and B. Smart (eds) *Women, Sexuality and Social Control*, London: Routledge & Kegan Paul.

—— (1978b) 'The state and the oppression of women', in A. Kuhn and A.M. Wolpe (eds) *Feminism and Materialism*, London: Routledge & Kegan Paul.

—— (1981) 'The homosexual role: postscript: "The homosexual role" revisited', M. McIntosh interviewed by J. Weeks and K. Plummer in K. Plummer (ed.) *The Making of the Modern Homosexual*, London: Hutchinson.

—— (1984) 'The family, regulation and the public sphere', in G. McLennan, D. Held and S. Hall (eds) *State and Society in Contemporary Britain*, Cambridge: Polity.

McIntyre, A. (1981) *After Virtue: A Study in Moral Theory*, London: Duckworth.

MacIntyre, S. (1976) ' "Who wants babies?" The social construction of "instincts" ', in L. Barker and S. Allen (eds) *Sexual Divisions and Society: Process and Change*, London: Tavistock.

MacKinnon, C.A. (1983) 'Feminism, Marxism and the state: toward feminist jurisprudence', *Signs* 8: 43–58.

Macmillan, I. (1989) 'Fallout after the Cleveland affair', *Community Care* 6, 11 May: 7.

McRobbie, A. (1981) *Feminism for Girls*, London: Routledge & Kegan Paul.

—— (1991) *Feminism and Youth Subculture*, London: Macmillan.

Maidment, S. (1983) 'Administrative procedures for the removal of parental rights', in H. Geach and E. Szwed (eds) *Providing Civil Justice for Children*, Sevenoaks: E. Arnold.

Malos, E. (1980) *The Politics of Housework*, London: Allison & Busby.

Mann, M. (1987) 'Ruling class strategies and citizenship', *Sociology* 21, 3: 339–54.

Marcus, S. (1966) *The Other Victorians: A Study of Sexuality and Pornography in Mid-nineteenth-century England*, London: Weidenfeld & Nicolson.

Marcuse, H. (1964) *One-dimensional Man*, Boston: Beacon Press.

—— (1969) *Essay on Liberation*, Harmondsworth: Penguin.

—— (1974) *Eros and Civilisation*, Boston: Beacon Press.

Margolis, D.R. (1989) 'Considering women's experience: a reformulation of power theory', *Theory and Society* 18: 387–416.

Marias, J. (1968) *America in the Fifties and Sixties*, Upper Darby, PA: Pennsylvania University Press.

Marshall, A. (1873) 'The future of the working class', paper quoted in A.C. Pigou (1925) *Memorials of Alfred Marshall*, London: Macmillan; and in T.H. Marshall (1950) in 'Citizenship and social class', in his *Sociology at the Crossroads*, Cambridge: Cambridge University Press.

Marshall, B. (1989) *Coming on Strong: Gay Politics and Culture*, London: Hyman/Unwin.

Marshall, G., Rose, D., Vogler, C. and Newby, H. (1985) 'Class, citizenship and distributional conflict', *British Journal of Sociology* 36, 2: 259–84.

—— (1987) 'Distributional struggle and moral order in a market society', *Sociology* 21, 1: 55–73.

—— (1988) *Social Class in Modern Britain*, London: Unwin Hyman.

Marshall, J. (1981) 'Pansies, perverts and macho men', in K. Plummer (ed.) *The Making of the Modern Homosexual*, London: Hutchinson.

—— (1989) 'Flaunting it', *Gay Times* January: 12–13.

Marshall, K. (1986) *Moral Panics and Victorian Values: Women and the Family in Thatcher's Britain*, 2nd edn, London: Junius.

Marshall, T.H. (1950) *Citizenship and Social Class and Other Essays*, Cambridge: Cambridge University Press.

Martin, B. (1981) *A Sociology of Contemporary Cultural Challenge*, Oxford: Blackwell.

Martin, N. (1989) 'Legislation and child sexual abuse – consideration and proposed changes in the law', in H. Blagg, J.A. Hughes and C. Wattam (eds) *Child Sexual Abuse*, London: Longman.

Martin, R. (1985) *Rawls and Rights*, Lawrence, KA: University of Kansas Press.

Martinson, F.M. (1976) 'Eroticism in infancy and childhood', *Journal of Sex Research* 12: 251–62.

Marx, K. (1904) *A Contribution to the Critique of Political Economy*, Chicago: Charles H. Kerr.

—— (1938) *Capital*, London: Allen & Unwin.

—— (1973) *Economic and Philosophical Manuscripts of 1844*, London: Lawrence & Wishart.

Masnick, G. and Barie, M.J. (1980) *The Nation's 'Families'*, Cambridge, MA: Joint Centre for Urban Studies of MIT and Harvard University.

Masters, W.H. and Johnson, V.E. (1966) *Human Sexual Response*, Boston: Little Brown.

—— (1970) *Human Sexual Inadequacy*, Boston: Little Brown.

—— (1979) *Homosexuality in Perspective*, Boston: Little Brown.

Mause, L. de (ed.) (1979) *The History of Childhood*, New York: Souvenir Press.

Mead, M. (1935) *Sex and Temperament in Three Primitive Societies*, London: Gollancz.

—— (1955) 'Theoretical setting', in M. Mead and M. Wolfenstein (eds) *Childhood in Contemporary Culture*, Chicago: University of Chicago Press.

—— (1975) 'Bisexuality: what is it all about?' *Redbook Magazine* January.

Meerloo, J. (1967) 'Change of sex and collaboration with the psychosis' *American Journal of Psychiatry* 124: 263–4.

Mellors, B. (1990) 'Gay liberation', *LSE Magazine* Summer: 31–2.

Merck, M. (1992) 'From Minneapolis to Westminster', in L. Segal and M. McIntosh (eds) *Sex Exposed*, London: Virago.

Meyer, J. and Hooper, J.E. (1974) 'The gender dysphoria syndromes', *Plastic and Reconstructive Surgery* 54: 444–51.

Middleton, C. (1975) 'Sexual inequality and stratification', in F. Parkin (ed.) *The Social Analysis of Class Structure*, London: Tavistock.

Mieli, M. (1980) *Homosexuality and Liberation: Elements of a Gay Critique*, transl. D. Fernbach, London: Gay Men's Press.

Miles, R. (1982) *Racism and Migrant Labour*, London: Routledge & Kegan Paul.

Mill, J.S. (1910) *On Liberty*, London: Routledge.

—— (1929) *On the Subjection of Women*, London: Dent.

Millett, K. (1972) *Sexual Politics*: London: Sphere.

—— (1981) 'Sexual revolution and the liberation of children', in D. T'Sang (ed.) *The Age Taboo*, London: Gay Men's Press.

Millot, B. (1988) 'Symbol, desire, power', *Theory, Culture and Society* 5, 4: 675–94.

Miner, J. and Blythe, E. (1988) *Coping with Child Sexual Abuse: A Guide for Teachers*, London: Longman.

Minor Problems (1983) Issue 1, 15 April.

Mishan, E. (1969) *The Costs of Economic Growth*, Harmondsworth: Penguin.

Mitchell, A. (1969) 'Priests, and prophets of permissiveness', in *The Guardian Enquiry* (ed.) *Permissive Britain*, London: Panther.

Mitchell, J. (1966) 'Women: the longest revolution', *New Left Review* 40, November–December: 11–37.

—— (1971) *Women's Estate*, Harmondsworth: Penguin.

—— (1975) *Psychoanalysis and Feminism*, Harmondsworth: Penguin.

Mitchell, J. and Rose, J. (1982) 'Feminine sexuality: an interview with J. Mitchell and J. Rose', *m/f* 8: 3–16.

Mitchell, W.E. (1977) 'The baby disturbers', in C.D. Bryant (ed.) *Sexual Deviance in Social Context*, New York: New Viewpoints.

Mitzel, J. (1980) *The Boston Sex Scandal*, Boston: Glad Day Books.

Moebius, P.J. (1900) 'Uber-Entartung', *Grenzfr. Nerv u. Seelenleb* 3: 95.

Mohr, J.C. (1978) *Abortion in America: The Origins and Evolution of National Policy*, New York: Oxford University Press.

Mohr, J.W., Turner, R.B. and Jerry, M.B. (1964) *Paedophilia and Exhibitionism*, Toronto: University of Toronto Press.

Moll, A. (1897/1953) *Libido Sexualis; Studies in Psycho-Sexual Laws of Love Verified by Case Histories*, New York: American Ethological Press.

Molyneux, M. (1980) 'Beyond the domestic labour debate', *New Left Review*, 116: 3–27.

Money, J. (1974) 'The new bisexual', *Time* 13 May: 79–80.

—— (1977) 'Bisexual, homosexual and heterosexual: society, law and medicine', *Journal of Homosexuality* 2: 229–33.

—— (1980) *Love and Sickness: The Science of Sex, Gender Differentiation and Pair Bonding*, Baltimore: Johns Hopkins Press.

Money, J. and Erhardt, A.H. (1972) *Man and Woman/Boy and Girl*, Baltimore: Johns Hopkins Press.

Money, J. and Gaskin, R. (1970–1) 'Sex re-assignment', *International Journal of Psychiatry* 9: 249–69.

Money, J. and Musaph, H. (eds) (1977) *Handbook of Sexology*, Amsterdam: Biomedical Press.

Money, J., Hampson, J.G. and Hampson, J.L. (1957) 'Imprinting and the establishment of gender role', *Archives of Neurology and Psychiatry* 77: 333–6.

Monter, W. (1981) 'Sodomy in early modern Switzerland', in S.J. Licata and R.B. Petersen (eds) *Historical Perspectives on Homosexuality*, New York: Haworth Press.

Moody, R. (1983) *Minor Problems* 1, 15 April: 4.

Moorhouse, H.F. (1983) 'American automobiles and workers' dreams', *Sociological Review* 31: 403–25.

Morgall, J. (1986) 'New office technology', *Feminist Review* (ed.) *Waged Work: A Reader*, London: Virago.

Morris, J. (1974) *Conundrum*, London: Faber & Faber.

Morris, M. (1982) 'A review of Michel Foucault's *La Volonté de savoir*', in M. Brake (ed.) *Human Sexual Relations*, Harmondsworth: Penguin.

Mort, F. (1980) 'Sexuality, regulation and contestation', in Gay Left Collective (ed.) *Homosexuality, Power and Politics*, London: Allison & Busby.

—— (1987) *Dangerous Sexualities: Medico-moral Politics in England Since 1830*, London: Routledge & Kegan Paul.

Mount, F. (1983) *The Subversive Family: An Alternative History of Love and Marriage*, London: Allen & Unwin.

Munter, C. (1984) 'Fat and the fantasy of perfection', in C.S. Vance (ed.) *Pleasure and Danger: Exploring Female Sexuality*, London: Routledge & Kegan Paul.

Murphy, T.F. (1984) 'Freud reconsidered: bisexuality, homosexuality and moral judgement', in J.P. de Cecco and M.G. Shiveley (eds) *Homosexual Identities: Critical Theoretical Issues*, New York: Haworth.

Murray, I. (1991) 'Opposing camps dig in for German battle over abortion', *The Times* 14 May: 11.

Nava, M. (1987) 'Everybody's views were just broadened: a girl's project and some responses to lesbianism', in *Feminist Review* (ed.) *Sexuality: A Reader*, London: Virago.

Nelson, S. (1988) *Incest: Fact and Myth*, Edinburgh: Stramullion Co-operative.

Nesbit, R.E. (1970) 'Who killed the student revolution?' *Encounter* 34, 2: 10–18.

Neumann, R.E. (1975) 'Masturbation, madness and the modern concept of childhood and adolescence', *Journal of Social History* 8: 1–27.

Newton, E. (1972) *Mother Camp: Female Impersonators in America*, New Jersey: Prentice-Hall.

Nichols, J. (1979) 'Butcher than thou: beyond machismo', in M.P. Levine (ed.) *Gay Men: The Sociology of Male Homosexuality*, New York: Harper.

Nicholson, M. and McLaughlin, C. (1987) 'Social constructionism and medical sociology: a reply to Mr. Bury', *Sociology of Health and Illness* 9, 2: 107–26.

Norburg, M. and Laub, D. (1977) 'Review of the Stanford experience: implications for treatment', Paper presented at the Fifth International Gender Dysphoria Symposium, 12 February, Norfolk, Virginia.

Norrie, K. (1988) 'Symbolic and meaningless legislation', *Journal of the Law Society of Scotland* September: 310–14.

—— (1989) 'How to promote homosexuality', *Gay Scotland* 44: 9.

Norris, P. (1987) *Politics and Sexual Equality: The Comparative Position of Women in Western Democracies*, Brighton: Wheatsheaf.

NSPCC (National Society for the Prevention of Cruelty to Children) (1989) *Child Abuse Trends in England and Wales: 1983–7*, London: NSPCC.

Oakley, A. (1972) *Sex, Gender and Society*, London: Temple-Smith.

—— (1976) *Housewife*, Harmondsworth: Penguin.

—— (1982) *Subject Women*, London: Fontana.

O'Carroll, T. (1980) *Paedophilia: The Radical Case*, London: Peter Owen.

Ochs, R. (1988) in interview, *Bisexuality: News, Views and Networking* 27 July.

O'Donovan, K. (1985) *Sexual Divisions in Law*, London: Weidenfeld & Nicolson.

Off Pink Collective (ed.) (1988) *Bisexual Lives*, London: Off Pink Publishing.

Offe, C. (1984) *Contradictions of the Welfare State*, edited by J. Keane, London: Hutchinson.

O'Higgins, J. (1982/3) 'An interview with Michel Foucault', *Salmagundi* 58–61: 11–24.

Oliver, D. (1991) 'Active citizenship in the 1990s', *Parliamentary Affairs: A Journal of Comparative Politics* 44, 2: 157–71.

Orlando, L. (1984) 'Loving whom we choose: bisexuality', *Gay Community News* 25 January: 8.

Orton, J. (1986) *The Joe Orton Diaries*, J. Lahr (ed.) London: Methuen.

O'Sullivan, S. (1979) 'Looking towards transvestite liberation', in L. Richmond and G. Noguera (eds) *The New Liberation Book*, New York: Ramparts Press.

—— (1987) 'Passionate beginnings: ideological politics 1969–72', in *Feminist Review* (ed.) *Sexuality: A Reader*, London: Virago.

Otitoju, F., Parris, M. and Weeks, J. (1988) 'Clause and effect: is there life after Clause 28?' *Marxism Today* 32, June: 22–8.

Pahl, J. (1990) 'Household spending, personal spending and the control of money in marriage', *Sociology* 24, 1: 119–38.

Palmer, E.L. and Dorr, A. (1980) *Children and the Faces of Television: Teaching, Violence and Selling*, New York: Academic Press.

Parsons, T. (1949) *Essays in Sociological Theory*, Glencoe, IL: Free Press.

—— (1952) 'Illness, therapy and the modern American family', *Journal of Social Issues* 8, 4.

—— (1959) 'Voting and the equilibrium of the American party system', in E. Burdick and A. Brodbeck (eds) *American Voting Behaviour*, Glencoe, IL: Free Press.

—— (1965) 'Full citizenship for the Negro American: a social problem', *Daedalus* 91, 4: 1015.

—— (1971) *The System of Modern Societies*, New Jersey: Prentice-Hall.

Parsons, T. and Bales, R.F. (1964) *Family Socialisation and Interaction Process*, London: Routledge & Kegan Paul.

Pauley, I.B. (1969) 'Adult manifestations of male transsexualism', in R. Green and J. Money (eds) *Transsexualism and Sex Re-assignment*, Baltimore: Johns Hopkins Press.

Pearson, G. (1983) *Hooligan: A History of Respectable Fears*, London: Macmillan.

Penelope, J. (1980) 'And now for the hard questions', *Sinister Wisdom* 3: 103.

Person, E. and Ovesey, L. (1974) 'The transsexual syndrome in males I and II', *American Journal of Psychotherapy* 28: 4–20, 174–93.

Petchesky, R.P. (1984) *Abortion and Women's Choice, the State, Sexuality and Reproductive Freedom*, Boston: Northeastern University Press.

Peters, J. (1976) 'Children who are victims of sexual assault and the psychology of offenders', *American Journal of Psychotherapy* 30, 3: 398–432.

Phillips, A. and Taylor, B. (1986) 'Sex and skill', in *Feminist Review* (ed.) *Waged Work: A Reader*, London: Virago.

Phillips, K. (1988) *Policing the Family*, London: Junius.

Piccone, P. (1988) 'Remembering 1968: mythology on the make', *Telos* 77, Fall: 7–43.

PIE (Paedophile Information Exchange) (1978) *Paedophilia: Some Questions and Answers*, London: PIE.

Pigou, A. (1925) *Memorial of Alfred Marshall*, London: Macmillan.

Pitman, D.J. (1971) 'The male house of prostitution', *Trans-Action* March–April: 21–7.

Plant, R. (1988) *Citizenship and Social Class: Citizenship Rights and Socialism*, London: The Fabian Society.

Pleck, J.H. (1981) *The Myth of Masculinity*, Cambridge, MA: MIT Press.

Plumb, A. (1990) 'The transgend-dance', in T. Geller (ed.) *Bisexuality: A Reader and Sourcebook*, New York: Times Change Press.

Plumb, J. (1972) *In the Light of History*, Harmondsworth: Penguin.

Plummer, K. (1975) *Sexual Stigma: An Interactionist Account*, London: Routledge & Kegan Paul.

—— (ed.) (1981) *The Making of the Modern Homosexual*, London: Hutchinson.

—— (1988) 'Organising AIDS', in P. Aggleton and H. Homans (eds) *Social Aspects of AIDS*, Lewes: Falmer Press.

Poster, M. (1984) *Foucault, Marxism and History: Mode of Production Versus Mode of Information*, Cambridge: Polity.

Prentice, T. (1990) 'AIDS: this time send the right message', *The Times* 17 October.

Prison Reform Trust (1990) *Sex Offenders in Prison*, London: Prison Reform Trust.

Rae, D. (1979) 'The egalitarian state: notes on a system of contradictory ideals', *Daedalus* Fall: 37.

Rakusen, J. (1976) 'Depo-provera: still for sale', *Spare Rib* 4 June.

Randell, J.B. (1973) *Sexual Variations*, Chicago: Priory Press.

Rapoport, R. and Rapoport, R. (1975) *Leisure and the Family Cycle*, London: Routledge & Kegan Paul.

Rastan, C. (1989) 'All dressed up for a trip with the girls', *Independent* 29 May: 14.

Rawls, J. (1972) *A Theory of Justice*, Oxford: Oxford University Press.

—— (1987) 'The basic liberties and their priority', in S. McMurrin (ed.) *Liberty, Equality and Law*, Salt Lake City and Cambridge: University of Utah Press/Campbridge University Press.

Raymond, J. (1979) *The Transsexual Empire*, London: Women's Press.

Rayner, C. (1978) *The Body Book*, London: Piccolo.

Rayside, D. and Bowler, S. (1988) 'Research note: public opinion and gay rights', *Canadian Review of Sociology and Anthropology* 25: 649–60.

Rechy, J. (1977) *The Sexual Outlaw*, New York: Grove Press.

Reich, W. (1961) *The Function of the Orgasm*, New York: Farrar, Strauss & Giroux.

—— (1969) *The Sexual Revolution: Towards a Self-governing Character Structure*, New York: Farrar, Strauss & Giroux.

Reiche, R. (1970) *Sexuality and Class Struggle*, London: New Left Books.

Reik, T. (1960) *Sex in Men and Women: Its Emotional Variations*, New York: Noonday Press.

Reiss, A.J. (1961) 'The social integration of queers and peers', *Social Problems* 9: 102–19.

Rentoul, J. (1987) *The Rich Get Richer*, London: Unwin.

Report of the Commission on Obscenity and Pornography (1970) New York: A *New York Times* Book: Bantam.

Reynolds, M. (1990) *Erotica: An Anthology of Women's Writing*, London: Pandora.

Reynolds, S. (1991) Review of F. Jameson *Postmodernism or the Cultural Logic of Late Capitalism*, Verso, in *Observer* 3 March: 59.

Rich, A. (1980) 'Compulsory heterosexuality and lesbian existence', *Signs* 5, 4.

Richardson, D. and Hart, J. (1981) 'The development and maintenance of a homosexual identity', in J. Hart and D. Richardson (eds) *The Theory and Practice of Homosexuality*, London: Routledge & Kegan Paul.

Riddell, C. (1980) *Divided Sisterhood: A Critical Review of Janice Raymond's 'The Transsexual Empire'*, Liverpool: News from Nowhere.

Riley, D. (1981) 'Pronatalism and working women', *History Workshop Journal* 11, Spring: 35–8.

Robarts, S. *et al.* (1981) *Positive Action for Women: The Next Step in Education, Training and Employment*, London: NCCL.

Roberts, M. (1980) Review of T. O'Carroll *Paedophilia: The Radical Case*, London: Peter Owen in *Gay News* 202.

Robertson, G. QC (1988) 'The Sections claws look less sharp now', *The Pink Paper*, 9 June.

Roche, M. (1987) 'Citizenship, social theory and social change', *Theory and Society* 16: 363–70.

Rock, P. (1973) *Deviant Behaviour*, London: Hutchinson.

Root, J. (1984) *Pictures of Women: Sexuality*, London: Pandora.

Rose, J. and Mitchell, J. (eds) (1982) *Feminine Sexuality – Jacques Lacan and the Ecole Freudienne*, London: Macmillan.

Rosen, I. (1979) *Sexual Deviation*, Oxford: Oxford University Press.

Ross, A. (1983) *The Married Homosexual Male*, London: Routledge & Kegan Paul.

Ross, M.W., Rogers, L.J. and McCulloch, H. (1978) 'Stigma, sex and society: a new look at gender differentiation and sexual variation', *Journal of Homosexuality* 3: 315–30.

Rossi, A. (1972) 'Abortion laws and their victims', in J.H. Gagnon and W.S. Simon (eds) *The Sexual Scene*, Chicago: Aldine.

Rossman, P. (1976) *Sexual Experience Between Men and Boys*, New York: Association Press.

Rothchild, J. and Wolf, S. (1976) *Children of the Counter-culture*, Garden City, NY: Anchor.

Rouse, R. (1990) 'Tea gowns and sympathy', *Sunday Correspondent* 15 July: 23.

Rowbotham, S. (1979) *The Women's Movement and Organising for Socialism: Beyond the Fragments*, Newcastle: Newcastle Socialist Centre.

—— (1989) *The Past Before Us: Feminism in Action Since the 1960s*, Harmondsworth: Penguin.

Rubin, G. (1984) 'Thinking sex: notes for a radical theory for the politics of sexuality', in C.S. Vance (ed.) *Pleasure and Danger: Exploring Female Sexuality*, London: Routledge & Kegan Paul.

Rubin, G. and Califia, P. (1981) 'Sadomasochism: fears, facts and fantasies', *Gay Community News Boston* 9, 5.

Ruddick, W. (1989) 'When does childhood begin?', in G. Scarre (ed.) *Children, Parents and Politics*, Cambridge: Cambridge University Press.
Rush, F. (1980) *The Best-kept Secret*, New York: Prentice-Hall.
Sagarin, E. (1969 *Odd Man In: Societies of Deviants in America*, Chicago: Quadrangle Books.
—— (1970) 'Languages of the homosexual subculture', *Medical Aspects of Human Sexuality* April: 12–16.
Sagarin, E. and Kelly, R.J. (1975) 'Sexual deviance and labelling perspectives', in W.R. Gove (ed.) *The Labelling of Deviance*, New York: Wiley.
Sahlins, M. (1976) *Culture and Practical Reason*, Chicago: University of Chicago Press.
Sandfort, T. (1982) *The Sexual Aspects of Paedophile Relations*, London: Pan/Spartacus.
Saslow, J.M. (1991) 'Homosexuality in the Renaissance: behaviour, identity and artistic expression', in M.B. Duberman, M. Vicinus and G. Chauncey Jr (eds) *Hidden from History: Reclaiming the Gay and Lesbian Past*, London: Penguin.
Scherker, M. (1989) 'Out on the streets: the story of Stonewall', *Gay Times* June: 26–8.
Schutz, A. (1962) *Collected Papers*, The Hague: Martinus Nijhoff.
Schwartz, L.B. (1963) 'Morals, offenses and the model penal code', *Columbia Law Review* 61, 1: 669–86.
Scott, J. (1978) *Wives Who Love Women*, New York: Walker.
Scruton, R. (1983) 'When intolerance must triumph', *The Times* 13 September.
—— (1984) *The Meaning of Conservatism*, London: Macmillan.
—— (1986) *Sexual Desire: A Philosophical Investigation*, London: Weidenfeld and Nicolson.
Seabrook, J. (1976) *A Lasting Relationship*, London: Allen Lane.
Search, G. (1988) *The Last Taboo: Sexual Abuse of Children*, Harmondsworth: Penguin.
Sebbar, L. (1981) *La Maman et le pédophile*, Paris: Editions Stock.
Seidler, V.J. (1987) 'Reason, desire and male sexuality', in P. Caplan (ed.) *The Cultural Construction of Sexuality*, London: Tavistock.
Seidman, S. (1989) 'Transfiguring sexual identity: AIDS and the contemporary construction of homosexuality', *Theory, Culture and Society* 6: 293–315.
Sennett, R. (1980) 'Destructive gemeinschaft', in R. Rocock *et al.* (eds) *An Introduction to Sociology*, Milton Keynes: Open University Press.
Shearer, A. (1987) *Woman: Her Changing Image: A Kaleidoscope of Five Decades*, Wellingborough: Thorson.
Shiers, J. (1988) 'One step to heaven', in B. Cant and S. Hemmings (eds) *Radical Records: Thirty Years of Lesbian and Gay History*, London: Routledge.
Shiner, L. (1982) 'Reading Foucault: anti-method and the genealogy of power–knowledge', *History and Theory* 21: 382–98.
Silbert, M. and Pines, A. (1981) 'Sexual abuse as an antecedent to prostitution', *Child Abuse and Neglect* 5: 407–11.

Siltanen, J. (1986) 'Domestic responsibilities and structuring of employment', in R. Crompton and M. Mann (eds) *Gender and Stratification*, Cambridge: Polity.

Silverman, K. (1984) 'Histoire d'O: the construction of a female subject', in C.S. Vance (ed.) *Pleasure and Danger: Exploring Female Sexuality*, London: Routledge.

Simon, W.S. and Gagnon, J.H. (1969) 'Psychosexual development', in D. Goslin (ed.) *Handbook of Socialization Theory and Research*, Chicago: Rand McNally.

Skocpol, T. (1986–7) 'A social issue in American politics: reflections on Kristin Luker's "Abortion and the Politics of Motherhood" ', *Politics and Society* 15, 2: 189–96.

Smart, C. (1981) 'Law and the control of women's sexuality: the case of the 1950s', in B. Hutter and G. Williams (eds) *Controlling Women: The Normal and the Deviant*, London: Croom Helm.

Smart, C. and Smart, B. (1978) 'Sexuality and social control', in C. Smart and B. Smart (eds) *Women, Sexuality and Social Control*, London: Routledge & Kegan Paul.

Smith, D. (1987) 'Fighting the backlash', *Gay Times* January: 14.

—— (1989) 'Tragic or toothless: Section 28 one year on', *Gay Times* June: 10–11.

Smith-Rosenberg, C. (1985) 'The abortion movement and the AWA: 1850–1880', in C. Rosenberg-Smith (ed.) *Disorderly Conduct: Visions of Gender in Victorian America*, New York: Alfred Knopf.

Snell, M. (1986) 'Equal pay and sex discrimination', in *Feminist Review* (ed.) *Waged Work: A Reader*, London: Virago.

Snell, M., Glucklich, P. and Povall, M. (1981) *Equal Pay and Opportunities*, Department of Employment Research Paper 20, London: HMSO.

Sniderman, P. (1986) 'Values under pressure: AIDS and civil liberties', Paper presented at the Annual Meeting of the American Political Science Association, Washington DC.

Snitow, A. (1983) *Desire: The Politics of Sexuality*, London: Virago.

Soble, A. (1983) *Pornography, Marxism and Feminism and the Future of Sexuality*, New Haven and London: Yale University Press.

Socarides, C. (1979) 'The desire for sexual transformation: a psychiatric evaluation of transsexualism', *American Journal of Psychiatry* 125: 1424.

Sontag, S. (1967) 'Notes on camp', in S. Sontag *Against Interpretation*, New York: Farrar, Strauss & Giroux; and S. Sontag (1983) *A Susan Sontag Reader*, Harmondsworth, Penguin.

—— (1969) 'The pornographic imagination', in *Styles of Radical Will*, New York: Farrar, Strauss and Giroux; and S. Sontag (1983) *A Susan Sontag Reader*, Harmondsworth: Penguin.

Spartacus International Gay Guide, various editions from the 1st (1970) to the 17th (1988), originally Brighton, now Berlin: Bruno Gmunder Verlag.

Spectator (1987) 'Decent and indecent', editorial, 14 March.

Spender, D. and Sarah, E. (1980) *Learning to Lose*, London: Women's Press.

Spender, S. (1988) *The Temple*, London: Faber & Faber.

Stanworth, M. (1984) *Gender and Schooling: A Study of Sexual Divisions in the Classroom*, London: Hutchinson in association with the Explorations in Feminism Collective.
—— (1987) *Reproductive Technologies: Gender, Motherhood and Medicine*, Cambridge: Polity.
Staver, S. (1987) 'Bisexuality spreads HIV to family, extent of transmission unclear', *American Medical News* 4 September: 3.
Stoller, R.J. (1968) *Sex and Gender: On the Development of Masculinity and Femininity*, New York: Aronson.
—— (1975) *Perversion: The Erotic Form of Hatred*, New York: Dell.
—— (1979) *Sexual Deviation*, New York: Oxford University Press.
Stones, R. (1989) *Where Babies Come From*, London: Dinosaur.
Summit, R. (1986) 'Beyond belief: the reluctant discovery of incest', in M. Kirkpatrick (ed.) *Women's Sexual Experience*, New York: Plenum.
Sunstein, C.R. (1991) 'Why markets don't stop discrimination', *Social Philosophy and Policy* 8, 2: 22–37.
Swedish National Board of Education (1986) *Sex Education in Swedish Schools*, May.
Szasz, T. (1980) *Sex. Facts, Frauds and Follies*, Oxford: Blackwell.
Talese, G. (1980) *Thy Neighbour's Wife: Sex in the World Today*, London: Collins.
Tarnowsky, B. (1898) *The Sexual Instinct and its Morbid Manifestations*, London: Charles Carrington.
Tatchell, P. (1990) *Out in Europe*, Channel 4 Television, London: Rouge.
—— (1992) *Europe in the Pink*, London: Gay Men's Press.
Taylor, G. Rattray (1953) *Sex in History*, London: Thames and Hudson.
Taylor, I., Walton, P. and Young, J. (1973) *The New Criminology: For a Social Theory of Deviance*, London: Routledge & Kegan Paul.
Taylor, P. (1981) *Perspectives on Paedophilia*, London: Batsford.
Teal, D. (1971) *The Gay Militants*, New York: Stein and Day.
Thompson, G. (1984) ' "Rolling back" the state?: Economic intervention 1975–1982', in G. McLennan, D. Held and S. Hall (eds) *State and Society in Contemporary Britain: A Critical Introduction*, Cambridge: Polity.
Tobin, G. and Wicker, R. (1972) *The Gay Crusaders*, New York: Paperback Library.
Townes, B.D., Ferguson, W.D. and Gillam, S. (1976) 'Differences in psychological sex adjustment and familial influences among homosexual and non-homosexual populations', *Journal of Homosexuality* 1: 261–72.
Tracey, M. and Morrison, D. (1979) *Whitehouse*, London: Macmillan.
Trumbach, R. (1987) 'Sodomitical subcultures, sodomitical roles and the gender revolution in the 18th century', in R.P. Maccubin (ed.) *'Tis Nature's Fault: Unauthorised Sexuality during the Enlightenment*, Cambridge: Cambridge University Press.
T'Sang, D. (ed.) (1981) *The Age Taboo: Gay Male Sexuality, Power and Consent*, London: Gay Men's Press.
Tucker, S. (1979) 'Sex, death and free speech', *Body Politic* 58, November.
—— (1987) 'Rawhide: the mystery and power of leather', *The Advocate* 472, 12 May: 40–7.

Turner, B.S. (1986) *Citizenship and Capitalism*, London: Allen & Unwin.

Tushnet, M. (1991) 'Change and continuity in the concept of civil rights: Thurgood, Marshall and affirmative action', *Philosophy and Policy* 8, 2: 150–71.

Tweedie, J. (1974) Review of J. Morris *Conundrum*, in *The Sunday Times* 5 May.

Udis-Kessler, A. (1990) 'The borderline bisexual blues', in J. Geller (ed.) *Bisexuality: A Reader and Sourcebook*, New York: Times Change Press.

Unger, R. (1975) *Knowledge and Politics*, New York: Free Press.

Urban, T. and Billings, D.B. (1982) 'The socio-medical construction of transsexualism: an interpretation and critique', *Social Problems* 29, 3: 266–82.

Urry, J. (1988) 'Cultural change and contemporary holiday-making', *Theory, Culture and Society* 5: 35–55.

—— (1990a) *The Tourist Gaze: Leisure and Travel in Contemporary Society*, London: Sage.

—— (1990b) 'The consumption of tourism', *Sociology* 24, 1: 23–35.

Valverde, M. (1985) *Sex, Power and Pleasure*, Toronto: Women's Press.

Vance, C.S. (ed.) (1984) *Pleasure and Danger: Exploring Female Sexuality*, London: Routledge & Kegan Paul.

—— (1989) 'Social construction theory: problems in the history of sexuality', in D. Altman *et al. Which Homosexuality? Essays from the International Scientific Conference on Lesbian and Gay Studies*, London and Amsterdam: Gay Men's Press and Uitgeverij An Dekker/Schorer.

Vandervelden, M., Freiberg, P. and Walter, D. (1987) 'GAY INC: the surprising health of gay businesses', *The Advocate* 467, 3 March: 40–9, 108–9.

Virkunnen, M. (1975) 'Victim precipitated paedophilia offences', *British Journal of Criminology* 15, 2: 175–80.

Walby, S. (1988) 'Gender politics and sociological theory', *Sociology* 22, 2: 215–32.

Walkerdine, V. (1991) *Schoolgirl Fictions*, London: Verso.

Walter, A. (ed.) (1980) *Come Together: The Years of Gay Liberation 1970–73*, London: Gay Men's Press.

Warde, A. (1990) 'Introduction to the sociology of consumption', *Sociology* 24, 1: 1–4.

Warnock, M. (1985) *A Question of Life: The Warnock Report on Human Fertilisation and Embryology*, Oxford: Basil Blackwell.

Watney, S. (1980) 'The ideology of the GLF', in Gay Left Collective (ed.) *Homosexuality, Power and Politics*, London: Allison & Busby.

—— (1987) *Policing Desire: Pornography, AIDS and the Media*, London: Comedia/Methuen.

—— (1988) 'AIDS: moral panic theory and homophobia', in P. Aggleton and H. Homans (eds) *Social Aspects of AIDS*, Lewes: Falmer Press.

—— (1989) 'Taking liberties', in E. Carter and S. Watney (eds) *Taking Liberties: AIDS and Cultural Politics*, London: Serpent's Tail.

Waugh, D. (1990) quoted in 'The eunuch's bequest', *Sunday Correspondent* 22 April.

Weber, M. (1947) *The Theory of Political and Economic Organisations*, Glencoe, IL: Free Press.

—— (1967) 'Class, status and party', in H.H. Gerth and C.W. Mills (eds) *From Max Weber*, London: Routledge & Kegan Paul.
Webster, P. (1984) 'The forbidden: eroticism and taboo', in C.S. Vance (ed.) *Pleasure and Danger: Exploring Female Sexuality*, London: Routledge and Kegan Paul.
Weeks, J. (1977) *Coming Out. Homosexual Politics in Britain from the Nineteenth Century to the Present*, London: Quartet.
—— (1978) Introduction to G. Hocquenghem *Homosexual Desire*, London: Allison & Busby.
—— (1980) 'Capitalism and the organisation of sex', in Gay Left Collective (ed.) *Homosexuality, Power and Politics*, London: Allison & Busby.
—— (1981a) 'Discourse, desire and sexual deviance', in K. Plummer (ed.) *The Making of the Modern Homosexual*, London: Hutchinson.
—— (1981b) *Sex, Politics and Society: The Regulation of Sexuality Since 1800*, London: Longman.
—— (1985) *Sexuality and its Discontents: Meanings, Myths and Modern Sexualities*. London: Routledge & Kegan Paul.
—— (1988) 'Love in a cold climate', in P. Aggleton and H. Homans (eds) *Social Aspects of AIDS*, Lewes: Falmer Press.
—— (1989) 'Against nature', in D. Altman *et al. Which Homosexuality?*, London and Amsterdam: Gay Men's Press and Uitgeverij An Dekker/Schorer.
Weinberg, G. (1973) *Society and the Healthy Homosexual*, New York: Anchor Books.
Weinberg, M.S. and Williams, C.J. (1974) *Male Homosexuals: Their Problems and Adaptations*, New York: Oxford University Press.
Weinreb, L. (1991) 'What are civil rights?' *Philosophy and Policy* 8, 2.
Weiss, J., Rogers, E., Darwin, M. and Dutton, C. (1955) ' A study of girl sex victims', *Psychiatric Quarterly* 29: 1–2.
Weitzman, L. (1985) *The Divorce Revolution: The Unexpected Social and Economic Consequences for Women and Children in America*, New York: Free Press.
Wellings, K. (1988) 'Perceptions of risk – media treatments of AIDS', in P. Aggleton and H. Homans (eds) *Social Aspects of AIDS*, Lewes: Falmer Press.
Werge, F. (1988) 'Swinging into action', *Pink Paper* 18 February: 5.
Wertham, F. (1953) *Seduction of the Innocent*, New York: Rinehart & Co.
Westergaard, J. (1973) 'Sociology and the myth of classlessness', in R. Blackburn (ed.) *Ideology in Social Science*, London: Fontana.
Westwood, G. (1952) *Society and the Homosexual*, London: Gollancz.
White, E. (1980) *States of Desire*, London: Andre Deutsch.
Whitehead, H. (1981) 'The bow and the burden strap: a new look at institutionalised homosexuality in native North America', in S.B. Ortner and H. Whitehead (eds) *Sexual Meanings*, Cambridge: Cambridge University Press.
Whitehouse, M. (1967) *Cleaning up T. V.*, London: Blandford.
Whiteley, C.H. and Whiteley, W.M. (1964) *The Permissive Morality*, London: Methuen.

Whitfield, R.C. (ed.) (1987) *Families Matter*, London: Hodder & Stoughton.
Whitham, F. (1977a) 'Childhood indications of male homosexuality', *Archives of Sexual Behaviour* 6: 89–96.
—— (1977b) 'The homosexual role: a reconsideration', *Journal of Sex Research* 13: 1–11.
Williams, R. (1983) 'Problems of the coming period', *New Left Review* 140, July/August: 7–18.
Williams, R. (1975) *The Long Revolution*, Harmondsworth: Penguin.
Willis, E. (1981) *Beginning to See the Light: Pieces of a Decade*, New York: Alfred Knopf.
Wilson, B.R. (1982) *Religion in Sociological Perspective*, Oxford: Oxford University Press.
Wilson, E. (1977) *Women and the Welfare State*, London: Tavistock.
—— (1981) 'Psychoanalysis: psychic law and order', *Feminist Review* 5.
—— (1987) 'Psychoanalysis: psychic law and order', *Feminist Review* (ed.) *Sexuality: A Reader*, London: Virago.
Wilson, G. (1983) *The Child Lovers: A Study of Paedophiles in Society*, London: P. Owen.
Wimbush, E. and Talbot, M. (1988) *Relative Freedoms: Women and Leisure*, Milton Keynes: Open University Press.
Wittman, C. (1977) 'A gay manifesto', in K. Jay and A. Young (eds) *Out of the Closets: Voices of Gay Liberation*, New York: Jove/HBJ.
Wittstock, M. (1987) 'The best of both worlds and still nothing: bisexuals come out to talk', *Rites*, quoted in T. Geller (ed.) *Bisexuality: A Reader and Sourcebook*, New York: Times Change Press.
Wolfe, T. (1979) 'The sexed up, doped up, hedonistic heaven of the "boom-boom" seventies', *Life*, December.
Wolfenden Report (1957) *The Report of the Committee on Homosexual Offences and Prostitution*, Cmnd 247, London: HMSO.
Wolin, R. (1986) 'Foucault's aesthetic decisionism', *Telos* 67, Spring: 71–86.
Wollen, P. (1979) 'Do children really need toys?', in M. Hoyles (ed.) *Changing Childhood*, London: Writers and Readers Publishing Co-operative.
Wolmar, C. (1988) 'Anti-gay law is a non-starter', *Observer* 21 May.
Wood, J. (1984) 'Groping towards sexism: boys' "sex talk"', in A. McRobbie and M. Nava (eds) *Gender and Generation*, London: Macmillan.
Woodhouse, A. (1989) *Sex, Gender and Transvestism*, London: Macmillan.
Wootton Report (1968) *Report of the Advisory Committee on Drug Dependence*, London: HMSO.
Worden, F.G. and Marsh J.T. (1955) 'Factors in a man seeking sex transformation: a preliminary report', *Journal of the American Medical Association* 157: 1291–8.
Wright, D. (1971) *The Psychology of Moral Behaviour*, Harmondsworth: Penguin.
Wright, M. (1990) *Young People's Rights*, London: Macdonald/Optima.
Yates, A. (1978) *Sex Without Shame*, London: Temple-Smith.

Yinger, J.M. (1960) 'Contraculture and subculture', *American Sociological Review* 25: 625–35.

Young, H. (1972) 'Politics outside the system', in D. McKie and C. Cook (eds) *The Decade of Disillusion*, London: Macmillan/St Martin's Press.

Younger, Lord (1972) *The Report of the Committee on Privacy*, Cmnd. 5012, London: HMSO.

Zukin, S (1990) 'Socio-spatial prototypes of a new organisation of consumption: the role of real cultural capital', *Sociology* 24,1: 37–56.

NAME INDEX

SUBJECT INDEX

abortion 252–9; attitudes to 84–5;
law reform 241; right of 61
Abortion Act (1967) 70, 254
accumulation strategies 51–2
Act Up 117
adoption 119–20
advertising and marketing 74,
137–8, 261–3
Advocate, The 104
age: of consent 118–19, 212,
213–15, 236; effect on
tolerance 81–2
agents provocateurs 121
AIDS: attitudes to 127; bisexuality
148, 160–5; construction of
138, 142; demonstrations
120–1; education 220;
educational campaigns 137–8,
161; effect on attitudes to
homosexuality 86; effect on
attitudes to sex 84; effect on
employment rights 124; effect
on gay communities 104–8;
HIV testing 118, 124, 125;
moral panic 142; patients 124;
rights 124–5; 'risk' groups
161–2; tourism 110–11
alienation 46
alter egos 187–8
ambisexuality 147–8
Amsterdam 106, 107; *see also*
Netherlands
anorexia 252
Anti-Sexist Men's Conference 171

ARC 124
Arena magazine 261
artificial insemination, attitudes
to 83
Association of London
Authorities 129
attitude surveys 82–7, 122
Australia 125

bath-houses 101, 102–3, 106, 107
BBC: *Weekend World* 128;
Woman's Hour 244
Beaumont Society 178–9, 184, 186
Belgium 202, 204–5
Betting and Gambling Act (1960)
69
Beveridge Plan 59
Bi-Monthly magazine 168
'bio-power' 13–14, 18, 25
biphobia 160
Bisexual and Married Gays
Group 168
Bisexual Information and
Counselling Service 168
bisexuality 147–73; AIDS 148,
160–5; attitudes to 147–8;
coming-out 169; explanations
for 151; Freud's approach
149–50; hostility to 151,
169–70; labelling 151–2,
170–2; 'new homosexuality'
96; political identity 171–2;
'scripts' 157–8, 169;
transsexualism 167

hegemonic projects 52
hermaphroditism 194
heterosexuality, AIDS 162–4
Hite Report 266
HIV: positive status 118, 124; testing 118, 124–5
Holland *see* Netherlands
Homicide Act (1957) 69
homosexuality: ages of consent 214; attitudes to 82–3, 84, 86–7, 122; bisexuality 96, 154–6; as condition or culture 143–4; dress 95, 99, 105; Foucault on 23; legal status 118; legislation 70, 101; masculinisation of 91, 94–5, 98–100; New Right approach 143; pre-adolescent male 154; role development 90–100; Scruton on 137; statistics 140; subculture development 90, 92; transsexuals 188, 192–3; virilisation 100; *see also* gay; lesbianism; Section 28
housewife 17, 38, 242–3

identity, gender 94, 177, 182, 187, 193
illegal/immoral distinction 52–4, 85
impersonators, female 181
imprisonment 119, 121
incest 207, 213
Indecency With Children Act (1960) 214
indecent assault 213, 214
individualism 172
Industrial Schools Amendment Act (1880) 212
industrial tribunals 123–4, 207–8
inheritance 17
intellectuals, Bohemian 93
interactionist analyses 27–33
International Gay Travel Association (IGTA) 108
intersexuality 93, 94
intolerance 81–2
Italy 120, 205

Johns Hopkins University 194

Kinky Gerlinky club 201
Klein Sexual Orientation Grid 156
korephilia 228

labelling 151–2, 170–2
labour: free wage 37–8; market discrimination 39–40; reproduction of 37–8; sexual division of 38; sexual minorities 40–1; women's roles 38–9, 41–2
Labour Campaign for Lesbian and Gay Rights 127, 141
Labour Party 7, 119
Lady Chatterley's Lover trial 67, 71
Last Exit to Brooklyn 71
legislation 53, 69–71, 120 123, 246; *see also* Section 28; *and individual Acts by name*
lesbianism: age of consent 214; attitudes to 86; lesbian continuum 272; marginalisation of 92; rights 118–20; tourism 108; transsexuals 188; *see also* homosexuality
liberation 1, 16–17; gay 92, 114, 140; sexual 65; women's 272
liberty: basic 56; civil 55; personal 79
Liberty Principle 238
Liverpool Corporation Act (1921) 183
Local Government Act (1988) *see* Section 28
London Bisexual Group 168
London Bisexual Women's Group 168
London School of Economics sit-in 74
Longford Report on Pornography 139
Luxembourg 205

'macho' male 94, 96
Manchester City Council 129
marriage: homosexual 118, 119; transsexual 203–7